T0215206

Communications in Computer and Information Science 520

Editorial Board

More information about this series at http://www.springer.com/series/7899

Yueming Lu · Xu Wu
Xi Zhang (Eds.)

Trustworthy Computing and Services

International Conference, ISCTCS 2014
Beijing, China, November 28–29, 2014
Revised Selected Papers

 Springer

Editors
Yueming Lu
Beijing University of Posts
    and Telecommuncations
Beijing
China

Xi Zhang
Beijing University of Posts
    and Telecommunications
Beijing
China

Xu Wu
Beijing University of Posts
    and Telecommunications
Beijing
China

ISSN 1865-0929   ISSN 1865-0937 (electronic)
Communications in Computer and Information Science
ISBN 978-3-662-47400-6   ISBN 978-3-662-47401-3   (eBook)
DOI 10.1007/978-3-662-47401-3

Library of Congress Control Number: 2015941360

Springer Heidelberg New York Dordrecht London

Printed on acid-free paper

Springer-Verlag GmbH Berlin Heidelberg is part of Springer Science+Business Media
(www.springer.com)

Preface

Trusted computing and services compromise one of the most promising and challenging technologies today and is the core technology of cloud computing, which is currently the focus of international competition; its standardization work is the premise and guarantee of the technology's successful application and promotion of the industry. The International Standard Conference on Trustworthy Computing and Services (ISCTCS) 2014 was hosted by the Key Laboratory of Trustworthy Distributed Computing and Service (BUPT), Ministry of Education, and National Software Testing Standards Working Group in order to lay the foundation for the establishment of the Trusted Computing Service Standards Working Group. Scholars, experts, and corporate leaders from around the world had the chance to share ideas on technologies of trustworthy computing and services as well as their evolution, application, and industrialization.

The main topics of this meeting include: architecture for trusted computing system, trusted computing platform, trusted system build, network and protocol security, mobile network security, network survivability and other critical theories, and standard systems; credible assessment, credible measurement and metrics, trusted systems, trusted networks, trusted mobile network, trusted routing, trusted software, trusted operating systems, trusted storage, fault-tolerant computing, and other key technologies; trusted e-commerce and e-government, trusted logistics, trusted Internet of Things, trusted cloud, and other trusted services and applications.

The conference began with an opening ceremony and the conference program featured a welcome speech, six keynote speeches, and two presentations by local and international experts. During the two-day program, all paper presentations were given in four parallel sessions. The conference ended with a closing ceremony. The conference received more than 279 papers, and each paper was carefully reviewed by the Program Committee members. Finally, 51 papers were selected.

On behalf of the Organizing and Program Committees of ISCTCS 2014, we would like to express our appreciation to all authors and attendees for participating in the conference. We also thank the sponsors, Program Committee members, supporting organizations, and helpers for making the conference a success. Without their efforts, the conference would not have been possible.

Finally, we trust everyone who attended enjoyed the conference program and also their stay in Beijing. We firmly look forward to the impact of ISCTCS 2014 in promoting the standardization work of trusted computing and services.

February 2015

Yueming Lu
Xu Wu
Xi Zhang

Organization

The International Standard Conference on Trustworthy Computing and Services (ISCTCS 2013) was organized by the Key Laboratory of Trustworthy Distributed Computing and Service of BUPT, Ministry of Education, and sponsored by the National Software Testing Standards Working Group.

General Chair

Binxing Fang   Key Laboratory of Trustworthy Distributed Computing and Service (BUPT), Ministry of Education

TPC Chair

Yueming Lu   Key Laboratory of Trustworthy Distributed Computing and Service (BUPT), Ministry of Education, China

Workshop Chair

National Software Testing Standards Working Group, China

Publication Chair

Xu Wu   Key Laboratory of Trustworthy Distributed Computing and Service (BUPT), Ministry of Education, China

Finance Chair

Beijing University of Posts and Telecommunications, China

Registration Chair

Beijing University of Posts and Telecommunications, China

Main Organizers

Beijing University of Posts and Telecommunications, China
National Software Testing Standards Working Group, China
National University of Defense Technology, China
Fraunhofer Institute for Open Communication Systems, Germany

ISCTCS Technical Program Committee

Axel Rennoch	Fraunhofer Institute for Open Communication Systems, Germany
Tomonori Aoyama	Keio University, Japan
Jørgen Bøegh	Beijing University of Posts and Telecommunications, Denmark
Enjie Liu	University of Bedfordshire, UK
Enrico Viola	ECLAT, Italy
Yukio Tanitsu	IBM Japan, Ltd., Japan
Ho-Won	Korea University, South Korea
Alain Renault	CRP Henri Tudor, Luxembourg
Juan Garbajosa	Technical University of Madrid, Spain
Nigel Bevan	Serco Usability Services, UK
Yuji Shinoki	Hitachi, Ltd., Software Division, Japan
Mitsuhiro Takahashi	DENKEN, Japan
Juan Carlos Granja	Granada University, Spain
Krishna Ricky	University of Montana, Suriname
Anakpa Manawa	Université de Lomé, Togo
Miandrilala	University of Antananarivo, Madagascar
Xin Chen	Nangjing University, China
Jianwei Yin	Zhejiang University, China
Yan Jia	National University of Defense Technology, China
Li Guo	Chinese Academy of Sciences, China
Hong Li Zhang	Harbin Institute of Technology, China
Xue Qi Cheng	Institute of Computing Technology, Chinese Academy of Science, China
Cong Wang	Key Laboratory of Trustworthy Distributed Computing and Service (BUPT), Ministry of Education, China
Tie Jun Lv	Beijing University of Posts and Telecommunications, China
Yue Ming Lu	Beijing University of Posts and Telecommunications, China
Chun Lu Wang	Beijing University of Posts and Telecommunications, China
Tian Le Zhang	Key Laboratory of Trustworthy Distributed Computing and Service (BUPT), Ministry of Education, China
Chuan Yi Liu	Key Laboratory of Trustworthy Distributed Computing and Service (BUPT), Ministry of Education, China
Dong Bin Wang	Key Laboratory of Trustworthy Distributed Computing and Service (BUPT), Ministry of Education, China
Jin Cui Yang	Key Laboratory of Trustworthy Distributed Computing and Service (BUPT), Ministry of Education, China
Xi Zhang	Key Laboratory of Trustworthy Distributed Computing and Service (BUPT), Ministry of Education, China
Yang Yang Zhang	Key Laboratory of Trustworthy Distributed Computing and Service (BUPT), Ministry of Education, China

Contents

XII   Contents

Cache Replacement Improving Based on User Group Interest Degree

Shuai Zhang[1,2(✉)], Yueming Lu[1,2], and Xi Zhang[1,2]

[1] School of Information and Communication Engineering,
Beijing University of Posts and Telecommunications, Beijing, China
{zs9075,ymlu,zhangx}@bupt.edu.cn
[2] Key Laboratory of Trustworthy Distributed Computing and Service (BUPT),
Ministry of Education, Beijing, China

Abstract. In order to reduce access latency and improve user experience, the current schemes include cache and prefetching technologies. The current cache replacement schemes only consider access time and access frequency, but ignore the user-group interest degree in access paths. This paper studies the visiting characteristics of user groups. Then a cache replacement improving algorithm is put forward called P-GDSF, which is based on the GDSF algorithm and joined the prediction mechanism due to user-group interest degree. The new algorithm takes most factors of Web objects into account. The simulation shows that our algorithm can achieve relatively higher hit rate and byte hit rate than the GDSF replacement algorithm in a certain cache space.

Keywords: Cache replacement algorithm · User-group interest degree · GDSF · Access path · Prefetching

1 Introduction

Because of the double limits of current network speed and dramatically increasing number of users, users often need to endure longer access latency. In order to reduce access latency and improve user experience, Web cache and prefetching technologies are the primary means of the current network improvements. Web cache technologies utilize the principle of temporal locality, which means the visited parts of document stored in a non-original server site. When a user sends a request again to a remote server site, he can obtain the desired information quickly with the help of cache. Temporal locality refers to that the shorter the distance between last access, the more likely the object is to be accessed again [1]. Web prefetching technologies utilizing the principle of spatial locality analyzes current and historical user requests and pro-actively predicts user future possible browsing pages. When users browse one Web page, the predicted contents will be deposited to local cache. So when they really want to access these pages, they only need to download pages from local cache. The advantage of employing prefetching is to complement the existing Web cache mechanisms and overcome the inherent limitations of Web cache in capitalizing on the spatial locality of Web accesses. The paper [2] shows that the integration of Web prefetching and caching holds the promise of reducing Web latency and improving the QoS of Web systems.

© Springer-Verlag Berlin Heidelberg 2015
Y. Lu et al. (Eds.): ISCTCS 2014, CCIS 520, pp. 1–7, 2015.
DOI: 10.1007/978-3-662-47401-3_1

At present, Web prefetching algorithms are roughly classified into the following three categories [3]:

(1) Based on access time, dominated by LRU (Least Recently Used) and the similar algorithms, replacing the least recently used contents at first;
(2) Based on access frequency, dominated by LFU (Least Frequently Used) and the similar algorithms, replacing the least used contents at first;
(3) Based on other properties, constructing the object evaluation function by the parameters of space size, object value and so on, such as SIZE, GDS (Greedy Dual Size), GDSF (GDS Frequency).

But the algorithms mentioned above ignore the user-group interest degree in access paths. Web browsing processes are affected by interest, hobbies and a variety of factors [4]. It is a hot research topic that using path mining techniques by log information predicts user future access in the era of big data. All the users are divided into a plurality of categories based on the browsing characteristics of each user, so that users of the same class have the same or similar browsing characteristics.

In this paper, we mine the distribution mode of user-group interest in the pages and compute the user-group interest degree. We obtain the interest degree of most users in the visited pages and the navigation patterns to predict user browsing paths. Using the average of accessing interval time based on GDSF avoids retaining a large number of objects without store of value. The simulation shows that our algorithm can achieve higher hit rate and byte hit rate than GDSF in a certain space.

2   A Cache Replacement Algorithm Model

Due to the limited storage capacity of Web cache, when cache memory is full, we need to replace some objects without store of value following some kind of policy. So the performance of cache depends on replacement policies [5].

Cache replacement problems can be described as follows:

Supposing that O is a set of data objects that all users can access, for any request object $d \in O$, there are corresponding object size S_d and retrieval cost C_d. Assuming that C is the cache capacity, there is a request sequence $R = (R_1, R_2, \ldots, R_n)$ leading to a cache state sequence $S = (S_1, S_2, \ldots, S_n)$, where the initial cache state is S_0, that is to say, there are no cache objects in this state. Setting C_{used} as the used cache capacity, for any state S_k ($k = 1, 2, \ldots, n$), it is defined as

$$S_k = \begin{cases} S_{k-1}; & if\, R_k \in S_{k-1} \\ S_{k-1} \cup \{R_k\}; & if\, R_k \notin S_{k-1}, C_{used} + S_d \leq C \\ (S_{k-1} - E_k) \cup \{R_k\}; & R_k \notin S_{k-1}, C_{used} + S_d > C \end{cases} \tag{1}$$

In the equation, $E_k(E_k \subset S_{k-1})$ is the set of the removed cache objects. All cache states migrating satisfies the Eq. (1) (Fig. 1).

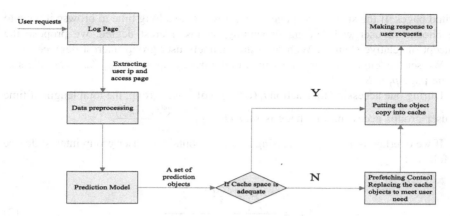

Fig. 1. Flow diagram of cache replacement problem

The basic idea of cache replacement problems is that if there is no enough space, we need to keep replacing the document whose weight is the smallest until there is enough space to store new documents.

3 The Cache Replacement Improving Algorithm

3.1 The User Group Mode

Because the Web log files contain user browsing information, we can understand user behaviors and make the users who have the similar access tendency into a class by quantitatively analyzing and mining Web access log files [6]. After understanding user needs and habits accurately, we can provide group users with the targeted services due to their interest.

Page groups are the set of the associated access to certain pages of a certain number of users. Page groups reflect user access habits [7].

A page group is defined as follows:

T is a set of user access transactions and D is the transactional database, which is constituted by the transaction T. A page group $p_k = \{p_1, p_2, \ldots, p_i\}$, $i = 1, 2, \ldots$ is the page node of user access. A user may have several access habits, namely, corresponding to several page groups during one event of accessing Web. Page groups provide a reliable basis for analyzing user access patterns. Through mining page groups corresponding to user groups by fuzzy clustering, users who have the similar access behaviors are classified as a class, forming a user group.

A user group is defined as follows:

$UG = \{u_1, u_2, \ldots, u_m\}$, where $m = 1, 2, \ldots, n$, u_m is a user.

In fact, an access user belongs to several user groups. On the contrary, one user group contains a number of access users. Supposing that $t(u_i) = <p_1, p_2, \ldots, p_j>$ is one of user access transactions, u stands for a set of users and u_i is the user who is accessing the page p_j. User-group interest degree relates to the size of a page, access time and access frequency [8]. Long browsing time indicates that a user have high interest in the visited pages. If the size of one page is big, it will take a long time to browse it. Due to the choose of user web surfing depending on his interest degree, we propose the concept of relative share of Web browsing, namely user-group interest degree.

We set the length of user access time to the page p_j as $L(UG_r, p_j)/S_j$, where the size of the page p_j is S_j.

During one accessing transaction t_i (UG_r, p_j) of a user group, the total length of time of user groups accessing one page is $sum(UG_r, p_j) = \sum_{i=1}^{max} \frac{L(UG_r, p_j)}{S_j}$.

If we overlay user groups accessing p_j, we can obtain the user-group interest degree as follows:

$$P = \frac{\sum_{r=1}^{max} \frac{sum(UG_r, p_j)}{S_j} \cdot k_j}{\sum_{r=1}^{N} \sum_{j=1}^{M} \left(\frac{sum(UG_r, p_j)}{S_j} \cdot k_j \right)} \tag{2}$$

In the Eq. (2), k_j refers to the access frequency to p_j.

3.2 The Average of Accessing Interval Time

For these objects we hardly or won't access in the future, we consider this class of objects no longer have store of value. If these things have always been stored in cache, the cache hit rate will be reduced. In this paper, we use the average of accessing interval time [9, 10] to solve this defect. T_k is the time interval between the accessing times k-1 and k. Supposing the object is accessed again after T_{k-1}, so we can get the average of accessing interval time as follows:

$$T_k = \lambda t_k + (1 - \lambda)T_{k-1} \tag{3}$$

In the Eq. (3), λ is an adjustable parameter whose value is between 0.5 and 1.

3.3 Our Mode

Our cache replacement improving algorithm is put forward which is based on the GDSF algorithm and joined the prediction mechanism due to user-group interest degree. We use the key formula as the objective formula described in cache replacement problems.

$$H = M + (P/T_k) \times (C_d/S_d) \tag{4}$$

In the equation, M represents the inflation factor; P represents the user-group interest degree to the page d; T_k represents the average of accessing interval time after accessing page d k times; C_d represents the cost of retrieving page d; S_d represents the size of the page d. The equation gives full consideration to user-group interest degree, size, the cost of retrieving objects and other factors.

4 Improving Cache Replacement Algorithm

4.1 Implementation Process

Input: A user access sequence $R=(R_1,R_2,...,R_n)$.

Output: The set of predicted objects Q.

(1) Setting the minimum user-group interest degree in the Q as $P_{min}=0$;

(2) new_page{ $p_1,p_2,...,p_n$ },

      calculating the user-group interest degree P_n of each page p_n;

      if($P_n>P_{min}$) {

              if (sizeof(Q)<threshold)

              the set of the predicted objects $Q=:Q+p_n$;

              else{

                    p_n randomly replacing the minimum user-group interest

                    degree p_{min} in the Q;

                    Resetting P_{min};

              }

        }

Input: The cache capacity of the system; The set of the predicted objects Q; The current request object d; A user access sequence $R=(R_1,R_2,...,R_n)$.

Output: The set of cache objects S.

(1) if IsInCache(d) calculating $H(d)$ corresponding to d

    else while (the cache space not enough to store object d)

      for (All objects d_i in cache)

          Setting H(d_i) corresponding to d_i, sorting $H_1<H_2<...<H_{i-1}<H_i$

          according to the value of H;

      for($j=H_1$; $j<H_i$; j++)

      {

          if (the object corresponding to j is in Q)

              j++;

          else replacing the object corresponding to j;

      }

(2) Putting d into the cache;

(3) Return the set of cache objects S.

4.2 The Simulation Experiment

The simulation experiments use the real web accessing log data [11]. In the experiment, the log documents are preprocessed at first, excluding the failure records, pictures and objects which can't be cached. Then we count the total number of user requests and select a certain size for cache space. If there is a user access sequence $R = (R_1, R_2, ..., R_n)$, we can output the set of predicted objects according to user-group interest degree and obtain the hit rate and byte hit rate of our algorithm and the GDSF replacement algorithm by statistics. The λ parameter in the average of accessing internal time is set to 0.6. Figures 2, 3 respectively shows the hit rate and byte hit rate of our algorithm compared with the GDSF replacement algorithm.

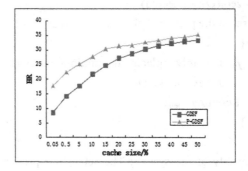

Fig. 2. Comparison of HR of two algorithms

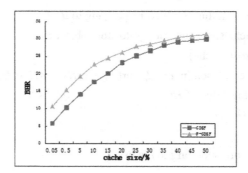

Fig. 3. Comparison of BHR of two algorithms

As shown in the experiment results, our algorithm can achieve relatively higher hit rate and byte hit rate than the GDSF replacement algorithm. The cache replacement improving algorithm uses user-group interest degree to construct the prediction model predicting the user access sequence. To some extent, the current cache replacement algorithms can be improved. With cache space increasing, there is enough space to store new request objects, so the performance advantages of our algorithm gradually reduce.

5 Conclusion

We mine the distribution mode of user group interest in the pages and compute the user-group interest degree transferring from one page to another one. Due to the visiting characteristics of user groups, we put forward a cache replacement improving algorithm which is based on the GDSF algorithm and joined the prediction mechanism. The new algorithm takes most factors of Web objects into account. The simulation shows that the current algorithm can achieve relatively higher hit rate and byte hit rate than the GDSF replacement algorithm in a certain cache space.

Acknowledgement. This work was supported by the Major Research Plan of the National Natural Science Foundation of China [91124002] and the Fundamental Research Funds for the Central Universities [2013RC0301].

References

1. Qinfen, H., Mingfa, Z., Jisheng, H.: WWW traffic access characteristic distribution research. J. Comput. Res. Dev. **38**(10), 1172–1180 (2001)
2. Shi, L., Han, Y., Ding, X., et al.: An SPN based integrated model for web prefetching and caching. J. Comput. Sci. Technol. **21**(4), 482–489 (2006)
3. Zhijie, B., Zhimin, G., Yu, J.: A survey of web prefetching. J. Comput. Res. Dev. **46**(2), 202–210 (2009)
4. Jia, C., Junhua, W.: Prediction for users' navigation based on Hybrid Markov Model. Computer Engineering and Design **30**(4), 903–908 (2009)
5. Lei, S., Caixia, M., Yingjie, H.: Web replacement policy based on prediction. Computer Applications **27**(8), 1842–1845 (2007)
6. Jia, J., Zhang, S., Meng, F., Wang, Y., Cai, L.: Emotional audio-visual speech synthesis based on PAD. IEEE Trans. Audio Speech Lang. Process. **19**(3), 570–582 (2011)
7. Yongkang, X., Shaoping, M.: Modeling user navigation sequences based on multi-Markov chains. Chin. J. Comput. **26**(11), 1510–1517 (2003)
8. Li, X., Wang, S.: New approach of mining user's preferred browsing paths based on Things Clustering Algorithm. Manuf. Autom., 2 (2013)
9. Lin, Y., Zhang, D., Qian, H.: A new web cache replacement algorithm. J. Softw. **12**(11), 1710–1715 (2001)
10. Huang, X., Zhong, Y.: Web Cache Replacement Algorithm Based on Multi-Markov Chains Prediction Model. Microelectron. Comput., 31(5) (2014)
11. Web caching and content delivery resources [EB/OL]. http://www.web-caching.com/. Accessed 17 October 2012

A Uighur Automatic Summarization Method Based on Sub-theme Division

Xiaodong Yan[✉]

China National Language Resource Monitoring & Research Center Minority
Languages Branch, Minzu University of China, Zhongguancun Street 27#,
Haidian District, Beijing 100081, China
yanxd3244@sina.com

Abstract. As a very important research focus of natural language processing,
automatic summarization can be used in many fields whether in improving the
quality of searching results on a search engine or as a means of public opinion
analysis. A method for Uighur automatic summarization is proposed in this
paper which is base on sub-theme division and weight value. And by experiments, we find that it can get good precision and recall rates.

Keywords: Automatic summarization · Sub-theme division · Weight
calculation

1 Introduction

In recent years, with the improvement of people's living standard, almost all minorities
in our country began to use Internet. They obtain effective information resource on
study, life and work and so on. Consequently many organizations and individuals have
created websites to provide information services which are described by their own
ethnic languages (including Uighur). Due to the existing Google, Baidu and other
major search engines are not suitable for unique characteristics of the text of Uighur or
other minorities language, search results of these Search Engine have never meet our
expectations (search for Uighur in Baidu is not supported and the correlation between
the pages of Google search results and the content of User query is very low, and
Uighur text always is Confused with the other Arabic text). So they all cannot meet the
majority of minority network users on information needs. Therefore searching and
obtaining Uighur information quickly accurately, comprehensively and conveniently is
the request of the information age.

Recently as the research hot spot, Internet public opinion analysis is widespread in
concern. In particular minority language network public opinion analysis is valued by
the national government. Automatic Summarization is also an indispensable method
and way of public opinion analysis.

© Springer-Verlag Berlin Heidelberg 2015
Y. Lu et al. (Eds.): ISCTCS 2014, CCIS 520, pp. 8–15, 2015.
DOI: 10.1007/978-3-662-47401-3_2

2   Related Researches

Automatic summarization research started early and has obtained a great amount of research results. In 1958, the United States, IBM's Luhn [1] in "The Automatic Creation of Literature Abstracts" first proposed automatic summarization. Early 1970s, Edmundson in University of Maryland proposed four weighting method [2, 3], Consolidating the words' weights in sentence, regarding their sum as the weights of this sentence, picking sentences as abstracts according to the weight. In 1989, U.S. GE Research Center Lisa F. Rauet developed a SCISOR system, the system generate the appropriate conceptual framework by analyzing the document theme and syntactic structure [4]. In 1995 a theme of "Summarizing Text" is published in special issue in international journals Information Processing & Management [5]. In 1991, Morris and Hirst presented the first computable model of vocabulary chain, it is word series consist of a set of adjacent words of a subject, provides important clues for dividing text structure and themes [6]. Then, Barzilay et have made other WordNet-based Lexical chain calculation method [7, 8]. Lexical chain can clearly represent the semantic relationships between words, providing an important basis for dividing text structure and analyzing themes. In 2004, the University of Michigan's Gunes Erkan etc. Put forward LexRank algorithm [9], it is a method calculating the weight of the sentence under graphical representation structure of text. Gunes Erkan achieved a abstracting system by using this method, and evaluate the system by using DUC2004 data sets, experimental results show that the system ranked first in the number of evaluation.

In Uighur automatic summarization a Uighur website automatic summary extraction method is proposed by Jepati which is based on statistics [10]. We learned from the past, all kinds of language automatic summarization methods and made a Uighur automatic summarization method based on the theme of division. In the following, we will describe it in detail.

3   A Uighur Automatic Summarization Method Based on Division of Sub-theme

3.1   Overview of the Method

A method for Uighur automatic summarization based on the division of sub-theme is presented in this paper. The main steps of the method are as following: text preprocessing, subtopics division, sentence weight calculation, redundant processing and summary generation.

3.1.1   Text Preprocessing
In preprocessing, first, clause and word segmentation is done. The stop words, rare words and modified word which is no practical significance in the text are all removed.

3.1.2   Sub-theme Division
In the division of sub-theme, first, vector space model is constructed by the unit of sentence, and the cosine of the angle between the vector is calculated as the element

values of text similarity matrix. Then according to the similarity matrix construct undirected weighted graph of the text, and the corresponding maximum spanning tree is obtained. Finally by using a modified K means clustering algorithm on maximum spanning tree, the clustering is completed and each sub-class we got represents a sub-theme.

3.1.3   Sentence Weight Calculation
When the weight of the sentence is calculated, each sub-theme will be represented as a graph structure and the LexRank Score of each sentence is calculated on sub-themes based on LexRank algorithm. Then the FeatureScored of each sentence is calculated. Finally, the weight of sentence is measured by the combination of these two parts.

3.1.4   Summary Generation
After the division of the sub-themes and the calculating weights of the sentence, Sub-themes are sorted from high to low according to the degree of importance. Then according to the order the highest weight of each sub-theme sentences is collected into the candidate Digest sentence set. In order to avoid repeat extracting a higher similar sentence next time, after extracting summary sentences from a sub-theme, the remaining weight of the sentence in this sub-theme is re-calculated.

The System Framework Figure of the method of Uighur document summarization based on the division of sub-theme which is mentioned in this paper is as shown in Fig. 1, and overall flow chart of it is shown in Fig. 2.

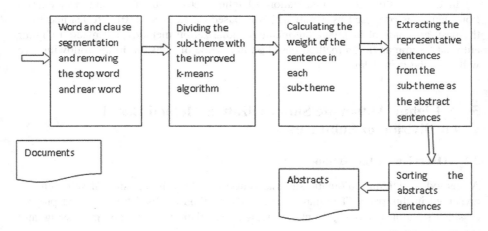

Fig. 1. System Framework Figure of the method of Uighur document summarization based on the division of sub-theme

3.2   Text Preprocessing

In the pretreatment process of the document, the main methods are speech tagging, filtering stop word and stemming. In addition to the above there are some other useful operations including deleting useless words, dictionary generation, text compression and stemming technology and so on.

- Speech tagging: nouns, verbs, adjectives, etc. can more accurately express a complete meaning and some parts of speech on expressing the central meaning of the article is not much useful. Such as conjunctions, Modal, function words, almost no meaning. So it is necessary to give nouns, verbs and other types of words weights. Of course, the introduction of part of speech tagging also has some disadvantages, not only increasing the execution time of the algorithm, but also not ensure that the chosen words can maximize express the central meaning of the article. However, after making part of speech tagging the amount of remaining keyword is further reduced. For the subsequent operations of feature extraction and the time and space to calculate weights can be reduced accordingly. After the part of speech tagging the number of each sentence and the location of each word in the sentence will be record.

- Filtering stop word: If the frequency of occurrences of the word is high but it hardly express the meaning of the text, the word is called stop words (stop words).such as " همم " ," بىلەن "," يەن ". If these words are in the vector representation, the dimension of feature vectors would be increased. Thereby the complexity of the algorithm will be increased. So first we will create stop word list, when in operation we will filter the stop words appeared in the text one by one, but the meaningful words are retained to build text vector model.

- Stemming: In order to improve the efficiency and accuracy of feature extraction we must do stemming in the title and text. Same meaning words are merged into a stem, for example, the following few words in Uyghur are all expressed "China", " جۇڭگودىن "," جۇڭگو "," جۇڭگونىڭ "," جۇڭگوغا "," جۇڭگونى ", so the words above are unified as " جۇڭگو ". After stemming the number of each sentence and the location of each word in the sentence will be record.

3.3 Division of Sub-Theme

In the research of our automatic summarization in this paper, in order to improve theme-coverage of Abstracts and reduce generation of redundancy, there are three major steps to achieve the subtheme division in this paper: the construction of similarity matrix, the generation of the largest tree and the clustering division of maximum spanning tree.

For a document, there are many construction methods of inter-sentence similarity matrix, such as the Hamming distance method, the absolute value of the reciprocal method, Euclidean distance method, scalar product method, absolute value of the index, the correlation coefficient method, geometric mean minimum, maximum minimum method, cosine method, and the arithmetic average minimum method. In this paper we use the cosine method to construct similarity matrix, as follows:

The text is divided into a set of sentences, expressed as $S = (S1, S2, S3, \ldots Sn)$, and as a set of samples which is waiting for be classified. Each sentence is a sample;

Each sentence is expressed as a vector whose components are the weight of feature words, the weights are calculated by using TFIDF algorithm, then we suppose the representation of m-dimensional vector of any two sentences Si and Sj is:

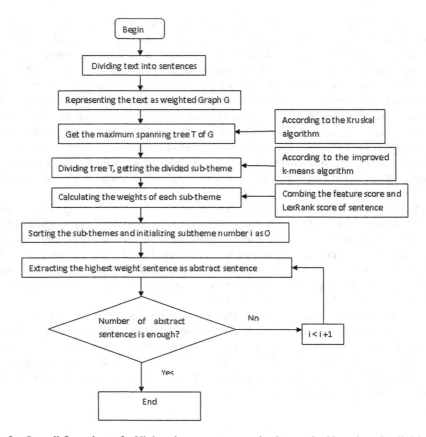

Fig. 2. Overall flow chart of a Uighur document summarization method based on the division of sub-theme

$$Si = (t_{i1}, t_{i1}, \ldots, t_{im}), \ Sj = (t_{j1}, t_{j2}, \ldots, t_{jm}),$$

Calculating the distance between two vectors according to the cosine equation, as the values of similarity matrix element, the formula is as follows:

$$r_{ij} = \frac{\sum_{k=1}^{m} x_{ik} x_{jk}}{\sqrt{\sum_{k=1}^{m} x_{ik}^2 \sum_{k=1}^{m} x_{ik}^2}} \tag{1}$$

Through the above steps, we can construct the similarity matrix of text, thus mading the foundation for the following generation and division of largest tree.

3.4   Calculation of Sentence Weight

After completion of the sub-theme division of the document, the next step is to determine the weight of sentences in each sub-theme and to provide the basis for extraction of abstract sentence. In our method, measurement of the weight of the sentence not only considers the sentence LexRankscore which is calculated by the LexRank algorithm, but also considers the importance of the sentence itself features, such as sentence length, location, sentence structure, clues word or title words and so on.

Next it will be described in detail. After completing sub-theme division of document, we can obtain sentences collection of each sub-theme. For each sub-theme, we can use the following procedure to calculate sentences LexRankscore based on LexRank algorithm:

① Each sentence within the sub-themes is expressed as vector space model whose component is the weights of feature words

② Calculating similarity between any two sentences in sub-theme by vector cosine;

$$sim(d_1, d_1) = \frac{\sum_{i=1}^{n} w_{1i} w_{2i},}{\sum_{i=1}^{m} w_{1i}^2 \sum_{i=1}^{n} w_{2i}^2} \qquad (2)$$

③ Taking the sentences in subtheme as the vertices. Using the similarity between sentences to measure the edge weights between vertices. Constructing corresponding graph structure of subtopics.

④ According to the graph structure of the sub-theme, iteratively calculating the significant value of each vertex using LexRank algorithm within subtheme until variation of significant degree value of each vertex is less than a threshold value Threshold. The final significant value as an indicator of measuring sentence importance denoted LexScore. Calculated as follows:

$$p(u) = \frac{d}{N} + (1 - d) \sum_{v \in adj(u)} \frac{w(u, v)}{\sum_{z \in adj(v)} w(z, v)} p(v) \qquad (3)$$

Wherein, p (u): significant value of vertex u;

Adj (u): a collection of vertices which adjacent to vertex u;
W (u, v): Edge weights between vertex u and vertex v, I.e., the similarity between corresponding sentences;
D: damping, located between [0.1, 0.2];
N: The total number of vertices which is in the graphic structure of sub-theme.

⑤ Repeating the above procedure, until sentences significant values of all subtheme are calculated.

Through the above steps, we can get LexRank algorithm based significant value sentence LexScore, the value is a measure of the overall importance of the sentence. It can be used as a important measure of the sentence weight.

3.5 Summary Generation

We can get sentences weights of all the sub-theme by subtheme division and the calculation method of sentences weight. Then according to the importance of sub-themes and the weight of each cub-topic sentences, we can complete the extraction of abstracts, which is a very critical step for automatic abstraction. Because extracting summary sentences generally have compression ratio (number of abstract sentence / number of sentence of the document), such as compression rate of 10 % or 20 %, the number of abstracts sentence is limited. In addition, each sub-theme of the document is not always important, therefore, when extracting summary sentences, in order to ensure that abstracts sentence can cover the important topics that descript in the document there will need to sort sub-themes before extraction according to the level of importance, so we can begin extracting from the most important sub-themes. Apparently, the importance of the sub-themes is decided mainly by the degree of importance of the sentences it contained. Therefore, in this article, we will take the sum of the weights of each sub-theme sentences as a measure of the importance of the sub-themes. Suppose there are n sentences in the sub-theme, the weight of sentences sf is represented by the form of (sf), then the importance of the sub-themes TopicScore can be calculated by the following formula:

$$TopicScore(T_k) = \sum_{i=1}^{n} w(s_i) \tag{4}$$

We can get the degree of importance of each sub-theme TopicScore by Eq. 4, and according this value we can sort the sub-theme in descending order. When the required abstraction sentence has a limited number, it can give priority to extract the highest weight sentences in the most important sub-theme. Thus ensuring the abstraction sentences can cover the important theme that expressed in the document. This paper presents a method of abstract generation, before extract abstract, all sub-themes are sorted in descending order according to the importance, then the sentence of each sub-theme are sorted in descending order by weight.

4 Experimental Results and Analysis

We compared the new abstract extraction method used in this system with Traditional abstract extraction method based on statistical [10]. In it we use the formula (5) to determine the precision and recall rate for comprehensive evaluation. As can be seen from Table 1, there is a good increase on the recall rate and precision rate in the new approach based on sub-theme division.

$$\text{Recall rate} = \frac{|s_a \cap s_r|}{s_r} \quad \text{precision rate} = \frac{|s_a \cap s_r|}{s_a} \tag{5}$$

Table 1. Comparisons of the experimental results based on traditional statistical method and on the sub-theme

results fields	Recall rate		Accuracy rate	
	Traditional approach	New approach	Traditional approach	New approach
Politics	0.56	0.72	0.45	0.68
News	0.50	0.55	0.46	0.51
Economy	0.51	0.63	0.52	0.58

Acknowledgement. The work in this paper is supported by the National Natural Science Foundation of China project "Research on Basic Theory and Key Technology of Cross Language Social Public Opinion Analysis"(61331013).

References

1. Luhn, H.P.: The automatic creation of literature abstracts. IBM J. Res. Dev. **2**(2), 159–165 (1958)
2. Edmundson, H.P.: New methods in automatic extracting. J. ACM **16**(2), 264–285 (1969)
3. Edmundson, H.P., Wyllys, R.E.: Automatic abstracting and indexing-survey and recommendations. Commun. ACM **4**(5), 226–234 (1961)
4. Ran, L.E., Jacobs, P.S., Zemik, U.: Information extracting and text summarizationusing lingusitic knowledge acquisition. Inf. Process. Manage. **25**(4), 419–428 (1989)
5. Jones, K.S., Brigitte, E.N.: Introduction:automatic summarizing. Inf. Process. Manage. **31**(5), 625–630 (1995)
6. Morris, J., Hirst, G.: Lexical Cohesion computed by thesaural relations as an indicator of the structure of text. Comput. Linguist. **17**, 21–48 (1991)
7. Elhadad, M.: Using lexical chains for text summarization. In: Proceedings of the Workshop on Intelligent Scalable Text Summarization, pp. 10−17. Madrid, Spain (1997)
8. Alam, H., Kumar, A., Nakamura, M.,et al.: Structured and unstructured document summarization: design of a commercial summarizer using lexical chains. In: The 7th International Conference on Document Analysis and Recognition. pp. 1147−1152. UK, Edinburgh, Scotland (2003)
9. Gunes, E., Radev, D.R.: LexRank: graph-based centrality as salience in text summarization. J. Artif. Intell. Res. **22**(12), 457–479 (2004)
10. A Jepati Corneille mention, Venera - Mu Shajiang: Research of statistics-based Uighur website Automatic Extraction of summary. Artificial Intelligence and Recognition Technology, 7(1): 185–188 (2011)

Accelerating DFA Construction
by Parallelizing Subset Construction

Yan Shao[1,2], Yanbing Liu[1(✉)], and Jianlong Tan[1]

[1] Institute of Information Engineering,
Chinese Academy of Sciences, Beijing, China
shaoyan@chinamobile.com
{liuyanbing, tanjianlong}@iie.ac.cn,
[2] China Mobile Information Security Center, Beijing, China

Abstract. Recently there have been increasing research interests on regular expression matching for its widely application in network systems to recognize predefined signatures in suspicious network traffic. Deterministic Finite Automaton (DFA) is the basic data structure for regular expression matching. Though DFA satisfies the need of real-time processing of network traffic in on-line systems, the construction of DFA is very time-consuming that prevents it from being applied on large sets of signature. In this article, we propose two approaches to parallelize the traditional sequential subset construction algorithm, which is used to convert a non-deterministic finite automaton (NFA) to an equivalent DFA, in order to accelerate DFA construction. The first proposed algorithm PRW is based on fine-grained locks on shared data structures to ensure multiple worker threads construct a DFA in parallel safely. The second proposed algorithm ARW splits the read and write accesses on shared data structures, and distributes the read operations and write operations to the multi-thread stage and the single-thread stage respectively. Experiment demonstrates the efficiency of our algorithms on real signatures of open source systems, and the speed-up ratio of PRW and ARW is up to 1.72 and 2.71 respectively with 4 worker threads.

Keywords: Automaton · DFA construction · Subset construction · Parallel algorithm

1 Introduction

Recent years, there have been increasing research interests on regular expression matching, which is widely used in network applications to search for predefined signatures against network traffic. Typical applications include network intrusion detection system, network firewall, traffic classification, anti-virus, anti-spam, etc.

Deterministic Finite Automaton (DFA) is a basic data structure for regular expression matching. A standard method to recognize a set of regular expressions with DFA consists of three steps: (i) translate the regular expressions into a combined Nondeterministic Finite Automata (NFA); (ii) perform subset construction to convert the NFA into a DFA; (iii) minimize the DFA [1]. Though DFA meets the requirement of real-time processing of network traffic in on-line systems, DFA construction is very

© Springer-Verlag Berlin Heidelberg 2015
Y. Lu et al. (Eds.): ISCTCS 2014, CCIS 520, pp. 16–24, 2015.
DOI: 10.1007/978-3-662-47401-3_3

time-consuming, especially for large sets of signatures. This limitation prevents DFA from being used in scenarios that require the signatures to take effect immediately. With the rapid development and widely application of multi-core technology, it is desperately desired to parallelize the sequential subset construction.

In this paper, we study the method to parallelize subset construction on multi-core shared-memory architecture. We propose two versions of parallel subset construction algorithm. The first proposed algorithm PRW (Parallel Reading and Writing) is based on fine-grained locks on shared data structures among multiple worker threads to ensure multi-thread safety in parallel DFA construction. The second proposed algorithm ARW (Alternating Reading and Writing) splits the read and write accesses on shared data structures, and distributes the read operations and write operations to the multi-thread stage and the single-thread stage respectively. We evaluate our proposed algorithms on real signatures from open source systems, and the speed-up ratio of PRW and ARW is up to 1.72 and 2.71 respectively with 4 worker threads.

This paper is organized as follows. Related work and the sequential subset construction algorithm are presented in Sects. 2 and 3. In Sects. 4 and 5, we proposed two versions of parallel subset construction algorithm to accelerate DFA construction. We carry out experiments in Sect. 6 and conclude the paper in Sect. 7.

2 Related Work

The sequential subset construction algorithm is introduced in [1] and [5]. Leslie [6] improves efficiency of subset construction with basic data structures. Leiss [7] proposes a NFA construction algorithm to reduce the size of its equivalent DFA. Chang and Paige [8] devise a novel method to represent NFAs, which enables efficient manipulation of NFA significantly. Chen and Su [9] propose an epsilon compressed NFA construction algorithm to enhance the performance of conversion from NFA to DFA by decreasing the epsilon edges and the corresponding states. Liu et al. [3] accelerates combined DFA construction by hierarchical merging of the DFAs of each single regular expression.

There are very few attempts to parallelize subset construction. As far as we are concerned, Choi and Burgstaller [10] are the first and only researchers study ways to effectively parallelize the subset construction algorithm. They design NFA and DFA data-structures to improve scalability and minimize overhead and present three different ways for synchronization.

3 Background: Sequential Subset Construction

Algorithm 1 describes the sequential subset construction algorithm. It starts with the ε-closure of the initial state of NFA. Then it explore the NFA for all reachable sets of NFA states, and generate DFA states during the exploration. Assuming the current NFA state set is S and the input character is $c \in \Sigma$, the next activated NFA state set is

$$T = \varepsilon - \text{closure}\left(\bigcup_{s \in S} \delta'(s, c)\right).$$ All the DFA states found are stored in a hash table

DStateHash, and the unexpanded NFA state sets are stored in a queue *Queue*. When a NFA state set T is activated, we search it in *DStateHash*. If T is not found, it indicates that T is a newly found DFA state, and then T is inserted to *DStateHash* and *Queue*. The subset construction algorithm terminates, when all states in *Queue* are expanded.

Algorithm 1: Sequential subset construction algorithm for NFA to DFA conversion.

Input: NFA $N=(Q', \Sigma, \delta', q_0', F')$
Output: DFA $D=(Q, \Sigma, \delta, q_0, F)$

```
1     I ← ε − closure(q₀')
2     push(Queue, I)
3     insert(DStateHash, I)
4     while Queue is not empty do
5        S←pop(Queue)
6        Q ← Q ∪ {S}
7        if S ∩ F' ≠ ∅ then
8           F ← F∪{S}
9        endif
10       for each c ∈ Σ do
11          T ← ε − closure(∪ₛ∈ₛ δ'(s,c))
12          δ(S,c) ← T
13          U←search(DStateHash, T)
14          if U is NIL then
15             insert(DStateHash, T)
16             push(Queue, T)
17          endif
18       endfor
19    enwhile
```

---

4   Parallelizing Subset Construction by Parallel Reading and Writing

We propose a direct and naïve version of parallel subset construction called PRW (Parallel Reading and Writing). The main idea is to parallelize the outer while-loop in subset construction (Algorithm 1 line 4−19). We start multiple threads and every thread get a unique element from *Queue* each time. All the threads have read and write access right to all data structure in order to explore reachable NFA state sets simultaneously. It is obvious that most operations are multi-thread safe, except getting an element from *Queue* (line 5), inserting an element into to *DStateHash* (line 15), and inserting an element into to Queue (line 16). We utilize fine-grained locks to maintain data synchronization, when updating *Queue* and *DStateHash*. The algorithm terminates, when *Queue* is empty at the beginning of iteration.

We employ separated Head and Tail locks to allow complete concurrency between en-queue and de-queue operations as demonstrated in [2]. A linear array of locks is applied to avoid race conditions when multiple worker threads accessing *DStateHash*. We assign a unique lock to each bucket in *DStateHash*, and the lock condition decides whether the bucket in *DStateHash* is available for read or write. When a worker thread finds a new reachable NFA state set T, it checks whether the bucket storing T is locked. If the lock is unlocked, the worker thread gains access right to the bucket and lock it.

Otherwise, the thread keeps waiting until another worker thread finishes its job and unlock the bucket. The idea is illustrated in Algorithm 2.

Algorithm 2: Access to *DStateHash* guarded by linear array of locks.

```
1    procedure AccessDStateHash(T)
2        key←hashfunc(T)
3        while DStateHash [key] is locked do
4            wait
5        endwhile
6        lock(DStateHash [key])
7        U←search(DStateHash, T)
8        if U is NIL then
9            insert(DStateHash, T)
10           push(Queue, T)
11       endif
12       unlock(DStateHash[key])
```

Algorithm 3: Multi-thread parallelizing stage of PRW.

```
1    start n worker threads and every
     worker thread do
2        while Queue is not empty do
3            S←pop(Queue)
4            Q ← Q ∪ {S}
5            if S ∩ F' ≠ ∅ then
6                F ← F∪{S}
7            endif
8            for each c ∈ Σ do
9                T ← ε − closure(∪ₛ∈ₛ δ'(s,c))
10               AccessDStateHash(T)
11               δ(S, c)←T
12           endfor
13       endwhile
```

$T \leftarrow \varepsilon - \text{closure}(\cup_{s \in S} \delta'(s, c))$

Algorithm 4: The multi-thread stage of ARW: operations executed by the *i*-th worker threads.

```
1    j←0
2    while Queue is not empty and j ≤
     SwitchingThreshold do
3        S←pop(Queue)
4        Q ← Q ∪ {S}
1        if S ∩ F' ≠ ∅ then
2            F ← F∪{S}
5        endif
3        for each c ∈ Σ do
6            T ← ε − closure(∪ₛ∈ₛ δ'(s,c))
7            U←search(DStateHash, T)
8            if U is NIL then
9                push (IndexTableⁱ, (T, S, c))
10               j← j+1
11           else
12               δ(S, c)←T
13           endif
14       endfor
15   endwhile
```

Algorithm 5: The single-thread stage of ARW: insert new DFA states into *DStateHash* and fill the transition table of DFA.

```
1    for i=1,..., n do
2        while IndexTableⁱ is not empty do
3            (T, S, c) ←pop(IndexTableⁱ)
4            insert(DStateHash, T)
5            push(Queue, T)
6            δ(S, c)←T
7        endwhile
8    endfor
```

There are two stages in PRW algorithm: the preprocessing stage and the multi-thread parallelizing stage. During the preprocessing stage, we generate at least n elements in *Queue* with sequential subset construction to ensure that every worker thread gets an element in *Queue*, where n is the number of worker threads in the multi-thread parallelizing stage. Then the multi-thread parallelizing stage begins, which is described in Algorithm 3. The multi-thread parallelizing stage terminates, when there is no element left in *Queue*.

5   Parallelizing Subset Construction by Alternating Reading and Writing

In PRW algorithm, when a worker thread has gained the access right to *DStateHash*, other worker threads have to wait even if the thread in processing only reads *DStateHash* without any updating operations. This phenomenon results in performance degradation. After analyzing the operations on *DStateHash*, we find out that there is a significant difference between the frequencies of read and write operations. We summarize this phenomenon in Theorem 1 as follows.

Theorem 1. In the subset construction, the ratio of the number of write operations in *DStateHash* to the number of total operations (including reads and writes) is $\frac{1}{1+|\Sigma|}$.

Proof. Every time a new DFA state is found, a write operation is performed in *DStateHash*. Thus the number of write operations is $|Q|$, where $|Q|$ is the number of DFA states. Each lookup in *DStateHash* incurs a read operation. *Queue* stores unexpanded NFA state sets, i.e. DFA states, so the number of elements in *Queue* is $|Q|$, which means the outer while-loop (Algorithm 1 line 4) repeats $|Q|$ times. The inner for-loop (Algorithm 1 line 9) repeats $|\Sigma|$ times. Thus the number of read operations is $|Q||\Sigma|$. Therefore, the ratio of the number of write operations in *DStateHash* to that of total operations (including reads and writes) is $\frac{|Q|}{|Q|+|Q||\Sigma|} = \frac{1}{1+|\Sigma|}$.   ∎

Usually, the size of input alphabet is $|\Sigma| = 256$, thus the write operations only accounts for $\frac{1}{1+|\Sigma|} = \frac{1}{1+256} = 0.39\,\%$ of all operations in *DStateHash*, while the read operations which are multi-thread safe account for 99.61 %. It indicates that most operations in *DStateHash* can be executed in parallel without locks.

Based on Theorem 1, we propose ARW (Alternating Reading and Writing) algorithm. It splits the read and write accesses in *DStateHash*, and distributes the read operations and write operations to the multi-thread stage and the single-thread stage respectively. These two stages execute in an alternating manner, until all of the reachable NFA state sets are discovered and explored.

ARW algorithm consists of three stages: the preprocessing stage, the multi-thread stage and the single-thread stage. The preprocessing stage is executed as same as that of PRW, so we do not cover it here again. When the preprocessing stage finishes, the multi-thread stage and the single-thread stage begin to run alternatively.

During the multi-thread stage, worker threads are only assigned with read access right of *DStateHash*. They execute the same operations described in Algorithm 4. The threads traverse the NFA and fill the transitions for DFA states that have been inserted to *DStateHash*. When worker threads encounter a new DFA state not in *DStateHash*, they record auxiliary information, including its equivalent NFA state set, previous state and input character. The auxiliary information is stored in *IndexTable* implemented as a queue. Every worker thread is assigned with separate *IndexTable* distinguished with superscript. When *Queue* is empty or the elements in the *IndexTable^i* is greater than a pre-set parameter (called switching threshold), the *i*-th thread terminates. ARW algorithm switches to the single-thread stage, when all the worker threads terminate.

All the DFA states newly found in the multi-thread stage are processed during the single-thread stage. There is only one worker thread, which has write access right to *DStateHash*. The new DFA states are inserted into to *DStateHash* and *Queue*, and the transition table is filled up based on *IndexTable*. The procedure of the single-thread stage is described in Algorithm 5. ARW algorithm terminates when the *IndexTable*s are empty right after the multi-thread stage, which means there is no more new DFA states and the DFA is fully constructed.

6 Experiment and Evaluation

We compare PRW and ARW with the original sequential subset construction in terms of construction time. We also evaluate their performance with different number of worker threads, as well as the performance of ARW with different switching thresholds.

The experiment is carried out on signature sets of regular expressions obtained from several open source systems, including L7-filter, BRO and SNORT. Their signatures are divided into 3 groups respectively. Liu et al. [3] proposes a method to accelerate DFA construction by hierarchical merging. We adopt this method in our experiments.

We implement all the algorithms in C ++ and compile them with Microsoft Visual Studio 2010 on Windows 7 (32-bit). The critical section from Windows API is used for all lock-based synchronization. The program runs on a hardware platform configured with Intel Core i5 2400 CPU (3.10 GHz, 2 CPUs × 4 core/CPU) and 4 GB memory.

6.1 Performance Comparison with Sequential Subset Construction

Table 1 presents the DFA construction time (in sec) of sequential subset construction, PRW and ARW on 9 groups of regular expression signatures, where the speed-up ratio is defined as the DFA construction time of sequential subset construction algorithm to that of PRW (or ARW). The number n of worker threads is set to 4.

PRW runs faster than the sequential subset construction, and the average speed-up ratio is 1.668, 1.226 and 1.171 on L7-filter, Snort and BRO respectively. It also indicates that PRW performs even better on the rule sets L7-filter 1 ∼ 3 and BRO 3, which correspond to DFAs with more than 240,000 states. With regard to smaller DFAs, the probability of multiple worker threads compete for the same buckets in *DStateHash* increases, resulting in more time spend on waiting.

ARW dramatically outperforms sequential subset construction and PRW. The average speed-up ratio is 2.436, 1.292 and 1.438 on L7-filter, Snort and BRO respectively. Similar to PRW, ARW performs better on huge DFAs, and achieves best acceleration performance on the rule sets L7-filter 1 ∼ 3 and BRO 3. With regard to smaller DFA, the switching between multi-thread stage and single-thread stage is more frequent. In result, the acceleration performance degrades because of thread switching.

6.2 Performance Evaluation with Different Number of Worker Threads

Since the number of worker threads n affects the performance of PRW and ARW, we test their performance with $n = 2, 4, 8$ respectively. Table 2 shows the results.

Table 1. DFA construction time of sequential subset construction, PRW and ARW. (The number of worker threads is $n = 4$.)

Rule set	# of rules	# of DFA states	Sequential subset construction	PRW ($n = 4$)	Speed-up ratio of PRW	ARW ($n = 4$)	Speed-up ratio of ARW
L7-fliter 1	52	249705	9.109	5.308	**1.716**	4.587	**1.986**
L7-fliter 2	21	1083358	34.009	20.912	**1.626**	13.040	**2.608**
L7-fliter 3	37	1542125	53.959	32.471	**1.662**	19.884	**2.714**
Snort 1	31	5389	0.698	0.579	1.206	0.598	1.167
Snort 2	24	8621	0.649	0.547	1.186	0.468	1.387
Snort 3	34	10194	0.891	0.693	1.286	0.674	1.322
BRO 1	217	6941	6.386	6.359	1.004	2.507	1.041
BRO 2	683	26042	9.392	9.088	1.033	8.192	1.105

Table 2. Speed-up ratio of PRW and ARW with different number of worker threads.

Rule set	PRW			ARW		
	$n = 2$	$n = 4$	$n = 8$	$n = 2$	$n = 4$	$n = 8$
L7-fliter 1	1.378	**1.716**	1.719	1.277	**1.986**	1.705
L7-fliter 2	1.366	**1.626**	1.633	1.517	**2.608**	2.440
L7-fliter 3	1.359	**1.662**	1.562	1.559	**2.714**	2.522
Snort 1	1.133	**1.206**	1.175	1.059	**1.167**	1.084
Snort 2	1.161	**1.186**	1.239	1.153	**1.387**	1.306
Snort 3	1.159	**1.286**	1.253	1.112	**1.322**	1.177
BRO 1	**1.023**	1.004	0.986	0.980	**1.041**	0.968
BRO 2	**1.212**	1.022	0.976	1.001	**1.105**	1.017
BRO 3	1.314	**1.569**	1.560	1.467	**2.168**	2.117

PRW achieves best speed-up ratio when $n = 4$ on all rule sets except BRO $1 \sim 2$. It is demonstrated in [4] that most transitions of DFAs lead back to the initial state or states nearby, i.e. the buckets containing these states are more frequently accessed. As n increases, the probability of multiple worker threads racing for certain buckets in *DStateHash* increases, which becomes the performance bottleneck.

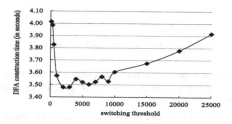
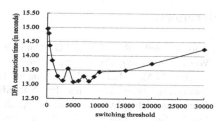

Fig. 1. DFA construction time of the final merging with different switching thresholds on L7-filter 1.

Fig. 2. DFA construction time of the final merging with different switching thresholds on L7-filter 2

ARW achieves best performance with $n = 4$ on all the rule sets. As the number of worker threads increases, the number of DFA states found during each multi-thread stage increases, resulting in more elements in the transition table filled during the single-thread stage. As a result, increasing the number of worker threads ($n > 4$) does not promise better performance enhancement.

6.3   Performance Evaluation with Different Switching Thresholds

With regard to ARW, the choice of switching threshold affects its performance. We test ARW with different switching thresholds on the regular expression signature sets L7-filter 1 and L7-filter 2, and the experiment results are showed in Figs. 1 and 2 respectively. It indicates that ARW achieves best performance when the switching threshold lies between 2500 and 7500. When the switching threshold is smaller than 2500, the switching between multi-thread stage and single-thread stage gets too frequently. When the switching threshold exceeds 7500, a great portion of the elements in the transition table are filled during the single-thread stage.

7   Conclusion

DFA is a basic data structure for regular expression matching in many network applications. However, constructing DFA with the traditional sequential subset construction algorithm is very time-inefficient. To attack this problem, we address the problem of parallel subset construction and propose two versions of improved algorithms. Experiment on real signatures demonstrates the efficiency of our algorithms. In the future, we plan to study the method of choosing the optimal switching threshold in ARW by exploiting the characteristics of regular expression signatures.

Acknowledgment. This work is partially supported by the "Strategic Priority Research Program" of the Chinese Academy of Sciences under grant No. XDA06030602 and the National Science Foundation of China (NSFC) under grant No. 61202477.

References

1. Aho, V., Sethi, R., Ullman, J.D.: Compilers: Principles, Techniques, and Tools. Addison-Wesley Publishing Co., Boston (1986)
2. Maged, M.M., Michael, L.S.: Simple, fast, and practical non-blocking and blocking concurrent queue algorithms. In: Proceedings of the 15th annual ACM symposium on Principles of distributed computing, pp. 267 − 275 (1996)
3. Liu, Y., Guo, L., Guo, M., Liu, P.: Accelerating DFA Construction by Hierarchical Merging. In: Proceedings of the 2011 IEEE Ninth International Symposium on Parallel and Distributed Processing with Applications (ISPA), pp. 1 − 6 (2011)
4. Becchi, M., Crowley, P.: An improved algorithm to accelerate regular expression evaluation. In: Proceedings of the 3rd ACM/IEEE Symposium on Architecture for networking and communications systems, pp. 145–154 (2007)
5. Hopcroft, J.E., Motwani, R., Ullman, J.D.: Introduction to automata theory, languages, and computation, 2nd edn. Addison Wesley, Boston (2000)
6. Leiss, E.: Constructing a finite automaton for a given regular expression. ACM SIGACT News 12(3), 81–87 (1980)
7. Leslie, T.: Efficient approaches to subset construction. Master thesis, the University of Waterloo, Canada (1995)
8. Chang, C.H., Paige, R.: From regular expressions to DFA's using compressed NFA's. In: Apostolico, A., Crochemore, M., Galil, Z., Manber, U. (eds.) Combinatorial Pattern Matching, vol. 644, pp. 90–110. Springer, Heidelberg (1992)
9. Chen, S., Su, J.: Protocol identification research based on content analysis. J. Nat. Univ. Def. Technol. 30(4), 82–87 (2008)
10. Choi, H., Burgstaller, B.: Non-blocking Parallel Subset construction on shared-memory multicore architectures. In: proceedings of the 11th Australasian symposium on parallel and distributed computing (AusPDC 2013), pp. 13 − 20 (2013)

A Novel Feature Selection Method Based on Category Distribution and Phrase Attributes

Yi Zheng[✉], Weihong Han, and Chengzhang Zhu

College of Computer Science,
National University of Defense Technology, Changsha, China
justice131@163.com

Abstract. A novel and effective feature selection method called CDPAB-FSM(category distribution and phrase attribute based feature selection method) for automatical Chinese web page classification was proposed. The method combined the distribution among categories with that within the category. As well, the length and position of the phrases to select were taken into account in order to distinguish the feature phrases from other unimportant ones. Experiments showed that CDPAB-FSM was suited for feature selection of Chinese web page classification and it achieved better classification results than TF-IDF did.

Keywords: TF-IDF · Feature selection method · Web page classification · ELM

1 Introduction

With the rapid development of information technology, the data on the Internet has accumulated at an amazing speed. According to CNNIC(China Internet Network Information Center), the number of Chinese web page has exceeded 150 billion since December of 2013. It raised a headache problem on how to organize and manage such large amount of data effectively. Luckily, the classification based on the text of these numerous web pages becomes one of the effective means to solve this problem. However, another problem comes after that, it is still a challenge to classify web pages for their high dimensional feature space at present. The dimensions range from thousands to tens of thousands and even to hundreds of thousands. This problem really brought troubles to exact and effective classification of web pages. Yet, since the feature space of most web pages distribute sparsely, it is possible to reduce the dimensions if we try to select the representative subset from feature space. This paper summarizes characteristics of most existed feature selection methods such as TF-IDF(Term Frequency-Inverse Document Frequency), MI(Mutual Information) and so on. For the purpose of selecting most representative feature phrases, we proposed a novel feature selection method which combines the distribution among categories with that within the category, meanwhile, we took the feature phrase attributes including the phrase's length and position in the web page it belongs to into consideration.

© Springer-Verlag Berlin Heidelberg 2015
Y. Lu et al. (Eds.): ISCTCS 2014, CCIS 520, pp. 25–32, 2015.
DOI: 10.1007/978-3-662-47401-3_4

Related experiments on Chinese web page classification show that the classifier based on our method achieves better classification results than that based on TF-IDF.

This paper is organized as follows. Section 2 describes related work on feature selection. Section 3 illustrates the proposed method and the ELM(Extreme Learning Machine) classifier. Section 4 shows the experimental results. Section 5 concludes the paper and provides direction for future improvement.

2   Related Work

Currently, the feature selection methods for web page classification mainly come from the document feature selection methods. There are several types as follows: (1) Term Frequency(TF) [7,12]. It selects feature phrases bases on the frequency it appears. (2) Document Frequency(DF). It selects feature phrases bases on the proportion of the documents it appears. (3) Mutual Information(MI) [6,8]. It gives priority to feature phrases which get more mutual information with the categories. (4) Information Gain(IG) [7,11]. The importance of a phrase is attached to the information amount it brings to the classfication system. (5) Chi-Square Statistic(CHI) [5]. The phrases are selected by their dependence on the categories. (6) Information Entropy(IE). It is a measurement of the amount of information in a certain category. Besides it is a key factor to select the feature phrases. In the meantime, many domestic scholars proposed improved methods based on methods above through their deep study and analysis. These improved methods are better adapted to Chinese web page classification, and listed as follows: (1) The improved method combines Term Frequency with Document Frequency. Term Frequency reflects its features within the document that the higher the phrases frequency is, the more it can represent the document. Document Frequency is the distribution of a phrase among the documents. The phrase which appears rarely among the document is more useful to distinguish the document it locates from others. In 1997, the classification experiment which combined Term Frequency with Document Frequency was done by Yang [10], thus confirmed advantages of the combined method. (2) Improved methods based on Mutual Information(MI). The distinction ability of a phrase depends on the ratio between the maximum and inferior amount of information the phrase can provide for the categories. (3) Improved Methods Based on Information Gain. Li Wenbing added a correction factor to the formula of Information Gain to balance the impact that information entropy brings to information gain. Besides, their experiment verified the sound effect of this improved method. (4) Improved Methods Based on Chi-Square Statistic. Li Mingjie proposed a novel means to integrate Chi-Square Statistic and Information Gain and get improved classfication results.

3   The Proposed Method CDPAB-FSM

The purpose of feature selection is to select a subset of phrases which can represent the categories. In other words, feature selection is to choose several phrases which appear frequently in a category and appear rarely in other categories. In this way, these selected phrases are able to distinguish the category it belongs to from others. In this paper, we proposed a novel method of calculating the synthetic weight of each phrase in categories. After calculating the synthetic weight of all the phrases in categories, we can easily determine whether to add a phrase to the feature phrases subset or not. More over, The synthetic weight formula is computed as follow:

$$Weight(t) = LenWeight(t) * PosWeight(t) * DA(t) * DW(t), \qquad (1)$$

where t is the phrase to calculate; $Weight(t)$ stands for the synthetic weight of it; $LenWeight(t)$ is the phrase t's length weight; $PosWeight(t)$ stands for the position weight of t; $DA(t)$ and $DW(t)$ refers to the distribution weight among categories and within a category. The details of the four parts are listed as follows.

3.1   Length Weight of Phrases(LenWeight)

The length of a phrase often determines the amount of information it carries. It means the longer a phrase is, the more information it carries. However, the long phrases are more inclined to appear fewer times. So in this paper, we take the length of phrases into consideration to avoid the omission of phrases which appear a few times but get long length. The length weight is formalized as follow:

$$LenWeight(t) = \log(Length(t)), \qquad (2)$$

where t is the phrase to calculate; $LenWeight(t)$ the phrase t's length weight; $Length(t)$ is the length of t.

3.2   Position Weight of Phrases(PosWeight)

The web pages are semi-structured documents which are made up of several tags and contents of tags. The importance of a phrase varies with the position it locates in. For example, the phrases in the tag "$\langle Title \rangle \langle /Title \rangle$" carry the theme information of the web page in most cases, whereas the content of the tag "$\langle body \rangle \langle /body \rangle$" contains much noise information. Based on this idea, we attached different weights to phrases in different tags as Table 1.

The position weight is formalized as follow:

$$PosWeight(t) = \frac{\sum_{i=1}^{m}(tf_i(t) * pos_i)}{tf(t)}, \qquad (3)$$

where t is the phrase to calculate; "$m = 10$" is the total number of tags; "i" is the sequence number in tags; $tf_i(t)$ stands for the frequence at which t appears in tag i; pos_i refers to the weight of tag i; $tf(t)$ is the total frequence of t in current document.

Table 1. Weight of Tags

Sequence	Tags	Meaning	Weight
1	$\langle Title \rangle$	title of web page	4.0
2	$\langle Meta \rangle$	Description	3.0
3	$\langle H1 \rangle$	Heading 1	2.0
4	$\langle H2 \rangle$	Heading 2	1.8
5	$\langle H3 \rangle$	Heading 3	1.6
6	$\langle H4 \rangle$	Heading 4	1.4
7	$\langle H5 \rangle$	Heading 5	1.2
8	$\langle H6 \rangle$	Heading 6	1.1
8	$\langle Strong \rangle\ \langle B \rangle\langle U \rangle\langle I \rangle\langle S \rangle$	Heading 6	1.1
10	$\langle Othertags \rangle$	Others	1.0

3.3   Distribution Among the Categories(DA)

The variance of a phrase's Term Frequency among all the categories is used as measurements of its distribution among the categories. The specific formula is as follow:

$$DA(t) = \frac{\frac{1}{n}\sum_{i=1}^{n}(tf_i(t) - \overline{tf(t)})^2}{\frac{1}{n}\sum_{i=1}^{n}(tf_i(t))^2},\qquad(4)$$

where t is the phrase to calculate; n is the number of categories; $tf_i(t)$ refers to the frequency it appears in category c_i ; $\overline{tf(t)}$ stands for the average frequency t appear in all categories, $\overline{tf(t)} = \frac{\sum_1^n tf_i(t)}{n}$.

3.4   Distribution Withing the Categories(DW)

Similarly, the variance of a phrase's Term Frequency within a category is also used as measurements of its distribution within the category. The formula to calculate the variance of category c_i is as follow:

$$DW(t) = 1 - Di(t) = 1 - \frac{\frac{1}{m}\sum_{j=1}^{m}(tf_{ij}(t) - \overline{tf_i(t)})^2}{\frac{1}{m}\sum_{j=1}^{m}(tf_{ij}(t))^2},\qquad(5)$$

where t is the phrase to calculate; m is the document number in category c_i; Di is the normalized inner variance; $tf_{ij}(t)$ is the Term Frequency of t in the j-th document of category c_i. $\overline{tf_i(t)}$ is the average Term Frequency of t in all the documents of category c_i, $\overline{tf_i(t)} = \frac{\sum_1^m tf_{ij}(t)}{m}$. The more uniformly t distributes among documents of category c_i, the better it can represent for c_i and the larger $1 - Di$ is. So we take $1 - Di$ as DW.

3.5   Classification Algorithm

ELM(Extreme Learning Machine) was adopted to the Chinese web page classification in this paper. ELM is one of the most excellent learning algorithms for single hidden layer feedforward neural networks(SLFNs). It randomly chose input weights and analytically determines output weights of SLFNs thus providing the best generalization performance at extremely fast learning speed [2,3,9]. Due to the advantages referred above, it has been widely used in related fields such as image and signal processing, face recognition since it was proposed [1,4,13]. Given a training set $\{(x_i, t_i)|x_i \in R^n, t_i \in R^m, i = 1, ..., N_1\}$, a SLFNs with N2 hidden neurons can be expressed as follow:

$$\sum_{j=1}^{N_2} \beta_j g(W_j X_i + b_j) = o_i, i = 1, ..., N_1, \tag{6}$$

where g(x) is the excitation function; β_j is the output weight; b_j is the offset of the i-th hidden unit. The learning goal of ELM is to find specific $\hat{w}_i, \hat{b}_i, \hat{\beta}_i$ $(i = 1, ..., N_2)$ such that

$$\left\| H(\hat{w}_1, w_{\hat{N}_2}, \hat{b}_1, b_{\hat{N}_2})\beta - T \right\| = \min_{w_i, b_i, \beta} \| H(w_1, w_{N_2}, b_1, b_{N_2})\beta - T \|. \tag{7}$$

which is equivalent to minimizing the cost function

$$\sum_{j=1}^{N_1} (\sum_{i=1}^{N_2} \beta_j g(w_i x_j + b_i) - t_j). \tag{8}$$

Besides, the learning process of ELM is as follow:
step1: The input weight W_j and bias b_j are assigned arbitrarily.
step2: The hidden layer output matrix H is calculated.
step3: The output weight β is calculated by the next formula:

$$\beta = H^\dagger T, \tag{9}$$

where † is the Moore-Penrose generalized inverse of H.

4   Experimental Result

We carried out comparative classification experiments with TF-IDF to verify the advantages of our method.

4.1   Corpus

The corpus for our experiments consists of Chinese web pages crawled from Sina, one of the four largest scale portal websites. Its channel categories are of certain authority for they are classified manually. We crawled 3000 pages in total including 12 categories as follows: sports, estate, tourism, finance, automobile, entertainment, city, education, buddhist, military, technology, games. Each category contains 300 web pages. Besides we use 250 of each category as training set and the remianing as test set.

4.2 Experimental Results

The input of the classifier is the web pages to be classified and the output is the classification result. Further more, specific procedures are as follows:

(1) Use our proposed method to select feature phrases from the training set.
(2) Denose the test web pages and then use ICTCLAS tokenizer to separate the denoising sentences into phrases.
(3) Get all the web pages structure formalized according to the tags in Table 1.
(4) Utilize vector space model to obtain the vector of the training and test web page struct according to the feature phrase set. The weight of each phrase is calculated by formula(3).
(5) Input the vectors of training and test set into the ELM classifier and record all the classification results.

At every run of the next experiments, the training set which occupied 4/5 of the entire data was randomly selected from the corpus. And the remaining data was used as test set. All the results displayed below are the average of 10 times repeated experiments.

Experiment 1: In this experiment, we discussed the effect of feature phrase scale on the classification results. The macro precision, macro recall rate, macro F1 value as well as micro precision is used to measure the experimental trends. Related results are presented in the Fig. 1. From the analysis of trends shown in Fig. 1, we can draw the following conclusions:

(1) The scale of feature phrases has potent effects on the classification results of ELM. In addition, the larger the scale of the feature phrases is, the better the results are at the beginning. However, when the scale of feature phrases exceeds 2000, the classification effect stays steady.
(2) Nearly in all scales of feature phrases, our proposed method CDPA-FSM achieved better classification results than TD-IDF did. This demonstrates the feasibility and advantages of CDPA-FSM.

Experiment 2: According to the results and conclusions we got in experiment1, the feature phrase scale at 2000 is a good choice where we can get better classification results and reduce the classification time cost as well. Thus, we set the feature phrase scale as 2000 in the following experiment2 and then compared the classification results between TF-IDF and CDPA-FSM. Details are shown in Table 2 and Fig. 2.

From the classification results displayed above, we can draw the following conclusions.

(1) Our novel method CDPA-FSM achieved higher precision and recall rate than TF-IDF did in most of the categories. Thus, the macro and micro index of CDPA-FSM are much better than those of TF-IDF. For example, the macro F1 of CDPA-FSM is 97.44 % far higher than 93.54 % of TF-IDF.
(2) As for category Estate, Entertainment and Technology, the evaluation indices are much lower than those of other categories. After analysis of original web

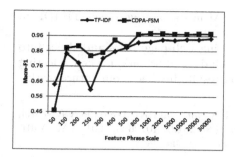

Fig. 1. results of experiment1.

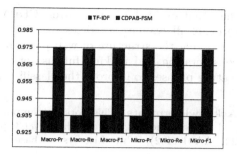

Fig. 2. comprehensive evaluation results.

Table 2. classification results (%)

Method \ Category	sport	est	tour	fina	auto	ent	city	edu	bud	mil	tech	game
Precision(TF-IDF)	93.7	91.6	95.5	97.6	99.8	91.7	90.6	95.9	99.9	94.3	77.9	96.3
Precision(CDPA-FSM)	98.9	94.0	98.9	98.6	100.0	98.6	98.6	97.3	100.0	96.7	90.1	98.2
Recall(TF-IDF)	91.8	84.4	87.2	97.4	99.0	91.8	93.2	96.4	99.2	98.4	86.2	97.4
Recall(CDPA-FSM)	96.8	93.4	93.8	97.8	99.8	97.6	98.8	97.0	99.6	98.8	96.6	99.2
F1(TF-IDF)	92.7	87.8	90.9	97.5	99.4	91.7	91.8	96.1	99.6	96.3	81.7	96.8
F1(CDPA-FSM)	97.8	93.6	96.2	98.1	99.9	98.0	98.7	97.1	99.8	97.7	93.2	98.7

pages of the three categories, we found the reason that the three categories contained few words but many pictures and advertisement contents in common. This unrelated information brought noises to the classifier so that the corresponding classification results were not so good as others.

5   Conclusion

Aimed at improving the accuracy and recall rate of Chinese web page classification, this paper presents a new method of feature selection which combines the phrases distribution among and within categories with its attributes. Besides, related Chinese web page classification experiments demonstrate the feasibility and advantages of our novel method CDPA-FSM. From these experiments, the relation between feature phrase scales and classification results is easily seen. On the one hand, if the feature phrase scale is too small to express the web page features, the precision and recall will be low. On the other hand, if the feature phrase scale is too large, noises will be brought in, leading to low precision and recall as well. So we discussed the impact of feature phrase scale on the classification results at first. Then contrast experiment was conducted to check the feasibility and improvement of CDPA-FSM. Chinese web page classification based on feature phrases selected by CDPA-FSM gets higher precision and recall than that of TF-IDF. More over, CDPA-FSM has advantages over TF-IDF in terms of all evaluation indices.

Taking the structure of web pages including web-page links and styles into consideration and making full use of this kind of information when selecting feature phrases to improve the classification results further is our future work.

Acknowledgments. This work was supported by National High Technology Research and Development Plan of China (863 plan)(No.2012AA012600, 2012AA01A401, 2012AA01A402), White List System based on Service Discovery.

References

1. Baboo, S.S., Sasikala, S.: Multicategory classification using an extreme learning machine for microarray gene expression cancer diagnosis. In: 2010 IEEE International Conference on Communication Control and Computing Technologies, pp. 748–757. IEEE (2010)
2. Cambria, E., Huang, G.B., Kasun, L.L.C., Zhou, H., Vong, C.M., Lin, J., Yin, J., Cai, Z., Liu, Q., Li, K., et al.: Extreme learning machines. IEEE Intell. Syst. **28**(6), 30–59 (2013)
3. Huang, G.B., Zhou, H., Ding, X., Zhang, R.: Extreme learning machine for regression and multiclass classification. IEEE Trans. Syst. Man Cybern. Part B: Cybern. **42**(2), 513–529 (2012)
4. Lan, Y., Hu, Z., Soh, Y.C., Huang, G.B.: An extreme learning machine approach for speaker recognition. Neural Comput. Appl. **22**(3–4), 417–425 (2013)
5. Mesleh, A.M.: Chi square feature extraction based svms arabic language text categorization system. J. Comput. Sci. **3**(6), 430 (2007)
6. Oveisi, F., Oveisi, S., Erfanian, A., Patras, I.: Tree-structured feature extraction using mutual information. IEEE Trans. Neural Netw. Learn. Syst. **23**(1), 127–137 (2012)
7. Patil, L.H., Atique, M.: A novel approach for feature selection method tf-idf in document clustering. In: 2013 IEEE 3rd International Advance Computing Conference, pp. 858–862. IEEE (2013)
8. Peng, H., Long, F., Ding, C.: Feature selection based on mutual information criteria of max-dependency, max-relevance, and min-redundancy. IEEE Trans. Pattern Anal. Mach. Intell. **27**(8), 1226–1238 (2005)
9. Xu, J., Zhou, H., Huang, G.B.: Extreme learning machine based fast object recognition. In: 15th International Conference on Information Fusion, pp. 1490–1496. IEEE (2012)
10. Yang, Y., Pedersen, J.O.: A comparative study on feature selection in text categorization. In: 1997 International Conference on Machine Learning, vol. 97, pp. 412–420 (1997)
11. Zhang, H., Ren, Y.g., Yang, X.: Research on text feature selection algorithm based on information gain and feature relation tree. In: 10th Web Information System and Application Conference. pp. 446–449. IEEE (2013)
12. Zhu, D., Xiao, J.: R-tfidf, a variety of tf-idf term weighting strategy in document categorization. In: Seventh International Conference on Semantics Knowledge and Grid, pp. 83–90. IEEE (2011)
13. Zong, W., Huang, G.B.: Face recognition based on extreme learning machine. Neurocomputing **74**(16), 2541–2551 (2011)

RayDroid: A Framework for Discovering Anomaly in Android

Fan Yang[✉], Yue Li, and Lidong Zhai

Institute of Information Engineering,
Chinese Academy of Sciences, Beijing, China
{yangfan,liyue,zhailidong}@iie.ac.cn

Abstract. Smartphone has completely improved our life and changed the world. However, the security of smartphone becomes a very serious problem to people's daily life. With the installation of more and more applications, people become nervous about what these applications do in their smartphones. To discover the anomaly that applications cause, we propose the design and implementation of a framework for discovering anomaly in Android named RayDroid, which monitors the behavior of applications and the flow of data both in Android Framework level and Linux kernel level, aiming to discover the anomaly of smartphones through the analysis. To prove its effectiveness, we also implement the prototype of RayDroid and show it's effective and efficient through the evaluation.

Keywords: Smartphone security · Anomaly discovery · Android

1 Introduction

Recently, the smartphone has become a very important tool in the daily life of many people. The convenience of the smartphone makes people more efficient both in life and work. However, it could be a threat to our life if its security can't be guaranteed. For example, as it is always around us and barely turned off, attackers can use the specific applications to track the victim's location through the smartphone's GPS [2]. Android [1] is the most popular operating system of the smartphone and occupies the largest market share. There are so many application stores, where developers can upload their applications. However, this has allowed malicious attackers to spread malwares through unofficial application stores.

Though Android provides a permission-based security model by restricting the behaviors of applications to address the security issues, the model is very weak. This is because most users don't look through the permissions while installing applications. Even some users notice that one application is applying more permission than it needs, they have to approve all of them if they want to use this application.

Against the weakness of Android's security model, there are many approaches that have been proposed by the researchers all over the world. In this paper we propose a new approach to solve the problem. We provide an anomaly discovery framework named RayDroid. It can discover the anomaly of smartphones through monitoring the behavior of applications and the flow of data both in Android Framework level and

© Springer-Verlag Berlin Heidelberg 2015
Y. Lu et al. (Eds.): ISCTCS 2014, CCIS 520, pp. 33–40, 2015.
DOI: 10.1007/978-3-662-47401-3_5

Linux kernel level, processing the log data of monitors and performing some analysis on it. As it doesn't depend on static signatures, RayDroid can discover the anomalies that have never shown up before, such as 0-day exploits and unknown malwares, which makes it a powerful weapon to defend the advanced attacks, such as APT.

Also, we implement one prototype of RayDroid to show our framework is effective. Our experimental results show that our system is capable of discovering the real anomaly that applications cause. We also perform an experiment on a mass of malwares and the result show the analytic technique is accurate and efficient.

This work is organized as follows. Section 2 describes the related work. In Sect. 3 we explain all the components of functionality and give an example of technique to implement some components. In Sect. 4, we present one prototype of RayDroid, which is implemented by us. In Sect. 5, we present the result of some data performed with a set of malicious applications. In Sect. 6 we conclude the work.

2   Related Work

Some security extensions have been proposed to improve the permission-based model, such as Kirin [3], which checks the combinations of permissions and denies the installation of the malwares, and Apex [4], which allows users to revoke some of permissions, in the cost of using a subset of functionalities.

However, while the priest climbs a post, the devil climbs ten. A series of researches on privilege escalation attack has been done to bypass the permission checking mechanism [5]. Although a lot of defenses have been proposed, including the researcher of this attack, who bring some methods to avoid this kind of attack. Besides, Xmandroid is proposed to address this issue through dynamic analysis of permission's pass between applications. However, they are all static and need to configure the policy based on signatures, which would produce false positives and affect the normal use when they are deployed in the wild.

Therefore, some dynamic approaches for detecting malicious applications have been proposed. The TaintDroid proposed in [6] performs dynamic information-flow tracking to identify privacy leaks. However, without the monitor of applications' behaviors and only focused on the privacy leaks, TaintDroid can't discover other anomalies, even the attack in [9], which is aimed at the privacy leaks. RayDroid monitors all applications' behaviors as well as the information-flow, so it can discover all kinds of anomalies.

The Andromaly [7] is a malware detection system that applies machine learning to analyze anomalous behavior. The Crowdroid [8] collects and analyzes the pattern of system calls made by running applications and applies clustering algorithms to differentiate between benign and malicious applications. Also, they are based on the static patterns and simply judge an application benign or malicious, which would cause false positives. In RayDroid, we don't judge an application benign or malicious and consider every application as a threat. Instead, we only focus on the anomaly of behavior and data in the device, and then report it to the end user.

Besides, there are some approaches of the dynamic analysis in sandbox [10]. First it performs static analysis dissembling Android APK files in order to detect

Malware patterns. Then, dynamic analysis is carried out, executing and monitoring Android applications in a totally secure environment, also known as Sandbox. During dynamic analysis, all the events occurring in the device (opened files, accessed files, battery consumption, etc.) were monitored. The main drawback of their system is that it simulates user interaction through ADB Monkey, which will never be as real as a user. Instead, RayDroid is deployed in the real world, which is able to discover the real anomalies that may cause damage to the user' interests.

3   Architecture

3.1   Components of Functionality

The anomaly discovery framework contains many components of functionality and it is extendible. Now, it contains four necessary components. And more and more components can be added to rich the functionality:

- Data collecting: This component of functionality is the essential prelude of anomaly discovery. It is in charge of collecting all the data that we need to discover the anomalies of smartphones. The data includes the behavioral log of applications, the internal information-flow of the privacy data, the export of the privacy data and so on. The technique to support this functionality can be diverse and different combinations of them can be applied. For example, you can change the source code of the framework in Android to monitor all the applications' behavior and the information-flow of the privacy data. Another option is to record the system call in Linux level to record the low-level information of smartphones. Our implementation of RayDroid uses the combination of both techniques above.
- Data processing: The data processing component's job is to process the collected data according to the demand of the anomaly analysis. In order to offer the fixed format data to anomaly analysis, a serial of data processing should be performed. To reduce the redundant network communication, we recommend that this component should be settled in the smartphone.
- Anomaly analysis: The anomaly analysis component's job is to analyze the data of app's behavior based on the policy that developers defined. However, not all data need to analyze immediately. Some data can be done in the cloud to save the energy of battery.
- Cloud processing: As the analysis is so energy consuming, some of anomaly analysis should be performed in the cloud. We recommend that the smartphone should upload the data to the cloud when the smartphone is in charge and connected to the Wi-Fi. And when the anomaly analysis in the cloud discovers an anomaly, it will report to the user as soon as possible.

3.2   Policy

The policy consists of the rules that define the anomaly and the rank of anomaly that decides where to analyze the log data. We make a policy language called RPL (RayDroid Policy Language) to define the anomaly.

We define a RPL as a combination of rules that indicates that the sequence of behaviors is an anomaly or not. However, the intersection (denoted by ∩) means that this is an anomaly only when both of rules are satisfied, while the inverter (denoted by-) means the rule should not satisfied. The purpose for the inverter is to exclude the normal use of the applications. For example, the use of the application developed for navigating may be considered as a tracking anomaly, so it should be excluded to reduce the false rate.

We define rule as R, and a rule is compose of one or more applications and a behavioral sequence. Besides, we define the application as A, and the behavioral sequence as BS. So the anomaly is:

$$An\ anomaly = R_1 \cap R_2 \cap R_3 \cap R_4 \cap \ldots \tag{1}$$

$$R_1 = \{A_1 + A_2 + A_3 \ldots\} \times BS_1 \tag{2}$$

The behavioral sequence is a sequence of the specific behaviors of applications, system or data. The behaviors includes accessing specific hardware (GPS, Wi-Fi, SD card, Bluetooth, camera), interacting with user, reading private data (contract, email, texts, call log, etc.), writing data, uploading data, downloading data and so on.

Based on the syntax of RPL, we can define a very simple tracking anomaly for example:

$$An\ simple\ tracking\ anomaly = R_1 \cap (-R_2) \cap (-R_3) \tag{3}$$

$$R_1 = All \times BS_1 \tag{4}$$

$$R_2 = BaiduMap \times BS_2 \tag{5}$$

$$R_3 = GoogleMap \times BS_3 \tag{6}$$

BS_1 = access the GPS, and upload data to any site;
BS_2 = interact with user, access the GPS, and upload data to the site of Baidu;
BS_3 = interact with user, access the GPS, and upload data to the site of Google.

Notice that the format of the specific behavior should be unified while implementing the RayDroid framework. And the component of data processing can process the data to the unified format. Here we don't give the specific format and everyone can define his own format while implementing the framework.

As to the rank of anomaly, we define some ranks of anomaly by default. For example, the anomaly of being tracked ranks first and should be analyzed in the smartphone, while the anomaly of being utilized as a host of the botnet ranks last and can be analyzed in the server. Some default anomalies are list in the Table 1.

Table 1. The default anomalies and the corresponding ranks

Anomaly	Describe	Rank
Tracking	Some applications access the GPS and send the information to unnormal site	5
Recording	Some applications record through the microphone and uploading the import information to a website	4
Espionage	Some applications stealing the important information from users' smartphone	4
Controlled	The smartphone is under controlled by attackers through the secret channel	3
Consumption	Some applications send messages or make calls automatic to cost users' money	2
Group anomaly	The smartphone of someone in the group has one or more anomalies	1

4 Implementation

In this section, we present our implementation of RayDroid. It performs real-time monitoring and analysis of applications' behaviors and the data in the device to discover the anomaly.

The implementation of RayDroid is shown in Fig. 1. The RayDroid is consisting of several key modules. The application named RayDroid is in charge of the interaction with users. It registers the Ray Event Listener in the Ray Monitor component (step 1). Then when a third-party application accesses the system resource like Application Msg, DVM variable pool, system methods, Binder kernel or network interface, it actually accesses them through a proxy that is called Ray Proxy (step 2). With the assistance of Ray Proxy, Ray Controller Service can collect the behaviors of applications and the information-flow according to the policy (step 3). Then Ray Controller Service formats the record data to a specific format and then passes them to the Ray Monitor (step 4). The Log manager in the Ray Monitor stores the entire formatted log for further analysis. The Ray analyst module in the Ray Monitor does the analysis work to discover the anomaly through the cooperation of the package splitter, the policy parser, the history checker and the synthetical analysis. As the RayDroid application has registered the Ray Event Listener in Ray Monitor, the Ray analyst could report the anomaly immediately after discovering it (step 5). Then the RayDroid notifies the user about the anomaly (step 6). In addition, the Ray analyst will upload the log data to the Ray Server when the smartphone is charging and connected to the Wi-Fi (step 7). After that, Ray Server does the deeper analysis in the server that is more powerful, so it can discover the anomaly that the smartphone can't. Finally, it reports the RayDroid application the anomaly it discovered, and then the RayDroid reminder the user immediately.

In Fig. 2, we show some parts of our modification and improvement above Android original framework. We use the standard service architecture of Android to modify. We establish the client end and the server end, and let them communicate with each other using Binder service. The class named SecurityManager is a class we added to monitor

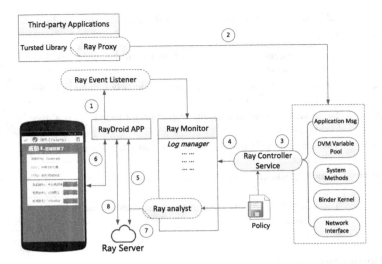

Fig. 1. The implementation of RayDroid

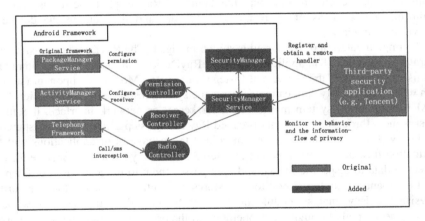

Fig. 2. The parts of our modification and improvement

all the behavior data and the information-flow of privacy. And the other classes are in charge of specific recording of the specific content.

5   Evaluation

We evaluated RayDroid through running our implementation in the Google Nexus. It can successfully discover a variety of anomalies, such as tracking users' location, stealing user' privacy, or recording voice and uploading it to servers [9].

We give the screenshot of our implementation in the Fig. 3, which shows the normal interface and the anomaly interface. When an anomaly is discovered, RayDroid will notify the user in several ways depending the rank of this anomaly. For the rank 5, our implementation chooses the "disturbed" way, which includes aloud ring and continual vibration. And when the user clicks the message, it will jump into the anomaly interface. Then user can click this anomaly to show the detail of the anomaly. However, for the rank 1, we just give a notification shown in the interface.

Fig. 3. The screenshot of our implementation

Table 2. Some malwares and the corresponding anomalies

Malware family	Anomaly	Website
LoveTrap	Espionage	www.coosh***.com[1]
Bgserv	Tracking	www.youl***.com
KMin	Consumption	su.5***.com
Plankton	Espionage	www.searchwebmob***.com
AnserverBot	Controlled	b4.cook***.co.cc

Notice, to avoid some unexpected problem caused to the owner, we hide some letters in the website.

In the meantime, we conduct a serial of experiments on a mass of malwares. These malwares belong to the famous malware family and we test them by running them respectively on a Google Nexus with our implementation of RayDroid built-in. Table 2 shows parts of the result.

6 Conclusion

In this paper we present an anomaly discovery framework called RayDroid. RayDroid can discover the anomaly happened in the smartphone through the monitoring of the behaviors of applications and the information-flow of data in the level of Android and Linux kernel. Then we elaborate the components of RayDroid and the policy language called RPL, which is used to define an anomaly. Furthermore, we show our implementation of the RayDroid and the technique we use. However, every developer can implement his own RayDroid according our elaboration of this framework and we encourage the cooperation with us on this research. Finally, we evaluate our implementation and show RayDroid is efficient and effective.

References

1. Google Android. http://www.android.com
2. Lineberry, A., Richardson, D.L., Wyatt, T.: These Aren't The Permissions You're Looking For. BlackHat, Las Vegas (2010)
3. Enck, W., Ongtang, M., McDaniel, P.: Mitigating android software misuse before it happens. Technical report NAS-TR-0094–2008, Pennsylvania State University (2008)
4. Nauman, M., Khan, S., Zhang, X.: Apex: extending android permission model and enforcement with user-defined runtime constraints. In: 5th ACM Symposium on Information, Computer and Communications Security (2010)
5. Davi, L., Dmitrienko, A., Sadeghi, A.-R., Winandy, M.: Privilege escalation attacks on android. In: Burmester, M., Tsudik, G., Magliveras, S., Ilić, I. (eds.) ISC 2010. LNCS, vol. 6531, pp. 346–360. Springer, Heidelberg (2011)
6. Enck, W., Gilbert, P., Chun, B., Cox, L., Jung, J., McDaniel, P., Sheth, A.: Taintdroid: an information-flow tracking system for realtime privacy monitoring on smartphones. In: Proceedings of USENIX OSDI (2010)
7. Shabtai, A., Kanonov, U., Elovici, Y., Glezer, C., Weiss, Y.: Andromaly: a behavioral malware detection framework for android devices. J. Intell. Inf. Syst. 38, 1–30 (2011)
8. Burguera, I., Zurutuza, U., Nadjm-Tehrani, S.: Crowdroid: behavior-based malware detection system for android. In: Proceedings of the 1st Workshop on Security and Privacy in Smartphones and Mobile Devices, CCS-SPSM'11 (2011)
9. Schlegel, R., Zhang, K., Zhou, X., Intwala, M., Kapadia, A., Wang, X.: Soundcomber: A stealthy and context-aware sound trojan for smartphones. In: 18th Annual Network and Distributed System Security Symposium (NDSS), pp. 17–33 (2011)
10. Bla͏sing, T., Schmidt, A.D., Batyuk, L., Camtepe, S.A., Albayrak, S.: An android application sandbox system for suspicious software detection. In: 5th International Conference on Malicious and Unwanted Software, Nancy, France (2010)

A Dynamic Load Balancing Strategy Based on Feedback for Cluster Rendering System

Qian Li[⊠], Weiguo Wu, Liang Gao, Lei Wang, and Jianhang Huang

Department of Computer Science and Technology,
Xi'an Jiaotong University, Xi'an, China
qian.l@stu.xjtu.edu.cn, wgwu@mail.xjtu.edu.cn

Abstract. In accordance with the issue of load imbalance in sort-first cluster rendering system, we present a dynamic load balancing strategy based on feedback. The proposed strategy improves the render history based load balancing method by the way of introducing load ratio, employing single exponential smoothing method and adding handling of the abrupt scene. The experiment verifies these improvement and illustrates that the proposed strategy can reduce the rendering time on exploding render model. Compared with the render history based load balancing method, the proposed strategy can divide load more uniformly among rendering nodes.

Keywords: Load balancing · Cluster rendering · Render farm · Feedback

1 Introduction

Currently, animation film industry is growing by leaps and bounds. Rendering is one key issue in the animation production, which is the process of creating an image from a model by means of computer programs and is actually a very complex and time consuming computation [1, 2]. Rendering application is very suitable for parallel processing in cluster computing environment.

However, the cluster rendering system face new issues, such as sharing data among different nodes and exchanging rendering information among processors [3]. Researchers gradually focus on intra-frame scheduling which divides each frame in more fine-grained level. Sort-first partitioned the screen in disjoint tiles that are rendered by the different rendering nodes. But it is very susceptible to load imbalance and the overall performance is limited by the slowest component [4].

In this paper, we overcome this issue by proposing a feedback based dynamic load balancing strategy which improves the render history based load balancing method, and the proposed load ratio and single exponential smoothing forecasting model based on time series improve the load balance, algorithm effectiveness and have ability of handling abrupt scene.

The rest of this paper is organized as follows: related works are introduced in Sect. 2. In Sect. 3, we analyze the problems of load balancing method based on render history. The proposed strategy is introduced in Sect. 4. We present the experimental results in Sect. 5. Section 6 concludes the paper.

© Springer-Verlag Berlin Heidelberg 2015
Y. Lu et al. (Eds.): ISCTCS 2014, CCIS 520, pp. 41–47, 2015.
DOI: 10.1007/978-3-662-47401-3_6

2   Related Works

Various methods have been proposed for balancing the rendering workload among a number of rendering nodes. Binary swap and direct send compositing schemes [5] are easy to implement and do a fair job of distributing the compositing workload among the render nodes. Also, many works have been done for the load balancing in the sort-first rendering cluster. The primitives are distributed among the nodes at the beginning of the rendering pipeline, by splitting the screen into regions and associating each region to rendering node [6]. Abraham et al. [3] proposed a time drawback based dynamic load balancing method which replicated the data set across all render nodes.

Compared with the Abraham algorithm, the render history based load balancing method [7] makes the following improvement. (1) It sets up the picture synthesis node which alleviates the load of main node and the architecture of rendering system becomes distinct. (2) The division method of screen region is based on one dimensional level which reduce the system overhead. But this method may bring extra overhead when adjusting the width of sub region and could not resolve the rendering of abrupt scene. Thus, this paper mainly focus these issues which will discussed in detail in Sect. 3.

3   Problem Statement

In render history based load balancing method, the screen region is divided on one dimensional level, i.e. horizontal or vertical direction, and then the number of sub regions is same with rendering nodes. Each rendering node records the rendering time of the sub region of the current frame. On the basis of these records, the Time-space algorithm have been opted to compute the partition of sub region of the next frame and the rendering nodes begin to rending each sub region according to the result of partition. The Time-space algorithm is described in Fig. 1.

We assume the frame k is divided equally into three sub regions. These sub regions are rendered by node R1, R2 and R3 and the corresponding time is 1 s, 2 s and 3 s. Thus, the load ratio of R1, R2 and R3 is 1:2:3. And then, the screen region of next frame will be divided according to this ratio and the task sent to rendering nodes will be reallocated.

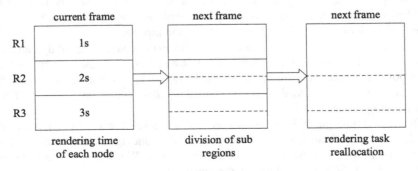

Fig. 1. The process of time-space algorithm

Compared with Abraham algorithm, the render history based load balancing method simplified the screen partition, but it still exists some disadvantages. (1) After the finish of each frame, this method adjusts and reallocates the sub region, and frequent adjustment and fast response may bring extra overhead and adjustment jolt. (2) The method of predicting the distribution of next frame according to previous frame cannot take full advantage of the historical frames and the prediction effect is less accurate. (3) This method could not resolve the rendering of abrupt scene. The abrupt scene break the continuity among frames and the sub region adjustment of next frame may cause load imbalance according to the time of previous frame, which is because the next frame is very different with previous frame and the light load of previous frame may transfer in the next frame. In the next section, we present some measure to resolve the above problems.

4 The Proposed Strategy

This section will propose some improvement approach from the aspect of enhancing the load balancing, algorithm effectiveness and handling of abrupt scene.

4.1 Load Ratio

We introduce the concept of load ratio which means the ratio of the latest finish rendering time of sub region and the expectation rendering time in a frame, which is shown in Eq. (1).

$$LR = \frac{T_l}{T_e} \tag{1}$$

LR means load ratio, T_l means the latest finish rendering time of sub region in a frame and T_e means the expectation rendering time, i.e. the time of sub regions which complete the sub rendering tasks simultaneously. In general, the LR is greater than 1. The smaller LR means the of load balance of sub regions. When the LR of the current frame locate in the appropriate scope, we will use the region partition of current frame to the next frame, otherwise, we will reallocated the sub region of next frame, which avoids the frequent adjustment of sub region, reduces the jolt and maintains the stability of system. In this paper, we set LR to 1.5 as the standard of adjustment.

4.2 Single Exponential Smoothing Method

To excavate the rendering information of history frames for predicting the partition of next frame, we present the single exponential smoothing method which is based on time series. This method takes advantage of all historical data and lets recent data make a greater impact on the predictive value. In this paper, we use this method every 5 frames to correct the prediction method based on render history, which make the prediction more effective.

4.3   Handling the Abrupt Scene

Abrupt scenes are inevitable in an animation series and the phase of abrupt scenes is actually continuous. Therefore, the judgment of opportunity is particularly important. According to the definition of load ratio, we can conclude that if the load ratio exceeds the threshold value the current time can be signal of arrival of abrupt scenes. The abrupt scenes break the continuity among frames. When the abrupt scenes have been judged by the load ratio, the screen region of the next frame will be divide equally to the render nodes, which avoids the calculation of partition and reduce the overhead of system.

4.4   Description of Proposed Strategy

In our strategy, horizontal partition is adopted and the size of each sub region is only related to the height. Firstly, the initialization of the first frame is done by way of dividing the region equally. And then, the load of each node of current frame and the expectation load of the next frame are calculated. Afterwards, if the current frame can be divisible with 5, the single exponential smoothing method is used, the next frame is to be rendered. Otherwise, the current load ratio is judged. If the LR is less than 1.5, the partition principle of next frame is consistent with method of sub region partition of the previous frame. Otherwise, the expectation load of the next frame will be calculated by difference value between the actual load of the current frame and the predictive load of previous frame. And if the LR is greater than 3, i.e. the abrupt scene is arrived, the region of the next frame will be divided equally.

5   Results and Analysis

In this section, we test our proposal with a complex scene exploding model which contain the exploding process from none to maximal effect, and the attribute is shown in Table 1.

Table 1. The attribute of exploding scene

Attribute name	Attribute value
Scene name	Exploding.ma
Number of frames	50
Number of nodes	5
Rendering engine	Maya

Compared with the render history based load balance method (RH method), we test the three improvement from the aspect of load balance, effectiveness and handling the abrupt scene. The result is shown in Fig. 2. Figure 2(a) shows the result of introducing load ratio (improvement 1), Fig. 2(b) shows the consequence of employing single exponential smoothing method (improvement 2), and Fig. 2(c) shows the effect of handling the abrupt scene (improvement 3).

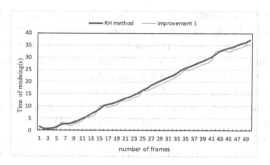

(a) The result of improvement 1

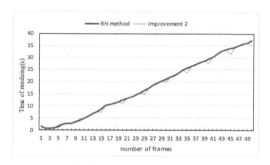

(b) The result of improvement 2

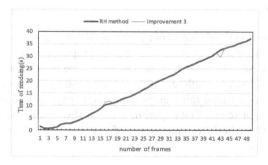

(c) The result of improvement 3

Fig. 2. The render time of each frame test of the improvement from the aspect of load balance, effectiveness and handling of abrupt scene

In Fig. 2(a), the render time of frame 6, 15 and 42 used with the proposed strategy is more than RH method. That is because that the load of the proposed strategy with load ratio changes after maintaining the same partition, i.e. the load ratio changes more than 1.5. And the proposed strategy with load ratio is superior to the RH method at the aspect of load balance. In Fig. 2(b), the previous 14 frames, the effect of adjustment is less than RH method which is due to the small render dataset. As the complexity of the scene increasing, the proposed strategy with single exponential smoothing method is greater than RH method every period of 5 frames. And in Fig. 2(c), the load of frame 17 is relatively concentrated and the method of dividing equally makes the load of each nodes imbalance. And the load of frame 43 is relatively decentralize and the process of abrupt scene is continuous, hence, the time is less than RH method.

And then we test the total effect of proposed strategy considered the three aspect in Fig. 3. The proposed strategy is superior to RH method and handles the phenomenon of abrupt condition in frame 43, but frame 17 with the concentrated scene cannot be resolved perfectly.

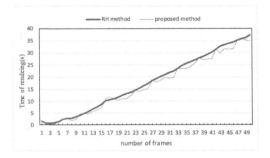

Fig. 3. The render time of each frame comparison of proposed strategy and RH method

6 Conclusions

In order to achieve load balance among the rendering nodes under the sort-first architecture cluster rendering system, this paper proposes a revised dynamic load balancing strategy based on feedback. According to the disadvantages of the render history based load balancing method, the proposed strategy improves the RH method by the way of introducing load ratio, employing single exponential smoothing method and handling the abrupt scene. The experiment result shows that the proposed strategy is superior to the RH method from the aspect of load balance, effectiveness and ability of handling abrupt scene.

Acknowledgement. This research is supported by Natural Science Foundation (No.61202041, No.91330117) and National 863 Program (No.2012AA01A306), P.R. China.

References

1. Baharon, M.R., Shi, Q., Llewellyn-Jones, D., Merabti, M.: Secure rendering process in cloud computing. In: Eleventh Annual International Conference on Privacy, Security and Trust (PST), pp. 82–87. IEEE Press, Tarragona (2013)

2. Chong, A., Sourin, A., Levinski, K., Merabti, M.: Grid-based computer animation rendering. In: Proceedings of the 4th International Conference on Computer Graphics and Interactive Techniques in Australasia and Southeast Asia, pp. 39–47. ACM, New York (2006)
3. Abraham, F., Celes, W., Cerqueira, R., Campos, J. L.: A load-balancing strategy for sort-first distributed rendering. In: 17th Brazilian Symposium on Computer Graphics and Image Processing, pp. 292–299. IEEE (2004)
4. Moloney, B., Ament, M., Weiskopf, D., Moller, T.H.: Sort-first parallel volume rendering. IEEE Trans. Vis. Comput. Graph. **17**(8), 1164–1177 (2010). IEEE
5. Eilemann, S., Pajarola, R.: Direct send compositing for parallel sort-last rendering. In: Proceedings of the 7th Eurographics Conference on Parallel Graphics and Visualization, pp. 29–36. ACM, Aire-la-Ville (2007)
6. Hui, C., Xiaoyong, L., Shuling, D.: A dynamic load balancing algorithm for sort-first rendering clusters. In: 2nd IEEE International Conference on Computer Science and Information Technology (ICCSIT), pp. 515–519. IEEE, Beijing (2009)
7. Shen, B.H., Jin, Z.F., Pan, R.F.: Load balancing method based on render history in cluster rendering. J. Comput. Appl. **26**(12), 2843–2847 (2006)

Extracting News Information Based on Webpage Segmentation and Parsing DOM Tree Reversely

Jing Li[1,2(✉)], Yueming Lu[1,2], and Xi Zhang[1,2]

[1] School of Information and Communication Engineering,
Beijing University of Posts and Telecommunications, Beijing, China
{lj_2013,ymlu,zhangx}@bupt.edu.cn
[2] Key Laboratory of Trustworthy Distributed Computing and Service (BUPT),
Ministry of Education, Beijing, China

Abstract. A new method of extracting news information based on webpage segmentation and parsing DOM tree reversely is presented and implemented in this paper, which intends to effectively extract news information for data mining. The method is proposed to get webpages' main DOM structure by segmenting webpages, further parse the main DOM structure reversely and finally extract news content, headlines, news agents and publication time. The experimental results show that the proposed method has achieved good performance on accuracy and meets the project demands.

Keywords: Webpage segmentation · Parsing DOM tree reversely · Extracting news information · Main DOM structure

1 Introduction

With increasing development of data mining and search engine technologies, the extraction technologies on webpage information including content, headlines, news agents and publication time become an increasingly hot topic. The information is not only a momentous corpus in the analysis of the net-mediated public sentiment, but also plays a vital role in the area of search engine technologies such as establishing indexes and removing duplicated web pages.

It is a phenomenon that in addition to this valuable information, a plenty of rubbish information consisting of advertisement, hyperlinks, copyright information can also be available at news webpages. Therefore, domestic and foreign researchers have carried much work of investigation and study on the webpage information extraction, and made considerable achievements.

Ying Bin and Yang Huizhi parse webpages into DOM trees, and then estimate webpage content judging by the weight of text characters and the density of link characters of each node in DOM trees in Ref. [1]. Zou Yongqiang and Zhong Zhinong locate webpage content depending on the news webpage features and the statistical regularity of the text blocks in Ref. [2]. However, the methods in the two mentioned Ref. [1, 2] are not suitable for the webpages with short content or continuous

Y. Lu et al. (Eds.): ISCTCS 2014, CCIS 520, pp. 48–55, 2015.
DOI: 10.1007/978-3-662-47401-3_7

hyperlinks. Chen Hansheng, Zeng Jianping and Zhang Shiyong restore each tag's display position of HTML documents in browser window by simulating part of the rendering process that web browser does, and then segment webpages in Ref. [3]. But the complexity is much higher.

But most of the existing information extraction technologies only extract news content without news headlines, news agents and publication time. Taking into account the fact that news agents, publication time and other information also have critical effect on the analysis of the net-mediated public sentiment, we put forward a method mixing webpage segmentation [4] with parsing DOM tree reversely [5] to extract news content, headlines, news agents and publication time from webpages.

2   Extracting News Information Based on Webpage Segmentation and Parsing DOM Tree Reversely

The method is to get webpages' main regions by segmenting webpages and then extract important news corpuses containing news content, headlines, news agents and publication time by parsing DOM tree reversely. It is more efficient and accurate to extract news information on the basis of webpages' main regions.

2.1   Webpage Segmentation

After analyzing news webpages from Sina, Tencent, Phoenix New Media,[1] Sohu and NetEase, it can be found that a news webpage is made up of four parts: the head, the foot, the left and the right. Generally, menus should be put on the head, and copyright information should be put on the foot. There are mostly a set of recommended news links and video links in the right. Ordinarily, webpages put their main parts on the upper-left half position and their related comments, pictures and links on the lower-left half position. Figure 1 demonstrates the layout of a news webpage from Sina.

Moreover, it is common that in webpage source codes, two CSS properties, which are *float: left* and *width: value* in CSS stylesheets, are used to add special effect to news webpages' left parts. And in a news webpage, the left div block is the only one with the two feature properties at the same time. Significantly, the *value* is determined as a pixel value over half of screens' width in the experiment. In this paper, the two CSS properties are defined as the feature properties.

Inspired by this, we design a flow chart showed in Fig. 2 to segment webpages. Taking a news webpage as an example, the detailed steps are as follows:

(1)   We use JSOUP to parse an HTML document firstly. JSOUP is a JAVA HTML parser. It can parse HTML from a URL, a file or a string, and provides an extremely efficient API. Its most prominent advantage is that JSOUP is as powerful as the JQuery selector. What's more, JSOUP can correctly deal with non-standard HTML tags such as non-closed tags.

---

[1] http://www.ifeng.com

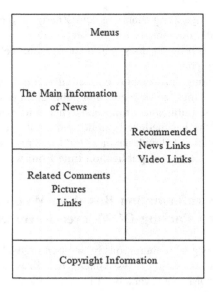

Fig. 1. The layout of a news webpage from Sina

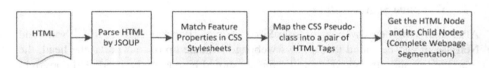

Fig. 2. The process of webpage segmentation

(2) We need to parse CSS stylesheets to search the two feature properties. As long as the two feature properties are matched successfully, we can stop parsing CSS stylesheets, record the CSS pseudo-class which contains the two feature properties and enter into the step (3). Otherwise, if there isn't a CSS pseudo-class with the feature properties to be matched until CSS stylesheets are traversed over, we output the whole DOM tree as the main region regardless of the step (3) and (4).

(3) Allowing for the fact that the webpage segmentation in this paper is aimed to obtain webpages' left parts, we only need to map the CSS pseudo-class recorded in the step (2) into a pair of HTML tags, instead of getting a complete DOM tree by parsing CSS stylesheets and merging all CSS pseudo-classes with corresponding HTML tags [4]. As a result, the time-consuming can be reduced greatly.

(4) We can get the HTML node mapped in the step (3) and its child nodes as the main region to finish segmenting the webpage.

2.2   Extracting News Information Reversely

After obtaining the main regions of news webpages from Sina, Tencent, Phoenix New Media, Sohu and NetEase by means of the above webpage segmentation, we analyze these main regions' DOM structure, and draw a conclusion that the DOM structure has strong similarity. As illustrated in Fig. 3, the main features of the DOM structure are summarized below:

Feature 1. News headlines are in a pair of <h1></h1> tags, represented as the title node (TITLE).

Feature 2. News agents and publication time are usually in a div block, represented as the info node (INFO).

Feature 3. News content is represented as a single div block, named the content node (CONTENT). In its child nodes, each paragraph of news content is a child p-node, and those videos or pictures of news content are represented as other div blocks.

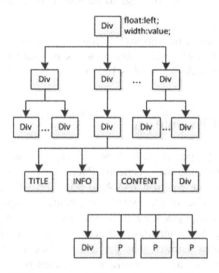

Fig. 3. The DOM structure of the main region of a news webpage

Inspired by this, this paper presents an idea of parsing DOM tree reversely. Firstly, we need to identify the content node (CONTENT) of a news webpage, and then search its headline node (TITLE), news agent and publication time node (INFO) reversely. Finally, the extracted results are text characters of CONTENT, TITLE and INFO. The detail steps are illustrated in Fig. 4 and are described below:

Identify CONTENT. In general, news webpage content is distributed in DOM trees' leaf nodes and wrapped in <p></p> tags [5]. Given that the feature is not exclusive, we can't well identify the difference between text nodes and non-text nodes by leaf nodes' tags. In the view of this, it is not practical to decide whether some nodes belong to news text nodes depending on whether they are leaf p-nodes.

As far as the above problem is concerned, we can firstly get rid of leaf p-nodes' <p></p> tags and their non-p sibling nodes (some div blocks of videos, pictures or layouts) from the main region's DOM structure of a news webpage. In this way, all leaf p-nodes' content is merged and their original parent node is turned into a new leaf node, and then we replace the new leaf node's tags with <t></t>. At this moment, news content is just in one leaf node of the DOM structure. Inspired by this, judging by the length of text characters in <t></t> tags, we can identify that the t-node with the maximum length is CONTENT.

Identify TITLE. Statistical analysis shows, TITLE and INFO are usually CONTENT's sibling nodes or child nodes of CONTENT's uncle nodes. If there is a node with <h1></h1> tags to be found in CONTENT's sibling nodes, we output the sibling node as TITLE. If there isn't, we traverse child nodes of CONTENT's uncle nodes until there is a node with <h1></h1> tags to be found. As a result, the found node is TITLE.

Identify INFO. Analogously, we can use regular expressions to match a time-formats node, while traversing CONTENT's sibling nodes or child nodes of CONTENT's uncle nodes. Finally, the node matched is INFO.

3 Experiment and Evaluation

In order to evaluate the proposed method, we select 2941 news webpages from five typical news websites including Sina, Tencent, Phoenix New Media, Sohu and NetEase in the validation experiment. We use JAVA to implement the proposed method. By manually counting the number of the correctly segmented webpages and the number of the correctly extracted webpages separately, the accuracies of segmenting the 2941 webpages and extracting their content, headlines, news agents and publication time are showed in Fig. 5. It demonstrates that the average accuracy of segmenting those webpages reaches 93.13 %, and the average accuracies of extracting their content, headlines, news agents and publication time are 92.28 %, 92.19 % and 89.56 % separately with the proposed method.

It should be noted that the performance of the webpage segmentation is satisfactory only in the condition that what we pick out for the experiment are news webpages from the five typical news websites. By comparison with segmenting those webpages, the accuracies of extracting news content and headlines are on the low side slightly due to the uncertain distribution of news webpage content and headlines. In addition, there are a series of webpages without news agents and publication time, leading to a little lower accuracy of extracting news agents and publication time.

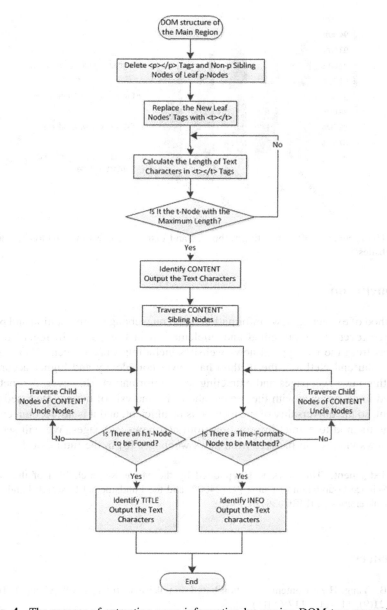

Fig. 4. The process of extracting news information by parsing DOM tree reversely

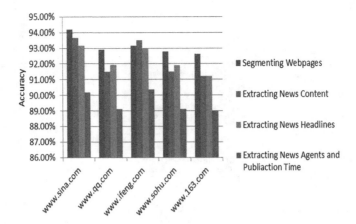

Fig. 5. The accuracies of segmenting webpages and extracting news information for different news websites

4 Conclusion

The method of extracting news information based on webpage segmentation and parsing DOM tree reversely is presented and implemented in this paper. In regard to those webpages from the five typical news websites including Sina, Tencent, Phoenix New Media, Sohu and NetEase, the method has lower complexity and higher accuracy in segmenting news webpages and extracting news information. However, the method is presented in accordance with the project about the analysis of the net-mediated public sentiment, so the universality of the method is insufficient, and it is not recommended to apply the method to extract information from non-news webpages. We will set out to extract news videos and pictures from news webpages [6] in the future work.

Acknowledgement. This work was supported by the Major Research Plan of the National Natural Science Foundation of China [91124002] and the Fundamental Research Funds for the Central Universities [2013RC0301].

References

1. Yin, B., Yang, H.Z.: Content extraction based on unknown structure web. Comput. Technol. Dev. **21**(9), 111-113, 117 (2011)
2. Zou, Y.Q., Zhong, Z.N.: An efficient approach to reduce noise in news webpages. Microcomput. Appl. **30**(16), 64–67, 71 (2011)
3. Chen, H.S., Zeng, J.P., Zhang, S.Y.: A position information-based web page segmentation method. Comput. Appl. Softw. **26**(7), 155–159 (2009)
4. Zhang, R.X., Song, M.Q., Gong, Y.L.: Parsing DOM tree reversely and extracting web main page information. Comput. Sci. **38**(4), 213–215, 225 (2011)

5. Li, J., Chen, J., Wang, L.F., Ni, H.: Approach to webpage segmentation and information extraction for vertical websites. Appl. Res. Comput. **30**(3), 844–847, 852 (2013)
6. Jia, J., Zhang, S., Meng, F., Wang, Y., Cai, L.: Emotional audio-visual speech synthesis based on PAD. IEEE Trans. Audio, Speech, Lang. Process. **19**(3), 570–582 (2011)

Enhancing Security and Robustness of P2P Caching System

Huailiang Peng, Majing Su$^{(\boxtimes)}$, Qiong Dai, and Jianlong Tan

Institute of Information Engineering Chinese Academy of Sciences, Beijing, China
{penghuailiang,sumajing}@iie.ac.cn

Abstract. At present, P2P caching system is widely used to reduce P2P traffic, but the security is always ignored. In this paper, we discuss three potential security issues: content poison, illegal files diffusion and malicious downloading. First, we propose content verification to ensure the correctness of data and defend against content poison attacks. Then, to prevent the spread of illegal files, we filter requests and responses by an info library and a feature library of known illegal files. Third, we present the strategies and introduce identity authentication to prevent malicious downloading from exhausting system's resources. Based on these considerations, we implement a novel P2P caching system to evaluate our designs. According to the result and analysis, we believe our strategies can promote the security and robustness of P2P caching system.

Keywords: Security issues · Content verification · Feature library · Info library · Identity authentication

1 Introduction

P2P technologies are applied widely in file sharing and live streaming, which generates huge amounts of traffics in the Internet. According to Sandvine Company's Global Internet Phenomena Report in recent four years, the P2P file-sharing traffic has a high percentage (about 50 %) in the Asia-pacific region [9], witch has resulted in some negative consequences to the Internet. At present, a popular solution is adopting P2P caching system in P2P networks. However, existing systems usually focus on the performance but neglect the security of system, which brings challenges of attacks.

In this paper, we discuss several potential threats on P2P caching system and present solutions to build a secure and robust P2P caching system. The concerned attacks of the paper are as follow: (a) **Content poison.** Attackers tamper and counterfeit some blocks and diffuse them into P2P networks, which destroy the correctness of contents and postpone downloads. (b) **Illegal files diffusion.** Because of the lack of central authority in P2P networks, it's convenient to disseminate illegal files, such as virus, infringing copies, etc. (c) **Malicious downloading.** By requesting huge amounts of contents incompletely, malicious users attempt to exhaust system's resources, such as connections and

© Springer-Verlag Berlin Heidelberg 2015
Y. Lu et al. (Eds.): ISCTCS 2014, CCIS 520, pp. 56–64, 2015.
DOI: 10.1007/978-3-662-47401-3_8

memory. In addition, attackers create a large amount of requests for less popular contents to produce an illusion of mendacious popularity.

Observing these issues, in this paper, we propose several corresponding strategies and implement a P2P caching system (P2PCache) to evaluate our designs. The main contributions of this paper are summarized as follow:

- To improve the reliability and security of the caching system, we propose an algorithm to verify the correctness of contents, which can prevent the diffusion of poisoned blocks efficiently.
- As for illegal files diffusion, we build an info library and a feature library to detect and filter the requests and the responses. And then, we forbid the illegal requests and pollute the illegal responses to prevent downloading.
- To combat against connection occupation and mendacious popularity of resource in malicious downloading and improve the robustness of the caching system, we propose guidance and regular clean-up mode.

2 Related Works

In this paper, we concern the security of P2P caching system and consider three security issues: content poison, illegal files diffusion and malicious downloading.

Researches in academia and industry have devoted themselves to adopt cache technology to reduce P2P traffic. For instance, Saleh and Hefeeda designed an P2P caching algorithm in 2006 [8] and implemented a caching system (PCache) in 2008 [3]. Additionally, there are some commercial P2P caching products, such as the PPCache [1]. However, all of them pay little attention to the security issues of P2P caching system. In terms of the security issues of the P2P network, a great deal of works have been done in recent years. In study [7], many popular attacks are surveyed, such as file poisoning and eclipse attack, etc. However, as for P2P caching system, some of them are unnecessary to concern. In this paper, we pay our primary attentions on content poison, illegal files diffusion and malicious downloading in designing the P2P caching system.

As for content poison, some detailed measurement studies have been undertaken and the impact of the attack is assessed by models in [4,6]. Additionally, the latest study [2,11] propose novel methods based on securing network coding to defend content poison. However, those methods are too complex to apply into P2P caching system. In our system, we propose the content verification to defend the attack and turn out it's efficient.

In terms of illegal files, the study [10] propose the technology of copyright protection by distribute false pieces with the same authentication keys as normal pieces. However, it's obvious that the method will result in lots of traffics, even though the file isn't sharing. In contrary, we propose our method by sending poison blocks just when we detect that they are been sharing.

3 Potential Attacks

In this section, we mainly discuss three typical security issues in P2P caching system: content poison, illegal files diffusion and malicious downloading.

3.1   Content Pollution

Content poison is a currently common form of pollution attack in P2P networks. With the intention of rendering content unusable, malicious users tamper the whole or part of files with white noise and diffuse them into P2P networks. When common users receive the poisoned blocks, unsuspecting users will accept poisoned blocks and the file will be unusable when downloaded completely.

For P2P caching system, the worse result will appears if poison blocks are indulged and cached. When a P2P caching system is adopted in networks, the files, requested by users in intranet, will be cached but the correctness can't be ensured. If the system caches block directly without considering its correctness, poisoned blocks will be cached as same as general blocks, which will accelerate the spread of poisoned blocks indubitably. In addition, if there are some malicious peers are attempting to pollute intranet, the caching system resources will be exhausted rapidly by poisoned blocks, and it will become the accessary involuntarily. Thus, we propose the content verification in our caching system.

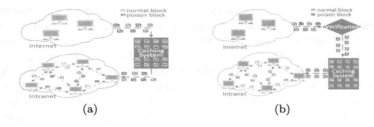

Fig. 1. The efficiency of content verification in P2P caching system: (a) P2P Caching System without Verification ; (b) P2P Caching System with Verification .

As shown in Fig. 1, the poisoned resources will be cached by P2P caching system and diffused in intranet without verification and all the pollutants will be rejected, when content verification is executed before caching blocks.

3.2   Illegal Files Diffusion

The detection and prevention of illegal files in the Internet have been a hot area of research for a long time, and there are some mature strategies and algorithms have been presented. However, because of the character of anonymity in P2P file sharing system, a confidential and convenient environment is offered for hackers to disseminate illegal files, including worms, viruses, etc. In addition, because no limits are imposed on using P2P file-sharing systems for users, infringing copies are spread crazily, which has resulted in huge financial lost. The P2P caching system provide an opportunity to detect and defense those illegal files and enhance the security of intranet. In Sect. 4, a strategy will be discussed and applied in our P2P caching system to combat with the attack.

3.3   Malicious Downloading

P2P caching system is similar to the traditional servers in the Internet, such as Web servers, where malicious attacks are in flood. Thus, it's inevitable that some attacks will be adopted to assault the P2P caching system. Additionally, the system is more likely to become a target, because we apply several strategies in our system to prevent content poison and illegal files diffusion. In this paper, we discuss the malicious downloading that is used to destroy availability and robustness of P2P caching system. For this attack, we consider two aspects: connection occupation and mendacious popularity of resource (Fig. 2).

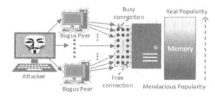

Fig. 2. The malicious downloading to P2P caching systems

Connection Occupied. First, attackers counterfeit lots of peers and establish huge amount of connections with the system so that it's too busy to respond any other queries. Additionally, as for every resource, bogus peers just request a tiny part but connections keep alive all the time, which will continuously consume system connections. Without any defensive measure, finite network connections of system will be exhausted.

Mendacious Popularity of Resource. To offer better service for users in intranet, P2P caching system usually cache the most popular contents, which give attackers an opportunity. Attackers create a huge amount of requests of less popular contents, which will result in an illusion of mendacious popularity, and the system will cache them unsuspiciously. Therefore, real popular contents will be lost and the decrease of free memory will cause low performance of system.

4   Defenses

To promote the security and robustness of the P2P caching system, we present corresponding methods to defend the above attacks in this section.

4.1   Content Verification

Because P2P caching system cannot ensure the reliability of the data sources, it's necessary to ensure correctness and integrality of content. Thus, we propose content validation algorithm (algorithm 1) to ensure the usability of contents and enhance the security of P2P caching system.

Algorithm 1. Content validation Algorithm

Input: One piece:P; Piece's hash in Torrent:H_t OR infohash of file:IH_r.
Output: TRUE/FALSE
1: **if** *Torrent is available* **then**
2:     $H = $ CalculateHash (P) ;
3:     **if** $H == H_t$ **then**
4:         Save(P, IH_r); return *TRUE*
5:     **end if**
6: **else**
7:     Search $(IH_r, P, $ MAP$)$;
8:     **if** *File is complete* **then**
9:         $Info = $ CalculateHash($file$);
10:         **if** $Info == IH_r$ **then**
11:             Save(P, IH_r); return *TRUE*
12:         **end if**
13:     **end if**
14: **end if**
    return *FALSE*

When our system saves one piece, the content verification is activated. Now we take BitTorrent protocol as an example to discuss the process. We classify the verification into two categories according to the reachability of Torrent file containing the hash of each piece: local verification and holistic verification.

As shown in Fig. 3, if the torrent file of resource can be accessed in the system (cached before), we just need to compute the hash of the piece by using the same algorithm as what used in protocol and compare it with the hash of this piece in torrent file. If the hash that we compute is the same with that in the torrent file, we can trust the piece and serve it to users in intranet. It is worth mentioning that the caching system can collect torrent file by crawling from Magnet URI or torrent publish sites when the torrent is not observed in the caching system and the target resource is not completely cached.

Besides, if the torrent file is not available but the file is downloaded completely (all pieces), holistic verification will be activated (Fig. 4). The caching system computes the infohash based on all pieces, and then we compares the result with the fixed infohash, which is the unique identification of file in P2P network and can be obtained from requests. When the verification fails, the caching system regards the resources (or pieces) as invalid and then prevents

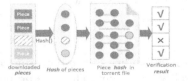

Fig. 3. Local verification

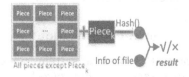

Fig. 4. Holistic verification

them from being shared among peers. Furthermore, the sources of fake resources (or pieces) can be considered as malicious nodes who are polluting the P2P network and our caching system blacklists them to the more serious consequence.

4.2 Legality Detection

Because of the anonymity in P2P networks, a more confidential environment is offered for bandits and hackers to disseminate illegal files. P2P caching system provide an opportunity to detect them. In this paper, we set up an info library and a feature library by known illegal files and design the strategy in two sides: infohash in request and content in response (Fig. 5).

First, if a request from intranet is found, we extract infohash from it and match infohash with the info library. The request will be allowed if and only if the matching result is rightful, otherwise, we prohibit the request and blacklist the user. However, there is a method adopted to trick our info library. Some attackers fill the illegal file with a little dispensable noise, which results in a new infohash but doesn't impact the essence of file. To further improve reliability of this strategy, we detect and analyze contents in responses by the feature library, which contains the features of known viruses, infringing files, and so on. Before cached, the file will be matched with the feature library and the infohash will be recorded into info library if the matching result shows that the file is illegal.

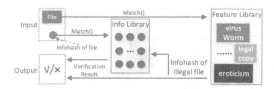

Fig. 5. The strategy of defense against illegal resource

As shown in Fig. 5, when an infohash is gained, it will be matched with info library and the file will be matched with feature library by some exiting matching algorithm, when it is downloaded completely. If the result show that overwhelming majority of the content is same with someone in resource library, the file will be considered as a latently illegalities and its infohash will be added into info library. When the result shows that infohash or file is illegal, two methods are alternative. First, the system can forbidden the downloading straightforward. What's more, we also can tamper the response by poisoned blocks, which is different with content poison that we only direct to illegal files.

4.3 Defense of Malicious Downloading

We propose a series of strategies to combat with malicious downloading attacks. For every file, the system records the logs once it's requested, which include who have downloaded it and the completion rate. First, to prevent attackers from exhausting the connection resources, we stop serving for users with two abnormal conditions: (1) the users only send keep-alive to the system; (2) users just request a tiny part of every resource. As for broadband consumption and mendacious popularity of file, attackers always achieve them by a mass of downloading requests. It's easy to detect and defend the attack without faking identity, because repetitive downloading is not allowed for one user. To detect bogus identity, we introduce identity authentication into our system. Referring to the study in [5], we verify the users by identity authentication mechanism and serve them just when identity is credible. Furthermore, the user will be blacklisted, once it's considered as malicious attacker.

5   Evaluation

To validate our designs, we implement a system (P2PCache) and deploy it on a 1 Gbps-bandwidth inter-domain export. In this section, we first introduce our testing environment, and then, the evaluations of our designs are discussed.

As Fig. 6 shown, we deploy the P2PCache on the export of a regional network. All modules in the network can be mounted and uninstalled independently, which make it convenient to evaluate every design and add new modules. We use uTorrent and aMuleas clients in our testing network.

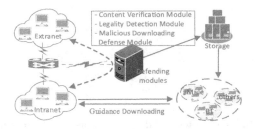

Fig. 6. The strategy of defense against illegal resource

Based on the test environment, we evaluate our defense strategies by simulating those attacks. To assess content verification, the nodes in the intranet start to request the contents, whose part blocks are poisoned and uploaded in the network. The result shows that poisoned blocks are cached and shared among nodes in the intranet when we uninstall the content verification module. In contrary, the poisoned blocks are abandoned by the caching system with mounting content verification module. Similarly, the nodes in the intranet request the illegal files sharing in the extranet with info library and feature library in P2PCache. The result turns out that all the illegal files can't be downloaded because of the defense module and the sources of illegal files are recorded. At last, the defending strategies against malicious downloading are evaluated. The result shows that the attackers who attempt to exhaust the resources of system by malicious downloading are detected and blacklisted.

6   Conclusion

In this paper, we discuss three potential attacks in P2P caching system: content poison, illegal files diffusion and malicious downloading, and propose optimization strategies to promote the security and robustness of the system.

First, to prevent content poison, we propose content verification to detect content's correctness and integrality. We verify piece by local verification when the Torrent file is available, otherwise, we use the holistic verification. And then, we detect the legality of file by two presupposed libraries: info library and feature library, which can prevent the spread of illegal files, such as infringing copies, eroticism and virus, etc. In addition, we propose strategies and introduce the identity authentication to deal with malicious downloading.

Guided by these innovations, we implement the P2PCache system and deploy it on a 1 Gbps-bandwidth inter-domain export. The results show that the system can detect poisoned blocks and the illegal files and prevent them from spreading, moreover, attackers of malicious downloading are detected and blacklisted.

Acknowledgement. This work is partially supported by the National High Technology Research and Development Program of China (863 Project) under grant No. 2012AA012502, the National Science Foundation of China (NSFC) under grant No. 61402475 and the Special Pilot Research of the Chinese Academy of Sciences under grant XDA06031000.

References

1. Fuchao, Z.: The research of ppcache system. Comput. Eng. Softw. **11**, 026 (2010)
2. He, M., Gong, Z., Chen, L., Wang, H., Dai, F., Liu, Z.: Securing network coding against pollution attacks in p2p converged ubiquitous networks. In: Peer-to-Peer Networking and Applications, pp. 1–9 (2013)
3. Hefeeda, M., Saleh, O.: Traffic modeling and proportional partial caching for peer-to-peer systems. IEEE/ACM Trans. Networking **16**(6), 1447–1460 (2008)
4. Liang, J., Kumar, R., Xi, Y., Ross, K.W.: Pollution in p2p file sharing systems. In: Proceedings of the IEEE 24th Annual Joint Conference of the IEEE Computer and Communications Societies. INFOCOM 2005, vol. 2, pp. 1174–1185. IEEE (2005)
5. Lou, X., Hwang, K.: Collusive piracy prevention in p2p content delivery networks. IEEE Trans. Comput. **58**(7), 970–983 (2009)
6. Montassier, G., Cholez, T., Doyen, G., Khatoun, R., Chrisment, I., Festor, O.: Content pollution quantification in large p2p networks: a measurement study on kad. In: 2011 IEEE International Conference on Peer-to-Peer Computing (P2P), pp. 30–33. IEEE (2011)
7. Prêtre, B.: Attacks on peer-to-peer networks. Dept. of Computer Science Swiss Federal Institute of Technology (ETH) Zurich Autumn (2005)
8. Saleh, O., Hefeeda, M.: Modeling and caching of peer-to-peer traffic. In: Proceedings of the 2006 14th IEEE International Conference on Network Protocols, 2006. ICNP 2006, pp. 249–258. IEEE (2006)
9. sandvine(2014): Global internet phenomena report: 1h 2014 (2014). https://www.sandvine.com/trends/global-internet-phenomena/

10. Wang, C.-H., Chiu, C.-Y.: Copyright protection in P2P networks by false pieces pollution. In: Calero, J.M.A., Yang, L.T., Mármol, F.G., García Villalba, L.J., Li, A.X., Wang, Y. (eds.) ATC 2011. LNCS, vol. 6906, pp. 215–227. Springer, Heidelberg (2011)
11. Xu, J., Wang, X., Zhao, J., Lim, A.O.: I-swifter: improving chunked network coding for peer-to-peer content distribution. Peer-to-Peer Networking Appl. 5(1), 30–39 (2012)

Minimizing the Negative Influence by Blocking Links in Social Networks

Qipeng Yao[1,2], Chuan Zhou[2](✉), Linbo Xiang[1], Yanan Cao[2], and Li Guo[2]

[1] Education Ministry Key Laboratory of Trustworthy Distributed Computing and
Service, Beijing University of Posts and Telecommunications, Beijing, China
yaoqipeng0706@gmail.com, xianglinbo0523@126.com
[2] Institute of Information Engineering, Chinese Academy of Sciences, Beijing, China
{zhouchuan,caoyanan,guoli}@iie.ac.cn

Abstract. In this paper, we address the problem of minimizing the negative influence of undesirable things by blocking a limited number of links in a network. When undesirable thing such as a rumor or an infection emerges in a social network and part of users have already been infected, our goal is to minimize the size of ultimately infected users by blocking k links. A greedy algorithm with accuracy guarantee and two efficient heuristics for finding approximate solutions to this problem are proposed. Using two real networks, we demonstrate experimentally that the greedy algorithm is more effective in terms of minimizing negative influence, while the heuristics based on betweenness and out-degree are orders of magnitude faster than the greedy algorithm in terms of running time.

Keywords: Negative influence · Blocking links · Social networks

1 Introduction

In the past decade, the online social networks are providing convenient platforms for information dissemination and marketing campaign, allowing ideas and behaviors to flow along the social relationships in the effective word-of-mouth manner [3,4,10]. From the functional point of perspective, networks can mediate diffusion including not only positive information such as innovations, hot topics, and novel ideas, but also negative information like malicious rumors and disinformation [7,11]. Take the rumor for example, even with a small number of its initial adopters, the quantity of the ultimately infected users can be large due to triggering a word-of-mouth cascade in the network. Therefore, it is an urgent research issue to design effective strategies for reducing the influence coverage of the negative information and minimizing the spread of the undesirable things.

Previous work studied strategies for reducing the spread size by removing nodes from a network. It has been shown in particular that the strategy of removing nodes in decreasing order of out-degree can often be effective [1,9,11]. Here notice that removal of nodes by necessity involves removal of links. Namely, the task of removing links is more fundamental than that of removing nodes.

© Springer-Verlag Berlin Heidelberg 2015
Y. Lu et al. (Eds.): ISCTCS 2014, CCIS 520, pp. 65–73, 2015.
DOI: 10.1007/978-3-662-47401-3_9

Therefore, preventing the spread of undesirable things by removing links from the underlying network is an important problem. Along this idea, Kimura et al. [7] aimed to minimize the spread of contaminant by blocking a limited number of links at the expense of lower diffusion capacity.

In this paper, we aim to minimize the spread of an existing undesirable thing by blocking a limited number of links in a network. More specifically, when some undesirable thing starts with some initial nodes and diffuses through the network under the independent cascade (IC) model [6], a widely-used fundamental probabilistic model of information diffusion, we consider finding a set of k links such that the resulting network by blocking those links to minimize the expected contamination area of the undesirable thing, where k is a given positive integer. We refer to this combinatorial optimization problem as the *negative influence minimization problem*. For this problem, we propose a greedy algorithm with accuracy guarantee for efficiently finding a good approximate solution. Using two large real networks include Facebook and Diggers, we experimentally demonstrate that the proposed greedy algorithm significantly outperforms link-removal heuristics that rely on the well-studied notions of betweenness and out-degree method.

The rest of the paper is organized as follows. Section 2 is devoted to related work. Section 3 reviews the IC model and introduces the problem formulation. In Sect. 4, we propose a greedy algorithm and two heuristics to find the approximate solution. In Sect. 5 we verify the performance of proposed algorithms by experiments. Section 6 concludes the paper.

2 Related Work

The research on finding influential nodes that are effective for the spread of information through a social network, namely Influence Maximization Problem, has attracted remarkable attention recently due to its novel idea of leveraging some social network users to propagate the awareness of products [3,6,12]. However, the problem of minimizing the negative influence of undesirable things gets less attention, although it is an important research issue.

Some related research work has been made on minimizing the influence of negative information. Previous work studied strategies for reducing the spread size by removing nodes from a network. It has been shown in particular that the strategies of removing nodes in decreasing order of out-degree can often be effective [1,9,11]. Kimura et al. proposed a links blocking method to minimize the expected contamination area of the network [7]. However, the fact of part nodes infected is not considered. Yu et al. addressed the problem of finding spread blockers are simply those nodes with high degree [5]. Budak et al. investigated the problem of influence limitation where a bad campaign starts propagation from a certain node in the network and use the notion of limiting campaigns to counteract the effect of misinformation [2]. Different from previous work, our research cares more about a specific contamination scenario in the social network, and how to minimize the negative influence by blocking a small set of links.

3   Problem Formulation

In this paper, we address the problem of minimizing the spread of undesirable things such as computer viruses and malicious rumors in a network represented by a directed graph $G = (V, E)$. Here, V and E are the sets of all the nodes and edges (or links) in the network, respectively. We assume the IC model to be a mathematical model for the diffusion process of some undesirable thing in the network, and investigate the negative influence minimization problem on G.

3.1   Independent Cascade Model

Consider a directed graph $G = (V, E)$ with N nodes in V and edge labels $pp : E \rightarrow [0, 1]$. For each edge $(u, v) \in E$, $pp(u, v)$ denotes the propagation probability that v is activated by u through the edge. If $(u, v) \notin E$, $pp(u, v) = 0$. Let $Par(v)$ be the set of parent nodes of v, i.e., $Par(v) := \{u \in V, (u, v) \in E\}$.

Given an initially infected set $S \subseteq V$, the IC model works as follows. Let $S_t \subseteq V$ be the set of nodes that are activated at step $t \geq 0$, with $S_0 = S$. Then, at step $t + 1$, each node $u \in S_t$ may infect its out-neighbors $v \in V \backslash \cup_{0 \leq i \leq t} S_i$ with an independent probability of $pp(u, v)$. Thus, a node $v \in V \backslash \cup_{0 \leq i \leq t} S_i$ is infected at step $t + 1$ with the probability $1 - \prod_{u \in S_t \cap Par(v)} (1 - pp(u, v))$. If node v is successfully infected, it is added into the set S_{t+1}. The process ends at a step τ with $S_\tau = \varnothing$. Obviously, the propagation process has $N - |S|$ steps at most, as there are at most $N - |S|$ nodes outside the initially infected set S. Let $S_{\tau+1} = \varnothing, \cdots, S_{N-|S|} = \varnothing$, if $\tau < N - |S|$. Note that each infected node only has one chance to infect its out-neighbors at the step right after itself is infected, and each node stays infected once it is infected by others.

Under the directed graph $G = (V, E)$, the negative influence spread of the initially infected set S, which is the ultimately expected number of infected nodes, is denoted as $\sigma(S|E)$ as follow,

$$\sigma(S|E) := \mathbb{E}_E^S \Big[\Big| \bigcup_{t=0}^{N-|S|} S_t \Big| \Big] \qquad (1)$$

where $\mathbb{E}_E^S$ is the expectation operator in the IC model with the initially infected set S and the graph links set E.

3.2   Negative Influence Minimization Problem

Now we present a mathematical definition for the *negative influence minimization problem*. Assume negative information spreads in the network $G = (V, E)$ with initially infected nodes $S \subseteq V$, our goal here is minimizing the number of ultimately infected nodes by blocking k edges (or links) set D in E, where $k \ (\ll |E|)$ is a given const. It can be represented as the following optimization problem:

$$\min_{D \subseteq E, |D| \leq k} \sigma(S|E \backslash D) \qquad (2)$$

where $\sigma(S|E\backslash D)$, defined like Eq. (1), denotes the influence (number of ultimately infected nodes) of S when the edge set D is blocked.

For a large network, any straightforward method for exactly solving the contamination minimization problem suffers from combinatorial explosion. Therefore, we consider approximately solving the problem.

4   Methodology

In this section, we propose a greedy algorithm based on maximum marginal gain rule for the contamination minimization problem on graph $G = (V, E)$. Let k be the number of links to be blocked in this problem. To demonstrate the effectiveness of it, we compare it against two classical centrality based influence evaluation methods.

Greedy Algorithm. To make better use of the greedy algorithm, we consider an equivalent optimization problem of Eq. (2) as follows,

$$\max_{D\subseteq E, |D|\leq k} f(D), \tag{3}$$

where

$$f(D) := \sigma(S|E) - \sigma(S|E\backslash D) \tag{4}$$

is defined as the **decreasing spread** after blocking edges set D when the initially infected set is S. The above alternative formulation has key properties as described in Theorem 1.

Theorem 1. *The decreasing spread function* $f : 2^E \to \mathbb{R}^+$ *is monotone and submodular with* $f(\emptyset) = 0$. *Theoretically, a non-negative real-valued function* f *on subsets of* E *is submodular, if* $f(D \cup \{e\}) - f(D) \geq f(D' \cup \{e\}) - f(D')$ *for all* $D \subseteq D' \subseteq E$ *and* $e \in E\backslash D'$. *And* f *is monotone, if* $f(D) \leq f(D')$ *for all* $D \subseteq D'$.

Proof. It is trivial that f is monotone with $f(\emptyset) = 0$. By definition of Eq. (4), in order to reach the submodularity of f, we need to prove that

$$\sigma(S|E\backslash D) - \sigma(S|E\backslash(D \cup \{e\})) \geq \sigma(S|E\backslash D') - \sigma(S|E\backslash(D' \cup \{e\})) \tag{5}$$

for all $D \subseteq D' \subseteq E$ and $e \in E\backslash D'$. Let $X(S, E\backslash D)$ be a random activation result (consisting of live edges [6], through which all activated nodes can be reached from S) in the network $(V, E\backslash D)$ with the initially infected set S. Then the influence spread from S can be measured as shown in Eq. (6)

$$\sigma(S|E\backslash D) = \mathbb{E}\Big[|X(S, E\backslash D)|\Big] \tag{6}$$

where $|X(S, E\backslash D)|$ means the number of nodes in activation result $X(S, E\backslash D)$. As we have the following equation

$$|X(S, E\backslash D)| - |X(S, E\backslash(D\cup\{e\}))| \geq |X(S, E\backslash D')| - |X(S, E\backslash(D'\cup\{e\}))| \tag{7}$$

works in all possible results, we finally get Eq. (5). Hence f is submodular.

By following the properties, the problem of finding a set D of size k that maximizes $f(D)$ can be approximated by the greedy algorithm in Algorithm 1. The algorithm iteratively selects a new edge e^* that maximizes the incremental change of $f(D)$ (or equivalently $-\sigma(S|E\backslash D)$) and includes it into the blocking edge set until k edges have been selected. It is shown that the algorithm guarantees an approximation ratio of $f(D)/f(D^*) \geq 1 - 1/e$, where D is the output of the greedy algorithm and D^* is the optimal solution [8].

Algorithm 1. $Greedy(G = (V, E), S, k)$

1: initial $D_0 = \emptyset$
2: **for** i = 1 to k **do**
3:     $e^* = \arg\max\limits_{e \in E \backslash D_{i-1}} \sigma\left(S\middle|E\backslash D_{i-1}\right) - \sigma\left(S\middle|E\backslash(D_{i-1}\cup\{e\})\right)$
4:     $D_i = D_{i-1} \cup \{e^*\}$
5: **end for**
6: output D_k

Comparison Methods. We compared the greedy method with two heuristics based on the well-studied notions of betweenness and outdegree in the field of complex network theory.

To minimize the influence of contaminant, a natural idea is to cut off the edges linking from infected set to uninfected set. Specifically, given the initially infected set S, define the out-edge set $O(S)$ like

$$O(S) := \{(u, v) \in E : u \in S \text{ and } v \in V \backslash S\} \tag{8}$$

We want to block k edges in the set $O(S)$ to minimize the negative influence. Since the set $O(S)$ is usually very large (i.e. $|O(S)| \gg k$), a natural question arises, *how to select k pivotal edges from the set $O(S)$ to block?* In this part, we introduce two scoring methods for the edges in $O(S)$, and then select k edges with the highest scores as the objectives to block.

Betweenness scoring method. Given the initially infected nodes S, the betweenness score $b(e)$ of a link $e \in O(S)$ is defined as follows:

$$b(e) = \sum_{u \in S, v \in V \backslash S} \frac{n(e; u, v)}{N(u, v)} \tag{9}$$

where $N(u, v)$ denotes the number of the shortest paths from node u to node v in G, and $n(e; u, v)$ denotes the number of those paths that pass e. Here we set $n(e; u, v)/N(u, v) = 0$ if $N(u, v) = 0$. We expect that blocking the links with the highest betweenness score can be effective for preventing the spread of contamination in the network. We refer to this method as the betweenness method.

Out-degree scoring method. Previous work has shown that simply removing nodes in order of decreasing out-degrees works well for preventing the spread of contamination in most real networks [1,9,11]. Thus, blocking links from contaminated nodes to high out-degrees looks promising for the contamination minimization problem. Here we focus on the contaminated nodes S. We define the out-degree score $o(e)$ of edge $e = (u, v) \in O(S)$ as the number of outgoing links from the node v to non-contaminative nodes. As a comparison method, we employ the method of blocking links $e \in O(S)$ in decreasing order of their out-degrees. We refer to this method as the out-degree method.

5 Experimental Results

We conduct experiments on two real-world data sets to evaluate the performance of greedy algorithm and compare it with that of betweenness and out-degree methods.

5.1 Data Sets

The data we use from Facebook is downloaded from the Stanford Large Network Dataset Collection. Nodes of the network are behalf of people and if a person i have a relationship with the other person j, the graph contains an directed edge from i to j. The Facebook data set contains 4,039 nodes and 88,234 edges. The Digger data set is available at http://arnetminer.org/heterinf. Digger is a heterogeneous network, including Digg stories, user actions (submit, digg, comment and reply) with respect to the stories, and friendship relations among users. The Diggers has 8,193 nodes and 56,440 edges.

5.2 Parameter Settings

In the IC Model, we assign a uniform probability p to each edge of the graph. Two propagation probabilities are used in our experiments: $p = 0.05$ and $p = 0.1$. The initially infected set S is chosen in the whole network uniformly with $|S| = 50$. Also we want to cut off 50 edges to minimiza the negative influence, i.e., $k = 50$.

5.3 Experimental Results

The results in Fig. 1 show that the *Greedy* algorithm outperforms the *Betweenness* and *Out-degree* methods on both data sets with different probabilities. The Betweenness takes the second place and the Out-degree comes last. By contrast, the performance of Betweenness gets very close to that of out-degree method.

In the first figure in Fig. 1. (a), we can observed that the greedy algorithm reduce the negative spread from 118 to 80 by blocking 50 links in the data set Diggers. Here note that blocking 50 edges means blocking 8.59 % of the links that connected to infected nodes in Diggers. Thus, by appropriately blocking about 8.59 % of the links, the greedy algorithm, betweenness heuristic, and out-degree heuristic reduce the negatibe spread by about 32 %, 19 % and 15 % respectively. The explanation of the other three figures are the same. Besides, we can draw a

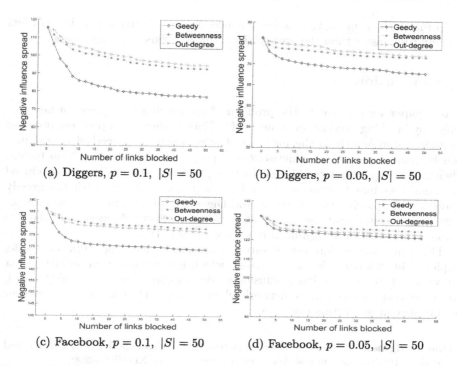

(a) Diggers, $p = 0.1$, $|S| = 50$ (b) Diggers, $p = 0.05$, $|S| = 50$

(c) Facebook, $p = 0.1$, $|S| = 50$ (d) Facebook, $p = 0.05$, $|S| = 50$

Fig. 1. The experimental results under different data sets and different propagation probabilities.

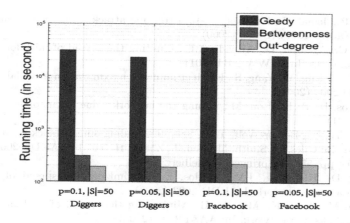

Fig. 2. The time comparsion among the three method.

conclusion from the experiment that our proposed methods perform better in the sparse networks, and their performance is unsatisfactory in the dense networks.

In Fig. 2, the running time of betweenness and out-degree heuristics is orders of magnitude faster than the greedy algorithm in terms of running time.

6 Conclusion

In this paper we investigate the problem of minimizing the spread of negative things by blocking links in social networks. This minimization problem provides an alternate approach to the problem of preventing the spread of contamination by removing nodes in a network. We proposed a greedy algorithm to find efficiently an approximate solution to this problem. Meanwhile we introduced two heuristics based betweenness and outdegree to compare with the greedy algorithm. Employing the Facebook and Diggers data sets, we have experimentally demonstrated that the greedy algorithm can effectively work, and the two proposed heuristics can significantly reduce running time.

There are several interesting future directions. First, the diffusion model employed in this paper is the IC model, which is a discrete time model. What can we do when the underlying diffusion model is a continuous time one? Second, how to extend it to a dynamic network when the network structure changes over time is also an interesting question.

Acknowledgments. This work was supported by the Strategic Leading Science and Technology Projects of Chinese Academy of Sciences (No. XDA06030200).

References

1. Albert, R., Jeong, H., Barabási, A.-L.: Error and attack tolerance of complex networks. Nature **406**, 378–382 (2000)
2. Budak, C., Agrawal, D., Abbadi, A.E.: Limiting the spread of misinformation in social networks. In: WWW 2011 (2011)
3. Chen, W., Wang, Y., Yang, S.: Efficient influence maximization in social networks. In: KDD 2009 (2009)
4. Domingos, P., Richardson, M.: Mining the network value of customers. In: KDD 2001 (2001)
5. Habiba, Yu, Y., Berger-Wolf, T.Y., Saia, J.: Finding spread blockers in dynamic networks. In: Giles, L., Smith, M., Yen, J., Zhang, H. (eds.) SNAKDD 2008. LNCS, vol. 5498, pp. 55–76. Springer, Heidelberg (2010)
6. Kempe, D., Kleinberg, J.M., Tardos, É.: Maximizing the spread of influence through a social network. In: KDD 2003 (2003)
7. Kimura, M., Saito, K., Motoda, H.: Minimizing the spread of contamination by blocking links in a network. In: AAAI 2008 (2008)
8. Nemhauser, G., Wolsey, L., Fisher, M.: An analysis of the approximations for maximizing submodular set functions. Math. Program. **14**, 265–294 (1978)
9. Newman, M.E.J., Forrest, S., Balthrop, J.: Email networks and the spread of computer viruses. Phys. Rev. E **66**, 035101 (2002)
10. Richardson, M., Domingos, P.: Mining knowledge-sharing sites for viral marketing. In: KDD 2002 (2002)

11. Wang, S., Zhao, X., Chen, Y., Li, Z., Zhang, K., Xia, J.: Negative influence minimizing by blocking nodes in social networks. In: AAAI (Late-Breaking Developments) (2013)
12. Zhou, C., Guo, L.: A note on influence maximization in social networks from local to global and beyond. Procedia Comput. Sci. **30**, 81–87 (2014)

Self-Adaptive Frequency Scaling Architecture for Intrusion Detection System

Qiuwen Lu[1,2,4], Zhou Zhou[2,4(✉)], Hongzhou Sha[2,3,4], Qingyun Liu[2,4],
and Hongcheng Sun[1]

[1] Beijing University of Chemical Technology, Beijing, China
luqiuwen@nelmail.iie.ac.cn, sunhc@mail.buct.edu.cn
[2] Institute of Information Engineering, Chinese Academy of Science,
Beijing, China
{zhouzhou,liuqingyun}@iie.ac.cn
[3] Beijing University of Posts and Telecommunications, Beijing, China
shahongzhou@nelmail.iie.ac.cn
[4] National Engineering Laboratory for Information Security Technologies,
Beijing, China

Abstract. Recently, Intrusion Detection Systems (IDS) have been deployed in the Internet for information security. Nevertheless, with the growing of Internet traffic, IDS becomes increasingly complicated and consumes much more energy. Existing studies concentrate on saving energy, but do not adapt to the change of network traffic. In this article, we propose a new method to adjust the frequency of IDS's devices' main processors automatically based on the prediction of the network traffic. It calculates optimal frequency scaling operation sequence via an internal sandbox model, so as to achieve energy saving purposes. Experiments show that our method can save 60 % power consumption generally.

Keywords: Green IDS · Sandbox model · Dynamic frequency scaling

1   Introduction

As the Internet traffic is growing up rapidly over time, the number of intrusion detection systems (IDS) devices in a trustworthy service is increasing [1]. Massive equipment run at their full rate all the time which consume large amounts of electrical energy. It causes huge waste of energy and brings the opportunity for the energy reduction since current link utilization is 30 % in average and below 45 % in peak [2]. This causes a huge waste of energy and bring the opportunity for reducing the energy consumption.

A lot of power management approaches have been proposed for substantial conservation in energy consumption, and can be classified into two categories: *smart standby* and *dynamic power scaling*. *Smart standby* methods maximize energy conservation by letting them fall asleep during the gaps of packets. However, these approaches may block the service called "network presence" that

© Springer-Verlag Berlin Heidelberg 2015
Y. Lu et al. (Eds.): ISCTCS 2014, CCIS 520, pp. 74–82, 2015.
DOI: 10.1007/978-3-662-47401-3_10

need to maintain network connectivity [3]. *Dynamic power scaling* approaches adapt the capacities of devices dynamically according to the actual or predicted traffic [4]. Some algorithms of them [5] switch frequency using fixed parameters given by users, which cannot adapt to the variational network traffic. Therefore, it is too complex for users to use these power scaling algorithms in practice.

To address this issue, we propose a *Self-Adaptive Dynamic Frequency Scaling Architecture* (SAFS) to reduce energy consumption. It predicts future network traffic based on historical data, and all the possible operation sequences which can be applied to the main processors are enumerated and sent to sandbox model with the predicted result. Then, the best operation sequence which be evaluated by an objective function will be applied. In this way, our approach is (1) self-adaptive to the network traffic (2) can keep a good trade-off between network performance and energy saving. Experiments indicates that our method can save around 60 % power consumption. We make the following contributions in this paper.

- First, we introduce a simplified sandbox model which simulates the procedure of packet receiving and processing in network devices.
- Secoud, we propose a novel scheme to tune the frequency of the main processor automatically based on the sandbox model.

2   Related Work

Many researchers concentrate on the method of reducing the energy consumption of network devices. These methods can be classified as two groups, as *smart standby* and *dynamic power scaling*.

Smart standby lets the complements of devices fall into sleep to reduce the energy consumption. M. Gupta and S. Singh [6] proposed a method by putting idle ports to sleep to save energy, but the method could only be effective when the device utilization rate is under 10 % according to [7]. G. Ananthanarayanan *et al.* [8] proposed a novel architecture for buffering ingress packets using shadow ports in low-power state.

Dynamic power scaling tune the frequency of the complements in devices dynamically to achieve the same goal. C. Gunaratne *et al.* [5] firstly raised the approach to tune the link rate of ethernet port. W. Meng *et al.* [9] proposed an approach by tuning the frequency of main processors. This method aimed to reduce the energy consumption by decreasing the ability of processors, which has been implemented on NetFPGA.

3   Self-Adaptive Frequency Scaling

In this section, we propose our approach in detail. The overview of our method are illustrated in Sect. 3.1 and the complements are proposed in Sects. 3.2–3.5.

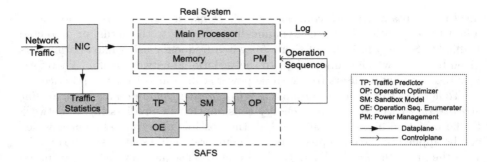

Fig. 1. The architecture of the SAFS

3.1 Overview

Our method is based on the idea of local optimization to adapt to the variation of network traffic. Different from dual-threshold method which set the fixed parameters on the buffer, our approach introduces a sandbox model to predict the behaviour of the system based on the predicted network traffic, then an optimized operation sequence applied in future will be concluded. As the traffic changing, the operation sequence can be recalculated to adapt to the future traffic. Therefore, our method can adapt to the traffic automatically.

Figure 1 illustrates the architecture of SAFS which can be which can be divided into 5 parts: real system, traffic predictor, operation sequence enumerator, sandbox model and operation optimizer. The whole system works as follows:

- As the network traffic being processed by real system, the statistical information of network traffic can be sent to the traffic predictor, and the traffic predictor predicts the trend of future network traffic;
- The operation sequence enumerator enumerates all the possible operation sequence and sends the result to the sandbox model with the predicted traffic trend. Then the sandbox model evaluates these sequences parallelly.
- The operation optimizer chooses the best sequence according to their performance and apply it in the real system.

3.2 Traffic Predictor

To calculate the operation sequence, we need to know the trend of the future traffic. Currently, ARMA (Autoregressive Moving Average) and FARIMA (Fractional Autoregressive Integrated Moving Average) [10] time series are the main model used to fit and predict the network traffic, which is well known and have good performance. Therefore, our work will force on other parts of the architecture.

The output of the traffic predictor N_t is a sequence in time,

$$N_t : \{N_{t^*}, N_{t^*+\Delta s}, N_{t^*+2\Delta s}, \ldots, N_{t^*+(m-1)\Delta s}\} \tag{1}$$

where Δs is the sample interval and have the length of m. t^* is start time of the sequence.

3.3 Operation Sequence Enumerator

The operation sequence enumerator gets all the possible frequency $F_{allow} = \{f_1, f_2, \ldots, f_n\}$ that the main processor can be set, and enumerates the operation sequence in time of $t_1, t_2, \ldots, t_m$,

$$F_1 = f_1, f_1, f_1, \ldots, f_1$$
$$F_2 = f_2, f_1, f_1, \ldots, f_1$$
$$\vdots$$
$$F_n = f_n, f_1, f_1, \ldots, f_1$$
$$F_{n+1} = f_1, f_2, f_1, \ldots, f_1$$
$$\vdots$$
$$F_{m \times n} = \underbrace{f_n, f_n, f_n, \ldots, f_n}_{m}$$

and we define an function $F_n(i)$ as the ith item of sequence F_n.

3.4 Sandbox Model

The sandbox model is used to evaluate the behaviour of the main processor in the real system with the particular network traffic and frequency sequence by simulation. The simulator in the sandbox model simulates the Producer-Consumer(P-C) system which exists widely in network devices. Packets came from the network are received and push it into a FIFO queue, then the worker pop the packets from FIFO queue and process the packets Fig. 2.

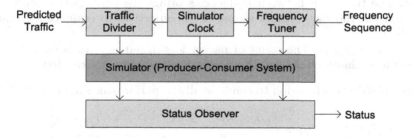

Fig. 2. The structure of sandbox model

The implementation of the sandbox model can be described as follows:

1. Get the simulator time t and Δt. Get the operation sequence F and the traffic sequence like Eq. (1).
2. Let $t^* = t$, get the traffic for the correct simulator time using traffic divider which divide the traffic N_{t^*} by $1/\Delta t$.

3. Get the ith item of the sequence in F as $F(i)$, and the frequency tuner set the processing capacity as $F(i)$.
4. Send $\hat{N}(t)$ into the packet generator. The packet generator generates the packets with length of $L(1), L(2), \ldots, L(n)$ until $\sum_{i=1}^{n} L(i) = \hat{N}(t)$.
5. The packets generated from packet generator is pushed into the FIFO buffer. and pop the $W(t)$ packets from FIFO buffer.
6. Let the simulator clock t equals $t + \Delta t$, and goto the step 3. When the t can be divided with no remainder by Δs, goto the step 2.

The system status observer can get the status of the system at each t. These status can be used to evaluate the performance of operation sequence, which will proposed in Sect. 3.5.

3.5 Operation Optimizer

Operation Optimizer selects the best operation sequence from the result of sandbox model and apply the sequence in the real system. The performance grade the sandbox model gives are listed below.

– *Energy Saving(E)*: We use the frequency to evaluate the energy saving instead of actual power, according to the linear relationship between energy consumption and the frequency. Thus, the energy consumption of devices could be modeled as

$$E = f_1 T_1 + f_2 T_2 + f_3 T_3 + \cdots + f_n T_n \tag{2}$$

where E is the energy consumption, $f_1, f_2, f_3, \ldots, f_n$ represents the frequency the processor can be tuned, and $T_1, T_2, T_3, \ldots, T_n$ denote the time spent in each frequency.
– *Switch Times(S)*: The switch of frequency in processor does not come without cost. The transition between frequencies brings the extra performance lost. So we treat the switch times as one of the objectives to evaluate the scaling method.
– *Packet Loss(P_{lost})*: The count of packet loss in our devices is an important grade to evaluate reliability. The packet loss would be unexpected.

We use an objective function to combine all the performance metrics as

$$f(E, S, P_{lost}, Q_l) = \begin{cases} \alpha E + \beta P_{lost} + \theta S, & Q_l < kQ_{max} \\ \alpha' E + \beta' P_{lost} + \theta' S + \xi' Q_l, & Q_l \geqslant kQ_{max} \end{cases} \tag{3}$$

with $\alpha + \beta + \theta = 1, \alpha' + \beta' + \theta' + \xi' = 1$, where Q_l is the length of the FIFO queue, and Q_{max} is the max length of the queue. $\alpha, \beta, \theta, \alpha', \beta', \theta', \xi'$ and k are the parameters of the objective function given by users.

Operation Optimizer gets all the sequence $F_1, F_2, F_3, \ldots, F_n$ and calculates the performance grade as Eq. (3). The best operation sequence $F|_{\min f(\cdot)}$ will be used in real system.

4 Experiment

4.1 Data Collection and Performance Metrics

We captured two cases of traffic spanning over a period of time of a total day. One of them is from the Internet link of a research institute and another is from the gateway of an office. The characters of traffic cases are listed in Table 1.

Table 1. Character of traffic cases

Name	Traffic Type	Sources	Bandwidth (Mbps)	Avg. Bit Rate(Mbps)	Avg. Pkt Length(B)
Case I	Core router	Institute	10,000	2,770.60	843
Case II	Home router	Office	100	6.68	913

There are three performance metrics for the devices that we studies which has been proposed in Sect. 3.5.

4.2 Experiment Setup

Our simulated experiments are finished on a PC. According to our datasets, we start the simulate at time in minutes of $t = 0$ and end up with $t = 1250$, which obtain the daily dynamic traffic pattern. The simulation clock step Δt are set as 0.1 min to reduce the cost of computing for the limited resource.

Table 2. The parameters of the simulator used in experiments

Simulator	CPU Frequency (pkts/Δt)	Queue Length (pkts)	Physical Interpretation
A	32,128	1,024	Simple CPU with small memory
B	32,128	2,048	Simple CPU with medium memory
C	32,128	4,096	Simple CPU with large memory
D	32,128	8,184	Simple CPU with huge memory
E	32,64,96,128	1,024	Complex CPU with small memory
F	32,64,96,128	2,048	Complex CPU with medium memory
G	32,64,96,128	4,096	Complex CPU with large memory
H	32,64,96,128	8,184	Complex CPU with huge memory

Table 2 lists the sets of parameters of the simulator, which represents the devices with different memory and CPUs to test the performance of the methods. The up-threshold of dual-threshold (DT) scaling method is set as Eq. (4) and the down-threshold is set as Eq. (5).

$$0, \frac{Q_l}{n} + \Delta L, 2\frac{Q_l}{n} + \Delta L, \ldots, (n-1)\frac{Q_l}{n} + \Delta L, Q_l \tag{4}$$

$$0, \frac{Q_l}{n} - \Delta L, 2\frac{Q_l}{n} - \Delta L, \ldots, (n-1)\frac{Q_l}{n} - \Delta L, Q_l \tag{5}$$

where Q_l, n are the length of the queue and the count of CPU frequencies for each simulator. In the following experiments, the ΔL is set as 10, and the parameters of Eq. (3) are set as $\alpha = 0.4, \beta = 0.2, \theta = 0.4, \alpha' = 0.1, \beta' = 0.3, \theta' = 0.2, \xi' = 0.4$ and $k = 0.8$ based on their importance of metrics.

4.3   Result

Figure 3 compares the performance of quad-threshold method (DT) [5] with SAFS in the Traffic Case I (Institute), which illustrates that SAFS has better performance with near 60 % energy saving comparing with peak in the huge memory simulator. Figure 3(a) shows the energy consumption of each method in each simulator, note that SAFS has good effect in Simulator C, D, F, G, H which have large memory and complex CPUs. Figure 3(b) shows the times of frequency

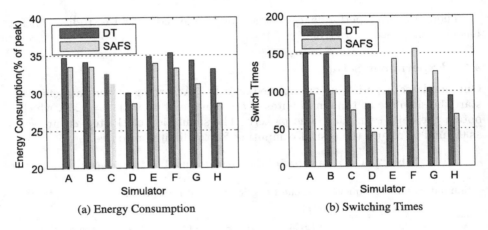

(a) Energy Consumption   (b) Switching Times

Fig. 3. The performance of SAFS and DT [5] in Traffic Case I(Institute)

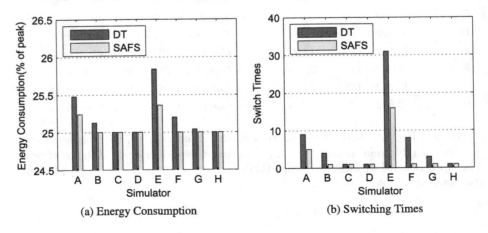

(a) Energy Consumption   (b) Switching Times

Fig. 4. The performance of SAFS and DT [5] in Traffic Case II (Office)

switch, which SAFS have better performance in Simulator D and H than DT. When it comes to the packet loss, our method lost on average of 633 packets at Simulator A, B, E, H, and both our method and dual-threshold method lose no packets in Simulator C, D, F, G, H.

Figure 4 shows the performance of SAFS in Traffic Case II (Office). SAFS has better performance on the energy consumption and switch times in Simulator A, B, C and E. In all the simulator, both SAFS and DT have no packet loss. SAFS and DT have the same performance in Simulator C, D, G, H because the traffic of Traffic Case II is too small for them which represents the machine with huge memory and have good computing power.

5   Conclusion

This paper is to design power scaling mechanism named by SAFS for energy efficient IDS devices, by adjusting frequency of the main processor in devices dynamically. Specially, SAFS employs a sandbox model firstly to evaluate the performance of the operation sequences that may be applied in real system, thus select the best one and finally use it in the next time period. Experiments indicate that SAFS effectively decreases the energy consumption of the main processor and the switching times. Consequently, our approach, SAFS, is much more effective for energy conservation in IDS devices.

Acknowledgments. This work was supported by The National Science and Technology Support Program (Grant No. 2012BAH46B02); The Strategic Priority Research Program of the Chinese Academy of Sciences under (Grant No. XDA06030200); The National Natural Science Foundation (Grant No. 61402474).

References

1. Di, P.R., Mancini, L.V.: Intrusion Detection Systems, vol. 38. Springer, Heidelberg (2008)
2. Chabarek, J., Sommers, J., Barford, P., Estan, C., Tsiang, D., Wright, S.: Power awareness in network design and routing. In: INFOCOM 2008, The 27th Conference on Computer Communications. IEEE (2008)
3. Bolla, R., Davoli, F., Bruschi, R., Christensen, K., Cucchietti, F., Singh, S.: The potential impact of green technologies in next-generation wireline networks: is there room for energy saving optimization? IEEE Commun. Mag. **49**(8), 80–86 (2011)
4. Song, T., Shi, X., Ma, X.: Fine-grained power scaling algorithms for energy efficient routers. In: Proceedings of the Tenth ACM/IEEE Symposium on Architectures for Networking and Communications Systems, pp. 197–206. ACM (2014)
5. Gunaratne, C., Christensen, K., Nordman, B., Suen, S.: Reducing the energy consumption of ethernet with adaptive link rate (ALR). IEEE Trans. Comput. **57**(4), 448–461 (2008)
6. Gupta, M., Singh, S.: Greening of the internet. In: Proceedings of the 2003 Conference on Applications, Technologies, Architectures, and Protocols for Computer Communications, pp. 19–26. ACM (2003)

7. Reviriego, P., Christensen, K., Rabanillo, J., Maestro, J.A.: An initial evaluation of energy efficient ethernet. IEEE Commun. Lett. **15**(5), 578–580 (2011)
8. Ananthanarayanan, G., Katz, R.H.: Greening the switch. In: Proceedings of the 2008 Conference on Power Aware Computing and Systems, p. 7. USENIX Association (2008)
9. Wei, M., Yi, W., Chengchen, H., Keqiang, H., Jun, L., Bin, L.: Greening the internet using multi-frequency scaling scheme. In: 2012 IEEE 26th International Conference on Advanced Information Networking and Applications (AINA), pp. 928–935. IEEE (2012)
10. Yantai, S., Zhigang, J., Lianfang, Z., Lei, W., Yang, O.W.W.: Traffic prediction using farima models. In: 1999 IEEE International Conference on Communications, ICC 1999, vol. 2, pp. 891–895 (1999)

Nonparametric Topic-Aware Sparsification of Influence Networks

Weiwei Feng[1]($\boxtimes$), Peng Wang[2], Chuan Zhou[1], Yue Hu[1], and Li Guo[1]

[1] Institute of Information Engineering, Chinese Academy of Sciences, Beijing, China
{fengweiwei,zhouchuan,huyue,guoli}@iie.ac.cn
[2] Institute of Computing Technology, Chinese Academy of Sciences, Beijing, China
peng860215@gmail.com

Abstract. In the last decade social networks are becoming denser and denser, which makes analyzing their structures and properties very difficult. However, for certain task, if we can remove the inactive users and irrelevant links, the network will be amazingly sparse and tractable. In this paper we propose the Nonparametric Topic-aware Sparsification (NTAS) algorithm, which can simplify social networks for a specific task. To determine whether a link is relevant to the task, we adopt nonparametric topic model to analyze the topic distribution of links and the task. We empirically demonstrate that our algorithm can return a more sparse network compared with other state-of-the-art methods in the task of network monitoring.

Keywords: Social network · Sparsification · HDP-LDA

1 Introduction

With the rapid growth of social networks, their scales become extraordinarily large. For example, there are about 1 billion Facebook users in 2012. Analyzing and monitoring social networks in such scale brings new challenges. To address this problem, the sparsification of social networks is one of promising solutions. On one hand, there is a large portion of inactive users; on the other hand, the propagation in networks is usually topic-aware, i.e., whether an item can be propagated through a link is largely determined by the interest or topic of the user. Hence, we can reverse the relevant part of networks for given information in order to reduce the analyzing and monitoring cost, which inspires us to study the problem of topic-aware network sparsification.

Compared to the traditional sparsity problems, the topic-aware sparsity meets several non-trivial challenges. First, mining the topics on social networks is difficult, as the number of topics is generally time-variant, and new topics emerge and evolve everyday. Second, determining the number of links to reserve is also a challenge. Therefore, we should balance the cost of monitoring a link and the risk of omitting a valuable link.

In this paper, we propose a Nonparametric Topic-Aware Sparsity algorithm (NTAS for short). NTAS aims at eliminating a large number of links in the

© Springer-Verlag Berlin Heidelberg 2015
Y. Lu et al. (Eds.): ISCTCS 2014, CCIS 520, pp. 83–90, 2015.
DOI: 10.1007/978-3-662-47401-3_11

network, and preserving only the links related to given topic. Note that we analyze the links instead of nodes of social network, that is because that information propagation is conducted by links, and a node can exhibit various types of behavior across its links. NTAS adopts the Latent Dirichlet Allocation based on Hierarchical Dirichlet Process (HDP-LDA) [1] to analysis the topic distribution of each link. The HDP-LDA is a nonparametric topic model which can recover proper number of topics. For certain topics, the NTAS reverse the *Top-N* related links based on the merit of Kullback-Leibler Divergence. And NTAS determines the proper reversed link number N which balance between the monitoring cost and omitting risk. In experiments, we demonstrate that our model can greatly reduce the scale of network without destructing the task of network monitoring.

The rest of the paper is organized as follows. Section 2 is devoted to the problem formulation and the NTAS algorithm. In Sect. 3 we conduct the experiment. We survey the related work in Sect. 4. We conclude out paper in Sect. 5.

2   Nonparametric Topic-Ware Sparsity on Social Network

2.1   Problem Definition

In this paper, a social network is denoted as $G = (V, E)$, where V corresponds to the whole set of individuals and E corresponds to social connections. Individuals perform actions, typically chatting with others. For each link $e_{u,v}$, the historical message set is denoted as $d_{e_{u,v}}$. The topic distribution for $d_{e_{u,v}}$ is denoted as $\theta_{e_{u,v}}$. Given a target information d' which we wish to monitor, we can get the sparse network $G' = (V', E')$ which is most economic to monitor. Here we assume that the cost C of monitoring a single link is identical. While the risk of omitting a link can be measured by the probability of the link propagating that type of information. The ultimate goal of our work is to find the reduced network which can minimize the cost, as written in Eq. (1).

$$\underset{G'=(V',E')}{\arg\min}\ C|E'| + \sum_{e_{u,v} \in E-E'} f(d_{e_{u,v}}, d') \tag{1}$$

2.2   Algorithm Description

Our nonparametric topic sparsity on social network is based on the following assumptions. First, information propagated on a link is mostly about the same topic. Second, the more relative the information with a link, the more probable that the link propagate the information. Based on the assumptions, the NTAS is conducted with the following steps. First, we analyze the topic distribution for each link and the target information in $G = (V, E)$ with HDP-LDA. Second, for the target message, we measure the probability of a link propagate it by the merit of KL-divergence. Third, we find the optimal sparse network with minimize cost (monitoring cost and omitting risk). In the following parts, we will present the details of the three steps.

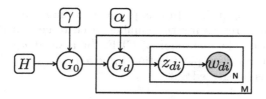

Fig. 1. Graphical model for HDP. γ, α_0 and H are hyper parameters. G_d denotes random measure at the document level while G_0 at the corpus level. z_{di} denotes the topic of word w_{di} while w_{di} denotes the ith word in document d.

2.3 Model the Network with Hierarchical Dirichlet Processes

In the first step, we adopt the hierarchical Dirichlet processes to learn the topic distribution $\theta_{e_{u,v}}$ for each link $e_{u,v}$. HDP-LDA is non-parametric topic model which can automatically determine the proper number of topic K based on the data at hand. It has been proved that HDP outperforms other unsupervised topic models, e.g. LDA [8] and LSA [10], on modeling large scale web texts.

This step contains three sub-steps. First, we collect all the messages on the links, which forms a document set $D = \{d_{e_{u,v},i} | e_{u,v} \in E, i = 1, \cdots, N_{e_{u,v}}\}$, where $N_{e_{u,v}}$ is the number of messages on link $e_{u,v}$. Second, we adopt HDP-LDA to learn the number of topic K and the topic distribution $\theta_{e_{u,v},i}$ for each message. Third, the topic distribution for link $\theta_{e_{u,v}}$ is calculated by averaging the topic distribution $\theta_{e_{u,v},i}$ and the topic distribution of the target information $\theta_{d'}$ is predicted (Fig. 1).

Model Description HDP defines a set of random measures G_d, one for each document, and a global random measure G_0. G_d models the topic distributions at the document level while G_0 at the corpus level. Each word w_{di} is associated with a topic z_{di} sampled from G_d. To share the topics across documents, the document-specific random measures G_d are drawn from the global measure with Dirichlet process $DP(\alpha, G_0)$, where α is a concentration factor. The global measure G_0 is also sampled from a corpus-level DP with a concentration parameter γ and a base probability measure H. In summary, we define the generative process of HDP as follows.

$$G_0|\gamma, H \sim DP(\gamma, H), \quad G_d|\alpha, G_0 \sim DP(\alpha, G_0)$$
$$z_{di}|G_d \sim G_d, \quad w_{di}|z_{di} \sim F(z_{di}) \tag{2}$$

HDP can be constructed with the Chinese Restaurant Franchise processes (CRF). In the metaphor of CRF, a restaurant franchise corresponds to a corpus, and each restaurant corresponds to a document. A global menu of dishes in the restaurant corresponds to a topic $\phi_1, \cdots, \phi_K$. A customer corresponds to a word in a document. And the process of a customer picking a table corresponds to generating a word with a topic. In particular, we need to maintain the counts of customers and tables. Here, n_{dbk} denotes the number of customers in the restaurant d at table b eating dish k and m_{dk} denotes the number of tables in the restaurant d serving dish k. In this paper, marginal counts are represented with dots. Thus, $n_{db\cdot}$ represents the number of customers in the restaurant d at table b, and so on. In metaphor of CRF, for a word w_{di}, the conditional distribution for the word's topic selection z_{di} given $z_{d1}, \cdots, z_{d,i-1}$ and G_0 as in Eq. (3), where G_d is integrated out.

$$z_{di}|z_{d,1:i-1}, \alpha, G_0 \sim \sum_{b=1}^{m_{d\cdot}} \frac{n_{db\cdot}}{i-1+\alpha} \delta_{\psi_{db}} + \frac{\alpha}{i-1+\alpha} G_0 \tag{3}$$

And the conditional distribution of $\psi_{db^{new}}$ is given in Eq. (4).

$$\psi_{db^{new}}|\psi_{1:d-1,\cdot,\cdot}, \psi_{d,1:m_{d\cdot}-1}, \gamma, H \sim \sum_{k \in K} \frac{m_{\cdot k}}{m_{\cdot\cdot}+\gamma} \delta_{\phi_k} + \frac{\gamma}{m_{\cdot\cdot}+\gamma} H \tag{4}$$

Eqs. (2), (3) and (4) together describe the CRF construction of HDP.

Model Inference We adopted the Gibbs sampling algorithm to infer the latent state of HDP. In Gibbs sampling scheme [11], the state of one variable is sampled with all the other states fixed. We sample the latent variables in sequence until convergence. In HDP, the latent variables of interests are the corpus-level topic distribution β, the topic for each word z_{di}, and the number of tables for each topic in document m_{kj}.

– **Sampling G_0.** Given CRF construction of HDP, the corpus-level topic distribution G_0 can be instantiated as $G_0 = \sum_k \beta_k \delta_{\phi_k} + \beta_u H$. And it is distributed as in Eq. (5):

$$\beta = (\beta_1, ..., \beta_K, \beta_u)|m_{\cdot,P\cdot}, \gamma \sim Dir(m_{\cdot 1}, ..., m_{\cdot K}, \gamma) \tag{5}$$

– **Sampling z_{ji}.** Given CRF construction of HDP, It can be realized by grouping together terms associated with each k.

$$p(z_{ji} = k|z^{-ji}, m, \beta) = \begin{cases} (n_{j\cdot k}^{-ji} + \alpha_0\beta_k)f_k^{-x_{ji}}(x_{ji}, w_{ji}) & \text{for existing } k, \\ \alpha_0\beta_u f_{k^{new}}^{-x_{ji}}(x_{ji}) & \text{for new topic } k = k^{new}. \end{cases} \tag{6}$$

– **Sampling m.** Given the CRF construction of HDP, the number of tables is determined by the scaling factors as well as the number of words in the documents. Antoniak (1974) [12] has shown that m_{jk} is distributed as in Eq. (7):

$$p(m_{jk} = m|z, m^{-jk} = k, \beta) = \frac{\Gamma(\alpha_0\beta_k)}{\Gamma(\alpha_0\beta_k + n_{j\cdot k})} s(n_{j\cdot k}, m)\alpha_0\beta_k{}^m \tag{7}$$

where $s(n, m)$ are unsigned Stirling number of the first kind.

Given the samples, the posterior of topic distribution of message j can be calculated as in Eq. (8)

$$\theta_j = (\theta_{j1}, \theta_{j2}, \cdots, \theta_{jK}) \sim Dir(n_{j\cdot 1} + \alpha_0\beta_1, n_{j\cdot 2} + \alpha_0\beta_2, \cdots, n_{j\cdot K} + \alpha_0\beta_K) \tag{8}$$

And the distributions of the link can be computed by averaging the distribution of messages on that link:

$$\theta_{e_{u,v}} = \frac{\sum_{i \in d_{e_{u,v}}} \theta_i}{N_{e_{u,v}}} \tag{9}$$

Prediction We have trained the model on a fully observed data of social network $G = (V, E)$ at hand, and get the word distribution for each topic denoted as ϕ_k, where $k = 1, 2, ..., K$ and K is the number of topics. We will use the ϕ_k to predict the topic distribution $\theta_{d'}$ for the new message d' with EM algorithm. In the E-step, given fixed ϕ_k and random topic distribution $\theta_{d'}$, we can compute the topic of every word z_{ji}. And in the M-step, we will compute the new $\theta_{d'}$ with the result from E step. The E-step and M-step is conducted iteratively until convergence. Then, we will get the topic distribution for new message denoted as $\theta_{d'}$ finally.

2.4 Measure the Propagation Probability

Intuitively, the probability of the link $e_{u,v}$ propagate the message d' is determined by two factors. First one is whether the link is active or not. Second one is whether the message is relevant to the link. It is known that the message and links propagate it are likely have the same topic, and the more relative they are, the higher probability the links will propagate the message. Thus, we adapt the KL divergence as the merit of the distance. The first factor can be measured by the number of historical messages on the link. And the second factor can be measured by the KL-divergence [9] between the topic distribution of links and the arriving messages, which is defined in Eq. (10):

$$p(d', e_{u,v}) \propto \frac{N_{e_{u,v}}}{D_{KL}(\theta_{d'}||\theta_{e_{u,v}})} = \frac{N_{e_{u,v}}}{\sum_{k=1}^{K} \theta_{d',k} log \frac{\theta_{d',k}}{\theta_{e_{u,v},k}}} \tag{10}$$

2.5 Get the Optimal Set of Links

As shown in Eq. (1), with the increase of link number, the cost for monitoring these links will grow and the risk for omitting will decrease, and vise versa. We assume that the benefit of monitoring a link can be measured by the probability of propagating that message. As the cost of monitoring a link is const. So the net profit of adding a link can be calculated by

$$P(e_{u,v}) = Rp(d', e_{u,v}) - C \tag{11}$$

Here R denotes the risk of omitting a link which conduct the message, and R varies with the specific application at hand. The optimal set of links can be got by choosing the links with positive net profit. While for applications with limited budget, we just reverse the *Top-N* edges.

In summary, NTAS is demonstrated in Algorithm 1.

Algorithm 1. Nonparametric Topic-aware Sparsification Algorithm

---

Input: Social network (SN) structure $G = (V, E)$;
1: Historical messages in SN $D_{u,v}, u, v \in V, (u, v) \in E$;
2: Target information d';
Output: Sparsity network E^o.

3: Collect all the messages on links, and forms the message set D;
4: **while** Not convergence //Gibbs sampling for model inference;
5:      Sample β with Eq.(5);
6:      For each word i in doc j, sample z_{ik} with Eq.(6);
7:      For each topic k in each doc j, sample m_{jk} with Eq.(7);
8: **end**
9: For each link $e_{u,v}$, calculate its topic distribution $\theta_{e_{u,v}}$ with Eq.(9);
10: Calculate the topic distribution with EM algorithm;
11: Calculate the probability of propagation of each link $p(\theta_{d'}, e_{u,v})$ with Eq.(10);
12: Calculate the net profit of monitoring each link with Eq.(11)
13: Reduce all the links with negative net profit, or reverse the *Top-N* links.

---

3   Experiment

In experiment, we test NTAS under the task of monitoring the malicious information on SINA weibo. We demonstrate that our algorithm outperforms other state-of-the-art methods.

Dataset. The data set is collected from Sina Weibo. It contains 10,125 users, 265,586 links and 1,253,421 messages.

Compared methods. We compare the proposed NTAS model with the following algorithms:

i. Sparsification of Infulence Networks(SPINE) [5]: SPINE is an efficiently greedy algorithm with two phases for eliminating links in the network.
ii. Activity Preserving Graph Simplification(APGS) [7]: It takes a *model-free* approach to find the most important pathways of the graph for understanding the information propagation.

3.1   Results

Figure 2(a) gives the comparison among NTAS, SPINE and APGS. Obviously, NTAS outperforms better than others on average. We can see that all of the algorithms are convergence after reducing the network to 45 %. To get the 90 % coverage of important links, the NTAS reduces the network to 15 % of original scale, the APGS reduces to 30 %, snd the SPINE reduces to 40 %. The reason for the superiority of NATS is that our method is more specific to topic-aware network sparsification.

Figure 2(b) presents the result of graphics before and after sparsification with NTAS on parts of network. The network, to be simplified, contains approximate

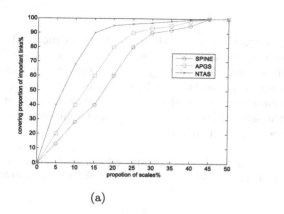

(a)   (b)

Fig. 2. Experiment results. Figure(a) illustrates the compared experiments among NTAS, SPINE and APGS. Figure(b) is the partial result for SINA Weibo. The figure above plots the original network (with 5000 edges), and the figure below plots the network (with 750 edges) simplified by NTAS.

5000 edges, and this number reduces to 750 after sparsification. This confirms the observations that information propagated along a link is mostly about the same topic and the more relative a message with a link, the more probable that this link propagate this message.

4   Related Work

Our goal is to identify subnetworks that preserve properties for a given purpose. Both the study of sparsification network and topic model are related to this study.

Topic modeling. Previous work like Mei *et al.* [2] Pathar *et al.* [3] used the topic model in the network for finding topical communities and text mining. A sequence of recent work has been done to analyze social network with topic model. Yin *et al.* [4] designed a *temporal context-aware mixture model* (TCAM) to model the user behaviors. TCAM is enable to find the user's favorite items by combining the topics related to user interests and topics related to temporal contexts. We adopt topic models as a tool to analysis measure for the relevance of a link to a target messages.

Network sparsity. Foti *et al.* [6] got the statistically significant edges by the empirical distribution used in real wold networks. Another greedy algorithm for simplifying directed network was given by Bonchi *et al.* [7]. Our work differentiate with the previous work in that we take latent topic of messages and links into account simultaneously. So the sparsification network is the most relevant network for that message.

5 Conclusion

To monitor a huge-scale social network for a specific purpose, it is more efficient to prune the network into a processable scale. In this paper, we present a novel nonparametric topic-ware network sparsity algorithm, which can reduce the complicated social network into a sub-network which is relevant to a specific information. Our experimental results on SINA weibo demonstrate that our method can greatly reduce the scale of the social network and achieve better results compared with other state-of-the-art methods.

Acknowledgments. This work was supported by the Strategic Leading Science and Technology Projects of Chinese Academy of Sciences (No. XDA06030200) and 863 projects (No.2011AA01A103).

References

1. Teh, Y.W., Jordan, M.I., Beal, M.J., Blei, D.M.: Hierarchical dirichlet processes. J. Am. Stat. Assoc. **101**, 1566–1581 (2006)
2. Mei, Q., Cai, D., Zhang, D., Zhai, C.: Topic modeling with network regularization. In: Proceedings of the 17th International Conference on World Wide Web, pp. 101–110. ACM (2008)
3. Pathak, N., DeLong, C., Banerjee, A., Erickson, K.: Social topic models for community extraction. In: In the 2nd SNA-KDD Workshop, vol. 8 (2008)
4. Yin, H., Cui, B., Chen, L., Hu, Z., Huang, Z.: A temporal context-aware model for user behavior modeling in social media systems (2014)
5. Mathioudakis, M., Bonchi, F., Castillo, C., Gionis, A., Ukkonen, A.: Sparsification of influence networks. In: Proceedings of the 17th ACM SIGKDD International Conference on Knowledge Discovery and Data Mining, pp. 529–537. ACM (2011)
6. Foti, N.J., Hughes, J.M., Rockmore, D.N.: Nonparametric sparsification of complex multiscale networks. PLoS one **6**(2), e16431 (2011)
7. Bonchi, F., Morales, G.D.F., Gionis, A., Ukkonen, A.: Activity preserving graph simplification. Data Min. Knowl. Disc. **27**(3), 321–343 (2013)
8. Blei, D.M., Ng, A.Y., Jordan, M.I.: Latent dirichlet allocation. J. Mach. Learn. Res. **3**, 993–1022 (2003)
9. Steyvers, M., Griffiths, T.: Probabilistic topic models. In: Handbook of Latent Semantic Analysis, pp. 424–440 (2007)
10. Dumais, S.T.: Latent semantic analysis. Annu. Rev. Inform. Sci. Technol. **38**(1), 188–230 (2004)
11. Casella, G., George, E.I.: Explaining the Gibbs sampler. Am. Stat. **46**(3), 167–174 (1992)
12. Antoniak, C.E.: Mixtures of Dirichlet processes with applications to Bayesian nonparametric problems. Ann. Stat. **2**(6), 1152–1174 (1974)

A Survey of Network Traffic Visualization in Detecting Network Security Threats

Xiaomei Liu[1,3], Yong Sun[1,3]([✉]), Liang Fang[2,3], Junpeng Liu[1,3],
and Lingjing Yu[1,3]

[1] Institute of Information Engineering, Chinese Academy of Science,
Beijing, China
[2] Beijing University of Posts and Telecommunications, Beijing, China
[3] National Engineering Laboratory for Information Security Technologies,
Beijing, China
{liuxiaomei,sunyong,liujunpeng,yulingjing}@iie.ac.cn,
fangliang@nelmail.iie.ac.cn

Abstract. Analyzing network traffic to detect network security threats has drawn attentions from security researchers for decades. However, the new characteristics of network traffic, such as explosive growth, more diverse attack types and higher dimension, have brought us new challenges. Because of these challenges, traditional detecting technologies like log analysis cannot directly identify threats from traffic in time. Visualization can straightly and quickly display multi-dimensional information of large network traffic. It can be our powerful weapon to meet the challenges. In this paper, we classify the network traffic into four layers. According to different layer, we systematically survey several well-known network traffic visualization systems. Then we analyze the advantages and disadvantages for each system and give out the comparisons. We also introduce the future works for network traffic visualization.

Keywords: Network traffic · Network security · Visualization

1 Introduction

The evolution of the network technologies has brought us more conveniences, while explosive growth of network traffic also comes up with it. According to the report by CISCO, the whole global network traffic will reach up to 1.3 ZB in 2016, which is much larger than we generate today. Would the number be larger? The answer is definitely yes. Meanwhile, network attacks hidden in the large network traffic have caused severe disastrous consequences. For example, as early as 2012, more than 68,000 DNS servers were utilized in a single DDoS attack. The traffic of network attacks has become even larger. In 2014, nearly 1/3 of the DDoS attack traffic reaches to 20 Gbps while the highest traffic can be over 200 Gbps. It brings us a challenge on how to identify network attacks from large network traffic directly and timely. Visualization technology has taken the researchers

© Springer-Verlag Berlin Heidelberg 2015
Y. Lu et al. (Eds.): ISCTCS 2014, CCIS 520, pp. 91–98, 2015.
DOI: 10.1007/978-3-662-47401-3_12

attention for it can straightly display the multi-dimensional information of the large network traffic in time.

Visualization transfers the invisible, unexpressed and abstract large data into visual images [1]. It can convert massive high-dimensional data to images and establish the image communications between human and data. By visualizing the network traffic, researchers can identify network patterns immediately and understand network traffic deeply. Meanwhile, researchers can find the hidden security threats, such as advanced persistent threat, internal threats and network cheating behavior, in the large network traffic. The advantages of visualizing the large network traffic are listed as follow:

- *Real-time:* Researchers can capture network traffic in real-time, extract the required properties of network traffic for visualizing, and update the visual graphics according to the updated data. In this way, researchers can identify network security threats more quickly.
- *High integrality:* All relevant data in the network traffic can be visualized to describe the continuous change over time. This not only helps to understand integral network patterns but also detects network security threats hidden in the network traffic more accurately.
- *Strong interactivity:* By using visualization technologies such as focus+context and dynamic queries etc., researchers can get more detailed information of the suspicious nodes for further analyzing. Besides, researchers can predict network attacks that have not occurred according to image schemas so as to guarantee the network security.

Although lots of visualization researches have made contributes to detect network security threats from traffic, a comprehensive survey of visualization trends and threats detection is absent.

Contributes and Outline: In this paper, we systematically survey several well-known network traffic visualization systems for detecting network security threats. Meanwhile, we highlight the development trend of visualization between systems. Firstly, we classify the network traffic into four layers and state the methods and steps for network traffic visualization. Secondly, we show how to visualize large network traffic for detecting security threats. Thirdly, we point out future works. We hope to provide research ideas and literature references for detecting network security threats by visualizing network traffic in the future.

2   Layers, Methods and Steps of Network Traffic Visualization

2.1   Layers of Network Traffic Visualization

It is difficult to visualize the entire network traffic because the traffic is abstract, complex and large. So we need to preprocess the network traffic to extract and visualize specific traffic attributes that are closely related to network attacks.

By summarizing and analyzing the related researches, we divide the current objects into four layers from top network traffic to bottom:

L1: visualization of bandwidth: Visualizing bandwidth to get the locations that consuming most network resources. Maybe most bandwidth is possessed by several illegal hosts.

L2: visualization of propagation delay: Propagation delay is the measurement of network connectivity and network performance. It can reflect the working state of network nodes to help researchers analyze abnormal network situations.

L3: visualization of communication paths: Communication paths represent the nodes that data go through from source to destination. It can reflect the dynamic changes of network topologies and help to detect abnormal network topologies like botnets, etc.

L4: visualization of packet attributes: Packet attributes include IP addresses, ports and protocols, etc. They are the most frequent objects of visualizing for detecting network abnormal behavior.

2.2   Methods and Research Steps of Network Traffic Visualization

According to the specific application status, we should select and design reasonable visualization methods to help us understand the different traffic. At present, the basic visualization methods include charts, 2D/3D graphics, 2D/scatter/circular plot, trajectory drawing, 3D geometry, topology, tree, etc. Most visual designs integrate the methods mentioned above with human-computer interaction technologies such as dynamic queries etc.

We can visualize network traffic as following steps [2]:

- S1. Data source selection
- S2. Visualization methods selection
- S3. Concurrent display of global and local information
- S4. Human-computer interaction design

3   Network Traffic Visualization

3.1   Visualization Based on Bandwidth

In order to achieve high quality network services, network administrators must allocate reasonable bandwidth for network applications. Through visualizing bandwidth, we can both quickly perceive the locations of consuming most network resources and identify the hosts that occupy illegal bandwidth. Initially, researchers just use ordinary histograms or pie-charts to display bandwidth. But such technologies cannot display high-dimensional and dynamic network traffic vividly. With the development of visualization, researchers begin to use the novel visual technologies to display the bandwidth. Oetiker [3] introduced MRTG which uses RRDtool to display bandwidth in form of charts. However, OPENGL can display bandwidth in 3D space [4]. Samak provided CISCO Net-Flow Analyzer which could analyze utilization of network bandwidth and would have alerts if it detects attack. Akamai shows the proportion of bandwidth of different areas around the world based on the global map and different colors represent different amount of bandwidth [5]. As is shown in Fig. 1, the redder color indicates the greater the traffic.

Fig. 1. Akamai - the proportion of traffic

3.2 Visualization Based on Communication Paths

As mentioned in Sect. 2.1, through visualizing communication paths we can find weak routing nodes and abnormal network topologies. However, with the increase of the traffic scale, it is difficult to visualize paths in 2D. Skitter visualizes communication paths based on a 3D earth model [6]. IP addresses in different positions are represented in different colored nodes. For example, yellow nodes represent the source nodes, while green nodes represent intermediate nodes or destination nodes. Communications between nodes are linked with lines. Skitter is used to measure the IP forwarding paths, evaluate the performance and topologies of Internet. More importantly, it helps researchers identify the abnormal topologies like botnets etc. In order to prevent topologies being too large,

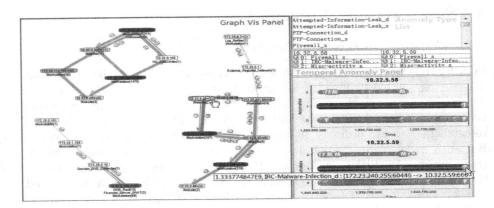

Fig. 2. Topologies display using compressed technology

Shi [7] uses the compressed technology which maps a set of IP addresses into a single node to reduce the display burden. As shown in Fig. 2, the main interface shows the compressed communication paths and the possible network anomalies, while the details of network anomalies are showed in the right.

3.3   Visualization Based on Propagation Delay

Although the success rate of transferring packets from source to destination is important, real-time transmission of the packets is also important. Propagation delay can reflect the speed of processing and forwarding packets of intermediate nodes. Then researchers can get suspicious network nodes through propagation delay. Akamai is one of the largest CDNs in the world [5]. It can test and show the slowest web connections between some important cities through a few of network behavior such as download etc. As shown in Fig. 3, every important city has two vertical bars. The bars represent both the current absolute time delay and the relative time delay compared with its historical average time delay. If the gap between current time delay and average time delay is very big, the web server may has been damaged by a malicious user. Then researchers should further analyze potential malicious network behavior.

Fig. 3. Akamai-propagation delay visualization

3.4   Visualization Based on Packet Attributes

Network traffic consists of packets that have basic attributes which are closely related to network attacks like source/destination IP address and port, protocol etc. Current network anomalies such as port scanning, worm attacks have obvious corresponding characteristics of one-to-many, many-to-one and many-to-many. We can quickly perceive them through visualizing IP address and port.

Both Spanning Cube of Potential Doom [8] and NetViewercite [9] map the entire IP addresses into the grid. The former shows the scanning activities in form of lines and detects malicious traffic by incomplete connections. The latter, however, uses different colors to represent the number of packets that go through the IP address over a period of time and uses polygons to classify IP addresses

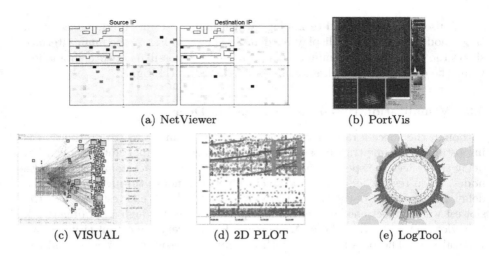

(a) NetViewer   (b) PortVis

(c) VISUAL   (d) 2D PLOT   (e) LogTool

Fig. 4. Visualization based on packet attributes

in the grid. NetViewer can monitor network anomalies such as the source IP-spoof, worm scan, etc. As shown in Fig. 4(a), the IANA reserved IP addresses are in the blue polygon. As we all know, the reserved IP addresses cannot serve as the destination address. Then we can monitor the source IP-spoof by using NetViewer. The two tools are difficult for researchers to further analyze network patterns because of the lack of human-computer interaction technology. Improvably, as shown in Fig. 4(b), PortVis [10] not only observe the information of all ports but also analyze specific ports in particular time by setting parameters and filtering details. VISUAL [11], VisFlowConnect [12] and NAV [13] visualize local hosts and remote hosts separately to determine the attack position accurately. VISUAL as shown in Fig. 4(c), local hosts are in the grid, while remote hosts are around outside the grid. Communications between them are represented by lines. VisFlowConnect and NAV use the parallel technology to depict the relationships between internal and external network and display detailed traffic information of specified nodes. We can know which remote host was scanning local hosts by using them. The common disadvantage of these tools is that visualizing large traffic may cause visual clutter. To avoid the visual clutter, NFlowVis [14] uses hierarchical edge bundles to classify traffic and reveals large-scale distributed attacks. Meanwhile, it connects an alarm of an intrusion detection system and sends alerts in time if network attacks are detected. Destination ports correlate to network connections and network behavior. As IDGraph [15] and n-dimensional histogram [16] observed, they can detect TCP SYN flooding. The former uses the traffic aggregation methods to visualize the destination IP addresses and ports to reveal it. While the later detects it by scanning each port and building an n-dimensional histogram to display unsuccessful connection number of destination ports. Gerth uses 2D PLOT to visualize destination ports to detect attacks [17]. As shown in Fig. 4(d), green represents mail, blue represents DNS, red represents scanning activities and orange represents SSH attacks, etc.

Flying Term [18] can find abnormal DNS query patterns and observe DNS dynamics over time by visualizing the query frequency of port 53. LogTool [19] as shown in Fig. 4(e), the time circle of a day is divided into 288 pieces. Each piece is a radial histogram that shows the proportions of uplink and downlink traffic. The dot-dash line inside the circle shows the number of HTTP(port 80) connection requests, so it can analyze users online surfing behavior.

4 Future Works

Although visualization has gained great achievements in quickly identifying network attacks from large network traffic, constructing a complete and practical visualization system to detect network security threats still faces many challenges.

- *Lack of a set of complete and systematic theories for the network traffic visualization.* Meanwhile, it is also difficult to choose a unified evaluation standard for verifying and evaluating the result provided by those visualization products. Because different users may have different needs, there is certain subjective for the evaluation standard. Above all, we need to put more attention on the theoretical research of network traffic visualization.
- *How to identify new network attacks by using network traffic visualization.* The network structure is getting more complex. The security threats are more varied. How to predict the attacks that have not occurred and how to find the new attacks in the normal flow are becoming very important.
- *How to design network traffic visualization system with high efficiency.* Because the scale of network traffic is getting more large, many systems cannot process and display such large data in real-time. We need to improve or redesign the algorithms for processing and visualizing the network traffic.

5 Conclusions

As a relatively mature technology, visualization has played an important role in many research fields. Aiming at identifying network security threats from large network traffic, we summarize and analyze the current visualization technologies from four aspects that are closely related to network attacks: (1) bandwidth, (2) propagation delay, (3) communication paths and (4) packet attributes. Though the existing works can partially handle the challenges brought by the new characteristics of the network traffic, there are still a lot of future works to be done. It will be our pleasure that our work could provide references for the future researches of network traffic visualization.

Acknowledgments. This work was supported by The National Science and Technology Support Program (Grant No. 2012BAH46B02); the National Natural Science Foundation (Grant No. 61402464, 61402474).

References

1. McCormick, B.H., Defanti, T.A., Brown, M.D.: Visualization in scientific computing. Comput. Graphics **21**(6), 1103–1109 (1987)
2. Lv, L., Zhang, J., Sun, J., He, P., Sun, L.: Survey of network security visualization techniques. Comput. Appl. **28**(8), 1924–1927 (2008)
3. Oetiker, T.: Multi router traffic grapher. http://oss.oetiker.ch/mrtg/
4. Yi, L., Ni, W., Han, Z.: Network traffic statistic analysis and visualization system. Microelectron. Comput. **24**(6), 153–155 (2007)
5. Popa, F.: Network traffic visualization. seminar innovative internet-technologien und mobilkommunikation, WS 2008/2009 Institut fr Informatik, Lehrstuhl Netzarchitekturen und Netzdienste Technische Universitt, Mnchen
6. CAIDA Skitter. http://www.caida.org/tools/measurement/skitter/
7. Shi, L., Liao, Q., Yang, C.: Investigating network traffic through compressed graph visualization. In: VAST 2012 Mini Challenge 2 Award: Good Adaptation of Graph Analysis Techniques (2012)
8. Lau, S.: The spinning cube of potential doom. Commun. ACM **47**(6), 25–26 (2004)
9. Kim, S.S., Narasimha Reddy, A.L.: NetViewer: a network traffic visualization and analysis tool. In: LISA 2005 Paper, A M University, Texas (2005)
10. McPherson, J., Ma, K.-L., Krystosk, P., Bartoletti, T., Christensen, M.: Portvis: a tool for port-based detection of security events. In: VizSEC/DMSEC 2004 Proceedings of the 2004 ACM Workshop on Visualization and Data Mining for Computer Security, pp. 73–81. ACM Press (2004)
11. Ball, R., Fink, G.A., North, C.: Home-centric visualization of network traffic for security administration. In: VizSEC/DMSEC04 Proceedings of the 2004 ACM Workshop on Visualization and Data Mining for Computer Security, pp. 55–64. ACM Press (2004)
12. Yin, X., Yurcik, W., Li, Y., Lakkaraju, K., Abad, C.: VisFlowConnect: providing security situational awareness by visualizing networks traffic flow. In: Proceedings of the IEEE 2004 (2004)
13. Allen, M., McLachlan, P.: NAV network analysis visualization, University of British Columbia, 29 May 2009
14. Fischer, F., Mansmann, F., Keim, D.A., Pietzko, S., Waldvogel, M.: Large-scale network monitoring for visual analysis of attacks. In: Goodall, J.R., Conti, G., Ma, K.-L. (eds.) VizSec 2008. LNCS, vol. 5210, pp. 111–118. Springer, Heidelberg (2008)
15. Ren, P., Gao, Y., Li, Z., Chen, Y., Watson, B.: IDGraph: intrusion detection and analysis using stream compositing. IEEE Comput. Graph. Appl. **26**, 28–39 (2006)
16. Bethel, E.W., Campbell, S., Dart, E.: Accelerating network traffic analytics using query-driven visualization. In: IEEE Symposium on Visual Analytics Science and Technology (2006)
17. Xiao, L., Gerth, J., Hanrahan, P.: Enhancing visual analysis of network traffic using knowledge representation. In: Proceedings of the IEEE Symposium on Visual Analytics Science and Technology (2006)
18. Ren, P., Kristoff, J., Gooch, B.: Visualizing DNS traffic. In: VizSEC 2006 Proceedings of the 3rd International Workshop on Visualization for Computer Security, pp. 23–30 (2006)
19. http://infosthetics.com/archives/2010/10/logtool_revealing_the_hidden_patterns_of_online_surfing_behavior.html

Sentinel: In Case of the Untrustworthy Behaviors Inside the Clouds

Dong Cui[1]([✉]), Chuanyi Liu[2], Meiqi Yang[3], and Jincui Yang[2]

[1] School of Computer Science, Beijing University of Posts and Telecommunications,
Beijing, China
cuidong1108@foxmail.com
[2] School of Software, Beijing University of Posts and Telecommunications,
Beijing, China
cy-liu04@mails.tsinghua.edu.cn
[3] School of Information, Renmin University of China, Beijing, China
740503175@qq.com

Abstract. Since compute cloud is the most important part of IAAS applications, there are a number of security issues associated with it, including the threat from untrustworthy administrators who may compromise the users' system without authorization and escape responsibility by deleting logs. Based on previous publication, ways to prevent destruction from administrators mainly fall into three broad categories: SSO(Single Sign On), administration rights distribution, log analyzing. However, any of these methods have strengths and weaknesses. In this document, we come up with a new method "Sentinel", which combines double-check and the log mechanism and can ensure the security of the system without weakening administrators' privileges. In our Sentinel, the administrators can only enter the management domain through a unified entrance. The Sentinel is able to detect and intersect destructive instruction and at the same time keep operation logs which are transparent to the administrators.

Keywords: Double-check · Sensitive instruction · Log · Compute cloud

1 Introduction

With the promotion of cloud computing, virtualization products have been greatly developed. C2(Compute Cloud), a significant part of the IAAS applications, lies at the bottom of cloud computing industry chain pyramid. It can effectively reduce operating costs, improve application compatibility, accelerate application deployment, improve service availability, increase resource utilization rate and schedule resources dynamically [1]. However, like cloud services, security issues turn to be a major bottleneck and get in the way of the development of C2. In order to attract potential users, cloud providers are inclined to prove themselves credible [2], but users may suffer from theft and attack from cloud providers' internal management personnel [3].

As for C2, major security issues from the administrators are as follows:

© Springer-Verlag Berlin Heidelberg 2015
Y. Lu et al. (Eds.): ISCTCS 2014, CCIS 520, pp. 99–106, 2015.
DOI: 10.1007/978-3-662-47401-3_13

1. Cloud platform roles and administration authority allocation may be a risk. Data center infrastructure, cloud platform management system and the VMM (Virtual Machine Monitor) all give the administrators corresponding management interfaces of cloud physical server and virtualization components. The VMM directly controls the physical hardware and runs on the layer with the highest processor access permission. Administrators always have root privilege in management domain (also called Domain0, a privilege VM(Virtual Machine) to control and manage C2), which makes it possible for them to destroy users' C2 without authorization.
2. When there is a breakdown or the administrators modify or delete logs on purpose, cloud platform do not have enough credible evidence confronted with audit and accountability. This is also because that the administrators often have the cloud platform physical server root privilege, which enables them to delete or modify logs to escape responsibility.

Technical difficulties to solve the problems above are:

1. Too coarse-grained permission division cannot limit the administrators' behavior to destroy C2 runtime environment. But too fine-grained permission division may deteriorate service quality and affect authorization efficiency. So it is clearly inappropriate to simply take back or reduce the administrators' privilege and expose too many low-level operation permissions to users.
2. Using fortress machine method to protect C2 needs protocol analysis. For example, SSH protocol analysis requires a great amount of work. Besides, there are many kinds of protocols and the analysis results are not portable.

To solve problems above, in this paper, we combine the double-check mechanism and the log mechanism to secure our C2 environment, and establish a "Sentinel" system based on the idea. Administrators are required to enter the management domain through a unified entrance. Sentinel will check every instruction from the administrators and stop it before any potential destruction. At the same time, Sentinel will keep administrators operation logs which is transparent to the administrators.

Main contributions of this article are listed below:

1. Forward proxy or reverse proxy in fortress machine needs protocol analysis. We copy the VMM cached data into Sentinel using ssh_connect interface provided by SSH protocol to avoid tedious protocol analysis.
2. In Sentinel, users can choose white list or black list or use both as they wish, switch between two mechanism are transparent to users.
3. Rewrite GateOne software, using GateOne terminal.py part as the SSO entrance of Sentinel system.

2   Related Work

Methods for protecting C2 from insider attacks roughly fall into three categories:

1. SSO: Single Sign On

SSO emphasizes filtering out insecurity factors at the entry point so that only trustworthy administrators can enter the management domain. Broker-based SSO benefits from centralized management but suffers from a heavy workload when reconstructing the old system. Agent-based SSO is portable but needs to design and implement new interface that is compatible with the original application. Token-based SSO enhances the security of the system but needs to add new components. Gateway-based SSO is easy to install and set up gateway, but is vulnerable to attack as well [4]. In China, the SSO system achieved by Dinghua He is independent from application, combining user information, user roles and system login information to generate a resource list related with web users, and use it for authentication when users login [5].

2. Separate and control administrators privileges

Nowadays management roles are often divided into super administrators and general administrators. Constructing a tree structure with different levels of privileges makes it possible to give different administrators different permissions, where super administrators have the highest privilege and general administrators can only manage local resources. Achieving fine-grained access control improves efficiency of authorization and eases administrators' workload in the centralized management system [6]. An example of this is the "separation of three powers" brought up by Yi Xu, which separates administrative privileges into database administrator, audit administrator and security administrator [7].

3. The traceability and accountability.

Related researches mainly focus on keeping logs. Revirt [8] is achieved in partially virtual environment, taking VM front-end and Domain0 back-end as intermediary to request data and logging these information. But we need to modify kernel VM, which mature commercial operating system does not support. V2E [9] virtual system is divided into main realm and recording realm. Malware runs in recording realm, while the rest still runs in main realm, so that it can keep logs from recorder. However, overheads for recording and translation at an instruction level are pretty high and will seriously affect system performance. XenLR, developed by Huazhong University of Science and Technology, is a Mini-OS that can record keyboard and mouse behavior sequence.

3 System Design

3.1 Design of Our Sentinel System

Sentinel system consists of three sub modules: SSO module, double-check module and log module. SSO module takes charge of administrators login, double-check module monitors the administrators instructions which is the core of Sentinel. Log module records administrators operation instructions as an auxiliary part.

As shown in Fig. 1, in order to manage C2 on the cloud platform, administrators often have root access to management domain. Domain0 is a privilege VM to control and manage C2, and is the only access to physical resources under VMM control. Administrators can create, modify and delete C2 instances in Domain0. Every instruction given by the administrators will be stored in the instruction

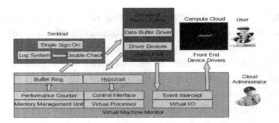

Fig. 1. Architecture of Sentinel system

cache at first, then transferred to data cache in management domain. Administrators can control users' C2 by connecting back-end driver in management domain and front-end driver through event channel.

We establish a unified login entrance between the VMM and C2. After administrators enter Domain0 through given SSO, Sentinel will take every instruction the administrators input from VMM instruction cache, save it to its own cache and identify what kind of instruction it is. Sentinel will perform a double-check on the instruction when Sentinel thinks it is dangerous. If double-check succeeds, the instruction will be sent to instruction cache in management domain and executed. If double-check fails, this instruction will be ignored. Logs of the administrators' instructions will be kept throughout the whole process. Because logs are stored in Sentinel, administrators have no permission to view, modify or delete logs, that it, logs are transparent to administrators.

3.2   Sensitive Instruction

In this paper, we define sensitive instructions as instructions that can harm even destroy the C2 runtime environment. For example, when the administrator gives an instruction "DeleteInstance" (shut down VM immediately) under root privilege, without Sentinel, this command will be executed immediately. This will kill all running processes of this instance and users will suffer a great loss from losing unsaved data.

In Sentinel, we distinguish between different kinds of instructions and users can put whatever they think threatening into the black list. In this prototype, we selected instructions shown in Table 1 as sensitive instructions in Sentinel.

Table 1. The sensitive instruction of black list

Cloud instruction	Stop instance, Modify instance attribute, etc.
Power-off	shutdown now, init 0, telinit 0, etc
Groups	groupadd, admin -d /home/user1 -s /bin/bash user1, etc.
Users	useradd user1, userdel -r user1, etc.
Others	history, chmod, chown, etc.

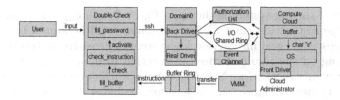

Fig. 2. Double-check mechanism

If the user has a higher demand for C2, he can also set his own white list, namely all the instructions except those in the white list require further authentication.

3.3 Double-Check Mechanism

Double-check mechanism means temporarily isolate the administrators' instruction and check if it is sensitive instruction. If it's general instruction, we allow it to execute normally. If not, further authorization from users is required. If users authorization succeeds, this instruction can execute. If fails, it will be ignored. Double-check mechanism can detect harmful instructions ahead of time and ask for the users' permission before the administrator can do any harm to the C2 environment.

The flow of double-check process is shown in Fig. 2. We suppose the administrator uses command line tool via keyboard. After the administrator issues one command, VMM Performance Counter will save the command to buffer ring. The instruction will be sent to Sentinel as a character stream in the fill_buffer module. Then, we'll match the instruction with the black list in the check_instruction module. If there is no match, the instruction will be sent via SSH to back-end driver of Domain0 to execute. Otherwise, fill_password module will be activated and authorization from user is needed. After users authorization, the fill_password module will evaluate the result to decide whether to send the instruction to Domain0 or to ignore the instruction and clear fill_buffer for next input.

3.4 Structure of Log System

The prototype design of the log system is a supplement to the double-check mechanism. The log system stores general instructions and sensitive instructions separately for later analysis.

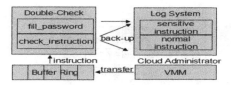

Fig. 3. Log system

Structure of the log system is shown in Fig. 3. It will copy necessary instructions from the instruction cache. Users' command will be stored in instruction cache and goes to general instruction log system or sensitive instruction log system depending on the result of check_instruction in double-check module. And if it is sensitive instruction, we also write down if it is executed or not.

We use 4 bytes to store the key value, 8 bytes to store administrator related information, 8 bytes to store instruction related information. For sensitive instruction log system, we add 1 extra byte to indicate if this command is executed. We also need to store the exact time when the administrator issues the command. We use the formula below to calculate the running time of the instruction and save it to the log system.

$$system\_time + ((tsc - tsc\_timestamp) << tsc\_shift) * tsc\_to\_system\_mul \quad (1)$$

System_time expresses time passed since the machine boots. Tsc_timestamp means time stamp counter(tsc) at last update of time interval. Tsc_shift saves shifting of cycle counter which is used to calculate current system time. Tsc_to_system_mul is the multiplier factor which expresses the corresponding relation between tsc and the system time.

4   Implementation and Evaluations

4.1   SSO Overview

We choose GateOne as our SSO unified login entrance. GateOne is a web-based terminal emulator and SSH client implemented with Html5. As shown in Fig. 4, GateOne service starts after loading tornado modules. First, server.py will look for init.py under applications repository and load terminal.py to log on to remote C2 server. Terminal.py communicates with remote cloud server through SSH plugins and sends instructions in the form of character stream.

Our double-check module and log system are both achieved in terminal.py and will be executed automatically when GateOne service starts.

4.2   Effectiveness

As shown in Fig. 5 at left, after the administrator logs on to Sentinel, available virtual machines that the administrator can access are displayed in the management interface. In this example, there are 2 users and 5 virtual machines.

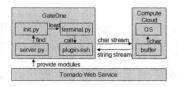

Fig. 4. Message transfer mechanism

Fig. 5. The effectiveness of Sentinel

The administrator can select one virtual machine at one time and establish connection. When the administrator gives a general instruction, Sentinel keeps silence. When the administrator gives a sensitive instruction, "DeleteInstance" in this example, Sentinel will suspend the instruction and prompt for user authorization password. If the password is wrong, Sentinel will print an error message and the instruction will be ignored.

The right part is an example of the log file in Sentinel. The third line shows that Bob issued DeleteInstance command but failed without user's authorization.

4.3   The Time Overhead of Sentinel

The time overhead of Sentinel mostly arises from loading black list to the system and checking if one instruction is in it. The former time is a constant, for we only load the black list once the first time we use it. So the time overhead mainly comes from the latter.

First, we set the size of black list to a fix number(100). Then we call a function in timeit module(Timer(function(), "from __main__ import function")) to calculate running time in double-check module. We select one sensitive instruction and one general instruction as experimental subjects and each experiment tests 100000 times in total to get rid of contingency. To cover as more cases as possible, we start from only general instructions and gradually increase the percentage of sensitive instructions. Results are shown in Fig. 6 at left. Execution time in double-check module of 100000 instructions falls between 16.62 us and 16.98 us which varies less than 2.12 %. Considering this is the total execution time of 100000 instructions, we believe the average overhead for one instruction is low enough to be unnoticeable for users.

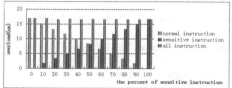 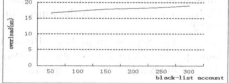

Fig. 6. The time overhead of Sentinel

With the increase instruction number in the black list, the time over-head remain at microsecond level, only increasing by 11.81 % (from 16.75 us to 18.99 us, shown in Fig. 6 at right) when the number of instructions in the black list increases 6 times (from 50 to 300). So even if the user chooses the white list, our prototype system, Sentinel can still provide stable high quality service.

5   Conclusions

Traditional ways to prevent untrustworthy behaviors from insiders are SSO, division of privileges, traceability and accountability. But integrating all methods into one system requires huge amount of work. Too fine-grained privilege division decreases management efficiency and traceability and accountability can only find the attackers afterwards. In this paper, we combine the double-check mechanism and the log mechanism to protect our C2, without weakening administrators' privileges. Sentinel can take measures beforehand with little time overheads when it detects potential danger.

Compared to other systems, out prototype Sentinel has the following two special features:

1. Dangerous instructions are isolated. We also provide white list for any users who have high security requirements. Only instructions in the white list can pass through Sentinel directly while others need further authorization from users.
2. High performance. Time overheads are very low which means high quality service is provided by our system.

References

1. Wang, Q.: Virtualization and cloud computing. PHEI (2011)
2. Liu, C.: A dynamic trustworthiness verification mechanism for trusted cloud execution environment. J. Softw. (2013)
3. Jansen, W.: Guidelines on security and privacy in public cloud computing. NIST, Washington, DC (2011)
4. Zhang, T.: Research and Design of Web-based SSO System. University of Science and Technology of China (2005)
5. He, D.: The Design and Implementation of SSO System Unrelated with Application. Builetin of Science and Technology (2012)
6. Li, H.: Research Based on the Fine-grained Access Control. ZhongShan University (2012)
7. Xu, Y.: The Separation of Three Rights Data Management. ESAS World (2009)
8. Dunlap, G.: ReVirt. University of Michigan (2008)
9. Artem Dinaburg.: Ether. Georgia Institute of Technology (2008)

Web-Based Heatmap of Physical Machines in Cloud Computing

Heng Chen[✉] and Xiaoshe Dong

Department of Computer Science and Technology, Xi'an Jiaotong University,
Xi'an, Shaanxi, China
{hengchen,xsdong}@mail.xjtu.edu.cn

Abstract. Cloud computing has become a flexible infrastructure for a variety of companies and organizations to develop and deploy their products. To provide a vision of physical machines for administrators and customers, this paper proposes a web-base heatmap of physical machines in cloud computing. It employs the browser-server architecture and utilizes distributed and asynchronous technologies to collect the temperature data. It divides the progress of heatmap drawing and keeps the user updated. It was tested in an experimental environment, the results show it functions well and achieves its goal.

Keywords: Heat map · Physical machine · Cloud computing

1 Introduction

Cloud computing has become a flexible infrastructure for a variety of companies and organizations to develop and deploy their products. The pay-as-you-go model makes customers with innovative ideas do not need a large capital outlays in hardware to deploy their product or engnieers to operate it [1]. Customers can easily adjust the number of resources according to the popularity of their products. Moreover, customers with large batch-oritented tasks can get results as quickly as their products can scale. For example, a task need to run 300 hours with one server. If this product has a good scalability, the task can run 1 hour with 300 servers. Cloud computing makes the latter cost no more than the former.

Many computing service providers including Amazon, Google, Microsoft, Yahoo and IBM are rapidly deploying data centers in various location around the world to provide cloud computing services. In industry these services are referred to Infrastructure as a Service (IaaS), Platform as a Service (PaaS), and Software as a Service (SaaS) respectively. For Iaas, cloud computing providers usually employ Virtual Machine (VM) technologies for consolidation and environment isolation purposes. Basically, the maximum number of VMs running on a physical machine (PM) is determined by the number of CPUs in the PM. From the viewpoint of customers, the operation of VMs is similar to PMs. Each customer can view the status of VMs and operate VMs via a Web-based control

© Springer-Verlag Berlin Heidelberg 2015
Y. Lu et al. (Eds.): ISCTCS 2014, CCIS 520, pp. 107–113, 2015.
DOI: 10.1007/978-3-662-47401-3_14

panel. The typical operations of a VM includes start, shutdown, reboot and transfer. The transfer operation means a customer can a VM from currently PM to another PM based on the characteristics of PMs such as load and temperature.

From the aspect of cloud computing provider, they hope their PMs can satisfy more customers with less cost. The main cost of cloud computing providers is the energy consumption of the compute equipment (PMs) and the associated cooling infrastructure [2]. Running more VMs on a PM increases the overall utilization and effiency of the equipment across the deployment. However, this strategy will dramatically increase the temperature of PMs which leads to more energy consumption in cooling. Thus, the creation, management and scheduling of VMs across PMs in a data center in a power-aware fashion is critical to reduce the overall operational costs [3]. However, the scheduling stategy related to the temperature of PMs is transparent to adminstrators of data centers and customers. Each of them has a requirement to view the status of PMs directly. Furthermore, some VMs can migrate from a hot PM to another PM with low temperature [4].

In this article, we introduce a Web-based Heatmap of Physical Machines in cloud computing (WHPM) which provide a method to visualize the temperature of PMs in a data center. WHPM is based on a browser-server architecture [5]. The browser side is responsible for providing the user interface, sending action events and rendering the heatmap. The server side collects the temperature data of PMs that users requested and generates the corresponding heatmap. WHPM supports multiple users to view a heatmap of a same set of PMs. To prevent the action of repeatly fetching the temperature of PMs in a short period, WHPM employs a database in server side to store the recent data of PMs.

The rest of this paper is organized as follows. Section 2 introduce the design principle and architecture of WHPM. The detailed implementation of WHPM is presented in Sect. 3. Section 4 concludes this paper with summary and future research directions.

2   Design Principle

The architecture of WHPM that includes three parts is depicted in Fig. 1. The left part means multiple users can access different heatmaps at the same time by using their browsers. The right part denotes N PMs in a data center. The key part which includes a Web server, database and the temperature fetching module locates in the middle. The arrows among three parts mean the network connections which can be Internet or Intranet.

Based on the architecture depicted in Fig. 1, the simple procedure for a user to view a heatmap of a set of PMs in a data center includes 5 steps. A user first log into a web-based control panel with a browser. Then, he/she sends the command of viewing heatmap after selecting a set of PMs. When the web server receives a heatmap request, it searchs the temperature data from the database for each PM in which the user interests. If the relevant data has expired or does not exist, the web server will call the moudle of data fetch to collect the realtime

Fig. 1. Architecture of WHPM

temperature data from there PMs. After the web server obtains the necessary data, it draw the heatmap. Finally, the user sees the interested heatmap in browser.

In order to fetch temperature data from PMs, each PM should have a method to sensor or collect its temperature. Typically this can be implemented either hardware or software approach. The former is supported by the Intelligent Platform Management Interface (IPMI) interface and the latter is implemented by installing a sensor tool such as lm-sensor on operating system. Since there are tens of thousands PMs in a data center, the data fetch module must employ a asynchronous mechnasim to collect data. With plenty of data, the heatmap can be drawed with a tool called RackDiag. However, the drawing phase that includes data rearrange, color legend and PMs plot costs a lot of time. Generally, both the data fetching phase and heatmap drawing phase consume more time which exceeds users' acceptable waiting time. As a user, he/she always wants to know what is happening after he/she sent a request. Therefore, the web server must inform the progress of heatmap. The browser of users can use AJAX technology get the intermediate status and show the progress to users.

3   Implementation

This section introduces the implementation of WHPM. The details are described in order from right to left based on the architecture showed in Fig. 1. We first introduce the implementation of the temperature fetching module. Then, we describe the heatmap drawing phase in detail. Next, we introduce the progress management of heatmap. The asynchronous request and response between users' browsers and the web server is described finally.

3.1   Temperature Fetching

A PM should have a hardware or software interface to sense its temperature. The hardware interface usually provides by IPMI which must be configured by the system administrator. The typical configuration includes a independant IP address which is different from the IP addresses in the operating system of a PM, a username and password. The software interface utilizes the lm-sensors which also need be installed and configured by the system administrator. In this paper, we use the hardware interface to sense temperature data from PMs.

The command of IPMI to get the temperature from a PM is "`impitool -I lanplus -H ipaddr -U user -P pass sdr type temperature`", in which `ipaddr`, `user` and `pass` denote the IP address of the PM's IPMI, username and password repesctively. The output of IPMI has multiple lines, each line represents the status of an entity and includes 5 fields splitted by "|" symbol. The 5th field denotes the specific temperature of an entity in the 4th field. A PM usually has several entities, we use the highest temperature to represent the temperature of the PM in order to simplify problem.

Considering a user may be interested in a lot of PMs, the data collecting phase should run in a distributed and asynchronous way. The celery tool [6] is used to implement the data collecting. For each PM, the data fetching module call the temperature celery task which aschronously obtains the PM's temperature with `ipmitool`. Since the celery task executes aschronously, WHPM saves the fresh temperature data into a database, in which each record includes the hostname or IP address of the PM, the temperature and the collecting time fields at least. After collecting all the required temperature data, WHPM call the heatmap drawing module to plot the heatmap that the user requested.

3.2   Heatmap Drawing

When the web server receives a user's heatmap request, it reads the temperature data of the PMs from database. If the temperature data of some PMs are expired or do not exist, the web server will call data fetching module described in Sect. 3.1. Therefore, when the heatmap drawing module is called by the web server, the temperature data read from the database are fresh and valid. With required temperature data, the heatmap drawing phase includes two parts as follows:

- Draw the legend of heatmap.
- Draw the heatmap of PMs based on their temperature.

The legend of heatmap is a color bar which is divided into 240 segments. Each segement of the color bar represents a specific temperature. To make the legend has a tight relation with the heatmap of the PMs, the temperatures of start, step and end of the legend should be calculated according to the temperatures of the PMs. The algorithm of legend calculation is given in Algorithm 1.

The Algorithm 1 includes two parts. The first part locating from 1st line to 12th line calculate the start, step and end temperature of PMs. The second part draws the legend color bar according to position and color of the 240 segments. The step of temperature in legend bar is calculated in line 1. Since the temperatures of PMs are varied, we cannot expect a reasonable step of temperature which will be used for drawing a marker in legend. Thus, WHPM uses an array to estimate the proper step of temperature. The array defined in line 2 can cover the temperature range from 0.1 to 500 degree which is enough for the temperature of PMs in cloud computing environment. The lines between 3 and 10 estimate the optimized step of temperature. After the optimized step is obtained, line 11 and 12 calculate the start and end of temperature in legend respectively. WHPM uses different color denotes the varied temperature.

Algorithm 1. Drawing the legend of a heatmp

Input: The minimum and maximum temperature $T_{\min}$ and $T_{\max}$;
Ouput: The start, step and end of the legend color bar T_{start}, T_{step} and T_{end}.

1: $T_{step} \leftarrow (T_{\max} - T_{\min})/10$
2: $M_{list} \leftarrow [0.01, 0.02, 0.05, 0.1, 0.2, 0.5, 1, 2, 5, 10, 25, 50]$
3: $prev \leftarrow 0$
4: **for** each $v \in M_{list}$ **do**
5:   **if** $T_{step} < v$ **then**
6:     $T_{step} \leftarrow M_{list}[prev]$
7:     **break**
8:   **end if**
9:   $prev \leftarrow prev + 1$
10: **end for**
11: $T_{start} \leftarrow \textbf{int}(\textbf{round}(T_{\min}/T_{step})) * T_{step}$
12: $T_{end} \leftarrow \textbf{int}(\textbf{round}(T_{\min}/T_{step})) * T_{step}$
13: $H_{step} \leftarrow 1/360$
14: **for** $n \in [0 : 240]$ **do**
15:   $P_{x,y} \leftarrow \textbf{GetRectPos}(n)$
16:   $color \leftarrow \textbf{GetRGBWithH}(n)$
17:   $\textbf{DrawColorBarRect}(P_{x,y}, color)$
18: **end for**

The line 15 and 16 get the position and color in legend for nth segment respectively. Then, line 17 draws the nth segment of the heatmap legend.

The heatmap of PMs is plotted with the help of the RackDiag tool [7], which needs a descriptive file of racks as the input file. The input file includes multiple racks. Each rack has the total number of PMs, the ID, location and height of each PM. The heatmap drawing is presented in Algorithm 2. Line 1 generates the input file F_{in} of RackDiag formation with the ID of PMs. The lines between 2 and 5 allocate the RGB color for each PM. Line 6 renders the F_{in} file with the RGB colors A. Here, the colored input file for heatmap has generated. Line 7 then call the RackDiag tool to generate the heatmap whose filename is F. Since the heatmap will be displayed in the browser, line 8 parse the dimension from the file F.

3.3 Progress Management

After a user sends a request of viewing heatmap, the web server will get the refresh data through reading the database or directly collecting from the PMs. Then, WHPM will use these data to draw the heatmap. Each of the two steps are time consuming. To prevent a user from waiting impatiently, the web server should tell the user what's going on in the background. Moreover, WHPM need to consider more than one user send requests to view a same set of PMs. For example, if a user U_a sends a request to view the heatmap of PM M_1 and the temperature data of M_1 in data is expired, the data fetching module call the IPMI to obtain the freshed temperature data. Before the data from M_1 is saved

Algorithm 2. Drawing heatmap

Input: The start, step and end of the legend color bar T_{start}, T_{step} and T_{end}; The number of PMs N, the array of ID I and temperature T.

Ouput: The filename, dimension of heatmap F and D.

1: $F_{\text{in}} \leftarrow$ **GenRackInput**$(I[0, N])$
2: $A[0, N] \leftarrow$ 'AABBCC'
3: **for** $n \in [0, N]$ **do**
4:     $A[n] \leftarrow$ **GetRGB**$(T[n], T_{\text{start}}, T_{\text{step}}, T_{\text{end}})$
5: **end for**
6: $F_{\text{in}} \leftarrow$ **RenderRackInput**(F_{in}, A)
7: $F \leftarrow$ **call** RackDiag **with** F_{in}
8: $D \leftarrow$ **ParseDimension**(F)

to the database, another user U_b also sends a similar request. In order to save energy and time, the status of data fetching should be recorded in database too.

To give each user a precise progress of heatmap drawing, WHPM defines three operation of heatmap, namely load map, refresh map and load plus refresh map. The difference between the load map and load plus refresh map is the former read the freshed temperature data from database, however, the temperature data read in the latter is expired. To simplify the problem, WHPM divides the whole process from 1 to 100. For example, the load map has the following progress $[(0, 5), (1, 20), (5, 20), (6, 25), (7, 15), (8, 15)]$. Each parenthesis in the bracket denotes a specific sub-task. The first element in the parenthesis represents the ID of a sub-task, the second element denotes the discrete time that this sub-task will spend. The meaning of the progress of load map is listed as follows:

- $(0, 5)$ means a browser sends the request spend 5 tiscrete time;
- $(1, 20)$ means reading data from database spend 20 discrete time;
- $(5, 20)$ means processing the temperature data need 20 discrete time;
- $(6, 25)$ means plotting heatmap need 25 discrete time;
- $(7, 15)$ means drawing legend of a heatmap need 15 discrete time;
- $(8, 15)$ means loading heatmap into browser need another 15 discrete time.

During each period defined in the discrete progress for every operation of heatmap, WHPM calls the **UpdateProgress** function to update the status of the heatmap progress. To support multiple users, WHPM makes a independant instance of heatmap progress for each user. Therefore, the browser of each user can get the precise progress by calling the instance of map progress with AJAX technology periodically.

3.4   Heatmap Display

With AJAX technology, a user can view the progress of generating heatmap. When the browser received the status of loading map to browser, it will display the heatmap with defined dimension. Since the size of heatmap maybe very large, the display zone of heatmap provides the zoom button. Moreover, users can draw and move the heatmap with mouse. It also has a refresh button, user can get a refreshed heatmap by press this button.

4   Conclusions

In this paper, a new web-based heatmap of physical machines in cloud computing is proposed. By using the distributed and asynchronous methods, the proposed mechanism can efficient collect the temperature data of physical machines in whichusers are interested. To let users know what is happening after they send requests, we divide the whole process and update the progress on time.

Although we have implement and test all the functions in this paper, we still need to consider the relation between the valid period time of temperature data and users' request frequency. A further research will focus on how to pre-fetch the information of physical machines and design a temperature-aware scheduling algorithm.

Acknowledgments. This research was supported in part by the National Natural Science Foundation of China under grant No. 61202041 and No. 61173039. Thanks for the great help.

References

1. Michael, A., Armando, F., Rean, G.: A view of cloud computing. Commun. ACM **53**(4), 50–58 (2010)
2. Srinivas D., Parveen S., Hongzhang L.: Real-time air quality monitoring through mobile sensing in metropolitan areas. In: UrbComp 2013, pp. 1–8. ACM, New York (2013)
3. Dhiman, G., Marchetti, G., Rosing, T.: vGreen: a system for energy-efficient management of virtual machines. ACM Trans. Des. Autom. Electron. Syst. **16**(1), 6–32 (2010)
4. Pakbaznia, E., Ghasemazar, M., Pedram, M.: Temperature-aware dynamic resource provisioning in a power-optimized datacenter. Design. In: Automation & Test in Europe Conference Exhibition, pp. 124–129. IEEE press, New York (2010)
5. Bjorn Z., Andreas K.: Applying heat maps in a web-based collaborative graph visualization, In: IEEE Information Visualization, pp. 1–2. IEEE Press, New York (2014)
6. Celery: Distributed Task Queue. http://www.celeryproject.org/
7. blockdiag - simple diagram images generator. http://blockdiag.com/en/index.html

RSA Encryption/Decryption Implementation Based on Zedboard

Xu Bai, Lei Jiang$^{(\boxtimes)}$, Xinxing Liu, and Jianlong Tan

Institute of Information Engineering Chinese Academy of Sciences,
Beijing, China
{baixu, jianglei, liuxinxing, tanjianlong}@iie.ac.cn

Abstract. This paper implements a 1024-bit RSA encryption/decryption system based on Zedboard, a product of Xilinx. It adopts some improved algorithms included limiting the intermediate product of multiplication and Chinese Remained Theorem(CRT) to improve the computing efficiency. It mainly optimizes the structure of system to satisfy the limited resource of Zedboard through the hardware-software codesign which makes the resource used effectively.

Keywords: RSA · Zedboard · CRT

1 Introduction

With more and more attention being paid to the information security technology, the RSA algorithm is becoming a hot topic in computer security field because of its security, high quality and public key. However, the range of the application is restricted by its computationally intensive structure and the difficulty in operating on very large integers.

The advantage of implementation of RSA [14] based on software is low cost, lightly simple. But it is not easy to meet the requirement of CPU's processing ability to achieve the satisfying encryption and decryption speed we want. By comparison, the implementation based on hardware provides higher speed to get the result and is more flexible to applying to much area. But this kind of platform also has some limitations such as high cost and difficulty in achieving. So we try to implement it on FPGA which own the both advantages [3–5].

This paper takes use of some improved algorithm to implement a 1024-bit RSA encryption/decryption system based on Zedboard with less resource and different structures because of the different complexity between encryption and decryption. The performance is satisfied through experiments.

2 Introduction of RSA Algorithm

The RSA algorithm is the most safe public-key cryptosystems nowadays. It is published by Ron Rivest, Adi Shamir, and Leonard Adleman. The security of RSA depends on a large number of decomposition: it is easy to multiply two large numbers

© Springer-Verlag Berlin Heidelberg 2015
Y. Lu et al. (Eds.): ISCTCS 2014, CCIS 520, pp. 114–121, 2015.
DOI: 10.1007/978-3-662-47401-3_15

but hard to compute the factorization of the product. The RSA algorithm includes three steps: key generation, encryption and decryption.

- Key Generation

  (a) Select two instinct prime integers p and q;
  (b) Calculate $n = p \times q$;
  (c) Calculate $\phi(n) = (p - 1) \times (q - 1)$;
  (d) Select an integer e such that $\gcd(\phi(n), e) = 1$, $1 < e < \varphi(n)$, so public key is $KU\{n, e\}$;
  (e) Select an integer d such that $d \times e \equiv 1 \pmod{\phi(n)}$, so private key is $KR\{n, d\}$;

- Encryption

  (a) Turn message M into an integer m such that $0 < m < n$ in some coding way;
  (b) Calculate $c = m^e \bmod n$, so the ciphertext is c.

- Decryption

  (c) Calculate $m = c^d \bmod n$;
  (d) Turn m into message M in same coding way.

From above description it is concluded that the present difficulty is how to implement modular exponentiation efficiently and accurately.

3 Implementation of RSA Algorithm

Modular exponentiation consists of modular multiplication. In the hardware area number processing is based on bit operation [16]. Suppose that A, B and N are all n-bit position integers and b_i is the i th bit of B. The hardware algorithm of modular multiplication is stated as follows:

```
Algorithm 1: Calculate C = A × B mod N, B = bn-1bn-2...b1b0;
Input        : A, B, N
Output       : C
Begin
1:    C = 0, T = A, i = 0
2:    While (i < n) do
3:       if (bi == 1) then
4:          C = C + T
5:       end if
6:       T = 2 × T
7:       i = i + 1
8:    end do
9:    while (C > N) do
10:      C = C - N
11:   end do
End
```

In algorithm 1, multiplication and modular arithmetic are separated. Line 4 is implemented by add operation. Line 6 is implemented by shift operation. Line 10 is implemented by subtraction operation. In practical applications add and subtraction operations both use 2n-bit adder so that they have the same complexity. Hence, algorithm 1 requires the 2n-bit adder to be used average 2n times in every modular multiplication and modular exponentiation needs much more. To increase the speed of encryption/decryption and optimize performance of RSA, algorithm could be improved in the following ways [1, 9, 10].

3.1 Modular Multiplication

In algorithm 1, the length of intermediate product C increasing from n-bit to 2n-bit leads to the arithmetic being more and more complex. Literature [1] proposes a new algorithm limiting the length to no more than 2^n to simplify the modular multiplication.

The new algorithm's main idea is to check if intermediate product C has carry digit – Carry(C). That is, to check if C is more than 2^n decides the operation to C. From literature [1] the Algorithm 1 is improved as follow:

Algorithm 2: Calculate $C = A \times B \mod N$, $B = b_{n-1}b_{n-2}...b_1b_0$;
Input   : A, B, N
Output   : C
Begin
```
1:     S = 2ⁿ mod N, C = 0, T = A, i = 0
```
1:     $S = 2^n \mod N$, $C = 0$, $T = A$, $i = 0$
2:     **While** ($i < n$) **do**
3:        **if** ($b_i == 1$) **then**
4:           $C = C + T$
5:           **While** Carry(C) **do**
6:              $C = C + S$
7:           **end do**
8:        **end if**
9:        $T = 2 \times T$
10:       **While** Carry(T) **do**
11:          $T = T + S$
12:       **end do**
13:       $i = i + 1$
14:    **end do**
15:    **if** $C > N$ **then**
16:       $C = C - N$
17:    **end if**
End

In Algorithm 2, line 4, 6, 11 are the primary factors that affect the performance of arithmetic. These steps just need n-bit adder and to compute modular multiplication once requires 0.5n times of $(1 + \frac{2}{3})n + \frac{2}{3}n = n$-bit add operation averagely based on the assumption that the probability of $b_i = 1$ is 50 % [1, 2]. So this algorithm increases the speed extremely.

3.2 Modular Exponentiation

Exponentiation is just a number multiplied by itself for many times. But the exponent e of encryption and d of decryption are both large integer, especially the length of d may be a thousand bits. It's impossible to calculate modular exponentiation one by one. So taking advantage of the characteristics of the same multiplier in exponentiation and the limited length of the product of modular multiplication, a high efficient algorithm is used in my system [15]. Suppose that A, B and N are all n-bit position integers and b_i is the i th bit of B. It is showed as following:

```
Algorithm 3: Calculate C = A^B mod N, B = b_{n-1}b_{n-2}...b_1b_0;
Input      : A, B, N
Output     : C
Begin
1:     C = 1, i = 0
2:     While (i < n) do
3:         if (b_i == 1) then
4:             C = A × C mod N
5:         end if
6:         A = A × A mod N
7:     end do
End
```

In Algorithm 3, line 4 and 6 are unrelated in order. So these two modular multiplications can be calculated in parallel to save the processing time and improve the performance. But this method will take more resource of FPGA. Restricted by the limited resource, the two steps are computed in serial in my system in finally.

3.3 Chinese Remainder Theorem (CRT)

In practice, public key exponent e is always a short bit-length integer in more efficient encryption – commonly $0 \times 10001 = 65537$ and so on. But private key exponent d is a long bit-length integer – commonly more than a thousand bits. Thus, it is necessary to optimize the algorithm of decryption. I choose Chinese Remainder Theorem (CRT) to improve the performance of decryption [6, 7].

CRT is a famous theory recorded in Chinese ancient book by Sunzi. It reduces the length of exponent of modular exponentiation. Suppose that m, d and n are all n-bit position integers and p, q are both 0.5n-bit position integers such that $n = p \times q$. The decryption algorithm is shown as following [11–13]:

Algorithm 4: Calculate c = m^d mod n;
Input   : m, d, n
Output   : c
Begin
1:     d1 = d % (p-1)
2:     d2 = d % (q-1)
3:     m1 ≡ m^{d1} mod p
4:     m2 ≡ m^{d2} mod q
5:     c1 ≡ q^{-1} mod p
6:     c2 ≡ p^{-1} mod q
7:     c ≡ (m1 × c1 × q + m2 × c2 × p) mod n
End

In the above algorithm the exponent in calculation is not n-bit-length but 0.5n-bit-length so that the times of modular multiplication to be used is reduced. The degree of parallelism is increased extremely. But because of the limited resource of Zedboard I do this operation in serial.

4 System Architecture and Performance Analysis

Zedboard is a product of Xilinx that belongs to Zynq–7000 AP SoC. Its basic structure is ARM + FPGA. The FPGA is XC7Z020 which has 53200 LUTs, 106400 registers. In Fig. 1 (from the software, Xilinx Platform Studio), Processing System (PS) is ARM and Programmable Logic (PL) is FPGA [8]. Being different from other FPGA product, Zynq-7000 series are famous for its containing a complete ARM processing system, namely dual-core Cortex^{TM} - A9 processor. FPGA is used as an extended subsystem to enhance the processing power. More than 100 Gb/s speed of intercom ensure the efficiency team working of ARM and FPGA [17]. This paper uses the PL principally and the PS works as a controller to manipulate the FPGA.

Compared with the computer, FPGA is more parallel. This hardware device is fit to implement large-scale computing in high frequency. In decryption the module of generating d1, d2, c1, c2 is used only once a time, so this work is done by a program of a PC as Host to optimize the performance of RSA in comprehensive consideration. FPGA is responsible for doing high-density 1024-bit modular exponentiation. This design makes every module to be used in a very high utilization rate.

In Zedboard the communication between ARM and FPGA uses an IP core of xillybus. The Host PC transmits parameters of n, p, q, e, d, c1, c2, d1, d2 to ARM on Zedboard through the network card. After that ARM control FPGA to complete encryption and decryption with the algorithms described above included limiting the intermediate product of multiplication and CRT. It is shown in Fig. 2.

The resource of XC7Z020 is limited, so this system uses some multiplex modules such as adder and modular multiplier, which reduces the degree of parallelism. This paper try my best to make sure every module works for all time so that none is free at any time. The utilization rate of FPGA LUTs is 48 % for encryption and 77 % for decryption. The results of experiments are shown in Table 1. In the experiments e is 65537 and d is any n-bit private key exponent with 50 MHz clock frequency on Zedboard.

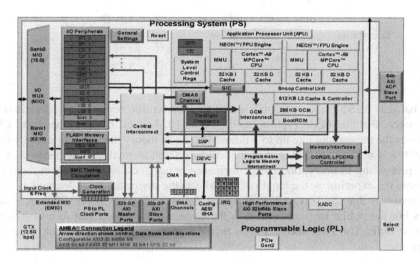

Fig. 1. Architecture of Zedboard

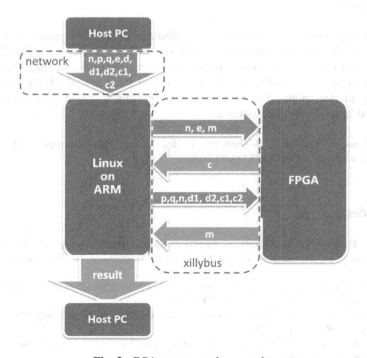

Fig. 2. RSA system work processing

Table 1. Experimental results

	n-bit	Numbers of clock cycles	Throughput (Kb/s)
Encryption	256	0.8×10^5	152.07
	512	1.8×10^5	138.62
	1024	4.3×10^5	115.47
Decryption	256	0.11×10^7	11.43
	512	0.34×10^7	7.21
	1024	1.5×10^7	3.22

That e is $65537 = 0 \times 10001$ means that encryption needs to do operations 16 times once. But that of decryption maybe needs 1024 times. On the other hand CRT improves the throughput rate up to 4 times [18]. So in theory the speed of encryption is $1024/16 \times 4 = 16$ times higher than that of decryption in total. In fact because of the serial processing in decryption the performance is not good as the result in theory.

From the experiment, the length of key affects the performance of decryption more. The season is that the private key exponent d is changed much for different experiments but the public key exponent e is the same. So the throughput of encryption is changed little. The data above shows that the performance of this RSA system is acceptable.

5   Conclusion

This paper implements 1024-bit RSA encryption and decryption system on Zedboard and optimizes the algorithm directed against the limited resource of XC7Z020. This algorithm improves the performance of modular exponentiation and reduces the times of add operation and modular multiply operation. It takes use of CRT to reduce the complexity of decryption. The next step is to pipeline this system to simplify the module and improve the performance.

Acknowledgment. This study is supported by the Special Pilot Research of the Chinese Academy of Sciences (Grant No. XDA06030200).

References

1. Su, F., Hwang, T.: Comments on iterative modular multiplication without magnitude comparison. In: Proceedings of the 6th National Conference on Information Security, pp. 21–22 (1996)
2. Chen, C.Y., Liu, T.C.: A fast modular multiplication method based on the lempel–ziv binary tree. Comput. Commun. **22**(9), 871–874 (1999)
3. Kaur, G., Arora, V.: An efficient implementation of RSA algorithm using FPGA and big prime digit. IJCCER **1**(4), 100–103 (2013)
4. Sahu, S.K., Pradhan, M.: FPGA implementation of RSA encryption system. Int. J. Comput. Appl. **19**(9), 10–12 (2011)

5. Anand, A., Praveen, P.: Implementation of RSA algorithm on FPGA. Int. J. Eng. Res. Technol. **1**(5) (2012)
6. Ito, Y., Nakano, K., Bo, S.: The parallel FDFM processor core approach for CRT-based RSA decryption. Int. J. Netw. Comput. **2**(1), 79–96 (2012)
7. Christofi, M., Chetali, B., Goubin, L.: Formal verification of an implementation of CRT-RSA vigilants algorithm. In: PROOFS Workshop: Pre-proceedings, p. 28 (2013)
8. Attili, S., Jain, S., Mitra, S.: PS and PL ethernet performance and jumbo frame support with PL ethernet in the Zynq-7000 AP SoC (2013)
9. Rao, G.R.C., Lakshmi, P., Shankar, N.R.: A new modular multiplication method in public key cryptosystem. IJ Netw. Secur. **15**(1), 23–27 (2013)
10. Sutter, G.D., Deschamps, J., Imaña, J.L.: Modular multiplication and exponentiation architectures for fast RSA cryptosystem based on digit serial computation. IEEE Trans. Ind. Electron. **58**(7), 3101–3109 (2011)
11. Menezes, A.J., Van Oorschot, P.C., Vanstone, S.A.: Handbook of Applied Cryptography. CRC Press, Boca Raton (2010)
12. Quisquater, J.J., Couvreur, C.: Fast decipherment algorithm for RSA public-key cryptosystem. Electron. Lett. **18**(21), 905–907 (1982)
13. Kim, C., Ha, J.C., Kim, S.-H., Kim, S., Yen, S.-M., Moon, S.-J.: A secure and practical CRT-based RSA to resist side channel attacks. In: Laganá, A., Gavrilova, M.L., Kumar, V., Mun, Y., Tan, C., Gervasi, O. (eds.) ICCSA 2004. LNCS, vol. 3043, pp. 150–158. Springer, Heidelberg (2004)
14. Rivest, R.L., Shamir, A., Adleman, L.: A method for obtaining digital signatures and public-key cryptosystems. Commun. ACM **21**(2), 120–126 (1978)
15. Nedjah, N., Mourelle, L.M.: Three hardware architectures for the binary modular exponentiation: sequential, parallel, and systolic. IEEE Trans. Circuits Syst. I: Regul. Pap. **53**(3), 627–633 (2006)
16. Takagi, N., Yajima, S.: Modular multiplication hardware algorithms with a redundant representation and their application to RSA cryptosystem. IEEE Trans. Comput. **41**(7), 887–891 (1992)
17. Lu, J., Jiang, Z., Ma, M.: Embedded System Hardware and Software Co-design Practical Guide based on XilinxZynq. China Machine Press, Beijing (2013)
18. Wu, C.H., Hong, J.H., Wu, C.W.: RSA cryptosystem design based on the chinese remainder theorem. In: Proceedings of the 2001 Asia and South Pacific Design Automation Conference, pp. 391–395. ACM (2001)

Security Risk Assessment of Rich Communication Services Over LTE

Xin He[1] and Huiyun Jing[2(✉)]

[1] National Computer Network Emergency Response Technical
Team/Coordination Center of China, Beijing, China
hexin@cert.org.cn
[2] China Academy of Telecommunication Research of MIIT, Beijing, China
jinghuiyun@catr.cn

Abstract. To deal with the threat of over the top (OTT) applications, many operators launch their own rich communication services over LTE. China Mobile also declares the overall commercial of rich communication services in 2015. The rich communication services integrate abundant multimedia, media and social characteristics into the traditional telecom services. While these characteristics provide a superior user experience, they also attract the scammers to utilize these services as the new channel of spreading digital misinformation, launching mass events, phishing and so on. Besides these, the LTE/SAE network and user terminals also pose much security challenges to the RCS services. In this paper, we firstly and systematically assess the security risk of rich communication services based on their three-tier architecture, which aims at improving the security of rich communication services.

Keywords: Rich communication services · LTE network · Security risk

1 Introduction

Recently, a large number of OTT applications are quickly occupying vast market, such as WhatsApp, Skype, twitter, Apple's iMessage. These OTT applications provide services over the Internet and bypass the distribution of traditional telecom operators. The rapid growth of OTT applications are having a negative impact on Short Message Service (SMS), Multimedia Messaging Service (MMS) and voice revenues for operators. To respond to this growing threat, Rich communication services under the Joyn brand are launched by many telecom operators, Vodafone, Telefonica, Orange and so on. China Mobile also aims to pre-commercial launch this new generation of converged communication for commercial use in the fourth quarter of 2014 and achieve overall commercial in 2015.

Rich communication services are the commercial implementations of Rich Communication Suite (RCS) Initiative [1]. RCS Initiative adds rich multimedia communication services features to existing mobile services, for example Enriched Messaging, Enriched Call and Enriched Phonebook. Enriched Messaging seamlessly integrates multiple message types (i.e. SMS, MMS, Instant messaging) and multiple media and formats. Enriched Phonebook is enrichment to the native mobile address book, which

© Springer-Verlag Berlin Heidelberg 2015
Y. Lu et al. (Eds.): ISCTCS 2014, CCIS 520, pp. 122–128, 2015.
DOI: 10.1007/978-3-662-47401-3_16

fully integrates social networks and other personalized services directly linked to the subscriber's phone number. Enriched call fully support VoLTE.

With the rapid deployment of LTE based networks, its characteristic of abundant capacity and good adaptability to IP based services will lead to LTE based networks greatly changing the environment for a typical user of mobile services. Regarding this tendency, operators begin to offer RCS services over LTE based networks. LTE based networks are essentially an open environment where various wireless access network and services share the core network. This openness of LTE poses much security challenges to the RCS services [2]. In addition, the security threats in traditional telecom services SMS and MMS are still existing in RCS services [3], like crank call, phishing, fraud, spam. Guaranteeing high level of security is one of the most important requirements in the successful deployment of RCS services over LTE. This means the security risk of RCS services should be comprehensively analyzed.

In this paper, we systematically assess the security risk of RCS services based on their hierarchical architecture. Firstly, we present an overview of the architecture for RCS services over LTE in Sect. 2. And then the security risk assessment for RCS services is given in Sect. 3. Finally, this paper concludes with Sect. 4.

2 Three-Tier Architecture of RCS Services Over LTE

Figure 1 represents the tree-tier architecture of RCS services over LTE. The top tier is the service layer, where the Application Servers (AS) of Enriched call, Enriched Messaging and Enriched Phonebook are situated. These AS deliver services via the standardized protocol as SIP to the middle tier, Network Layer.

In the middle tier, IP Multimedia Subsystem (IMS) independent of access and separating service control from multimedia transmission, provides LTE network with the core function and infrastructure of delivering IP multimedia services. LTE network consists of the Evolved Packet Core (EPC) and the E-UTRAN. EPC, core network of LTE, is all-IP network. Based on this characteristic, EPC supports the mobility and interoperability between multiple heterogeneous access networks, including E-UTRA (LTE air interface), 3 GPP legacy systems (for example GERAN or UTRAN, air interface of GPRS and UMTS respectively), but also non-3 GPP systems (for example WiMAX).

The lowest tier is user terminal layer. For facilitating the RCS end-user services, the mobile terminal supporting RCS and LTE is indispensable. The RCS services may be explicitly embedded in devices as delivered, or obtained through downloading client application (App).

3 Security Risk of RCS Services Over LTE

According to the above mentioned three-tier architecture, the security risk of each layer is separately explored.

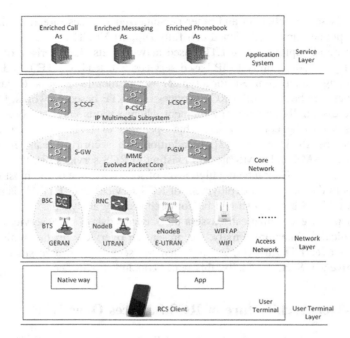

Fig. 1. Three-tier architecture of RCS services over LTE

3.1   Security Risk of Service Layer

(1) Security risk of traditional telecom functions in RCS services

RCS services are the upgrade to the traditional circuit-switch based voice and short messaging services. They retain all the capability of traditional telecom services "call, message and contacts". Thus there will be growing prevalence of the severe security risks of traditional telecom services.

The findings of the GSMA indicated that crank call, spam, phishing and fraud are pressing issues throughout the world, especially in Asia, where up to 50 % of all SMS traffic is spam [3]. Since RCS offers enhanced call and messaging services allowing users to call or send messages to both individuals, the convenience and return on investment (ROI) of the services could be exploited by scammers. Furthermore, the massive multimedia information with various formats and the social attribute will aggravate these risks and increase the difficulty of hedging them.

(2) Security risk of social media and network attributes in RCS Services

RCS services add internet media and online social features on the basis of traditional telecom functions. These characteristics lead to the information content security risk of social media and network still popular in RCS services.

Social media and network can rapidly spread both accurate and inaccurate information in wide rage. This feature may be easily exploited by subversives to make and spread digital misinformation, plan and organize network group incidents. These misleading information and unexpected mass incidents can rip through the public consciousness, devastate social stability and cause great challenges to the government administration.

Since RCS brings the official account into Enriched Phonebook and introduces ground chat in Enriched Messaging, these social media and network attributes in RCS are attractive to subversives spreading rumors or launching group events. And the multimedia properties of RCS services will further aggravate these security risks.

(3) Security risk of consumer privacy and user communication data

The RCS services record the personal information, contact list, call logs, message history, blacklist and other sensitive information of consumer. And for facilitating the synchronization of these information between multiple terminals, telecom operators may allow users to backup these information in the remote Cloud platform. Due to the high value of these information and the substantial vulnerability of Cloud platform, hackers or aggressors may have great interest in stealing these information from Cloud platform. Once these user personal information is stolen and sold on the black market, the security of consumer privacy is seriously damaged.

Besides the security risks of consumer privacy, the user communication data transmitted by RCS also faces great security risks of being leaked. To achieving the balance of security, efficiency and cost, the exiting mobile communication networks only encrypt user communication data in the wireless network. The user communication data is not protected by encryption in core network. This can be utilized by hackers or aggressors to eavesdrop, corrupt and delete user communication data through attacking core network. Since EPC, the core network of LTE, is open and all-IP network rather than the closed and circuit-switched network, it is easier for hackers to intrude EPC than the core networks of 2 G and 3 G. Thus the user communication data of RCS services are faced with serious security risks. If the end-to-end encryption is used to protect user communication data, which will increase the difficulty of detecting internet rumors, harmful information, internet mass events, crank call, spam and so on.

(4) Security risk of RCS application servers

Besides the above mentioned risks, the vulnerability of software system, operating system, hardware of the RCS Application Servers (AS) can also cause security risk for RCS services. These vulnerability can be utilized by hackers to compel RCS AS to knock off work or steal confidential information. And the RCS AS can be directly accessed through Internet, which makes the attacks to RCS AS easier. These attacks destroy the usability, reliability and confidentiality of RCS services.

3.2   Security Risk of Network Layer

Since network is the communication carrier of RCS services, the connectivity and efficiency of network directly affect the normal operation of RCS services. Here we emphatically explore the security risk caused by intruding the wireless network LTE and IP Multimedia Subsystem (IMS).

(1) Security risk of LTE
Similar to IMS, 3GPP also has devised security schemes for LTE to solve the potential security problem. For example, Evolved Packet System Authentication and Key Agreement (EPS AKA) is proposed to achieve the mutual authentication between User Equipment (UE) and Mobility Management Entity (MME). Though these schemes benefit increasing the security of LTE, there are still some security vulnerabilities in the current LTE/LTE-A networks, which need to be further analyzed. These vulnerabilities are existing intensively in LTE architecture and LTE access procedure.

For increasing the efficiency and compatibility, the LTE network employs the flat IP-based architecture. This leads to the vulnerability to the traditional attacks of Internet emerging in LTE, such as the vulnerability to IP address spoofing, Deny of Service (DoS) attack, viruses and so on. Moreover, the base stations also causes some other weaknesses. Because of the unsecure place where the base stations are laid and the all-IP nature of the LTE networks, the base stations can be easily controlled by hacker and be utilized to attack the core network.

In LTE access procedure, the EPS AKA is able to prevent some attacks, like Man-in-the-Middle (MitM) attacks, redirection attacks [4]. However, EPS AKA can not prevent DoS attacks [5]. Furthermore, EPS AKA lacks a privacy protection [6], which results in the disclosure of the International mobile Subscriber Identity (IMSI). IMSI is a unique identification used to identify the user of a cellular network. Once IMSI is stolen by the hacker, the user privacy can be easily obtained, such as user location information, conversation information. And based on the information, the hacker can disguise the real UE to launch the DoS attack to the core network.

(2) Security risk of IMS
Though the IMS Authentication and Key Agreement (AKA) has been employed by 3 GPP committee to ensure the IMS security, there are still vulnerability existing in IMS security mechanism. Some vulnerabilities derive from IMS AKA. Since IMS AKA is based on EAP AKA scheme, IMS AKA has the similar shortcomings with EAP AKA, such as the vulnerability to the MitM attacks, lack of SQN synchronization, and extra bandwidth consumption [4]. In addition, the IMS security mechanism is found to be vulnerable to DoS attacks is vulnerable to several types of DoS attack [7].

3.3   Security Risk of User Terminal Layer

RCS services can be obtained by purchasing the mobile devices natively supporting RCS or downloading RCS client from APP store.

(1) Security risk of using the smartphone natively supporting RCS
While smartphones become essential to the daily social fabric of our lives, they begin to be the hot target for attackers to steal the sensitive information of user, push advertisement, deducting fee and so on [8]. This causes the number of vulnerabilities in smartphone operating systems to evidently rise. As soon as a new version of a smartphone operating system (OS) is launched, attackers urgently look for new vulnerabilities.

In case of using devices natively supporting RCS, hackers exploit the discovered or new vulnerabilities of various smartphone OS (Android, IOS or Windows Phone) to attack user devices. Once the devices have been maliciously compromised, RCS communication data and log and other personal data is exposed, leaving the owner violated and picking up the pieces.

(2) Security risk of using RCS client
Recently, the software reverse engineering technologies and tools have rapid development. Attackers may exploit these technologies and tools to launch diverse types of hacks and tampering attacks to mobile apps [9], such as disabled or circumvented security, unlocked or modified features, free pirated copies, ad-removed versions, source code/IP theft, and illegal malware-infested versions.

In case of using RCS client, attackers can decompile the original RCS application, changes the code in order to incorporate the malicious code, repackages the applications and republishes them in the app market. Users usually cannot differentiate between the tampered applications and the original mobile applications including the RCS client. Thus attackers entice users to download and install the malicious repackaged RCS APP on the device. Then the tampered RCS APP help attacker steal users' private information and potentially wreak havoc on your life and finances.

4 Conclusion

For systematically assessing the security risk of RCS services, we propose the three-tier architecture including service layer, network layer and user terminal layer. And then we analyze the security risk of each layer. In the service layer, information content security risk caused by maliciously using the functions of RCS services, data security risk of user information and operation security risk of RCS application server are respectively analyzed. In the network layer, we describe the operation security risk caused by utilizing the vulnerabilities of the wireless network LTE and IMS. In user terminal layer, we point out that the security risk of RCS services in user terminal layer are mainly caused by the vulnerability of the intelligent mobile operating system and the maliciously repackaging RCS client.

Acknowledgement. This work was supported by the National Key Technology Research and Development Program of the Ministry of Science and Technology of China [2012BAH46B02].

References

1. Henry, K., Liu, Q., Pasquereau, S.: Rich communication suite. In: International Conference on Intelligence in Next Generation Networks (2009)
2. Park, Y., Park, T.: A survey of security threats on 4G networks. In: IEEE GlOBECOM Workshops (2007)
3. Cook, N.: Rich communications suite: opportunities and threats. Comput. Fraud Secur. **4**, 9–11 (2012)

4. Cao, J., Ma, M., Li, H., et al.: A survey on security aspects for LTE and LTE-a networks. IEEE Commun. Surv. Tutor. **16**(1), 283–302 (2014)
5. Da, Y., Wushao, W.: Non-access-stratum request attack in E-UTRAN. In: Computing, Communications and Applications Conference (2012)
6. Forsberg, D., Huang, L., Tsuyoshi, K., Alanara, S.: Enhancing security and privacy in 3GPP E-UTRAN radio interface. In: Personal, Indoor and Mobile Radio Communications (2007)
7. Kambourakis, G., Kolias, C., Gritzalis, S., Park, J.: DoS attacks exploiting signaling in UMTS and IMS. Comput. Commun. **34**(3), 226–235 (2011)
8. Felt, A., Finifter, M., Chin, E., et al.: A survey of mobile malware in the wild. In: ACM Workshop on Security and Privacy in Smartphones and Mobile Devices (2011)
9. Barrera, D., Van, P.: Secure software installation on smartphones. IEEE Secur. Priv. **9**(3), 42–48 (2001)

CAS: Content Attribution System
for Network Forensics

Yan Chen[1,2,3], Yiguo Pu[1,2,3($\boxtimes$)], Xiaojun Chen[1,3], Jinqiao Shi[1,3],
and Xiaojie Yu[1,2,3]

[1] Institute of Information Engineering, CAS, Beijing, China
{chenyan, puyiguo, chenxiaojun}@iie.ac.cn
[2] University of Chinese Academy of Sciences, Beijing, China
[3] Chinese National Engineering Laboratory for Information Security
Technologies, Beijing, China

Abstract. With increasing attention has been taken into network forensics, tools that can help investigators find evidences that indicate whether sensitive information has been transferred on wire and when, how it happened via querying some excerpts become very important. Storing raw network traffic for upcoming queries is unrealistic because of huge volume of network traffic. Payload attribution system (PAS) storing payload in Bloom filters alleviates demand of storage but provide limited transport layer information for forensics. In this paper, a content attribution system (CAS) via enhanced winnowing multihashing Bloom filters (EWMB) is proposed to store the digest of huge volume of content and session indexes of application-level information related with content, and provides capabilities of content querying and attribution tracing. Experimental results show that CAS can achieve good data reduction and shorten query time vastly via adding time-index for Bloom filters with low false positive.

Keywords: Network forensics · Content attribution · Winnowing · Bloom filter

1 Introduction

Cybercrime today is alive and well on the Internet and growing both in scope and sophistication [1]. While there is much excellent work going on targeted at preventing cybercrime, unfortunately there is the parallel need to develop good tools to aid law enforcement in investigating network traffic [2]. We need this kind of tools to determine whether excerpts of possible transmission content have appeared on network, give their sources, destinations and application session info to judge perpetrators or victims of network security incidents.

The most directed method to develop this kind of tools is to capture and log all the raw network traffic. Even full packet traces can be collected with commodity hardware, it is extremely unrealistic to make process to analyze terabyte of such data. Then, the improved method is to storage the hashes of raw network traffic. However, the method can only answer query of the entire content of packages but not the excerpts of transmission content. Shanmugasundaram et al. proposed the Hierarchical Bloom Filter

© Springer-Verlag Berlin Heidelberg 2015
Y. Lu et al. (Eds.): ISCTCS 2014, CCIS 520, pp. 129–136, 2015.
DOI: 10.1007/978-3-662-47401-3_17

(HBF) which store hashes of payloads instead of actual network traffic [3]. Subsequently, more and more researchers began to engage in the study of PAS. With viruses, worms, and vulnerability exploits, payload attribution system can identify packets that propagate worm or sensitive data. However, payload attribution system may be not useful in further judging victims or perpetrators of network security incidents for network forensics because of working on network layer.

In this paper, we proposed a content attribution system (CAS), which can obtain information entity of communication and session information to provide capabilities of content querying and attribution tracing. Our mainly contributions in this paper are shown as following:

- A content attribution system is designed for excerpts query and attribution trace. CAS used two EWMBs, one EWMB stored hashes of content blocks for excerpts query, and another EWMB stored hashes of blocks concatenated with session indexes of blocks to trace the context of suspicious sessions.
- An enhanced winnowing multihashing Bloom filter (EWMB) is provided for content attribution system. EWMB combines consecutive small blocks and can achieve lower false positive rate than winnowing mutihashing Bloom filters (WMH) which is one of the best of known Bloom filter algorithms.
- A prototype system of CAS is implemented, which executes excerpts query more effectively by using time-index EWMBs. Experiments demonstrated that the system can improve query efficiency 30 times at cost of about 10 % more storage in contrast to the system without time-index Bloom filters.

The rest of this paper is organized as follows: the following section discusses related work in detail. Section 3 describes the design and implementation of a Content Attribution System. In Sect. 4, we present the experiments and results of the prototype system. Finally we conclude with a summary and future work in Sect. 5.

2   Related Work

The overall method of CAS is to divide the content into blocks and store them in a Bloom filter. In this section, we first give a short introduction of Bloom filters and describe the winnowing, which is technique for block partition. Then, we retrospect the work related to payload attribution system.

A Bloom filter is a simple space-efficient randomized data structure for representing a set in order to support membership queries firstly proposed by Burton Bloom in [4]. It allows false positives but the space savings often outweigh this drawback when the probability of an error is made sufficiently low [5]. The components of a Bloom filter include an m-bit bit vector and k independent random hash functions. An approximation of the false positive rate α is given in [6], as Eq. (1), after n distinct elements were inserted into the Bloom filter.

$$\left(1 - \left[1 - \frac{1}{m}\right]^{kn}\right)^k \approx \left(1 - e^{-\frac{kn}{m}}\right)^k \tag{1}$$

Winnowing is an efficient fingerprinting algorithm enabling accurate detection of full and partial copies between documents [7]. It works as follows: for a document to be detected, the algorithm divides it into several substrings of length k (k-gram, the length of self-set), then calculates the hash value for each sub-string, and finally selects some subsets of these hash values by certain selection strategies as the fingerprinting of the document. The selection strategies may be set as follows: Select all hash values equals 0 mod p or define of a window size of w to split the hash values.

Since Shanmugasundaram et al. presented the concept of payload attribution system and designed the Hierarchical Bloom Filter data structure, extensive research about PAS has been conducted over the past few years. A PAS based on an HBF is a key module for a distributed network forensics system called ForNet [3]. Throughout the development of the attribution system, this method used by the system, which monitors network traffic, creates hash-based digests of payload, and archives them periodically is a great leap forward. Subsequently, another group has offered a variant technique for the same problem. They proposed an alternative data structure, the Rolling Bloom Filter (RBF) [8] to use in the payload attribution system. Recently, there has been an important research effort to improve the PAS, which can generally be grouped into two broad categories: (1) improvement of the block dividing method. (2) implementation of more complex queries (e.g., wildcard queries) [9, 10].

However, these methods can only achieve the source and/or the destination of some instance of traffic because they work at the level of individual packets. For further judging the victims or the perpetrators of network security incidents, access to find evidences that indicate whether sensitive information has been transferred on wire and when, how it happened is not enough.

3   Content Attribution System via EWMB

This section will look into the inside of our content attribution system based on EWMB. Firstly the architecture will be shown and then an Enhanced Winnowing Multihashing Bloom Filter (EWMB) is described in detail.

Before we proceed, we want to make an explanation of terminology. Content Attribution System storage the hashes of reassembled network packets to attribute the session information including all meta-information for an excerpt of possible communication content.

3.1   Overview of CAS's Architecture

As shown as Fig. 1, CAS's architecture is composed of three process phases and two main storage area.

Data reassembling take raw data on wire as input to reassemble the raw net-work packets into application session, such as http session, skype session etc. many mature and open source tools (Wireshark[1] etc.) can be used to complete this work.

---

[1] Wireshark is a free and open-source packet analyzer. It is used for network troubleshooting, analysis, software and communications protocol development, and education.

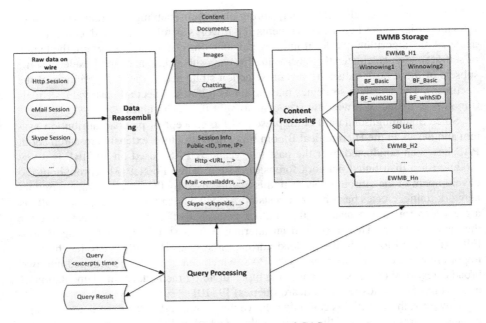

Fig. 1. Frame diagram of CAS

The first data storage is the application session information outputted by data reassembling. It is separated into two groups, the content and the session info. Content denotes the information entity of communication, such as the documents, images embedded in the emails. Session info includes all meta-information about the application session which carries the communication content. Http Session info may include the URL, cookies, content media type etc. All session info must include some public attributions such as session IDs that will be used for session tracing, and session time which would be used as time index for query efficiently.

The second data storage is the archive units for content and session info by EWMB. During content processing, CAS stores blocks of the content into a EWMB and saves session info into a SID list for each time interval. For each winnowing method of EWMB, different digests are inserted into different Bloom filters separately. Hashes of content blocks are inserted into BF_Basic and each of content blocks is inserted into BF_withSID concatenated with SessionID.

In query processing given an excerpt and search parameters (e.g., possible time interval, candidate SIDs), all the archive units within the time interval have to be retrieved. We query each archive unit with the blocked excerpt, if we get a positive answer, then we query the unit with the blocked excerpt concatenated each candidate SessionID and get all positive answers.

3.2   Enhanced Winnowing Multihashing Bloom Filters (EWMB)

An Enhanced Winnowing Multihashing Bloom Filter (EWMB) based on WMH is used for content attribution system mentioned in Sect. 3.1.

A WMH method uses multiple instances of Winnowing Block Shingling (WBS) in order to reduce the probability of false positives. A WBS method is based on the idea of winnowing described in Sect. 2 to choose boundaries of blocks and use shingling to determine whether two blocks appeared consecutively in the same file.

Two kinds of window sizes slide the whole document to choose boundaries. Blocks are composed of the bytes between consecutive pairs of boundaries and the prefix (the beginning of size o of the next block) of the next block called shingling. Finally the blocks are inserted into a Bloom filter. See Fig. 2(a).

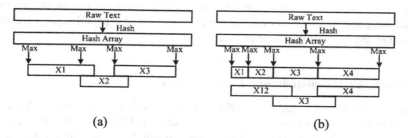

(a)   (b)

Fig. 2. Illustrations of WBS and EWMB

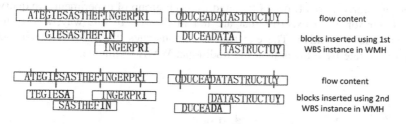

Fig. 3. An example of WMH

When querying for an excerpt, the only difference is that we query the Bloom filter for blocks instead of inserting them. Assuming the WMH uses t instances of WBS, both document processing and excerpt querying are completed for all the instances. If all the blocks are found in each of the instances, final answer to the query is positive. Figure 3 shows an example of processing document and querying in a WMH method.

WMH guarantees that there is at least one block boundary in any winnowing window. Therefore, the size of the block has been controlled distributing between $[1, w+o+1]$ in a WMH. These small blocks not only waste the storage space of a Bloom filter, but also increase false positives of querying. Based on this, we propose an enhanced version of WMH which we call EWMB to address the problem of the small blocks. In EWMB, we form concatenate blocks which consist of blocks selected by each WBS instance. Specifically, we use each instance WBS method to select block boundaries firstly, and concatenate small blocks, of which length is lower than the pre-set threshold, with the next block until the length meets the threshold. Finally, con-catenate blocks with a shingling of size o of the next block are inserted into a Bloom filter. See Fig. 2(b).

This modification does not increase the compute pressure compared with the WMH method, and has a significant effect on increasing space utilization and accuracy. In our experiments in Sect. 4, we implement the EWMB method and display the improved effect of our enhanced method.

4   Experiments and Results

In this section we discuss some experiments and show performance of the prototype CAS we have implemented to evaluate the effectiveness. All experiments were tested by selecting the best combination of parameters.

4.1   Block Size Distribution and False Positives

The distributions of block sizes with a slide window size (w) of 64 bytes in a WMH are exhibited in Fig. 4. The output block size takes values in $[1, w]$. In EWMB, we set the slide window size (w) as 64 byte, and the minimum length (m) as 32 bytes. We can see that the window size is gracefully controlled in $[m, w + m - 1]$.

Figure 5 provides the comparison of our method and WMH mechanism. 10000 excerpts are stored into a Bloom filter, and for each group of experiment, we query the Bloom Filter for 1000 excerpts that are not in the set. In this way, a yes answer represents a false positive. The experiment demonstrates that EWMB obtains lower false positive rate by 6 times than the traditional WMH technique.

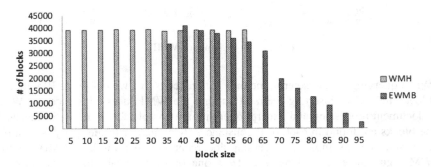

Fig. 4. The distributions of block sizes for two different methods of blocking mechanism after processing the same data set. The abscissa stands for interval values of block size, for example, 10 means that the length of a block takes values in [6, 10].

4.2 Different Time Interval

In this experiment, we use traditional search engine, CAS of 1 h-interval time index and CAS without time index to compare the performance of the system. Table 1 shows that CAS outperforms the traditional search engine greatly and the short time interval of CAS achieves good data reduction and shortens query time vastly with low false positive by adding time-index for Bloom filters. The experiment demonstrates that the system can improve query efficiency 30 times at cost of about 10 % more storage in contrast to the system without time-index Bloom filters.

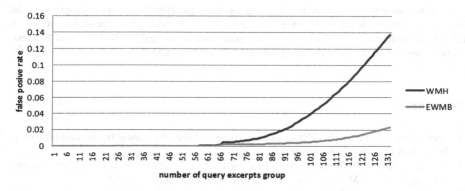

Fig. 5. False positive rate comparison of WMH and EWMB

Table 1. Performance for different time interval of CAS. 33830 documents from one day's network traffic have been collected, and they need 4258.71 MB storage space. In order to store these documents into one Bloom filter without time index, based on the Eq. (1) selecting the best combination of parameters to gain lowest false positive, the Bloom filter needs 234.38 MB storage space. Let random variable X denote the amount of documents in an hour, which we assume is drawn from Poissonian distribution. Then, X will not be greater than 1551 in the possibility of 99 %, when $\lambda = 33830/24 = 1409$. Finally, the Bloom filter needs 257.86 MB storage space with additional demand for SID.

Method	Doc (Number)	Storage (MB)	Query time(s)	Accuracy
ORIGN_ElasticSearch	33,830	4258.71	2.0	100 %
CAS_NoTimeIndex	33,830	234.38	5.77	99 %
CAS_TimeIndex	1,551	257.86	0.16	100 %

5 Conclusion and Future Work

In this paper, we describe and design content attribution system (CAS). Unlike previous system, our system can be used to judge victims or perpetrators of network security incidents. For example, we may only possess a fragment of a secret file transferred over the network and we want to know when, where and how it happened. In order to complete a content attribution system, we propose a lowest rate of false-positive hash-based digesting data structure—EWMB. The best of our approach allow data reduction ratios more than 100:1 reducing the storage pressure and give no false-positive answer for querying excerpts of 256 byte effectively. When the length of the excerpt is increased and the information of the query is more, the answer of the attribution is more accurate. Furthermore, the system can be used by any untrusted party without disclosing any original privacy information. In the future, we can focus on encrypted transmission and various attacks to make the system more robust.

Acknowledgements. This work is supported by Strategic Priority Research Program of the Chinese Academy of Sciences (Grant No. XDA06030200), National High Technology Research and Development Program of China, 863 Program (Grant No. 2012AA013101) and National Science Fund for Distinguished Young Scholars (Grant No. 61303260).

References

1. Richardson, R., Peters, S.: CSI Computer crime and security survey shows average cyber-losses jumping after five-year decline (2007)
2. Ponec, M., Giura, P., Wein, J., et al.: New payload attribution methods for network forensic investigations. ACM Trans. Inf. Syst. Secur. (TISSEC) **13**(2), 15 (2010)
3. Shanmugasundaram, K., Brönnimann, H., Memon, N.: Payload attribution via hierarchical bloom filters. In: Proceedings of the 11th ACM Conference on Computer and Communications Security, pp. 31–41. ACM (2004)
4. Bloom, B.H.: Space/time trade-offs in hash coding with allowable errors. Commun. ACM **13**(7), 422–426 (1970)
5. Broder, A., Mitzenmacher, M.: Network applications of Bloom filters: a survey. Internet Math. **1**(4), 485–509 (2004)
6. Mitzenmacher, M.: Compressed bloom filters. IEEE/ACM Trans. Networking (TON) **10**(5), 604–612 (2002)
7. Schleimer, S., Wilkerson, D.S., Aiken, A.: Winnowing: local algorithms for document fingerprinting. In: Proceedings of the 2003 ACM SIGMOD International Conference on Management of Data, pp. 76–85. ACM (2003)
8. Cho, C.Y., Lee, S.Y., Tan, C.P., et al.: Network forensics on packet fingerprints. In: Fischer-Hübner, S., Rannenberg, K., Yngström, L., Lindskog, S. (eds.) Security and Privacy in Dynamic Environments. IFIP, vol. 201, pp. 401–412. Springer, Boston (2006)
9. Wei, Y., Fei, X., Chen, X., Shi, J., Qing, S.: Winnowing Multihashing Structure with Wildcard Query. In: Han, W., Huang, Z., Hu, C., Zhang, H., Guo, L. (eds.) APWeb 2014 Workshops. LNCS, vol. 8710, pp. 265–281. Springer, Heidelberg (2014)
10. Haghighat, M.H., Tavakoli, M., Kharrazi, M.: Payload attribution via character dependent multi-bloom filters. IEEE Trans. Inf. Forensics Secur. **8**(5), 705–716 (2013)

Tracking and Analysis of Hot Words and Posts for University Campus

Xuefeng Du and Xiaodong Yan[✉]

China National Language Resource Monitoring & Research Center Minority
Languages Branch, MINZU University of China, Zhongguancun Street 27#,
Haidian District, Beijing 100081, China
yanxd3244@sina.com

Abstract. In this paper we mainly analysis the posts on MINZU University campus forum, including displaying and tracking the hot words, hot posts and other data, and the statistics of the keywords. We also analyzed the users on the forum, tracking his motion and finding the relations between the users and readers. By this, we can find the public opinion in students timely and find some imminent events. It is helpful for teachers and administrators of university.

Keywords: Hot words · Imminent events · Public opinion

1 Introduction

According to the survey of the 34th China Internet Network Information Center (CNNIC), As of June 2014, The number of Internet users in China has reached 632 million, increased by nearly 2699 people, and 1.1 percentage points, compared to the end of 2013. Meanwhile, according to the survey, the first half of 2014 Chinese Internet users online time per week has increased 0.9 h more than the end of 2013, has reached 25.6 h. With the dramatic increase of the number of Internet users, the network information resources are also having a very rapid growth rate. Early on, users can simply browse news, send and receive messages through the network, but with the popularity and development of the network of knowledge and technology, blog, forum, website development has become even more active recently, therefore, comments, opinions and other information in such site has increasingly become a part of life of Internet users.

However, the quality of information in such site varies greatly: there are many illegal, false statements, which is easy to mislead people. So with the dramatic increase of the amount of information, how to manage information on these websites, extract and analyze the information on the website has becoming a more and more urgent needs. Although the network facilitated people's lives, effective network management and supervision are needed.

In addition to the existence of some of the community forum website, major colleges and universities have also created their own forum website in recent years, such as "cun" of the MINZU University. The information gathering and analysis in this paper is mainly based on the "cun" of MINZU University forum.

© Springer-Verlag Berlin Heidelberg 2015
Y. Lu et al. (Eds.): ISCTCS 2014, CCIS 520, pp. 137–143, 2015.
DOI: 10.1007/978-3-662-47401-3_18

2 System Requirements Analysis

System Requirements System is supposed to be completed in the beginning; it determines what the system should show. "Needs analysis" in software engineering determines the computer "what to do" [1].

2.1 System Overview

This system is to be implemented a system that can detect sensitive word, and track the author of every post. At first the web crawlers crawling on the "cun" forum, then analysis and count the information appeared in the posts, we can easily know the hot topics and sensitive events. The system includes hot words discovery module, hot posts found module, the characters find module (Fig. 1).

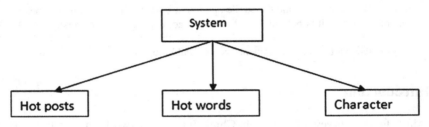

Fig. 1. System requirements overview figure

2.2 Hot Posts

Hot posts module includes hot posts found, policy documents, sensitive events, warning information and emergency events. Its function is to display the corresponding post information and links to the original URL.

2.3 Hot Words

Hot words modules include hot words found, named entities, sensitive word. And its function is to dynamically display hot words that appear in the site.

2.4 Characters

Characters module includes post author and important figure, the main function is to show an author posting history and detect those posts that have important people's name.

3 System Design

The mission of system design is design the structure of software system and define programming environment. Its purpose is clear software system "how to do" [1].

3.1 System Technical Architecture Design

The system uses B / S structure, namely Browser / Server architecture [2]. Uses Struts framework and JDBC technology development. The database is MySQL database [3].

   B / S architecture is an architecture that combined by Internet technology and database technology. On the one hand, it has a strong system independence and platform independence, as long as the client can directly access the browser, regardless of operating system, and do not need to install, etc., in addition its development efficiency is very high.

   MVC is short by Model View Controller; it's a software design model. MVC can manage the code by separate the business logic, data and display. And MVC gathered all of the business into a component so that the users do not need to re-write the code when they improving and customization interface and user interaction at the same time. MVC is developed to map the unique conventional input, processing and output of the functional structure of graphical user interface logic [4, 5]. Model is a section that used for processing the application logic and data. Model is usually responsible for storing data in the database. View is part of the application that processes the data displaying. Typically the view is created based on the model data. Controller is part of the application that processes user interaction. Typically the controller is responsible for reading data, control user input, and transmit data to the models.

   Struts framework is an open source framework for the Apache Software Foundation, which implements the view layer, business layer and control layer. It is a classic model of MVC framework [6, 7].

   In Struts, once the Web application starts, the controller ActionServlet class will be automatically loaded and initialized, after receiving an HTTP request, the controller first reads the configuration information related to the Struts configuration file struts-config.xml, then distributed the HTTP request to the corresponding Action object, and at the same time, fill the requested page corresponding to the ActionFormBean, thus completing the processing requested by the user [8, 9].

3.2 System Function Architecture Design

Based on the contents of the system needs analysis, the main system is divided into three major business needs modules, namely: hot posts found module, hot words and characters found module.

3.2.1 Hot Posts

Hot Posts found module includes hot posts found, policy documents, sensitive events, such as warning information and emergencies sub-module (Fig. 2).

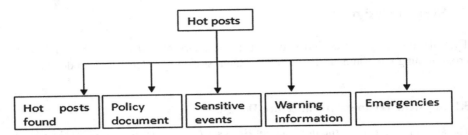

Fig. 2. Hot posts discovery module function

(1) Hot posts found module's main function is to find the most read forum posts, it should display hot posts within one day, three days, one week or one month;

(2) The main function of the policy document is find policy document released by the Forum in the campus network; it can display one day, three days, one week, and one month policy documents related posts;

(3) The main function of sensitive events is to find those posts is related to sensitive events, such as exam-related, rallies, meetings, etc.

(4) The main function of warning information is found those posts with some criticism related or sensitive events may happen;

(5) The main function of emergency is finding some more serious nature of the post, such as fights, fraud or other news.

3.2.2   Hot Words

Hot words modules include hot words found, named entities, sensitive words three sub-modules (Fig. 3).

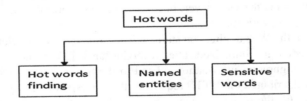

Fig. 3. Hot words modules

The main function of Hot words finding modules is to show the hot words that appeared in recent days, and show how many times it appeared in recent days whit a curve;

Named entities module includes names, places, organization name.

Sensitive words module main function is warning function, its category is divided into 1, 2, 3, 4-class, such as life, politics, pornography and other vocabulary.

3.2.3   Character Module

Character module includes post author, search and important figure two sub-modules, so that achieve such figures tracking (Fig. 4).

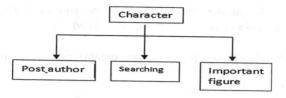

Fig. 4. Character module

The main function of the post author is that you can find its posting record; The main function of Search is that it can search the authors in this forum then show every posts he or she posted in forum. And by the way the topology diagram shows the response of people who associated with the post; The main function of important figure is getting the posts that their names have appeared.

System implementation:

Previous sections of this article have introduced the requirements analysis and system design, this section will discuss the specific implementation of the system.

Server hardware environment:

RAM: 1 G;

Hard driver: 250 G.

Server software environment:

Operating System: Windows Server 2003;

Database: MySQL;

JDK version JDK1.7;

Client Operating Environment:

Any operating system platform, only a browser and network support is needed.

4   System Function Implement

4.1   Hot Posts Module Implement

Hot posts module is divided into five sub-modules, such as hot posts, policy documents, sensitive events, warning information and emergencies. Hot posts module shows the posts that ranked by read times; Policy documents module shows the posts on policy of campus; Sensitive event shows those sensitive posts according to the browse quantity. The sensitive posts here are those posts including sensitive words (we defined according to our rule) in them; Warning information shows the posts which are serious enough for our attention; Emergency events shows those posts which are in focus in short time.

4.2   Hot Words Module Implement

1. Hot words finding

Hot words module shows those words that have a high frequency of occurrence in the forum.

When a word is clicked, the page will jump to the word detail page, showing the number of occurrences of nearly 90 days, and related post.

2. Named entity
   Named entity mainly displays people names, organization names that appear in the forums

3. Sensitive words
   Sensitive words mainly shows sensitive word in the forums may appear so that can get a warning.

4.3   Character Module Implement

1. Posts author
   This module shows all of authors in the forum, and ranked by the amount of posts they published. When an author was clicked, the page will jump to a page shows all of the posts she or he published. We can also search the authors, and then get those who replied him by a topology, and all of posts he published.

2. Important figure
   This module displays the important names such as school leaders. When a name was clicked, the page will jump to a page that shows all of the posts that have this name.

5   Conclusion

In this paper a campus network public opinion analysis system is developed for the "village outside village" of MUC (MINZU University) forum. In it we mainly analysis the posts on MINZU University campus forum, including displaying and tracking the hot words, hot posts and other data, and the statistics of the keywords, important figure tracking, sensitive events finding and emergencies discovery and so on.

We use struts + MVC development model for system development, and we also use simple and lightweight MySQL database for development. The system is based on B / S architecture. So it's simple to use, its content of information at a glance, and can be viewed on any platform. However, due to the development time is short, and the technical level, so the interface can have a greater improvement and function can also be more and more perfect. For the system will be revised and improved in subsequent development.

Acknowledgement. The work in this paper is supported by the National Natural Science Foundation of China project "Research on Basic Theory and Key Technology of Cross Language Social Public Opinion Analysis" (61331013).

References

1. Pressman, R.S., et.al,: Software engineering: research methods of practitioner. Machinery Industry Press (2007)

2. Tian, K., Xie, S., Fang, M.: Solutions of J2EE data persistence layer. Comput. Eng. **29**(22), 93–95 (2004)
3. Xia, L.: Principle and implementation of MVC design patterns and [D]. Jilin University (2004)
4. Wang, L., Cai, Z.: Web application developing by JSP. Comput. Appl. **21**(10), 88–89 (2001)
5. ban Ke, H.: Comparative study on two kinds of generic java web development framework. Comput. Knowl. Technol. Acad. Exch. **6**(7), 5249–5251 (2010)
6. Wang, G.: Technical analysis of struts framework. Changchun Teachers Coll. Nat. Sci. **31**(9), 25–28 (2012)
7. Zhang, S.-H., Ma, Y.: Struts framework based on MVC design pattern. Mod. Comput. (Prof. Ed.) **10**, 33–35 (2004)
8. Gui, Y., Yan, F.: Struts development portal and project practice. People Post Press (2005)

Software Vulnerability Severity Evaluation Based on Economic Losses

Yunxue Yang[⊠], Shuyuan Jin, and Xiaowei He

CAS Key Laboratory of Network Data Science and Technology,
Institute of Computing Technology, Chinese Academy of Sciences,
Beijing, China
{yangyunxue,hexiaowei}@software.ict.ac.cn,
jinshuyuan@ict.ac.cn

Abstract. Enterprises suffer economic losses due to vulnerability exploitation. The aim of this paper is to propose a comprehensive software vulnerability severity evaluation model incorporating technical assessment and circumstances information of enterprises, especially economic losses caused by vulnerability exploitation. We use analytic hierarchy process to establish the model and get weights of evaluation factors, obtaining both of qualitative severity ranking levels and quantitative severity scores of vulnerabilities. Through case study, we show that evaluation values are accurate and effective and consequently, our model can be used for security improvement prioritization.

Keywords: Software vulnerability · Vulnerability evaluation · Economic losses · Analytic hierarchy process · CVSS

1 Introduction

Cyber security incidents cause huge economic losses for enterprises. According to the survey results conducted by Kaspersky Lab and B2B International in 2013 [1], large companies lost $2.4 million on average due to a successful targeted attack and for a medium-size or small company, this meant about $92,000 in financial losses.

The frequent security incidents during recent years are mostly due to hacker attacks using security vulnerabilities. As an exemplary case, in March 2014, the domestic Internet security monitoring platform wooyun.org disclosed a security vulnerability in Ctrip.com International and through the vulnerability, users' personal and private information could be obtained, making it possible for hackers to use the users' credit cards, according to wooyun.org. On the other hand, security vulnerabilities are intrinsic to software systems. The National Vulnerability Database (NVD) [2] announced that 13 new vulnerabilities per day on average were reported in 2013 and the total number was 4,794.

In order to guarantee the effectiveness both of patches and mitigation actions, companies need to improve the vulnerability processes. The method for processing a vulnerability should correspond to the severity of the vulnerability. Vulnerability severity assessment prioritizes vulnerabilities according to their dangers and related attributes, and the representative is Common Vulnerability Scoring System (CVSS).

© Springer-Verlag Berlin Heidelberg 2015
Y. Lu et al. (Eds.): ISCTCS 2014, CCIS 520, pp. 144–151, 2015.
DOI: 10.1007/978-3-662-47401-3_19

CVSS is the standard method for ranking IT vulnerabilities and helps organizations prioritize security vulnerabilities by communicating the base, temporal and environmental attributes of a vulnerability [3]. However, the base metric group is used only and the temporal metric group and environmental metric group are not generally used in a real-world situation [4].

Due to ignoring circumstances information of the enterprise influenced by vulnerability exploits, CVSS scores do not match security requirements of enterprises exactly. Previous research has acknowledged the problem and advises that the CVSS should be used cautiously [5]. Moreover, technically critical vulnerabilities do not always make great economic impact on the organization. Therefore, in order to develop reasonable approaches for vulnerability severity assessment accordant with the practical situation, it is necessary to comprehensively consider the characteristics of the enterprises, especially the economic losses caused by a vulnerability exploit. Our work is to fill the gap and the contribution is two-fold. First, a set of economic loss metrics captures the economic impact of vulnerability exploits on the enterprises. Second, in order to rate vulnerabilities, we propose a model of vulnerability severity assessment aggregating the technical metrics and economic loss metrics.

The remainder of this paper is organized as follows: Sect. 2 discusses about the related work of the vulnerability assessment. Section 3 proposes the economic loss metrics. Section 4 is the vulnerability severity assessment model. Section 5 is about implementation of the model and contains case study. Section 6 provides conclusions for the work.

2 Related Work

2.1 Common Vulnerability Scoring System

CVSS quantitatively describes and compares the severity of a vulnerability on the basis of defined attributes. The base score is the most important metric group in CVSS and represents the risk level of a vulnerability and the difficulty of exploiting. The base score is composed of impact subscore and exploitability subscore. The value range of the base score is [0, 10]. The range [0, 3.9] represents that the severity of a vulnerability is low and [4.0, 6.9] and [7.0, 10] represent medium and high respectively.

CVSS provides two optional metric groups: temporal metric group explains the severity of a vulnerability that change over time and environmental metric group represents the characteristics of vulnerabilities with respect to the user's environment.

2.2 Existing Vulnerability Evaluation Methods

The researches that study vulnerabilities severity evaluation have increased recent years. In [6], the authors use a case-control study method of medicine for verifying whether the CVSS score does really match the severity of the vulnerability exploitation in a real-world context. In [7], the authors apply fuzzy analytic hierarchy process to software vulnerabilities assessment and ranking, and moreover, the authors consider the subjectivity of humans in reality and construct the fuzzy integral decision making model. Liu et al. propose the Vulnerability Rating and Scoring System (VRSS) based on the CVSS [8, 9]. VRSS combines advantages of the current scoring systems and prioritizes vulnerabilities. The closest to our work is [10], in which the authors propose to assess vulnerability severity from the point of view of the economic loss. But they do not provide detailed descriptions of how to reasonably calculate weights of metrics effecting the vulnerability severity assessment.

3   Economic Loss Metrics

The proposed economic loss metrics capture the effect of exploits on the economy and quantify damage caused by network attacks incidents. Before providing details about the proposed economic loss metrics, we introduce the economic loss levels first.

3.1   Economic Loss Levels

Quantitative score is objective relative to qualitative rating. However, the quantitative score cannot reflect the vulnerability severity intuitively. We propose to use a scale of 4 possible values to evaluate the economic loss: low, medium, high and critical. Exact values are related to the particular business. Enterprises should define the interval value C_x according to their own circumstances. The economic loss levels are shown as in **Table 1**.

Table 1.   Economic loss levels

Qualitative scale	Monetized scale (RMB)	Quantitative scale
Low	$[0, C_{medium}]$	3.5
Medium	$[C_{medium}, C_{high}]$	6.1
High	$[C_{high}, C_{critical}]$	7.1
Critical	$[C_{critical}, \infty]$	10

3.2   Economic Loss Metrics and Values

We define the economic loss metrics based on the work of [10] and [11].

Definition 1 Revenue loss. Computer systems make revenues for enterprises. Let c denotes the number of customers and r the average revenue per user with respect to a transaction. There are two main reasons will cause revenue losses: system services unavailable and customer churn caused by long service response time. Let A denotes the availability of system services and therefore, $A = 1$ denotes availability and $A = 0$ means unavailability. Consequently, the revenue loss caused by system services unavailable is:

$$RevL = c \times r \times (1 - A) \tag{1}$$

Definition 2 Data loss. Data leakage causes property damage for enterprises. The data loss caused by data leakage can be calculated by formulation (2), where *avr* denotes the average value of each data record and *nlr* the number of missing records.

$$DL = avr \times nlr \tag{2}$$

Definition 3 Reputation loss. It is hard to measure reputation losses of a business caused by vulnerability exploits. The method for measuring the reputation losses is the historical impact of vulnerability exploits and security incidents on stock price for companies [10]. Let *ise* be the average historical impact, and the formulation of the reputation loss is (3), where P_t is the stock average price during the period of time *t* prior to the attack incident and P_{after} the stock price after the attack incident. Moreover, if *ise* ≤ 0, then it is set to 0.

$$ise = \frac{\sum_{t=0}^{n} P_t}{n} - P_{after} \tag{3}$$

Definition 4 Customer loss. If the security incident happened in the enterprise is announced, customers who are sensitive to security will terminate business relationships with the enterprise. Therefore, this will cause customer losses and the formulation is (4), where *ssc* is the number of customers sensitive to the security and acr_t the average customer revenue during the period of time *t*.

$$CL = ssc \times arc_t \tag{4}$$

Definition 5 Investment loss. Investment losses are similar to customer losses. If the security incident happened in the enterprise is announced, investors who are sensitive to security will halt investments. The formulation of the investment loss is (5), where *ssi* the number of investors who are sensitive to security and ai_t the average investment during the period of time *t*.

$$IL = ssi \times ai_t \tag{5}$$

4 Vulnerability Severity Evaluation Model

In order to propose the vulnerability severity evaluation model based on economic losses caused by cyber security incidents, we define three aspects for the vulnerability severity assessment: economic loss metrics, user security requirements metrics and CVSS base metrics. There are not inconsistent criteria amongst these metrics but only "cost" criteria for which the values need to be minimized in an ideal situation. Therefore, this is a typical problem that can be addressed by using Multi-criteria decision-making analysis (MCDA). Analytic Hierarchy Process (AHP) is the most widely used and accurate MCDA method [10]. It was developed by Thomas L. Saaty [12] in the 1970 s. AHP is especially suitable for the problems cannot be addressed by using quantitative analysis only. To represent a decision problem, AHP decomposes the problem into several subproblems and uses a hierarchic structure to illustrate the problem. The important feature of AHP is the combination of qualitative and quantitative analysis and it expresses and handles subjective judgment through quantities.

Saaty proposed four basic steps to address the AHP problems, including hierarchy construction, paired comparisons, priority analysis and consistency verification. The procedure can be summarized as:

1. Construct a hierarchy at different levels of decision goal, criteria and alternatives.
2. Compare each element in the same level by using paired comparisons to obtain priorities of the objectives at each level of the hierarchy.
3. Synthesize local priorities into global priorities for the hierarchy.
4. Check the consistency by computing the consistency index and consistency ration.

On the basis of the procedure, the proposed vulnerability severity evaluation model is shown below (**Fig.** 1). In the next section, we will illustrate how to use the proposed model to calculate the severity score and rank the severity level for a vulnerability.

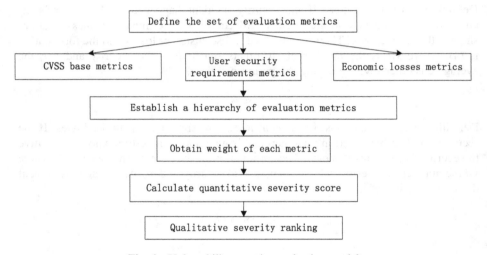

Fig. 1. Vulnerability severity evaluation model

5 Case Study

The vulnerability information source of the case study is the NVD. We choose the vulnerability CVE-2014-3376 as an evaluation target. This vulnerability allows remote attackers to cause a denial of service via a malformed RSVP packet and the CVSS score is 5.0 (medium). Considering a small and medium sized company whose availability requirement is high, we evaluate the severity of the vulnerability according to environmental characteristics of the company.

Step 1: Establish the hierarchical structure of vulnerability severity assessment as shown in **Fig.** 2.

Step 2: Construct judgment matrices. Using pairwise comparisons, the judgment matrix G of criteria level with respect to objective level is $G = \begin{bmatrix} 1 & 1/2 & 1 \\ 2 & 1 & 2 \\ 1 & 1/2 & 1 \end{bmatrix}$, and judgment matrices C_1, C_2 and C_3 of alternatives level with respect to criteria level are

$$C_1 = \begin{bmatrix} 1 & 5 & 5 \\ 1/5 & 1 & 1 \\ 1/5 & 1 & 1 \end{bmatrix}, \quad C_2 = \begin{bmatrix} 1 & 1 & 1/2 \\ 1 & 1 & 1/2 \\ 2 & 2 & 2 \end{bmatrix} \quad \text{and} \quad C_3 = \begin{bmatrix} 1 & 2 & 3 & 5 & 6 \\ 1/2 & 1 & 3 & 4 & 5 \\ 1/3 & 1/3 & 1 & 3 & 5 \\ 1/5 & 1/4 & 1/3 & 1 & 2 \\ 1/6 & 1/5 & 1/5 & 1/2 & 1 \end{bmatrix}$$

respectively.

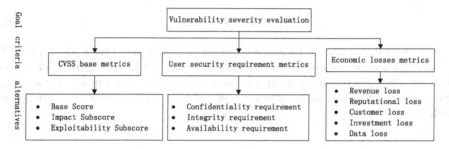

Fig. 2. Hierarchical structure of vulnerability severity assessment

Step 3: Hierarchical single arrangement and consistency check. Using Matlab, we obtain the largest eigenvalues and eigenvectors of matrices G, C_1, C_2 and C_3 as shown in **Table** 2. For example, the largest eigenvalue λ_{max} of the judgment matrix G is 3, the corresponding eigenvector $W = (0.25, 0.50, 0.25)^T$, the consistency index $C = \frac{\lambda_{max} - n}{n-1}$ and the random consistency ratio $C_R = 0 < 0.10$. Therefore, weights of CVSS metrics, user security requirements metrics and economic losses metrics with respect to vulnerability severity assessment are 0.25, 0.5 and 0.25 respectively.

Table 2. Hierarchical single arrangement and consistency check

Matrices	Eigenvalues	Eigenvectors	Consistency check
G	$\lambda_{max} = 3.00$	$W = (0.25, 0.50, 0.25)^T$	$C_R = 0.00 < 0.10$
C_1	$\lambda_{max} = 3.00$	$W = (0.71, 0.14, 0.14)^T$	$C_R = 0.00 < 0.10$
C_2	$\lambda_{max} = 3.00$	$W = (0.25, 0.50, 0.25)^T$	$C_R = 0.00 < 0.10$
C_3	$\lambda_{max} = 5.18$	$W = (0.42, 0.05, 0.07, 0.17, 0.30)^T$	$C_R = 0.04 < 0.10$

Step 4: Hierarchical total arrangement and combination consistency check. The result of hierarchical total arrangement is as shown in **Table** 3. The consistency check of hierarchical total arrangement is $C = 0$ and the random consistency ratio is

$C_R = 0 < 0.10$. Hence, the global weight of each metric with respect to vulnerability severity assessment is 0.18, 0.04, 0.03, 0.12, 0.12, 0.25, 0.10, 0.01, 0.02, 0.04 and 0.07 respectively.

Table 3. Hierarchical total arrangement and combination consistency check

Metrics	BS	IS	ES	CRq	IRq	ARq	RevL	RepL	CusL	InvL	DaL
Weights	0.18	0.04	0.03	0.12	0.12	0.25	0.10	0.01	0.02	0.04	0.07

Step 5: Vulnerability risk quantization value and ranking. Assuming the scoring sample matrix of the vulnerability is $S = [52.9106610109.59.51010]^T$. Therefore, the risk quantization value of vulnerability CVE-2014-3376 is:

$$P_v = W \times S = 7.8537 \tag{6}$$

The result shows that the qualitative severity ranking level of the CVE-2014-3376 is High. We evaluate vulnerabilities CVE-2014-6055, CVE-2014-3361, CVE-2014-0548 and CVE-2013-2848 by using the same method and obtain qualitative severity ranking level and quantitative severity score of each vulnerability is as shown in **Table** 4.

Table 4. Vulnerability comparison

Cases	Vulnerability scoring	Severity ranking
CVE-2014-6055	6.6750	High
Multiple stack-based buffer overflows in LibVNCServer 0.9.9.		
CVE-2014-3361	5.3371	Medium
The ALG module in Cisco IOS does not properly implement SIP over NAT, allowing remote attackers to cause a denial of service.		
CVE-2014-0548	6.9855	High
Adobe series allow remote attackers to bypass the Same Origin Policy via unspecified vectors.		
CVE-2013-2848	3.4755	Low
The XSS Auditor in Google Chrome before might allow remote attackers to obtain sensitive information via unspecified vectors.		

6   Conclusion

In order to improve the effectiveness of security vulnerabilities processing and identify vulnerabilities prioritization, it is necessary to evaluate the severity levels of security vulnerabilities. The current methods of vulnerability severity assessment have not considered circumstances information of the enterprise and economic loss caused by a vulnerability exploit. To this end, we propose a comprehensive method of vulnerability severity evaluation integrating technical metrics and economic loss metrics, and therefore evaluating the vulnerability severity according to the particular circumstances of the enterprise. The result of the case study shows that the proposed method can assess the vulnerabilities severity effectively and accurately. As the future work, we will consider other possible economic metrics and evaluate the potential cost savings that can be obtained by using our method.

Acknowledgement. This work is supported by the National Natural Science Foundation of China under Grant No. 61402437.

References

1. Global Corporate IT Security Risks (2013). http://media.kaspersky.com/en/business-security/Kaspersky_Global_IT_Security_Risks_Survey_report_Eng_final.pdf
2. National Vulnerability Database. http://nvd.nist.gov/
3. Common Vulnerability Scoring System (CVSS-SIG). http://www.first.org/cvss
4. Frigault, M., Wang, L.Y., Singhal, A., Jajodia, S.: Measuring network security using dynamic Bayesian network. In: ACM Conference on Computer and Communications Security, pp. 23 − 30 (2008)
5. Cheng, P.S., Wang, L.Y., Jajodia, S., Singhal, A.: Aggregating CVSS base scores for semantics-rich network security metrics. In: 2012 IEEE 31st International Symposium on Reliable Distributed Systems (SRDS 2012), Irvine, CA, USA, 8 − 11 October 2012
6. Allodi, L., Massacci, F.: Comparing vulnerability severity and exploits using case-control studies. ACM Trans. Inf. Syst. Secur. **17**(1), 1–20 (2014)
7. Huang, C.C., Lin, F.Y., Lin, F.Y.-S., Sun, Y.S.: A novel approach to evaluate software vulnerability prioritization. J. Syst. Softw. **86**, 2822–2840 (2013)
8. Liu, Q.X., Zhang, Y.Q.: VRSS: a new system for rating and scoring vulnerabilities. Comput. Commun. **34**(3), 264–273 (2011)
9. Liu, Q.X., Zhang, Y.Q., Kong, Y., Wu, Q.R.: Improving VRSS-based vulnerability prioritization using analytic hierarchy process. J. Syst. Softw. **85**, 1699–1708 (2012)
10. Ghani, H., Luna, J., Suri, N.: Quantitative assessment of software vulnerabilities based on economic-driven security metrics. In: 2013 International Conference on Risks and Security of Internet and Systems (CRiSIS), IEEE Computer Society, p. 8 (2013)
11. Innerhofer-Oberperfler, F., Breu, R.: An empirically derived loss taxonomy based on publicly known security incidents. In: 4th International Conference on Availability, Reliability and Security (ARES), vol. 1 and 2, pp. 66–73 (2009)
12. Saaty, T.L.: How to make a decision: the analytic hierarchy process. Eur. J. Oper. Res. **48**, 9–26 (1990)

A Tibetan Word Sense Disambiguation Method Based on HowNet and Chinese-Tibetan Parallel Corpora

Xinmin Jiang[1(✉)], Lirong Qiu[1], and Yeqing Li[2]

[1] School of Information Engineering, Minzu University of China, Beijing, China
jiang_xinmin@yeah.net
[2] Inner Mongolia University of Finance and Economics, Hohhot, China

Abstract. In natural language, it is a common phenomenon that words are ambiguous. How to make computer understand its right meaning in the specific context environment is the driving force for research on word sense disambiguation. Making use of Tibetan-Chinese bilingual corpora and HowNet semantic knowledge base, this paper puts forward a word sense disambiguation method that can select a right Chinese interpretation for Tibetan words with multiple Chinese translation in the specific context. Study of word sense disambiguation method proposed in this paper will have a positive role in promoting the study of Tibetan-Chinese machine translation and cross-language information retrieval.

Keywords: Tibetan language information processing · Word sense disambiguation · Parallel corpora · HowNet

1 Introduction

In natural language, there is a universal phenomenon that one word has several interpretations, which is called the semantic diversity of natural language vocabulary. For example, the English word "bear" can be translated into two Chinese word: " 熊" (bear, an animal) and " 忍受" (endure); the Chinese word " 冲洗" can be translated into two English words: "Develop" (for instance, develop this photo) and "wash". The Tibetan language also have this kind of phenomenon. The Tibetan word " འོང་བ" can be interpreted as " 开发" (develop) and " 驱逐" (drive out) in Chinese. Human can quickly determine the intended meaning of words according to the words' context. But this is a very difficult problem for computer.

Word sense disambiguation (WSD) is a research that is to study how to make the computer to realize meaning's recognition in the specific language environment. Word sense disambiguation has two necessary steps: (1) we need to describe the meaning of words in dictionaries, and then we can use these descriptions to train algorithm; (2) Using this algorithm to remove the ambiguity of words in corpus automatically [1].

There are more word sense disambiguation research in the field of English and Chinese, but Tibetan' related research is few. To solve this problem, this paper proposes the word sense disambiguation method that is based on HowNet and Tibetan-Chinese bilingual parallel corpus. This method makes use of semantic information that

Y. Lu et al. (Eds.): ISCTCS 2014, CCIS 520, pp. 152–159, 2015.
DOI: 10.1007/978-3-662-47401-3_20

are provided by Chinese semantic knowledge base which is called as HowNet to calculate the semantic similarity and relevance between the multiple meanings of the ambiguous Tibetan words and the context that these words are located. So we can select the appropriate meaning according to the calculation results.

2   Related Work

Due to statistical natural language processing technology's development, word sense disambiguation methods based on rules are now little researched. After entering the period of studying the method of word sense disambiguation with the statistical strategy, most of the research is on monolingual corpora annotation, and this is directly concerned with the lack of parallel corpora. In particular, most of research are mainly focused on the optimization of disambiguation method and construction of tagged corpus.

In the study of English word sense disambiguation, Hwee Tou Ng uses supervised method to develop a tool called IMS (It make sense) for any English text for word sense disambiguation [2]. The method that are used in this tool obtains 73 % of the accuracy on the SensEval-3 test. Chengliang Li eliminates the ambiguity of vocabulary with the help of Wikipedia which contains lots of knowledge [3], and this method opens up a new research direction for the research of word sense disambiguation from the perspective of knowledge.

In the study of Chinese word sense disambiguation, Jingzhou He uses a maximum entropy model to focus on the feature template's selection problem of Chinese word sense disambiguation [4]. Zhizhuo Yang proposes a network diagram word sense disambiguation that are based on the word distance [5]. This method not only consider the strength of the semantic relations between words, but also consider their actual distance in ambiguous sentences.

Currently in Tibetan areas, we have not searched the published results about Tibetan automatic word sense disambiguation and annotation that are based on the Chinese-Tibetan parallel corpora.

3   Specific Method

3.1   Overview

At present, word sense disambiguation techniques mainly include the method that are based on dictionary, supervised and unsupervised method. Supervised Word sense tagging relies on large-scale, high quality word corpus as training data. According to the training data, we can calculate the co-occurrence probability of an ambiguous word's context and the vocabulary of a specific word. So the word sense disambiguation can be converted to a classification problem. Unsupervised Word sense tagging method does not require a dictionary knowledge, nor does it needs word sense tagging corpus, but only directly depends on a massive scale corpus to learn and derive the meaning of words, so as to achieve the purpose of word sense disambiguation.

Related studies [6] show that supervised word sense disambiguation method is superior to unsupervised methods.

In Tibetan area, because there is no large-scale semantic annotation training corpus, even it is very difficult for us to obtain an unmarked corpus, so the realization of completely supervised and unsupervised methods is not very high. In view of the above reasons, this paper adopts the method of combining Chinese-Tibetan dictionary, semantic knowledge base and Tibetan-Chinese bilingual translation information to research the Tibetan word sense disambiguation method.

3.2   Introduction of HowNet

HowNet is a semantic knowledge base for English and Chinese words that can reveal the relationship between concepts and concepts as well as the property of concept. HowNet uses its unique Knowledge Dictionary Mark-up Language (KDML) to describe words' definition. HowNet represents a word with the following content as shown in Table 1:

Table 1. Word's represent in HowNet

Description Flag	Description
Chinese Word	宗教运动
English Word	Religious movement
DEF	{fact|事情: CoEvent={function|活动},domain={religion|宗教}}

Semantic knowledge base plays an important role in this study. The word sense disambiguation method that are proposed by this paper needs to calculate the semantic similarity and relevance between current candidate word meaning and the current context. We need to select the appropriate meaning according to the results of calculation, and regard this meaning as the right meaning of the ambiguous word in the current Tibetan sentences.

3.3   Process of Word Sense Disambiguation

The knowledge-based word sense methods have been widely used in English, and WordNet and Wikipedia are popular knowledge resource. The Chinese word sense disambiguation's research focus also tends to the method that are based on knowledge base. This is mainly because Chinese is a parataxis language, and the absence of the actual word sense tagging of corpus. This study aims to provide services for Tibetan-Chinese bilingual translation and information retrieval research, so we hope to reference some successful experiences in Chinese word sense disambiguation, to select the right Chinese interpretations for Tibetan ambiguous words in the specific context environment. In this paper, the main content of the word sense disambiguation method is shown in Fig. 1.

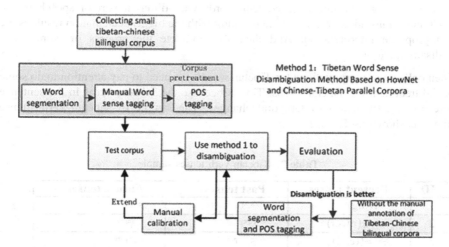

Fig. 1. The process of word sense disambiguation

Data preprocessing.

The study in this paper is based on bilingual corpus. First of all, we need to collect small Tibetan-Chinese bilingual aligned corpus, and then we need to do some pretreatment like word segmentation, manual word sense tagging and part of speech tagging. Manual word sense tagging is to provide a testing standard for the method of word sense disambiguation. The part of speech tagging for the corpus is for two reasons: (1) Help with the collection of interpretations; (2) Help with the calculation of word similarity and relevance.

Method of Word Sense Disambiguation.

After data preprocessing, the selection of Tibetan word needs to go through the following steps:

1. Extracting Chinese interpretations for the content words in the Tibetan sentences that are pending (Function words are not the research content of this paper). If one Tibetan word has multiple meanings, this word will be marked as ambiguous word, and we need go to step 2.
2. Processing the Tibetan words that are marked as ambiguous words one by one. We need to calculate the similarity between the interpretations of Tibetan word and the word that have the same part of speech as the current Tibetan word in Chinese translation. We can select the appropriate meaning for ambiguous words according to the calculation result. The selection criteria is that words semantic similarity computation results need to be larger than α (The value of α needs to take lot of experiments to make sure). If the number of eligible interpretation is greater than 1,

we need go to step 3. If the value is less than or equal to 1, we can pick up the greatest semantic similarity computation result as the correct meaning.

3. Calculating the relevance between the candidate meaning of the current Tibetan ambiguous words and other content words with different part of speech in the Chinese translation. We select the meaning with the biggest calculation result as the appropriate interpretation. And then we complete the process of word sense disambiguation.

When collecting interpretations for Tibetan words, we need to pay attention to do some special treatment for Tibetan verbs. This is because the Tibetan verbs in the sentence there are usually words of temporal changes. The sample of Tibetan verbs' tense change is shown as Table 2.

Table 2. Tibetan verb tenses sample

ID	Present tenses	Past tenses	Future tenses
1	ཀྲོག་(dig)	བཀྲོགས་པ་	བཀྲོག་བ་
2	འཛོལ་བ་(meet)	བཙལ་བ་	གཞལ་བ་
3	ཀློག་ བ་(read)	བཀླགས་པ་	བཀླག་ པ་

This paper builds the Tibetan verb tenses reference library which is aimed at that Tibetan verbs have several different form. When we need to deal with verbs in Tibetan sentences, we should search our reference library to find the original form of this Tibetan word.

The calculation of word semantic similarity in the step (1) can be calculated with the Formula (1) [7]. $\beta_i(1 \leq i \leq 3)$ are weight parameters, and they should comply with the following conditions: $\beta_1 + \beta_2 + \beta_3 = 1$, $\beta_1 \geq \beta_2 \geq \beta_3$.

$$sim(w_1, w_2) = \sum_{i=1}^{3} \beta_i \prod_{j=1}^{i} sim_j(w_1, w_2) \tag{1}$$

$$sim_1(w_1, w_2) = \frac{\gamma \times h}{dis(w_1, w_2) + \gamma \times h} \tag{2}$$

$$sim_3(w_1, w_2) = \frac{\sum sim_3^i(p_1, p_2)}{n} \tag{3}$$

n is the comparison number of relationship description

We can use Formula (2) to calculate $sim_1(w_1, w_2)$ in Formula (1). $sim_1(w_1, w_2)$ represents the similarity of main feature of basic feature in HowNet. $dis(w_1, w_2)$ represents semantic distance between w_1 and w_2. The parameter h represents the height of public parent sememe of two main sememes in two words' definition. γ is an adjustable parameter. We can use the calculation method that are proposed by reference [8] to calculate $sim_2(w_1, w_2)$ which represents similarity of the secondary feature of basic sememe between words. Using the Formula (3) to calculate $sim_3(w_1, w_2)$ which represents the similarity calculation of the relationship feature. $sim_3^i(p_1, p_2)$ represents the number of relationship description that have the same content.

There are multiple terms in Chinese translation with the same part of speech (especially the nouns and adjectives). When we need to calculate the similarity between the interpretations of Tibetan word and the word that have the same part of speech as the current Tibetan word in Chinese translation, we need to calculate the similarity between candidate interpretations and every Chinese word that meets the POS requirement. And then the average value of all calculation results will be regarded as the evaluation criteria of the candidate interpretation.

Under normal circumstances, after passing through the words semantic similarity computation with POS, we can get the right candidate senses. In less ideal conditions, after word similarity calculation was completed, there is still more than one candidate meanings with similar results. In this case, we need to continue to calculate the relevance between candidate interpretations and other content words that have different part of speech in Chinese translation. Since this goal does not lies in the study of highly precise semantic relevance computing methods, this paper selects 4 dynamic roles to calculate this kind of relevance. These dynamic roles are "domain", "MaterialOf", "CoEvent" and "RelateTo". Extracting the four dynamic roles' content of the two concepts that need to calculate the relevance. This paper uses Formula (4) to calculate this kind of correlation.

$$rel(w_1, w_2) = \sum_{i=1}^{4} \varphi_i \times sim_i(p_1, p_2) \tag{4}$$

φ_i is adjustable parameter in Formula (4), usually used as a weight parameter, and meet the following conditions: $\sum_{i=1}^{3} \varphi_i = 1$. $sim_1(p_1, p_2)$ represents the similarity of the dynamic role called "domain" in HowNet; $sim_2(p_1, p_2)$ represents the similarity of the dynamic role called "MaterialOf"; $sim_3(p_1, p_2)$ represents the similarity of the dynamic role "RelateTo"; $sim_4(p_1, p_2)$ represents the similarity of the dynamic role called "CoEvent". Similarity can be calculated according to the formula (1). When we are calculating the relevance, there are more than one words with different part of speech information, so we need to calculate the average of relevance of the same candidate interpretation. As a result, we can select the candidate interpretation that has the highest relevance result as the appropriate interpretation.

A situation which these definitions are lack of related dynamic roles may exist in the process of extracting the necessary contents to calculate the relevance. At this point, we ignore the correlation calculation process, and select the candidate interpretation with highest similarity result as the right interpretation.

Expansion of the Tagged Corpus.

After using the word sense disambiguation method that is shown in Fig. 1 to deal with the tagged corpus, we can evaluate the effectiveness of the disambiguation method according to the meanings that have been tagged in advance. Under the condition of disambiguation effect is good, we can deal with the Tibetan-Chinese corpus which are not tagged with the appropriate interpretation. So we can expand the tagged corpus. This corpus can lay an important foundation for more accurate word sense disambiguation in the future.

4 Discussion

This paper learn from the design ideas of word sense tagging in Chinese-English bilingual corpora. Word sense disambiguation methods' effectiveness based on HowNet have been proven [9]. In addition, due to the lack of corpus resources in minority language, some word sense disambiguation method that can achieve good results in the area of English can't be used in the field of minority language. So this paper proposes a Tibetan Word Sense Disambiguation Method Based on HowNet and Chinese-Tibetan Parallel Corpora.

In this paper, the research method is ultimately based on the method of knowledge and dictionary, so this method is inevitably plagued by inherent drawback which is the problem of unknown word. Due to the development of language, dictionary or knowledge base that are built by human can't cover all words in one of languages. Because the Tibetan Word sense disambiguation method itself is at an early stage of the research, this article does not do some additional processing on this problem.

The proposed method requires a sentence level aligned bilingual corpus that are annotated with the right word sense manually. But the meaning tagging process is relatively slow, there are no one test corpus that is ready to use. So this article just puts forward the research method, and does not give the related experimental results.

5 The Future Work

At present, due to the lack of basic resources, which leads to the related research methods and temporarily cannot prove its validity through the experiment, so now the priority is the construction of corpus resource. Only under the condition of perfecting the basic corpus resources, we can actually demonstrate the effectiveness of semantic disambiguation method. And we also hope that we can design a more accurate similarity and relevance calculation method in the future study.

Acknowledgement. Our work is supported by the National nature science foundation of Mongolia (No. 2013MS0901) and the Program for New Century Excellent Talents in University (NCET-12-0579)

References

1. Wu, Y.: Introduction to some terms on word sense disambiguation. In: Terminology Standardization & Information Technology, vol. 3, pp. 18–20 (2010)

2. Chan, Y.S., Ng, H.T., Chiang, D.: Word sense disambiguation improves statistical machine translation. In: Proceedings of Annual Meeting-Association for Computational Linguistics (2007)
3. Li, C., Sun, A., Datta, A.: A Generalized Method for Word Sense Disambiguation Based on Wikipedia. In: Clough, P., Foley, C., Gurrin, C., Jones, G.J., Kraaij, W., Lee, H., Mudoch, V. (eds.) ECIR 2011. LNCS, vol. 6611, pp. 653–664. Springer, Heidelberg (2011)
4. Jingzhou, H., Wang, H.: Chinese word sense disambiguation based on maximum entropy model with feature selection. J. Softw. **21**(6), 1287–1295 (2010)
5. Yang, Z., Huang, H.: Graph based word sense disambiguation method using distance between words. J. Softw. **23**(4), 776–785 (2012)
6. McCarthy, D., Koeling, R., Weeds, J., et al.: Finding predominant word senses in untagged text. In: Proceedings of the 42nd Annual Meeting on Association for Computational Linguistics, Association for Computational Linguistics (2004)
7. Liu, Q., Li, S.: The calculation method of word semantic similarity based on HowNet, CLSW2002, Taipei, May 2002
8. Xia, T.: Study on chinese words semantic similarity computation. Comput. Eng. **33**(6), 191–194 (2007)
9. Liu, D., Yang, E.: Word sense tagging in chinese-english parallel corpus. J. Chin. Inf. Process. **19**(6), 50–56 (2006)

SFAPCC: A Secure and Flexible Architecture for Public Cloud Computing

Baohui Li[1,2,3], Kefu Xu[2,3(✉)], Chuang Zhang[2,3], and Yue Hu[2,3]

[1] Beijing University of Posts and Telecommunications, Beijing, China
libh@nelmail.iie.ac.cn
[2] Institute of Information Engeering, Chinese Academy of Science,
Beijing, China
[3] National Engeering Laboratory of Information Security, Beijing, China
{xukefu,zhangchuang,huyue}@iie.ac.cn

Abstract. Cloud computing platforms, such as Amazon EC2, provide organizations or enterprises with flexible resources at low cost. Indeed, this technology is currently taking us into a new era in terms of the remote off-site handling our data. However, while existing offerings are useful for providing basic computation and storage resources, they fail to provide the security that most of customers would like. In this work, we identify two challenges for public cloud computing, and we argue that more comprehensive controls over public cloud computing services need to be provided for users. Towards this goal, this paper proposes a secure and flexible architecture, called SFAPCC, to address these challenges. Security analysis shows that our architecture realize logical isolation for different tenants, and improve flexibility for public cloud.

Keywords: Public cloud · Security · Flexibility · Architecture

1 Introduction

With the large scale proliferation of the internet around the world, applications can now be delivered as services over the internet, more significantly, this could reduce the overall cost for resources integration and other reasons. In the last few years, due to the reemergence of virtualization as an efficient method of flexibly sharing resources, cloud computing has rapidly grown in popularity. Furthermore, cloud computing is so technologically elegant, and conceptually simple that even a CEO can easily grasp it, making it a better choice for organizations, such as enterprises and governments, to transfer their business to the convenient cloud computing platform. So far, we have seen widespread adoption for public web services, moving computing and data away from portable PCs and desktop into large data centers [1]. However, security is one of the major issues which obstructs the growth of cloud computing, and complications with data privacy and data protection continue to plague the market. As a consequence, most of organizations, which do have the needs to utilize cloud computing, are

Y. Lu et al. (Eds.): ISCTCS 2014, CCIS 520, pp. 160–165, 2015.
DOI: 10.1007/978-3-662-47401-3_21

reluctant to deploy their business, especially, the company's mission-critical data and intellectual property in the hands of a third party.

Based on scalability, interoperability, quality of service and the delivery models of cloud computing, it can be divided into private, public and hybrid cloud. Due to the fact that private cloud services are dedicated to a single organization, the hardware, data storage, and network can be designed to assure high levels of security, meaning that private cloud has better security assurance than public cloud. So, this paper focuses on the security of public cloud. Especially, public cloud faces two secure challenges which have to be solved urgently to alleviate the trepidation of organizations.

- Data flows among organizations can not be effectively controlled in public cloud. Data flows in public cloud could go arbitrarily every corner, and thus increased the ways through which malware penetrate into the target tissue essily.
- Due to resource sharing, the internal activities within an organization, such as pesky software bugs cause sporadic crashes, could affect another tissue locating in the same cloud. For example, different organization's virtual machines, locating on the same physical machine, can not determine whether they should aid their neighbors automatically. If they help their neighor blindly, a catastrophic problem of chain reaction may happen [2].

To address the above problems, this paper proposes a secure and flexible architecture for public cloud computing. Details about the two challenges and our solution method are discussed in later sections. We feel that our paper provides the following contributions:

- we identify two challenges that have to be addressed urgently in public cloud computing (Sect. 2).
- we propose a new secure and flexible architecture do deal with the two challenges (Sect. 3).

The rest of this paper is organized as follows. To begin with, we will provide a brief background and related works on the two challenges in Sect. 2. Section 3 describes the design proposed by this paper in details, followed by a security analysis. At last, we conclude this paper in Sect. 4.

2   Background and Related Work

This section presents two challenges that has to be dealt with urgently, and discirbes the related works with them.

2.1   Problem Statement

Uncontroled Data Flows. Data from one virtual machine can reach anyone in the pulic cloud, missing global security rules which define data flow directions among cloud. Thus, many problems arises, for example, attackers may distribute malicious software to construct botnets easily.

Uncontroled Assitiance Mechanism. A key motivation for moving applications into the cloud is the ease with which new resources can be allocated or moved. Due to pesky software bugs, load increases or other reasons, cloud service inevitably fails to work smoothly. When the cloud computing operating system detects high workload on the flooded service, it will start to provide more resources to cope with the additional workload. However, during recent years, many problems have arised due to blindly assistance [3–6]. Take gmail accident [6] as an example, workers took offline a few gmail servers for routine maintenance, but overloaded service affected requested routers for underestimate after a recent upgrade. Then, recovery pushed traffic to other request routers blindly, as a consequence, overload begun to spread. At last, within minutes, google's gmail suffered a loss of function of a large area.

2.2   Related Work

Virtual firewall is a software appliance that controls communications between virtual machines, running entirely within a virtualized environment [7]. Like a traditional network firewall, a virtual firewall inspects packets and blocks unapproved communication among virtual machines based on security policy rules. For a virtual firewall to work effectively, companies first need to define their network security policies which specify how they can be used and who can use them, and stipulate the actions to be taken when communications violated certain security policies. But, due to the complexity of the network topology, it is very confused for cloud systems administrator to determine where is the just right place to set up a firewall, balancing between efficiency and safety.

For the problem that recovery may replicate small accidents to other servers recursively until the entire cloud service fails in a catastrophic outage, Guo et al. [2] proposes that considering the system holistically is a must when failure occurs. Bryan [8] dealt with dynamic instabilities caused by multiplexed hardware resource pools or unpredictable interactions. But, these works do not give us a criterion whether to assist a weak neighbor when a small event occurs.

3   SFAPCC: A Secure and Flexible Architecture for Public Cloud

In this section, we give a detailed description for our architecture SFAPCC, followed by a security analysis.

3.1   Architecture Overview

Cloud computing service providers have the obligation and required ability to prevent attacks among tenants. And most importantly, this ability should not restrict the elasticity of their cloud. As is pointed out by [9], public cloud service has many advantages, such as simplicity, low cost and no maintenance. However, compared with private cloud, it perceives weaker security. Combining the

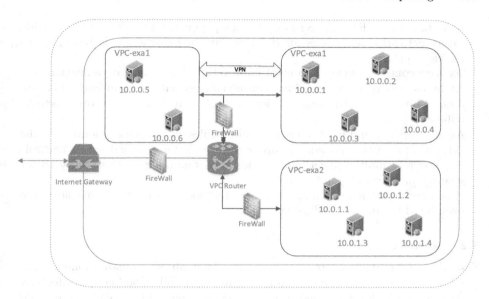

Fig. 1. Secure and flexible architeture for public cloud computing

advantages of both public cloud and private cloud, we design SFAPCC showed by Fig. 1 to achieve the target of satisfying the two needs at the same time.

SFAPCC builds virtual private clouds in public cloud, leveraging existing virtualization technologies at the server, router, and network levels to create dynamic resource pools. Virtual private cloud is a combination of cloud computing resources with a virtual private network infrastructure to give users the abstraction of a private set of cloud resources by taking dynamically configurable pools of cloud resources. As is shown by Fig. 1, VPC-exa1 and VPC-exa2 are logically isolated, and their communications are be controlled by setting virtual firewalls between them.

The key components of SFAPCC can be listed as below:

- Try to put machines belonging to the same organization within a physical area. Resources within the same organizations can be dynamically changed to meet the needs of different people or respond to emergencies jointly.
  Virtual networks can be implemented in several ways, such as OpenStack Neutroni [10], VMware/Niciras NVP [11], and IBM DOVE [12]. In our prototype, we utilize Xen [13] to virtualize servers, and VLANs are used to partition the local area networks within each cloud data center.
- Based on the consideration of scalability, it is unavoidable to allocate machines cross-physical areas. Virtual private clouds belonging to the same tenant use tunnels to provide secure communication channels via the creation of secure, virtually dedicated paths within the provider network, presenting a unified pool of resources. As is illustrated by Fig. 1 that VPC-exa1's separate physical portions are connected by VPNs.
  Tunnels are established among the virtual devices to decouple the virtual network from the physical network, using serveral tunneling techniques, such

as VxLAN, NVGRE, and STT [8]. In this paper, we use VPNs [8] to provide covert network connections for different virtual private clouds belonging to the same enterprise.

- Security control policies to control information flow among organizations are set by the cloud service provider, considering security domain and other factors. While, within the organization, tenants can design their own security policies.

  An enterprise would need to create firewall rules within public cloud or at the gateways to its own network in order to provide fine grained access controls and securely limit connectivity. In this way, tenants gain the ability to set security policies independently.

- Resources from different organizations, but locating on the same host, are prohibited to support each other.

3.2   Security Analysis

Security. Our architecture makes public cloud absorb private cloud's security features. *On the one hand*, data flows among public cloud can be effectivly controlled, using domain-based or other security polies. Our architecture could achieve a hierarchical control of information flows in public cloud, reducing the avenues of malicious acts of penetration or other attacks, and eventually, reducing the probability of attacks among organizations. *On the other hand*, the secure responsibility between cloud service providers and tenants separated. Cloud service providers are responsible for providing platforms of virtual private clouds and tunnels, while tenants obtain the flexibility of setting security policies independently, making certain companies feel that data is more secure by having it reside in-house.

Flexibility. Our work lays the basis for virtual resources flow autonomously, preventing the emergence of chain reactions. Only machines affiliating with the same organization are permitted to support each other, otherwise, prohibited. As a result, we can make sudden failures confined to a certain range in the worst case, preventing it from affecting the entire cloud data center.

4   Conclusion

In order to enhance the security and flexibility of public cloud systems, in this work we first identify and describe two challenges urgently needing to be solved. For the challenges existing in the cloud, we propose a secure and flexible architecture to build virtual private clouds for one organization. And virtual private clouds locating in different physical places are connected by tunnels, such as VPN. Only machines belonging to the same organization are permitted to surpport each other. Security analysis shows that our work make tenents feel that the data is more secure by having it resided in-house. Furthermore, it limits a sudden problem to specific range, preventing from extending to the whole public cloud.

References

1. Dikaiakos, M.D., Katsaros, D., Mehra, P., Pallis, G., Vakali, A.: Cloud computing: distributed internet computing for it and scientific research. IEEE Internet Comput. **13**(5), 10–13 (2009)
2. Guo, Z., McDirmid, S., Yang, M., Zhuang, L., Zhang, P., Luo, Y., Bergan, T., Bodik, P., Musuvathi, M., Zhang, Z., et al.: Failure recovery: when the cure is worse than the disease. In: Proceedings of the 14th USENIX Conference on Hot Topics in Operating Systems (USENIX 2013). Santa Ana Pueblo: ACM Press, pp. 1–6 (2013)
3. Microsoft. Summary of windows azure service disruption on feb 29th, 2012. http://blogs.msdn.com/b/windowsazure/archive/-2012/03/09/summary-of-windows-azure-service-disruption-on-feb-29th-2012.aspx
4. Amazon. Summary of the amazon ec2, amazon ebs, and amazon rds service event in the eu west region. April 2011. http://aws.amazon.com/message/65648/
5. Facebook. More details on todays outage. September 2010. http://www.facebook.com/notes/facebook-engineering/more-details-on-todays-outage/431441338919
6. Google. More on todays gmail issue. September 2009. http://googleappengine.blogspot.jp/2012/10/about-todays-app-engine-outage.html
7. Luo, S., Lin, Z., Chen, X., Yang, Z., Chen, J.: Virtualization security for cloud computing service. In: 2011 International Conference on Cloud and Service Computing (CSC), pp. 174–179. IEEE (2011)
8. Ford, B.: Icebergs in the clouds: the other risks of cloud computing. In: USENIX Workshop on Hot Topics in Cloud Computing (HotCloud) (2012)
9. Inc., Aerohive Networks. Public or private cloud: The choice is yours. whitepaper (2013)
10. openstack, October 2014. www.openstack.org
11. TechCrunch, August 2012. http://techcrunch.com/2012/07/23/vmware-buys-nicira-for-1-26-billion-and-gives-more-clues-about-cloud-strategy/
12. Lewin-Eytan, L., Barabash, K., Cohen, R., Jain, V., Levin, A.: Designing modular overlay solutions for network virtualization. IBM Technical Paper (2012)
13. Barham, P., Dragovic, B., Fraser, K., Hand, S., Harris, T., Ho, A., Neugebauer, R., Pratt, I., Warfield, A.: Xen and the art of virtualization. ACM SIGOPS Operating Syst. Rev. **37**(5), 164–177 (2003)

Towards Enumeration of NTFS Using USN Journals Under UEFI

Zilu Zhang[1,2,3(✉)], Jinqiao Shi[1,2], and Lanlan Hu[1,2]

[1] Institute of Information Engineering, Chinese Academy of Sciences,
Beijing, China
[2] National Engineering Laboratory for Information Security Technologies,
Beijing, China
[3] University of Chinese Academy of Sciences, Beijing, China
{zhangzilu,shijinqiao,hulanlan}@iie.ac.cn

Abstract. To manage and protect the increasingly files, file-system-status monitoring has become more useful nowadays. Since most of existing file-system -status monitoring systems are based on OS level, they still cannot take effect when malicious attacks manage to take control of computers during the booting process. So file-system-status monitoring systems before the OS booting has become an urgent requirement. A key problem of file-system-status monitoring systems is to enumerate all the files in the system. Considering NTFS file system is the most popular file system and UEFI has become a new standard specification of BIOS, we put forward an implementation of an enumeration engine of NTFS file system under UEFI using the USN journal, and experiments shows that our engine could enumerate all the files.

Keywords: NTFS · UEFI · USN journal · Enumeration of file system

1 Introduction

Nowadays, the applications on computers have become increasingly various and the number of files on computers has been increasing. To manage and protect these increasingly files, file-system-status monitoring systems has become more useful nowadays. Since most of existing file-system-status monitoring systems are running on OS level, they still cannot take effect when malicious attacks manage to take control of computers during the booting process. So file-system-status monitoring systems before the OS booting has become an urgent requirement. A key problem of file system status monitoring is to enumerate all the files in the system.

Since 1990s, Windows operating-system has been very popular in our daily life. Thus, NTFS, which is the common file system under Windows operating system also play an important role. Meanwhile, to make the file-system-status monitoring take effect before OS booting, technical on BIOS level is of a great importance. In recent years, Unified Extensible Firmware Interface (UEFI), as a software interface specification between an operating system and platform firmware designed to replace legacy BIOS, has become more and more popular.

© Springer-Verlag Berlin Heidelberg 2015
Y. Lu et al. (Eds.): ISCTCS 2014, CCIS 520, pp. 166–174, 2015.
DOI: 10.1007/978-3-662-47401-3_22

In this paper, considering NTFS file system is the most popular file system and UEFI has become new standard specification of BIOS, we put forward an implementation of a enumeration system of NTFS file system under UEFI using the USN journal, and the experiments shows that our engine could enumerate all the files. The remainders of this paper are organized as follows: Sect. 2 introduce the background and related works. Section 3 is mainly about the implementation and solving way of the key problem of the engine. Section 4 is the experiments of the engine. Section 5 give an conclusion.

2 Background and Related Works

2.1 NTFS File System and USN Journal

2.1.1 NTFS File System

Data in NTFS can be generally divided into four parts (as the Fig. 5 shows): (1) Partition boot sector (boot sector, also called BPB), this part is Shared with all disk format, and takes up a sector. (2) The Master File Table (MFT), it is the record In NTFS, location of the file is determined by the MFT (Master File Table). MFT is a corresponding database which is consist of a series of file record. Each file in the volume has at least one file record, and contains at least one or more attributes. In general, it takes 12 % space of the volume. (3) The System files. NTFS System has 16 System files and 8 reserved files totally. (4) The data area. This area is offered to user space.

Each file in NTFS has a unique identifier that called MFT file reference. The file reference number consists of two parts: one is the file index number, the second is file sequence number. File index number is 48-bit and is corresponding to the position of the file in the MFT. File sequence number increases with each reuse of file record.

The enumeration and parsing on NTFS also has a lot of research recently. Paper [7] designs an NTFS file parsing system (working after the OS booting) in computer forensics vision. In practice, "Everything" is a fast filename search engine under windows, but it cannot be valid before the operating system boot. Besides, 'Everything' is not an open source software, thus normal programmer cannot use its SDK to implement their own function.

2.1.2 Analysis of USN Journal

The USN Journal (Update Sequence Number Journal), as the name implies, is a database to store all the changed information of the volume of NTFS . Every NTFS volume has its own USN journal database. It include several useful information like parent MFT reference, filename and the information about the changes.

Under Windows, there are several ways to view the USN journal. One way is to use the CMD command "FSUTIL". The command must obey following format (just as Fig. 1 shows):

Fsutil usn enumdata < file ref# > < lowUsn > < highUsn > < volume pathname>.

You can also use winAPI to do view the USN journal. Paper [6] shows how to use the winAPI DeviceIoControl to create and query the USN journal.

   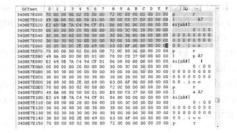

Fig. 1. Fsutil command under Windows   **Fig. 2.** $Extend$UsnJrnl$J in Winhex

Actually, all the USN journals are stored in the NTFS metafile named $Extend $UsnJrnl, It begins as an empty file. Whenever a change is made to the volume, a record is added to the file. Each record is identified by a 64-bit Update Sequence Number or USN. We can see the meta $Extend $UsnJrnl in Winhex (Just as Fig. 2 shows). The selected part of picture is one USN record.

The data structure of USN journal is as Table 1:

Table 1. The data structure of $Extend $UsnJrnl$J

Offset	Size	Description
0 × 00	4	Size of entry
0 × 04	2	Major Version
0 × 06	2	Minor Version
0 × 08	8	MFT Reference
0 × 10	8	Parent MFT Reference
0 × 18	8	Offset of this entry in $J
0 × 20	8	Timestamp
0 × 28	4	Reason
0 × 2B	4	SourceInfo
0 × 30	4	SecurityID
0 × 34	4	FileAttributes
0 × 38	2	Size of filename (in bytes)
0 × 3A	2	Offset to filename
0 × 3C	V	Filename
V + 0 × 3C	P	Padding (align to 8 bytes)

2.2 UEFI and Related Works

UEFI (Unified Extensible Firmware Interface) is a specification designed to replace legacy BIOS. In Recent years, UEFI has been popularized in our daily life. [1].

UEFI provide a standard environment for the running of computer before OS booting. The design of the UEFI based mainly on the following elements: traditional architecture, system partition, protocol, UEFI boot services And UEFI runtime services. UEFI data tables, runtime services and boot Services are independent of the platform architecture. The framework of UEFI is shown as Fig. 3.

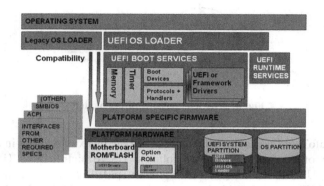

Fig. 3. The framework of UEFI [1]

There are many studies about the attack and defence under UEFI. Paper [3] and Paper [10] respectively put forwards up the method of attacking EFI (predecessor of UEFI) and UEFI, but not including the specific implementation ways. Paper [11] put forwards a bootkit method through PCI under UEFI, including both the project and technical overview. On the other hand, there are many study towards detection and defence under UEFI. Paper [12] analysis the work mechanism and key technology of UEFI and build a theory model of UEFI bootkit. Paper [13] and Paper [14] gives the method and implementation of UEFI bootkit detection in practice. To make a conclusion of the security of UEFI, Paper [9] review the study about threats and security of UEFI in recent years and provide analysis of the UEFI security issues comprehensively.

To make a conclusion of this section, these related works did a great job on their research. However, their work place emphasis on enumeration of files in the system under OS or bootkit technical under UEFI. There is still lack of research on file-status-monitoring system that is pre-booting.

3   Implemention of the System Archaitecture

The implementation of the system can be devided into 3 parts: USN journal locating module, index construction module and file query module. Figure 4 shows the relationships between them.

USN journal locating module find the disk and list all the clusters the address of USN journals in the disk. Index construction module get the USN records from the address of USN journals and construct index for all the disks. File query module is offer to the user to query the file rapidly.

There are two types of table in the system: USNBasicInfoTable and US-NRecordInfoTable. USNBasicInfoTable stores the start address of USN journal.

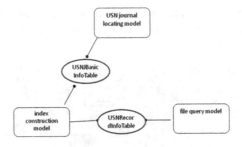

Fig. 4. The relationships of the modules

USNRecordInfoTable stores the USN records and the index of the files in all the disks. The structure of the two tables is as follows: USNBasicInfoTable {id, diskNum, startaddress}, USNRecordInfo{id, MftReference, pMftRefernce, fileName, pMftID-diskNum}. USNRecordInfoTable is a ordered table (sorted by key MftReference).

When our system get executed first time, the USN journal locating module will get the basic information of the USN journals and story it into USNBasicInfoTable. The index construction module will read USNBasicInfoTable and extract all the USN records, and construct the index of all the files according to the USN records. The index constructed will be stored in USNRecordInfoTable Then the file query module will be in work. Every time getting a query from the user, file query module will read US-NRecordInfoTable to get the file address.

The implementation of the 3 modules is just as follows.

3.1   USN Journal Locating Module

The main task of this module is to construct the process is just as follows:

Step.1.   Enumerate all the devices. In A practiced Way, use the UEFI function LibLocateHandle() to get the handles of EfiDevicePathProtocol.

Step.2.   For all the devices got in step.1.read the BPB of them and check if they are NTFS format. In A practiced Way, use Handleprotocol () function to get the DiskIO and BlockIO of them,and use ReadDisk() function to get the BPB.

Step.3.   Find the logical address of $Extend record According to BPB information and the cluster number. ($Extend is the 12nd file in NTFS according to the standard for most of the prastic situation, it's address is 11times of cluster size offset to the loacation of MFT)

Step.4.   Analysis 0×90 attribute of $Extend and find the MFT reference of the file named $UsnJrnl. Caculate the logical address of $UsnJrnl (use the MFT reference mutiply bytes per sector mutiply 2)

Step.5.   Go to the address of $UsnJrnl and analysis 0×80 attribute. Follow the datarun in attribute 0×80 named $J and list all the clusters where $J is in.

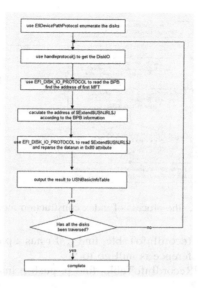

Fig. 5. the process of USN journal locating module

3.2   Index Construction Module

The main task of this module is to construct the index according to the USN records. The process is just as follows:

Step.1.   Fill into USNRecordInfoTable with record (0X5000000000005, NULL,"."). Here 0X5000000000005 represents the root address of the disk.

Step.2.   Through cyclic traversal, analysis the USN journals according to the datastructure as Table 2 shows.

Step.2.1.   Get frn, pfrn and filename, using the data in every USN record (the offset is 0×8, 0×10, $0 \times 3c$)

Step.2.2.   Find the record in USNRecordInfoTable whose MFTReference value equals pfrn,take its ID as pMftID (use bisearch according by the key MFTReference)

Step.2.3.   Insert the MFTReference, pMFTReference, filename and pMftID as a record into USNRecordInfoTable (Fig. 6).

3.3   File Query Module

The main task of this module is to output the object file according to the index constructed. The process is just as follows:

Step.1.   Build a stack S to restore the content structure of current query.

Step.2.   Search the USNRecordInfoTable by filename, hit the MftReference r that corresponds a filename matching with the key word.

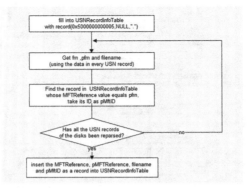

Fig. 6. the process of index construction module

Step.3.   Query the USNRecordInfoTable, find r, if r has a pMftReference p, going to 4. If r's pMftReference is null go to 5.

Step.4.   Query the USNRecordInfoTable, find p, push p into the stack S. Set r = p, and go to step 2.

Step.5.   Read the stack S from top to bottom, the result is the path P. Output P to the user (Fig. 7).

4   Experiments and Discussing

We implement the method on a virtual simulative environment of UEFI. The results of the every query will be written into a file locating in the simulative EFI partition. Figure 8. Is the output of our engine when accepting the query "WINDDK" while

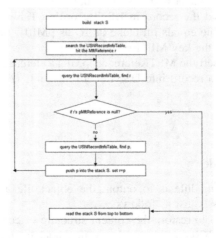

Fig. 7. The process of file query module

Fig. 9. Is the output of OS search engine when accepting the query "WINDDK". As is shown, our engine returns the result correctly.

NAME   PATH   MFTreference
srcindex.htm C:\WINDDK\3790.1830   0x000100000003d52f
srcindex.htm D:\C\WINDDK\3790.1830   0x00002000000007e7
srcindex.htm D:\WINDDK37   0x0006000000001763
srcindex.txt D: 0x5000000000000005

Fig. 8. The output of our engine

Fig. 9. The output of OS system

5 Conclusions

Through detailed analysis on the Memory Principle of the USN journals and UEFI implement technical, This paper propose and implement an engine to enumerate NTFS file system under UEFI using USN journals. It offer an interface for the follow-up systems. In the experiments, the result is outputted correctly. What is insufficient is that the implementation is under a simulative environment. Implementation under real environment will have a sight different with the simulative environment. This will be presented in our future work.

References

1. UEFI Specification2.4.1. Avalible: http://uefi.org/specifications
2. UEFI Technology: say hello to the windows 8 bootkit. Avalible: http://www.saferbytes.it/2012/09/18/uefi-technology-say-hello-tothe-windows-8-bootkit/
3. Heasman J.: Hacking the Extensible Firmware Interface (2007). http://www.ngssoftware.com/research/papers/BH-DC-07-Heasman.pdf
4. Jinqian, L., Yue, Z.: The main data structure of NTFS file system. J. Comput. Eng. Appl. **19**(2), 116–130 (2003)
5. MSDN: Volume Management Control Codes, Avalible: http://msdn.microsoft.com/en-us/library/aa365729(v=vs.85).aspx
6. En., K.Z. Gao., C.Q.: Analysis and implementation of NTFS file In: 2010 Second International Workshop on System Based on Computer Forensics Education Technology and Computer Science (ETCS), Issue Date: 6–7 March 2010
7. Bulygin, Y., Furtak, A., Bazhaniuk, O.: A Tale of One Software Bypass of Windows 8 Secure Boot. Black Hat, USA (2013)
8. Sergeev, A., Minchenkov, V., Yakovlev, A.: Too young to be secure: Analysis of UEFI threats and vulnerabilities. In: Proceedings of the 14th Open Innovations Association (FRUCT) (2013)
9. Wen-bin, T., Yue-fei, Z., Jia-yong, C.: Research on attack method of unified extensible firmware interface. J. Comput. Eng. **38**(13), 99–101 (2012)
10. Chifflier, P.: UEFI and PCIbootkits. PacSec2013

11. Tang-Wenbin, C-Xi.: Analysis and Detection of UEFI Bootkit. Computer Science[J], October 2012
12. Si-yuan, F., Gong-shen, L., Jian-hua, L.: Research of malicious code defense technology based on UEFI firmware. Comput. Eng. **38**(9), 117–120 (2012)
13. Zhengwei, J., Xiaozhen, W.: UEFI malicious behavior detection model based on minimal attack tree. Comput. Eng. Appl. **48**(32), 14–17 (2012)
14. Everything searching engine. Avalible: http://www.voidtools.com/

Trusted Cloud Service Certification and Evaluation

Wei Li[(⊠)] and Feng Cao

Beijing Key Laboratory of Cloud Computing Standard and Verification,
China Academy of Telecommunication Research of MIIT,
No. 52, Huayuan Road, Haidian District, Beijing, China
{liwei, caofeng}@ritt.cn

Abstract. In recent years, cloud computing service is used widespread for information systems. The significant thing for costumers is distinguishing trusted cloud. However, since this new technology covers Internet, CT and IT fields how to defines and assessment trusted cloud is very complicated. Many organizations have offered metrics for evaluating cloud, while few of them is accepted as standard, let alone those for trusted cloud. This paper proposes a new framework including 17 indicators in terms of data security, service quality and rights protection, to evaluate trusted cloud service. Additionally, this framework has been the standard of China Communication Standard Alliance, and applied in Trusted Cloud Certification of China.

Keyword: Trusted cloud service certification

1 Introduction

In these days, it is common that more and more customers choose cloud services for their systems. The essential thing for customers is which one is trusted. The current researches for evaluating cloud focus on particular cloud service and performance indexes, such as [1, 2]. While CATR's report [3] shows that customers select the trusted cloud not only from performance and cost aspects, but also mostly concern about data security. Thus the definition of trust should be explicit and the evaluating system should comprise data security indicators. In additional, information systems usually base on different kinds of cloud services. For example, in China, customers usually use Alibaba's VM service and Qiniu's Storage service for one system. As VM and Storage are not comparable, different cloud services need unified but slight different index system, which make the task for evaluating trusted cloud is more complicated. To solve these problems, we design a new framework including 17 indicators in terms of data security, service quality and rights protection, to evaluate and certificate different kinds of trusted cloud service. Firstly, in Sect. 2, this paper specifies the clear boundary and outlines the framework of "trusted" and "service", which has been the standard YDB144-2014 < Cloud Service Agreement Reference Framework > [4] of CCSA. Section 3 presents assessment methods of indicators which have been used

© Springer-Verlag Berlin Heidelberg 2015
Y. Lu et al. (Eds.): ISCTCS 2014, CCIS 520, pp. 175–182, 2015.
DOI: 10.1007/978-3-662-47401-3_23

for trusted cloud service certification in China. Section 4 shows the results of certified cloud services using these evaluating methods.

2 Framework

2.1 Definition of Trusted Cloud Service

According to technical report [5], trusted cloud services are those satisfying the following three aspects:

1. Completeness: whether CSP commits related indicators in agreement to customers.
2. Regularity: whether the indicators are specified regularly in agreement.
3. Authenticity: whether CSP has the abilities to reach the level of commitment.

2.2 Evaluating Framework

The framework for evaluating the above three aspects of trusted cloud service comprise 3 categories indicators in terms of Data Control and Security, Service Quality & Performance and Rights Protection Clause. The definitions of 17 indicators are as follows:

- Data Control and Security
  - Data Durability: the probability that data saved and not lost during the contract period, i.e., the monthly intact Data /(monthly intact Data + monthly lost data).
  - Data Destructibility: if the user requires, CSPs shall delete all the data completely before they discard and resell the data or device, and the data cannot be recovered.
  - Data Migration: users can control data migration and make sure that data can be imported and exported when cloud services are enabled or disabled.
  - Data privacy: CSPs shall have encryption, isolation and other means to ensure user data that in the same resource pool is not visible mutually.
  - Right to know the data: the degree of right to know the data storage location and usage that shall be committed by CSPs.
  - Service Auditability: under necessary conditions if compliance, or security forensic investigation or other reasons requires, CSPs can provide related information: for example, running logs of key components, operating records of the maintenance personnel.
- Service Quality and performance
  - Service Function: CSPs commit to the user the specific functions of the services.
  - Service Availability: the monthly probability of the available time for user using cloud service during the contract period, that is, actual monthly available time / month (the actual available time + unavailable time). Where the unavailable time is defined as since the time the user cannot use cloud services, or the time the

subscribed cloud services cannot run correctly, till the cloud service is restored to normal levels, if the this period is more than X minutes, then it is unavailable time, the value of X are determined by CSPs with the specific cloud services.

- Service Resource Elasticity Capability: the capability of the time of expanding or shrinking for unit storage unit or computing resources, and the largest expansion.
- Failure Recovery Ability: the ability by CSPs for users to recover the failure in case of failure.
- Network Access Performance: the deviation between the actual value and the purchase value of network bandwidth should not be more than 5 %
- Service Billing Accuracy: CSPs charge users by the actual purchase and quantity.
- Rights Protection Clause
  - Service change and termination clause: the rights and obligations that both parties shall have and undertake in case of service change or termination for some reason.
  - Service indemnity clause: if Service Availability fails to meet the compensation levels in the SLA, the specific indemnity will be provided by CSP.
  - User constraint clause: users shall undertake their limits of authority and comply with the constraints proposed by the service provider.
  - Service provider disclaimer clause: CSPs shall inform the users of its own disclaimer clause and formally announce it by website and other means.

This framework can be used for the following cloud services. While for different services, the meaning of "data" may have slight difference, for example, the data in Object Storage Service means customers' object data; and that of Application Hosting Container Service means the code hosting on the service. Additionally, for some services, Data Durability is not necessary, such as caching storage.

- IaaS: Virtual Machine, Object Storage, Database, Block Storage, Caching Storage;
- PaaS: Application Hosting Container;
- SaaS: Online Application.

3 Assessment Methods

The assessment metrics system uses three kinds of methods. Those are:

- SLA and Documents Review: by offering the service related SLA, instruction, technical framework documents, users' white book, etc.; CSPs should prove they can satisfy the first and second requirement in Sect. 2.1. More details of this method could be found in [4, 5].
- Technical Testing & Operating System inspection: using technical tools to test measurable indicators to judge whether their abilities are authenticable, that is required as the third requirement in Sect. 2.1.

- Monitoring: installing agent or through VM's api to monitoring sustainable index, particularly for service availability and performance to verify whether they could reach the SLA level in actual.

The matches of indexes and methods are showing in Table 1. Section 3.1 and Sect. 3.2 will explicit technical testing, operating system inspection and monitoring methods.

Table 1. Assessment method for indicators

Trusted Indicators	SLA and documents review	Technical testing & operating system inspection	Monitoring
Data durability	Yes	Yes	
Data destructibility	Yes		
Data migration	Yes	Yes	
Data privacy	Yes	Yes	
Right to know the data	Yes		
Service auditability	Yes		
Service function	Yes	Yes	
Service availability	Yes	Yes	Yes
Service resource elasticity capability	Yes	Yes	
Failure recovery ability	Yes	Yes	
Network access performance	Yes	Yes	
Service billing accuracy	Yes	Yes	
Performance	Yes	Yes	Yes
Service change and termination clause	Yes		
Service indemnity clause	Yes		
User constraint clause	Yes		
Service provider disclaimer clause	Yes		

3.1   Technical Testing and Operational System Inspection

All the metrics simulating users are black-box methods. As examples, this section mainly illustrates testing methods of data durability, service availability, data migration, data privacy and network performance. Other indicators' technical testing and operational system inspection are explicated in [5].

Data Durability. This indicator will be inspection in two aspects, which are the theoretical probability and the actual probability:

- The theoretical probability is calculated as following formulas:
  If m block data have n block data redundancy, T1 is recovery time and T2 is mean time to failure, then a single block of data loss rate R is:

$$R = \text{T1} / (\text{T1} + \text{T2}) \tag{1}$$

The theoretical probability is

$$C_m^n * R^n * (1 - R)^{(m-n)} \tag{2}$$

- The actual probability is calculate as following formula:
  The monthly durability of every user is set as

$$x_{ij} = \frac{z_{ij} - y_{ij}}{z_{ij}} \times 100\%, \tag{3}$$

In which, z_{ij} is the total data quantity of the jth user in the ith month, y_{ij} is the total data loss of the jth user in the ith month, i is the ith month, j is the jth user.

Service Availability. This indicator will be inspection in two aspects, which are the theoretical probability and the actual probability:

- The theoretical probability is calculated as following formula:

$$A = A1 \times A2$$
$$A1 = a_{11} \times a_{12} \times a_{13} \times a_{14} \times a_{15} \tag{4}$$
$$A2 = a_{21} \times a_{22} \times a_{23}$$

In which, A is Service availability, A1 is infrastructure availability, A2 is software availability, a_{11} is IDC availability, a_{12} is power system availability, a_{13} is server availability, a_{14} is network equipment availability, a_{15} is air conditioning system availability, a_{21} is virtualization software availability, a_{22} is virtualization management software and a_{23} is cluster software availability.

- The actual probability is calculate as following formula:
  The monthly durability of every user is set as

$$x_{ij} = \frac{y_{ij}}{y_{ij} + z_{ij}} \times 100\% \tag{5}$$

In which, z_{ij} is the downtime of the jth user in the ith month, y_{ij} is the total usable time of the jth user in the ith month, i is the ith month, j is the jth user;

Data Migration. The methods of data migration for different services are various. Here take the VM service data migration testing as an example, and others services testing methods are presented in [5]. Test topology as shown in the Fig. 1, the cloud host image file template are used for import and export verification between the service provider's cloud computing platforms and cloud computing local verification platform. The test file and application should be consistent in the migration. The verification platform support KVM, Xen, Vmware, etc., virtual solutions.

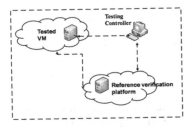

Fig. 1. Data migration test topology

Data Privacy. For VM service data privacy testing, topology as shown in the Fig. 2, using the ping command and the port scanning tool to test whether different users have cloud host network isolation, in addition, we can also test whether one user has group isolation mechanism.

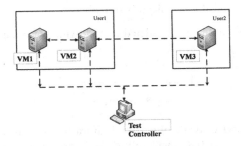

Fig. 2. Data privacy test topology

3.2 Monitoring

Monitoring for cloud services are focus on performance including CPU, disk I/O, memory and network indexes, and the system are illustrated in Fig. 3. Performance testing and monitoring methods are as follows:

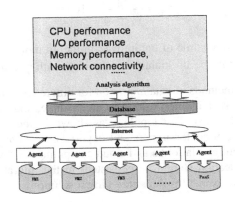

Fig. 3. Monitoring system

- CPU: Run the specified number of transactions to test the CPU value of TPS. To put in details, record the time of computing 1000000 bits after the PI decimal point.
- I/O: Write the large file to the disk sequentially and randomly, and record statistic of read and write IO bytes per second, which is IOPS number.
- Memory: Write the large file to the memory sequentially and randomly, and do a statistic of read and write IO bytes per second, which is IOPS number.
- Network: Test the bandwidth maximum throughput and stability.

4 Certification Results

The above evaluating methods have been applied in the Trusted Cloud Certification of China. So far, 35 cloud services by 19 CSPs have been certified and 34 cloud services by 23 CSPs are being certified. Table 2 gives the results of certified trusted cloud services. More results are summarized in [6].

Table 2. Certied trusted cloud services

Elastic Computing (16)	Object Storage (9)	Database (8)	PaaS (1)	Block Storage (1)
Alibaba ECS	Alibaba OSS	Alibaba RDS(MySQL)		
China Telecom	China Telecom OOS			
China Mobile	China Mobile			
		Tencent NoSQL		
		Tencent MySQL		
UCloud Uhost		UCloud UDB (MySQL)		
	Sina Storage	Sina MySQL	Sina SAE	
	Baidu BCS	Baidu MySQL		
JD J CS	JD JSS			
ChinaCache				ChinaCache
21vianet	21viane	21viane SQL Server		
Net constellation	Net constellation			
Huawei	Huawei			
Kingsoft				
Inspur				
GDS				
Qihoo 360				
Youole		Youole		
SISDC				
China Mobile Gansu Province				

5 Conclusion

Above all, this paper proposes definition and a framework of evaluating for different kinds of trusted cloud services, the 17 indicators of which are in terms of three categories which are Data Control and Security, Service Quality & Performance and Rights Protection Clause. The evaluating methods are variety including SLA and Documents Review, Technical Testing & Operating System inspection and Monitoring. The framework and evaluating methods have been applied in China Trusted Cloud

Certification, and most Chinese CSPs have attended the certification. In the future, we will focus on performance and data security testing to improve this framework.

References

1. Garg, S.K., Versteeg, S., Buyya, R.: A framework for ranking of cloud computing services. Future Gener. Comput. Sys. **29**, 1012–1023 (2013)
2. Open Data Center Alliance, Inc.: Open Data Center Alliance Usage: Standard Units of Measure for IaaS (2011)
3. China Academy of Telecommunication Research of MIIT Senior Engineer, The Survey of China Public Cloud Market (2012)
4. China Communication Standard Alliance. Cloud Service Agreement Reference Framework. YDB144–2014 (2014)
5. Data Center Alliance. Assessment Method for Trusted Cloud Service Certification: Virtual Machine, Object Storage, Database, Block Storage, Caching Storage, Application Hosting Container and Online Application. Technical report (2014)
6. Data Center Alliance. Trusted Cloud Best Practice (2014)
7. DMTF CIMI. Cloud Infrastructure Management Interface (2013)

Enhanced AllJoyn Network
with Centralized Management

Linghan Li[(⊠)], Yonghua Li, Jiaru Lin, and Tianle Zhang

Key Lab of Universal Wireless Communitions (BUPT), Ministry of Education,
Beijing, China
{llh,liyonghua,jrlin,tlezhang}@bupt.edu.cn

Abstract. The Internet of things is an exciting vision which promises to connect people with things and things with each other in ways. AllJoyn system is proposed to establish the network at the right moment. The structure has been changed in this paper to realize centralized management and security, from bus to star topology, which make it more suitable for users, after changing the mechanics of the original system.

Keywords: Iot · AllJoyn · Centralized management · Security

1 Introduction

IoT (Internet of things) is a new Internet concept that tries to connect everything that can be connected to the Internet, where everything refers to people, cars, televisions (TVs), smart cameras, microwaves, sensors, and basically anything that has Internet-connection capability [6]. When things are connected to a network, they can work together in cooperation to provide the ideal service as a whole, not as a collection of independently working devices [7]. But there still exists many difficulties, like information exchanging across different kind of networks, devices random access and the need of strong support of various systems, platforms, networks and even programming languages. AllJoyn framework is brought into being when the occasion calls for it.

The AllJoyn open-source software system provides a framework for enabling communication among IoT devices across heterogeneous distributed software systems [1]. The AllJoyn system is a proximity-based, peer-to-peer communication platform for devices in a distributed system, which enables applications running on IoT devices to advertise, discover and connect to each other for making use of services offered on these devices. Peers can be connected over different access networks such as Wi-Fi, Bluetooth and PLC (in the future). AllJoyn-enabled devices run one or more AllJoyn applications and form a peer-to-peer AllJoyn network. The AllJoyn framework enables these applications to expose their functionality over the network via discoverable interfaces which are the contracts that define the functionality provided by the application. An AllJoyn application can play the role of a provider (or called server), a consumer (or called client) or both depending upon the service model. Provider applications implement services and advertise them over the AllJoyn network. Consumer applications interested in these services discover them via the AllJoyn network.

Y. Lu et al. (Eds.): ISCTCS 2014, CCIS 520, pp. 183–188, 2015.
DOI: 10.1007/978-3-662-47401-3_24

Consumer applications then connect to provider applications to make use of these services as desired. An AllJoyn application can act as both provider and consumer at the same time. This means that the app can advertise a certain set of services it supports, and can also discover and make use of services provided by other apps in the proximal AllJoyn network.

The AllJoyn framework's characteristic provides an ecosystem where various parties can continue by adding new features and enhancements to the AllJoyn system. It supports OS independence via an OS abstraction layer allowing the AllJoyn framework and its applications to run on multiple OS platforms. The AllJoyn framework supports most standard Linux distributions, Android 2.2 and later, common versions of Microsoft Windows OS, Apple iOS, Apple OS X and embedded OSs such as OpenWRT and RTOSs like ThreadX. The AllJoyn also supports multiple programming languages for writing applications and services for IoT devices, which enable a wide ecosystem for developing AllJoyn applications and services. The AllJoyn framework currently, supports C, C ++, Java, C#, JavaScript and Objective-C [1].

Figure 1 demonstrates an AllJoyn network with 4 devices. Device 1 and Device 2 have only Provider applications providing AllJoyn services. Device 3 has only consumer applications consuming services from other provider devices. Device 4 has an application which acts as both provider and consumer. The application on Device 4 consumes services from the application on Device 2. It also provides services which get consumed by applications on Device 3. Arrow directions are from provider to consumer indicating consumption of services [3].

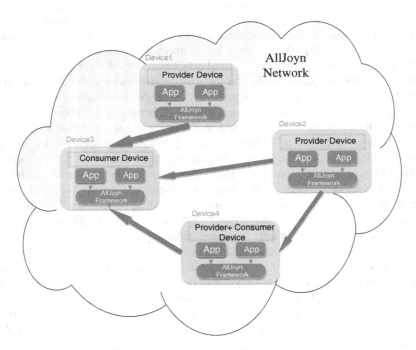

Fig. 1. An example of Alljoyn network

2   The Mechanics of the AllJoyn

2.1   Key Concepts of AllJoyn System

AllJoyn router: responsible for communication with other AllJoyn Routers and moves AllJoyn messages across the system. Performs work on behalf of an AllJoyn Thin Library. Can either be bundled into an application, on Android, iOS, etc. or can be a standalone process. This allows data to flow between applications at the lower level [2].

AllJoyn bus: a term used to describe the connection between applications and how data flows between applications at a lower level [2].

AllJoyn bus attachments: connects your app with the AllJoyn framework so API calls and callbacks can occur [2].

AllJoyn unique name: the AllJoyn router assigns a unique temporary name to each connecting application to enable addressing for individual applications [2].

AllJoyn well-known name: a consistent way to refer to a service (or collection of services) offered over the AllJoyn bus [2].

AllJoyn session: a group of applications that are connected, allowing them to exchange data [2].

2.2   The Work Flow of AllJoyn

Figure 2 shows the basic structure of the AllJoyn system as an example. The most basic abstraction in the AllJoyn framework is the software bus that ties everything together. The virtual distributed bus is implemented by AllJoyn routing nodes which are background programs running on each device. Providers and consumers (as peers) connect to the bus via bus attachments. The bus attachments live in the local processes of the consumers and providers and provide the interprocess communication that is required to talk to the local AllJoyn router.

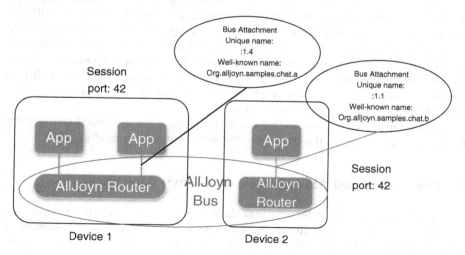

Fig. 2. The sample of basic structure of AllJoyn

Each bus attachment is assigned a unique name by AllJoyn system as the example shows above. A bus attachment can request to be granted a unique human-readable bus name that it can use to advertise itself to the rest of the AllJoyn network. This well-known bus name lives in a namespace that looks like a reversed domain name and encourages self-management of the namespace. The existence of a bus attachment of a specific name implies the further existence of at least one bus object that implements at least one interface specified by a name.

On one hand, after requesting and being granted the well-known bus name, an application will typically advertise the name as a provider to allow another applications to discover its service as consumers. The provider makes an advertise request to its local router. The router, based on input from the provider, decides what network medium-specific mechanism it should use to advertise the service and begins doing so. On the other hand, when a prospective consumer wants to locate a provider for consumption, it issues a find name request [3]. Its local router device, again based on input from the consumer, determines the best way to search and probes for advertisements. Once the devices move into proximity, they begin hearing each other's advertisements and discovery requests over whichever media are enabled.

The consumer and provider sides of the developing scenario both use methods and callbacks on their bus attachment object to make the requests to orchestrate the advertisement and discovery process. Before remote methods manage being called, a communication session must be formed to effectively join the separate bus segments. Advertisement and discovery are different from session establishment. One can receive an advertisement and take no action. It is only when an advertisement is received, and a consumer decides to take action to join a communication session, that the busses are logically joined into one. To accomplish this, a provider must create a communication session and advertise its existence; and a consumer must receive that advertisement and request to join the implied session. After both sides join the established session, the information exchanging begins, consumers are able to call remote services.

But there exist a few disadvantages. Because the original AllJoyn network topology is bus, there is no central control and management. The user information of AllJoyn-enabled devices can't be collected and stored as a log, the users' behavior can't be analyzed resulting lack of personalized services. Besides, as any two of the all devices in AllJoyn network could join in the same session and exchange information immediately without any protection, the AllJoyn architecture doesn't have the ability to ensure the security of every device in the network, anyone who join the proximal network are allowed to operate any devices.

So in the next section, some improvements are proposed to add central management to the AllJoyn system. At the same time, the security would be reinforced.

3   The Centralized Management of AllJoyn Appliances

Centralized management is brought into the system, which is the creative and core improvement and motivated mainly by the requirement of tight and management of AllJoyn appliances [5]. To achieve centralized management, the topology structure of the original AllJoyn network has to be transformed.

Any application connected to the traditional bus as a node can communicate with the nodes in network, like Fig. 3. The appliances connect to the bus over different access networks as motioned before. This topology is obviously not suitable for centralized management. As a result, AllJoyn appliances operating in the proximal area like home or office are managed by the only node which is called gateway server. So considering the goal above, the star topology is the exact mode and the node in the center is the gateway server, every appliance node connect to it to communicate with others, just as Fig. 4 shows below. A managing system in this open centralized management environment must be capable of supporting a number of different management protocols [8].

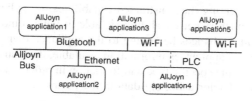

Fig. 3. The AllJoyn bus topology.

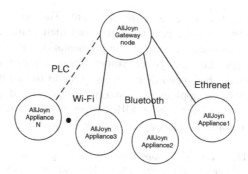

Fig. 4. The AllJoyn star topology

In order to transform the architecture, the mechanics of AllJoyn has to be modified. The auto advertisement is canceled in all the appliance nodes except the gateway. The gateway node acts as the only provider in the proximal network, providing the register and connect service to all the other appliances. The gateway server broadcast the service advertisement into the AllJoyn network, the other applications fetch the advertisement and analysis the information in the data packet, then sending the return value to the gateway server. After establishing the connection between gateway node and appliance nodes, they all join the same session, communicating through the exact same session port. The unregistered appliance are refused to connect with the gateway, so that the privacy of the users can be ensured as well as the security of the network. The entire AllJoyn network consists of a lot proximal networks, becoming a tree topology. When the appliances are called, the information is recorded and stored in the gateway node.

Acting as the appliances manager, the gateway server has the ability to control the entrance of AllJoyn network. Users can manipulate all the appliances through the gateway server in a centralized management manner. Once the appliance service request from the user is received, the gateway server sends the request to the corresponding appliance. As diverse access technologies such as Wi-Fi, BT, Ethernet and PLC can be used for appliances, to facilitate the centralized management of AllJoyn appliances, it is useful if the centralized gateway server supports multiple access technologies [5].

Appliance owners may share appliances functions/services with others under the protection of authority control. Appliance owners want to ensure that specific functions or services provided by their own appliances are not allowed for others to use. So that specific functions or services of an AllJoyn appliance can be accessed and used by authorized users. Considering the constrained capabilities of appliances, however, the gateway server with much richer capabilities is able to have some form of mandated control strategy for all appliances belonging to the appliance owner.

To collect and record appliances information available, there should be a file stored in the gateway server in the specific type and formation in order to transmit to the cloud and analyze the user behavior using big data in the future.

4 Conclusion

AllJoyn can promote gateway services development. The AllJoyn gateway service framework fulfills users' requirements of centralized management of AllJoyn appliances. It moves more complicated logic and implementation into the AllJoyn gateway server device and keeps the AllJoyn consumer device simpler and at lower cost. Management of appliances by a centralized gateway server device reduces the resource requirement on the AllJoyn appliances, resulting in gateway deployment with reasonable cost. The security of the whole AllJoyn network has been enhanced and the operation information stored in gateway server can be analyzed.

Acknowledgement. This work was supported by Beijing Natural Science Foundation (No. 4132015) and "Eleventh Five-year Plan" for Sci & Tech Research of China (No. 2012BAH38X), P. R. China.

References

1. Allseen-Alliance. https://allseenalliance.org/developer-resources
2. Allseen-Alliance. https://allseenalliance.org/alljoyn-framework-tutorial
3. Allseen-Alliance. https://allseenalliance.org/developer-resources/alljoyn/docsdownloads
4. Allseen-Alliance. https://wiki.allseenalliance.org/smarthome/overview
5. Abdelwahab, S., Hamdaoui, B., Guizani, M., Rayes, A.: Enabling smart cloud services through remote sensing. Internet Everything Enabler 1(3), 276–288 (2014)
6. Kobayashi, S., Koshizuka, N., Sakamura K.: An internet of things (IoT) architecture for embedded appliances. In: Humanitarian Technology Conference, pp. 314–319 (2013)
7. Willems, R.C.: centralized management in a distributed world. In: Network Operations and Management Symposium, pp. 819–830 (1994)

A Method of Evaluating Distributed Storage System Reliability

Hongjie Huang[✉] and Shuqiang Yang

School of Computer Science, National University of Defense Technology,
Changsha 410073, China
oj.nero@163.com, sqyang9999@126.com

Abstract. After analyzing evaluation methods of the data storage system reliability, we found there is not a set of generally accepted evaluation criteria for distributed storage system reliability. Based on reliability theory and probability method, a model is provided in this paper to evaluate the reliability of a given distributed system. This model evaluates the data reliability of the system by calculating successfully reading data probability and successfully writing data probability of the system. And then it provide a set of acceptable evaluation criteria for distributed storage system reliability.

Keywords: Distributed storage system · Data reliability · Successfully accessing data probability

1 Introduction

With the rapid development of information technology, data, generated by computers, show an explosive growth. The storage requirement of massive data drives the surge of distributed storage technology. As a series of distributed storage system emerged, the distributed storage systems based on large clusters are widely employed [1].

Reliability is an important indicator for evaluating system performance. For storage system, reliability should focus on data reliability of the system. It describes the capacity of storage system to provide data accessing services as required over specified time. Therefore, study on data reliability of distributed storage system plays a significant role in evaluating distributed storage systems.

In the new distributed storage system, like Hadoop, the data to store are divided into several data blocks with a certain specific size by system. Each data block will have specific numbers of copies, which will be stored on independent storage nodes. References [2,3] And the system protects data from disaster through its consistency and dynamically maintaining the numbers of copies. Traditional storage systems adopt backup-restore methods to secure data. Namely, systems require external backup systems to back up the data on its primary system, so the data can be recovered from the backup system when data are lost. Chervenak et al. [4] Compared with traditional storage system, distributed

© Springer-Verlag Berlin Heidelberg 2015
Y. Lu et al. (Eds.): ISCTCS 2014, CCIS 520, pp. 189–196, 2015.
DOI: 10.1007/978-3-662-47401-3_25

storage system does not have an external backup system. When the distributed storage system suffered a disaster, we wonder to know whether data on system are reliable or not and how is its reliability. However, there is not a set of generally accepted evaluation criteria for distributed storage system reliability.

Researches on data reliability of distributed storage system are done, and now we propose a method of evaluating distributed storage system reliability, providing a set of acceptable evaluation criteria for distributed storage system reliability.

2   Related Work

Reliability of computer system has been a topic of concern. Now it is generally accepted that reliability of computer system is measured by MTTF (Mean Time To Failure), which means how long the system could work properly before a failure occurs. Maintainability is measured by MTTR (MTTR, Mean Time To Repair), which means how long it takes to repair the system after system failure, while availability is measured by $MTTF/(MTTF + MTTR) * 100\%$. Rausand and Hoyland [5] Without an external backup system, once some data are lost, the distributed storage system would not be restored and no longer to provide data accessing services. Since there is still not a generally accepted evaluation criteria for distributed storage system reliability, the study on data reliability of distributed storage system will continue.

Traditional storage system uses backup-restore methods to secure data. A generally accepted method of evaluating storage system reliability is using RTO (Recovery Time Objective) and RPO (Recovery Point Objective) as evaluation indexes. References [6, 7] RTO describes how much time the system could provide data accessing services properly. RTO is bigger, and its reliability is higher. RPO describes the latest data backup point before a disaster. And then data written between RPO and disaster moment will be lost, so that if RPO more close to disaster moment, less data will lost and its reliability will be higher. However, this data reliability calculation model only applies to the storage system which external backup system is always available. Nowadays, distributed storage systems store massive data. For example, Google processes data of hundreds of Petabyte (PB), Facebook generates log data of over 10 PB per month. Chen et al. [8] Suppose that it uses external backup system, when disaster occurs and we have to uses external backup system to restore. Its long consuming time makes it unacceptable. Therefore, the current distributed storage system secure stored data through its own mechanisms instead of external backup system. A conclusion can be drawn that evaluation indexes of RTO and RPO are not applicable to distributed storage system.

According to the international standard SHARE78, disaster backup technical solution is divided into seven levels, which specifies several indexes including RTO, RPO, data loss, disaster recovery center, backup mode, host state, etc. Liu and Qi [9] This standard applies to evaluate reliability of the system in which level, but unable to explain whether each index meet its requirement. Therefore, this standard does not apply to the evaluation of distributed storage system either.

Reference [10] proposed a simple probability model and the model based on the failure probability density function for data reliability of distributed storage system. The simple probability model assumes that all nodes are independent of each other, and their failure probability is fixed, and each node is in normal state or failed state. Different states of each node constitute the system status. This model is to calculate the probability of each state and accumulate all the probability which meet the requirements. The result is the index of data reliability. This model describes the probability that the system does not lost data. The calculation is simple and easy, so it's applicable to simple and quick assessment. The model based on the failure probability density function assumes that each node has its probability density function $f(t)$, and node failure probability at time T is $f(t)$ integral from Time 0 to Time T. As the simple probability model, this model is to calculate the probability of each state and accumulate all the probability which meet the requirements. The result is the index of data reliability. This model describes the probability that the system does not lost data and takes the effect of time on the failure probability of each node into account. It evaluates the capacity of system to secure data but not access data.

Data reliability of distributed storage system describes the capacity of distributed storage system to provide data accessing services as required over specified time. As a result, we constructed a model focusing on the capacity of system to provide data accessing services properly. We referenced to node failure probability density function $f(t)$ in [10] and analyzed the relationship between nodes. Then we construct a system data reliability model, which evaluates distributed storage system by successfully reading data probability and successfully writing data probability of the system.

3 Successfully Accessing Data Probability Model

3.1 Basic Idea

Data reliability of distributed storage system describes the capacity of distributed storage system to provide data accessing services as required. If we measure data reliability of a distributed storage system from the view of a system user, we mainly consider following two aspects.

1. The capacity of system to provide reading data services
2. The capacity of system to provide writing data services

We propose to use successfully reading data probability and successfully writing data probability to evaluate the capacity of above two aspects.

A distributed storage system is constituted of multiple server nodes. When the user stores data into it, it will divide data into several data blocks with a certain specific size. Each data block will have specific numbers of copies, which will be stored on independent storage nodes.

Considering the system processes data in units of data blocks, we can analyze the system from data blocks. Every data block is stored on independent nodes.

We could calculate successfully accessing data probability of each data block, which is referenced to [10]. In addition, we could work out successfully accessing data probability of system.

For a node in the distributed storage system, its failure time is uncertain, which is not only associated with properties of the node itself, but also affected by the working status of the node. Therefore, each node has its failure probability density function $f(t)$, and we can get node failure probability at time T [10] as below.

$$F(T) = \int_o^T f(t)dt. \tag{1}$$

The calculation methods of successfully reading data probability of system and successfully writing data probability of system will be given in detail in following sections.

3.2   Successfully Reading Data Probability of System

When we discuss system whether providing reading data services properly, we should consider two aspects. Firstly, whether the data block to read exists and whether the copy is intact or not. Secondly, if the data block exists, whether there will be failures in reading process.

In distributed storage system, every data block has specific numbers of copies on different nodes. If one of the nodes fails, we assume that the data stored on the node is not available. If all the nodes which store copies of one data block work properly, we believe the data block is intact. However, if one of the nodes which store copies of one data block fails, we assume that some copies of the data block is lost and the system will maintain the copies based on its consistency strategy. Moreover, if all the nodes which store copies of one data block fail, we believe this data block is lost and it is impossible to restore.

Supposing there are n copies of a data block, each data block is restored on n different nodes. The status of these nodes can be represented as an n-dimensional vector $\theta = (s_1, s_2, s_3, ..., s_n)$, $s_i \in \{0, 1\}$. $s_i = 0$ represents the i-th node failed, and $s_i = 1$ represents the i-th node working properly. Because of the independent nodes, the occurrence probability P_θ of status θ at time T is shown as below,

$$P_\theta = \prod_{i=1, s_i=0}^{n} F_i(T) \prod_{i=1, s_i=1}^{n} (1 - F_i(T)). \tag{2}$$

where $F_i(T)$ is the i-th node failure probability at time T.

In distributed storage systems, if copies of the data block exists, the storage system will select an available copy to provide reading data services according to the copy selection strategy. If the node of the copy fails in the reading process, the reading process will fail this time.

As supposing above, the status of nodes is an n-dimensional vextor θ. According to the copy selection strategy, every available node has different probability

e_i to be selected. And the successfully reading data probability P_Π under status θ is shown as below,

$$P_\Pi = \sum_{i=1, s_i=1}^{n} (1 - F_i(T))e_i. \tag{3}$$

where $F_i(T)$ is the i-th node failure probability at time T.

Moreover, the successfully reading data probability of a data block under status θ is $\gamma P_\theta P_\pi$. γ is a coefficient which describes how the system maintaining copies operation affects the data accessing services when some copies are lost. There are 2^n cases in total for status θ. And the successfully reading data probability P_{rb} of the data block is

$$P_{rb} = \sum_{j=1}^{2^n} \gamma_j P_{\theta_j} P_{\pi_j}. \tag{4}$$

Supposing there are N nodes in the system ($N \geq n$), every data block selects n nodes to store copies and there will be $S = C_N^n$ cases for the combination of selected nodes. Based on the data distribution strategy, each combination has probability c_k to be selected. And the successfully reading data probability P_r of system is

$$P_r = \sum_{k=1}^{S} P_{rb_k} c_k. \tag{5}$$

The value range of successfully reading data probability P_r of system is from 0 to 1. The greater the probability P_r that the system provides data reading services more properly, the higher the data reliability of system is; on the contrary, the lower the data reliability of system is.

3.3 Successfully Writing Data Probability of System

In distributed storage systems, the data to store is divided into several data blocks by system. Every data block will have specific numbers of copies, which will be stored on independent storage nodes. The successfully writing data probability of system is related to the copies consistency strategy of system. In writing process, a data block should be written into specific numbers of nodes, which is specified by system copies consistency strategy. Some copies consistency strategy require only one or two nodes are written [11], but some copies consistency strategy require most of or all nodes [12].

Supposing there are n copies for a data block in the system, n nodes will be selected to store copies. The status of these nodes can be represented as an n-dimensional vector $\varphi = (u_1, u_2, u_3, ..., u_n), u_i \in \{0, 1\}$. $u_i = 0$ represents the i-th node will fail in writing process, and $u_i = 1$ represents the i-th node will work properly. And the successfully writing data probability P_φ of these n nodes is shown as below,

$$P_\varphi = \sum_{\varphi} (\prod_{i=1, u_i=0}^{n} F_i(T) \prod_{i=1, u_i=1}^{n} (1 - F_i(T))). \tag{6}$$

where $F_i(T)$ is the i-th node failure probability at time T. The status φ involved in the calculation should be the status which number of properly working nodes satisfied the number specified by the copies consistency strategy.

As supposing as last section, there are N nodes in the system $(N \geq n)$, every data block selects n nodes to store copies and there will be $S = C_N^n$ cases for the combination of selected nodes. According to the data distribution strategy, each combination has probability c_k to be selected. And the successfully writing data probability P_w of system is

$$P_w = \sum_{k=1}^{S} P_{\varphi_k} c_k. \tag{7}$$

The value range of successfully writing data probability P_w of system is from 0 to 1. The greater the probability P_w that the system provides data writing services more properly, the higher the data reliability of system is; on the contrary, the lower the data reliability of system is.

In conclusion, we have constructed a system data reliability model for distributed storage systems. This model evaluates the data reliability of the system by calculating successfully reading data probability and successfully writing data probability of the system.

4 Experiment

According to the model above, we suppose that there are 10 nodes in the distributed storage system and the number of copies is 3. The copies distribution strategy adopts balanced distribution. All node failure probabilities are a fixed constant. The system maintaining copies operation does not affect the data accessing services when some copies is lost ($\gamma = 1$). Increasing the node failure

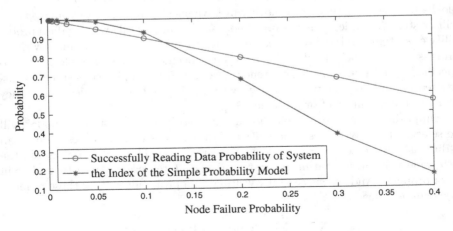

Fig. 1. Curves of the successfully reading data probability of system

probabilities, the curve of the successfully reading data probability of system should decline. Experimental results are shown in Fig. 1.

This experiment use the simple probability model in [10] for comparison. As shown in Fig. 1, the successfully reading data probability of system is decreasing, while the node failure probabilities is increasing. So we can believe that the data reliability of system also decreases as expected.

Then each node failure probability is fixed at 0.1. And a data block should be written into all nodes. Increasing the number of copies, the curve of the successfully reading data probability of system should rise, but the curve of the successfully writing data probability of system should decline. Experimental results are shown in Fig. 2.

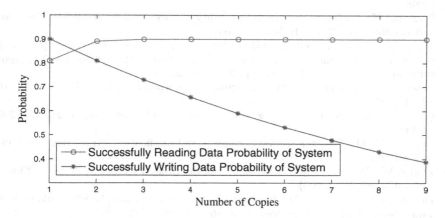

Fig. 2. Curves of successfully accessing data probability of system

As shown in Fig. 2, the successfully reading data probability of system is increasing with the number of copies increasing, and the successfully writing data probability of system is decreasing with the number of copies increasing as expected.

5   Conclusion

In this paper, we analyzed the characteristics of a distributed storage system and traditional methods of evaluating data storage system reliability. Then, we constructed a successfully accessing data probability model to evaluate the data reliability of system by calculating successfully reading data probability and successfully writing data probability of system. This model is simple and easy to apply to a distributed storage system. We think it could become a set of acceptable evaluation criteria for distributed storage system reliability.

Acknowledgments. This work is supported by National High Technology Research and Development Plan of China (863 plan) (No. 2012AA012600, 2012AA01A401, 2012AA01A402).

References

1. Hsu, C.W., Wang, C.W., Shieh, S.: Reliability and Security of Large Scale Data Storage in Cloud Computing. The Reliability Society 2010 Annual Technical Report. pp. 1–7 (2010)
2. Ghemawat, S., Gobioff, H., Leung, S.-T.: The google file system. ACM SIGOPS Oper. Syst. Rev. **37**, 29–43 (2003)
3. Shvachko, K., Kuang, H., Radia, S., Chansler, R.: The hadoop distributed file system. In: 2010 IEEE 26th Symposium on Mass Storage Systems and Technologies (MSST), pp. 1–10 (2010)
4. Chervenak, A., Vellanki, V., Zachary, K.: Protecting file systems: a survey of backup techniques. In: Joint NASA IEEE Mass Storage Conference, pp. 17–32 (1998)
5. Rausand, M., Hoyland, A.: System Reliability Theory: Models, Statistical Methods, and Applications. Wiley, Hoboken (2004)
6. Yang, Q., Xiao, W., Ren, J.: TRAP-Array: a disk array architecture providing timely recovery to any point-in-time. In: Proceeding of the International Symposium on Computer Architecture, pp. 289–300 (2006)
7. Benton, D.: Disaster recovery: a pragmatists viewpoint. Disaster Recover. J. **20**, 79–81 (2007)
8. Chen, M., Mao, S., Liu, Y.: Big data: a survey. Mob. Netw. Appl. **19**, 171–209 (2014)
9. Liu, Y., Qi, M.: Disaster recovery: concept and application. Appl. Res. Comput. **6**, 7–10 (2002)
10. Zhang, W., Ma, J., Yang, X.: Reliability of distributed storage systems. J. Xidian Univ. **36**, 480–485 (2009)
11. DeCandia, G., Hastorun, D., Jampani, M.: Dynamo: amazons highly available key-value store. ACM SIGOPS Oper. Syst. Rev. **41**, 205–220 (2007)
12. Borthakur, D.: HDFS architecture guide. Hadoop Apache Proj. **53**, 3–14 (2008)

DDoS Detection Based on Second-Order Features and Machine Learning

Xiaowei He[1(✉)], Shuyuan Jin[1], Yunxue Yang[1], and Huiqiang Chi[2]

[1] CAS Key Laboratory of Network Data Science and Technology,
Institute of Computing Technology, Chinese Academy of Sciences,
Beijing, China
hexiaowei@software.ict.ac.cn
[2] School of Mechanical Engineering, University of Shanghai for Science
and Technology, Shanghai, China

Abstract. In recent years, there appeared several new forms of DDoS attacks, such as DDoS using botnet, DNS Amplification attack and NTP Amplification attack, posing a great threat to network security and seriously affecting the stability and reliability of the network. Therefore, detecting the DDoS attacks accurately and timely has positive significance to mitigate DDoS attacks as soon as possible and reduce the impact of DDoS attacks. Previously, most of the researchers focused on extracting features of traffic and finding effective approaches to detect DDoS attack, while ignoring the correlativity between features. This paper applies second-order features to machine learning algorithms in order to study the correlativity between features and use sliding window mechanism to improve the model. We use KDD CUP 99 dataset for evaluating the methods. The evaluation results show that the correlativity between features can accurately differentiate DDoS attacks from normal traffic.

Keywords: Covariance matrix · Second-order feature · Machine learning · Anomaly detection

1 Introduction

In recent years, there appeared several new forms of DDoS attack, such as DDoS using botnet, DNS Amplification attack, NTP Amplification attack and so on, posing a great threat to network security and seriously affecting the stable and reliable operation of the network. In March 2013, Europe's anti-spam company Spamhaus suffered a large scale DDoS attack with attack traffic as high as 300 Gbps, which was the largest attack traffic in the history. Hackers used the DNS reflection technology and open DNS servers to launch the attack. In February 2014, some companies protected by Incapsula Company suffered the biggest DDoS attack in history, which reached at its peak 400 Gbps of attack traffic. DDoS attack has become an important weapon for business competition and even cyber warfare between countries.

DDoS (Distributed denial-of-service) attack aims to make network service unavailable by occupying network bandwidth and consuming targets' resources. Thus DDoS attack will cause the traffic of target network abnormal. There are two ways to detect cyber-attack: misuse detection and anomaly detection [1]. In misuse detection approaches,

© Springer-Verlag Berlin Heidelberg 2015
Y. Lu et al. (Eds.): ISCTCS 2014, CCIS 520, pp. 197–205, 2015.
DOI: 10.1007/978-3-662-47401-3_26

we define abnormal network behavior at first, and then any other behavior will be treated as normal behavior. Misuse detection approaches can detect known attacks and differentiate attack types effectively, but it has a fatal flaw that it cannot detect unknown attacks. Compared with misuse detection, anomaly detection can detect unknown attacks [2]. Anomaly detection approaches learns a norm profile for the normal behavior from normal traffic, and any other behavior deviated much from the norm profile is anomaly. However, anomaly detection has difficult in distinguishing the specific type of attack.

In this paper, we have improved the existing covariance matrix model by applying a sliding window mechanism. We compared the covariance matrix model without sliding window and that with sliding window by applying machine learning algorithms to KDD CUP 99 dataset. The result showed that the improved model can identify attack more quickly and more accurately. Moreover, we discussed the impact of the sequence length and sliding window size in the covariance matrix model.

The remainder of this paper is organized as follows: Sect. 2 discusses about the related works. Section 3 introduces the methods of the improved covariance matrix model describing the correlativity between traffic features. In Sect. 4, we compared the two models based on experimental results. At last, we concluded our work in Sect. 5.

2   Related Works

Among anomaly detection methods, machine learning is the most widely used technique in recent years [3], such as Markov models [4], Naïve Bayesian classifier [5]. For combining the advantages of different algorithms, more and more researchers applied two or more different algorithms to anomaly detection, Reif, M. [6] combined decision trees and parametric densities, Ndong, J. [7] use combined statistical methods to decrease the false alarm rates.

Daniel S. Yeung proposed a covariance matrix model to detect various flooding. Daniel used second-order features to characterize the detected flooding attacks [1]. But the covariance matrix model used in detection is not timely and the correlativity between records in time series is not considered fully.

Anomaly detection based on machine learning need to extract features of cyber flow. These traffic features can be divided into three classes: packet-based features, connection-based features and interval-based features. This paper discusses the correlativity between interval-based features.

How to extract flow features that can distinguish normal traffic from abnormal traffic included different kinds of attacks is always a challenge in intrusion detection domain. Daniel S. Yeung [1] put forward a covariance matrix model which extracted second-order features characterizing the correlativity between features based on one-order interval-based features. The covariance matrix model extend n records of p features to one record of $p(p + 1)/2$ features. This approach reduced the number of records and increased the length of feature vector. In one word, this method obtains a longer feature vector at the sacrifice of the number of flow records.

In this paper, the covariance matrix model is improved by introducing a sliding windows. With the improved covariance matrix model, anomaly detection become more accurate and timely.

3   The Improved Covariance Matrix Model

This paper uses the covariance matrix model to extend fundamental one-order features to second-order features characterizing the correlativity between one-order features, from p-dimension to $p(p + 1)/2$-dimension. In [1], the sequence length n is set for 150, and the relationship between network flow feature vectors on the time series and their flow feature matrices is illustrated as follows [1].

The covariance matrix model computes once every 5 min if time interval is 2 s and the number of feature vectors in each network flow feature matrix is 150. So when there is abnormal traffic in the network, the detection model of covariance matrix cannot alert in time. And because there is no overlap between traffic feature matrices, the correlativity between feature records on time series is not fully considered. For example, the correlativity between feature vector x_{m-1} and feature vector x_{m+1} in Fig. 1 is not reflected. For solving this problem, we introduces the sliding window algorithm.

$$x_1, x_2, x_3, \ldots, x_m \quad x_{m+1}, x_{m+2}, \ldots, x_{2m} \qquad x_{k(m+1)}, \ldots, x_{2km}$$

Fig. 1. Network flow feature matrices without overlap

In order to detect DDoS attacks timely and keep the correlativity between adjacent network flow feature matrices, we apply sliding window algorithm to the covariance matrix model. In the improved model, the IDS compute the covariance matrix and judge whether it is abnormal or not every s feature records, where s is the number of feature records moving forwards every time on time series. For example, when s is two, the relationship between network flow feature vectors on time series and their network flow feature matrices is illustrated as Fig. 2.

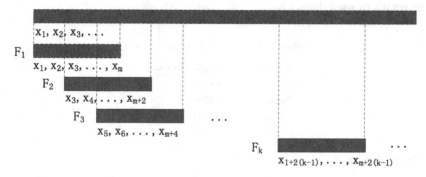

F_1 $x_1, x_2, x_3, \ldots$

$x_1, x_2, x_3, \ldots, x_m$

F_2

$x_3, x_4, \ldots, x_{m+2}$

F_3

$x_5, x_6, \ldots, x_{m+4}$

F_k

$x_{1+2(k-1)}, \ldots, x_{m+2(k-1)}$

Fig. 2. Overlapping network flow feature matrices

4   Experiment and Evaluation

In this section, to verify the improved covariance matrix model, several experiments are performed based on KDD CUP 99 dataset and three machine learning algorithms, which are Decision tree, Naïve Bayes and KNN.

4.1   Dataset

The KDD CUP 99 dataset is made for The Third International Knowledge Discovery and Data Mining Tools Competition. Afterwards, the KDD CUP 99 dataset is widely used for the evaluation of intrusion detection algorithm. The dataset extracts 41 features describing different traffic behavior, and only nine of them are time-based features. According to [8], we select 4 important features in our experiments as described in Table 1.

Table 1. Four important features from [8]

Feature name	Description	Type
Count	number of connections to the same host as the current connection in the past two seconds	continuous
serror_rate	% of connections that have "SYN" errors	continuous
srv_count	number of connections to the same service as the current connection in the past two seconds	continuous
srv_rerror_rate	% of connections that have "REJ" errors	continuous

This paper uses a subset of KDD CUP dataset: kddcup.data_10 %. We only use the data labeled as normal, Smurf or Neptune for evaluating the detection approaches and the improved covariance matrix model. As the number of records whose label is pod, back, land and teardrop is too little, we did not use these attacks records. In Table 2, we list the details of used dataset.

Table 2. Dataset used in experiments

Label	Sample number
Normal	97278
Smurf	280790
Neptune	107201

4.2   Experiments

We extend 4-dimension feature vector to 10-dimension feature vector in both the training and testing phase at first. Secondly, we train the classifier using 10-dimension feature vector as the input of classification algorithm. Finally, we examine the classifier and evaluate the performance of different machine learning algorithms.

Scikit-learn is a python module. It is very convenient and helpful for researchers using machine learning algorithms. We make use of sklearn module and four features of Table 1 to obtain the optimal sequence length n and moving steps in covariance matrix model. For measuring the accuracy of the classifier, F-Measure is used for evaluating the testing result. Besides, we care about whether the classifier can distinguish the attack type or not, so we adopted a CC_RATE (Correctly Classified Rate, defined as follows) to identify the precision of the attack types of classification.

$$CC\_rate = \frac{The\ number\ of\ records\ that\ accurately}{The\ size\ of\ test\ set} \tag{1}$$

The dataset listed in Table 2 is divided into two parts randomly. Nine-tenth of it is used for training the decision tree classifier, and the left is used for testing. This process is run ten times randomly. At last, we compute the average of F1-Measure value of ten times and the average of CC_RATE.

A. Covariance matrix model. According to the way illustrated in Fig. 1, we construct flow feature matrix, where the feature number p is 4 and the sequence length n is 10, 20, 30... 300. Using decision tree algorithm, we get the relationship between accuracy and n as Fig. 3. From Fig. 3 we find that the detection accuracy has little relationships with the sequence length n.

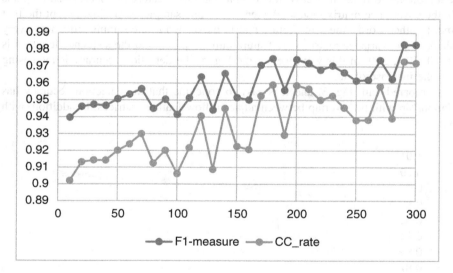

Fig. 3. Relationships between sequence length and accuracy with decision tree and the covariance matrix model

For a further discussion, we use the other two machine learning algorithms: Naïve Bayes and KNN, and the comparison as Fig. 4. The Fig. 4 shows that the detection accuracy has a slight increase with the increase of the sequence length, only with Naïve Bayes algorithm, they has a positive correlation.

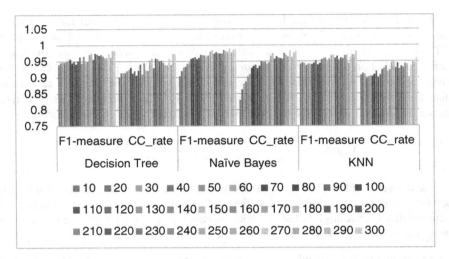

Fig. 4. Relationships between sequence length and accuracy with machine learning and the covariance matrix model

B. Improved covariance matrix model. On the basis of Fig. 2, we take into consideration the correlativity between two adjacent traffic feature matrices. Assuming s is 10, the covariance matrix model take ten new traffic samples each time except the first time. In other words, the flow feature matrix moves ten traffic samples forwards every calculating covariance matrix. The feature number p is 4 and the sequence length n is 10, 20, 30... 300. In this way, we get the Fig. 5, the detection accuracy is increasing with the increase of n.

Compared with Fig. 3, and it is easy to conclude that the detection accuracy has relationship with the overlap between adjacent flow feature matrices. In addition, with

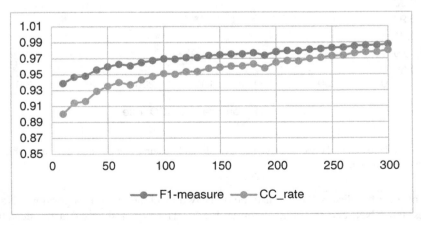

Fig. 5. Relationships between sequence length and accuracy with decision tree and the improved covariance matrix model

the increase of the sequence length n, the detection accuracy increase more stable than that in Fig. 3.

In the same way, we get the relations between the sequence length and the detection accuracy using the other two kinds of machine learning algorithms: Naïve Bayes and KNN, as shown in Fig. 6.

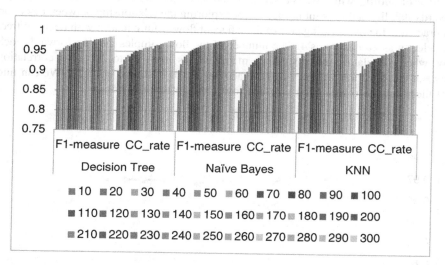

Fig. 6. Relationships between sequence length and accuracy with machine learning and the improved covariance matrix model

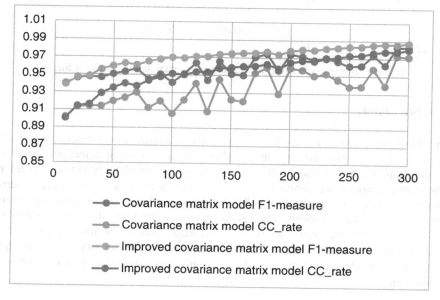

Fig. 7. Comparison of the two models using decision tree

By combining Fig. 3 and 5, we get Fig. 7. It is easy to find that the detection accuracy rate curve of the improved model is smoother and more perfect. One of the most import reason that the curve grows more stable is the application of the correlativity between two adjacent traffic feature matrices.

C. Size of sliding window. We set n to 200 since the detection accuracy is tending towards stability at that point in Fig. 7. For exploring the relationship between detection accuracy and the overlapping size of the adjacent flow feature matrix with decision tree, we select n as 200 and p as 4. The number of the flow samples moving forwards each time when calculating the covariance matrix varies from 10 to 200. The correlation between the detection accuracy and the Moving Steps is shown in Fig. 8. We can find that the small the overlapping size, the lower the detection accuracy.

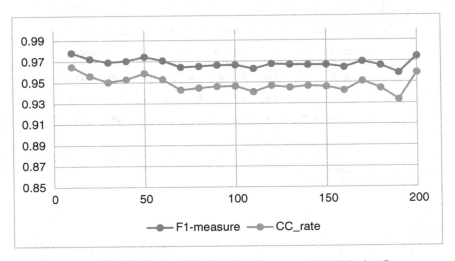

Fig. 8. Correlation between the detection accuracy and the Moving Steps

5   Conclusion

This paper applies covariance matrix model to characterize the correlativity between time-based features and increases the number of features used in detection algorithm. For detecting attack behavior in time and keeping the correlativity between adjacent flow feature matrices, we improved the covariance matrix model with sliding window algorithm. Finally, we use the KDD CUP 99 dataset and machine learning algorithms to conduct several experiments. The results show that the correlativity between time-based features not only can effectively differentiate DoS attack traffic from normal traffic, but also can identify specific DoS attack types. Our future work will apply this method to more DoS attack types and performing this experiment in a real network environment.

Acknowledgement. This work is supported by the Natural Science Foundation of China (Grant No. 61202058).

References

1. Yeung, D.S., Jin, S.: Covariance matrix modeling and detecting various flooding attacks. IEEE Trans. Syst. Man Cybern. Part A Syst. Hum. **13**, 222–232 (2007)
2. Denning, D.E.: An intrusion-detection model. IEEE Trans. Softw. Eng. **13**, 222–232 (1987)
3. García-Teodoro, P., Díaz-Verdejo, J., Maciá-Fernández, G., Vázquez, E.: Anomaly-based network intrusion detection: techniques, systems and challenges. Comput. Secur. **28**(1–2), 18–28 (2009). ISSN: 0167-4048
4. Tan, X., Xi, H.: Hidden semi-markov model for anomaly detection. Appl. Math. Comput. **205** (2), 562–567 (2008). ISSN: 0096-3003
5. Vijayasarathy, R., Raghavan, S.V., Ravindran, B.: A system approach to network modeling for DDoS detection using a Naïve Bayesian classifier. In: 2011 Third International Conference on Communication Systems and Networks (COMSNETS), pp. 1–10, 4–8 January 2011
6. Reif, M., Goldstein, M., Stahl, A., Breuel, T.M.: Anomaly detection by combining decision trees and parametric densities. In: 2008 19th International Conference on Pattern Recognition, ICPR 2008, pp. 1–4, 8–11 December 2008
7. Ndong, J., Salamatian, K.: A robust anomaly detection technique using combined statistical methods. In: Proceedings of the 2011 Ninth Annual Communication Networks and Services Research Conference (CNSR 2011). IEEE Computer Society, Washington, pp. 101–108
8. Chebrolu, S., Abraham, A., Thomas, J.P.: Feature deduction and ensemble design of intrusion detection systems. Comput. Secur. **24**(4), 295–307 (2005)

Construction of Software and Hardware Resource Pool in Data Center Using Virtualization

Na Ye[1(✉)], Lili Dong[1], Genqing Bian[1], and Jian Li[2]

[1] School of Information and Control Engineering,
Xi'an University of Architecture and Technology, Xi'an, China
yenanaye2003@126.com, {donglilixjd, bgq_00}@163.com
[2] Shaanxi Electricity Information Communication Co. Ltd., Xi'an, China
ali88.vip@qq.com

Abstract. With the development of enterprise informationization, the information systems become more complexity and their maintenance is becoming more difficult, the infrastructures are frequently expanded while the ratio of the utilization of software and hardware resources is relatively low. To address the issue, a method of constructing software and hardware pools in the data center using cloud computing and virtualization technologies is proposed in the paper. The design of key fields in resource pool construction are described, which includes server field design, network field design, storage field design, safety field design, data backup field design and the software's entering- in-pool design. The application of the proposed construction method to the data center of a provincial electric power company shows that the method could produce a certain administrative and economic benefits.

Keywords: Cloud computing · Virtualization · Resource pool · Data center

1 Introduction

With the improvement of the enterprise information construction, the counts and types of the information systems are increased sustainably, and the scale of the information communication infrastructure is expanded gradually. Take an electrical company for an example, it has 82 information systems, 375 servers, and the occupation rate of the server cabinets is 96.19 %, but the availability of the software and hardware resources is very low. The average utilization rate of the servers' CPU is about 8 % and that of the memory is 41.3 %. Moreover, large amount of equipment are still purchased every year and many information systems are put into operation. The growth of the requirement of the infrastructure construction and the information system maintenance leads to the increasing of cost and the complexity of maintenance and resource waste.

To address the problems, software and hardware resource pool construction using the cloud computing and virtualization technology is an efficient way. Cloud computing is a network-based computing model through which the shared software and hardware resources could be provided to computers and other equipment on demand [1]. It provides three types of services, that is, taking the Infrastructure as a Service (IaaS),

© Springer-Verlag Berlin Heidelberg 2015
Y. Lu et al. (Eds.): ISCTCS 2014, CCIS 520, pp. 206–212, 2015.
DOI: 10.1007/978-3-662-47401-3_27

the Platform as a Service (PaaS), and the Software as a Service (SaaS) [2–4]. The construction of resource pool in the data center is the key to implement cloud computing [1, 5]. The computing resources, storage resources and network resources in the data center are constructed into a dynamic virtual resource pool using virtualization technique so that the automatic deployment, dynamic extension and on-demand allocation of cloud resources can be easily achieved.

2 Resource Pool Design

In resource pool construction, some key points should be considered. On the hardware pool construction, the aspects to be considered include the server field design, network field design, storage field design, safety field design and data backup field design. On the software pool construction, the requirements coming from different softwares including databases, middlewares and some special applications when they are entering the pool should be considered.

2.1 Hardware Resource Pool Construction

2.1.1 The Logical Architecture

From the composing of the resource pool, the hardware resource pool generally can be classed into X86 virtual pool, X86 physical pool and minicomputer pool. These three types of pools which are connected to the cloud resource management platform through the adapter for unified management provide resources for application systems with different requirements. The logical architecture of the hardware resource pool is shown in Fig. 1.

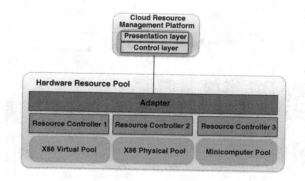

Fig. 1. Logical architecture of the hardware resource pool

In the X86 virtual pool, the servers, network components and storage devices are put into a pool using virtualization technique shielding the concrete hardware characteristics. The X86 physical pool is used to support those systems which are not suitable to run in the virtual pool, or which have high requirement for the computing resources or which depend on some special devices such as dongles and COM components. The minicomputer pool composed of various types of minicomputer is fit for the data process services requiring high reliability and throughput such as OLTP/OLAP.

2.1.2   Server Field Design

The server field refers to the combination of servers which have the same function. In order to reduce the resource fragments and improve the resource availability, the X86 virtual pool is uniformly scheduled through the virtualization management platform with the adapter in the cloud. The deployment architecture is shown in Fig. 2. The X86 physical pool and minicomputer pool need not to be virtualized and only monitoring tools are needed to be installed.

2.1.3   Network Field Design

According to the application, the network resources can be divided into application network, management network and storage network [7]. In accordance with the information system classified protection requirement, the network resource pool is classified to Level 2 protection area and Level 3 protection area. The two areas are isolated by physical devices in order to guarantee the network safety. The network resources are uniformly managed through VLAN plan, IP plan and port plan. Figure 3 shows the safety isolation design on the application network, management network and storage network according to the classified protection requirement.

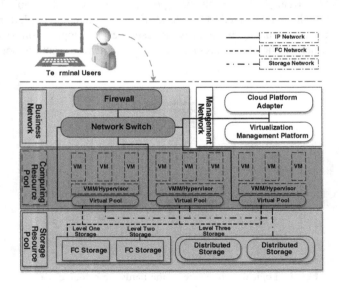

Fig. 2. Deploy architecture for the X86 virtual pool

2.1.4   Storage Field Design

The storage resource pool is divided into Level 1 storage, Level 2 storage and Level 3 storage according to the requirements of computing resource and business systems.

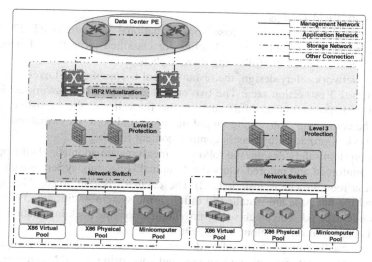

Fig. 3. Design of the network field

Level 1 storage provides high centralized storage and is mainly used to store business data. Level 2 storage is designed to meet the needs of virtual machine images for storage resource. Level 3 storage is a distributed storage and used to store virtual machine templates, ISO files of operation systems, copies of virtual machines, install packages of commonly used softwares and other data from applications with mess-storage requirement. Through the storage virtualization, the physical storages are detached from their logical representation, which shields the bottom hardwares and brings benefits like storage flexibility, unified schedule and strong extensibility. The design of storage resource pool is shown in Fig. 4.

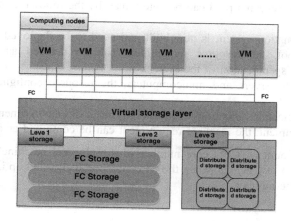

Fig. 4. Design of the storage field

2.1.5   Safety Field Design

The design of the safety field is based on the national standard GB/T 22239-2008 "Information security technology— Baseline for classified protection of information system" [8] and includes the following three aspects.

On the Network safety design, the resource pool is classified to Level 2 protection area and Level 3 protection area. The two areas are isolated by network devices and facilitated with protection methods such as the firewall and the intrusion detection system. The communication among virtual machines and between virtual machine and outer network is protected by access control, content filtering etc.

On the system safety design, the following measures are adopted: (1) the operating system is reinforced and tailored. Only the "minimal" operating system which satisfies the business requirement is installed. (2) The database is reinforced. The operating system and the database are installed in different file system partitions. (3) The safety patches are reinforced. The patch server providing automatic pack installation, test and rollback is deployed on the cloud management node.

On the virtualization platform safety design, the network's division into application network, management network and storage network using VLAN technique implements the data isolation of the three types of networks.

2.1.6   Data Backup Field Design

For the backup method, the SAN(Storage Area Network) Server-Free strategy [9, 10] is adopted because it can transfer data directly from the bottom storage array to the backup media and the backup data stream need not go through the production server so that the backup process will not occupy the CPU resource and other resources on the production server.

2.2   Software Resource Pool Construction

The software resource pool is mainly composed by databases, middlewares and other special applications and services. The resource requirement of application systems when entering the resource pool can be determined by the following methods:

(1) If the information system is new built and need to be deployed directly in the resource pool, the resource requirement can be decided according to the requirement specification of the system.
(2) For the X86 servers and minicomputers, the resource configuration will not change.
(3) For the applications migrating from the physical X86 environment to the virtual X86 environment, the resource requirement can be computed as follows:

- CPU amount = ⌈CPU core number of the physical machine*the maximum utilization of CPU*2⌉, when the CPU number after round up is odd, then add one to the number.

- Memory capacity = ⌈the memory capacity of the physical machine *the maximum utilizaiton of the memory*2⌉
- Disk capacity = the required disk capacity in the physical machine * 120 %.

3 Experimental Evaluation and Analysis

In order to verify the effect of the proposed method, we applied it to the information system data center of some provincial electric power company and achieved the following benefits:

(1) Hardware cost reduction. Through virtualization the resources of the servers are dynamically allocated and multiple virtual machines are running in one physical machine to support multiple application systems, which improves greatly the share and reuse of server resources and decreases the purchase of new devices. The average virtualization rate of the physical servers is 1:6 and the cost of investment on hardware is reduced by 40 % every year.
(2) Energy cost reduction. Less physical servers are needed to support the application systems running on the original physical environment. According to the statistics, the electricity power is reduced by 50 % after the resource pool construction.
(3) Room space saving. Because of the improvement of the resource utilization, the physical room space is reduced by 60 % while keeping the same computing ability.
(4) The management and maintenance cost is effectively reduced through the centralized management of the cloud resource management platform.

4 Conclusion

Aimed at the problems caused by the increasing demand for infrastructure construction and information system management in the enterprise informationization, the software and hardware resource pool construction based on cloud computing and virtualization in the enterprise data center is studied in the paper. The design of the server field, network field, storage field, safety field and data backup field in hardware resource pool construction and the resource requirement evaluation in software resource pool construction are discussed detailedly. The proposed method is verified in the data center construction of some provincial electric power company.

Acknowledgement. The authors would like to thank the reviewers for their detailed reviews and constructive comments. This work was supported in part by the Natural Science Basic Research Plan in Shaanxi Province of China under Grant No. 2013JM8021, the Xi'an Technology Transfer Promotion Project under Grant No. CXY1348-(1) and the Yulin Science and Technology Project under Grant No. CXY12-2-07.

References

1. Han, Q., Muhammad, S., Jieyao, L., Abdulla, G., Zulkanain, A.R., Torki, A.A.: Data center network architecture in cloud computing: review, taxonomy, and open research issues. J. Zhejiang Univ. Sci. C Comput. Electron. **15**(9), 776–793 (2014)
2. Chao-Tung, Y., Wen-Chung, S., Chih-Lin, H., Fuu-Cheng, J., William, C.-C.C.: On construction of a distributed data storage system in cloud. Computing, .1–26 (2014)
3. Wei, F., Xuezhi, W., Wubin, P., Shengjun, X.: Cloud computing: conceptions, key technologies and application. J. Nanjing Univ. Inf. Sci. Technol.: Nat. Sci. Ed. **4**(4), 351–361 (2012)
4. Qiongfen, Q., Chunlin, L., Xiaoqing, Z., Layuan, L.: Survey of virtual resource management in cloud data center. Appl. Res. Comput. **29**(7), 2411–2415 (2012)
5. Sai, L., Xurong, L., Linrui, W.: Computing clouds resources pool model research based on queue theory. Comput. Technol. Dev. **22**(12), 87–89 (2012)
6. Maricela-Georgiana, A.: Advantages and challenges of adopting cloud computing from an enterprise perspective. In: Proceedings of the 7th International Conference Interdisciplinary in Engineering (INTER-ENG 2013), pp.529–534 (2014)
7. Brendan, J., Rolf, S.: Resource management in clouds: survey and research challenges. J. Netw. Syst. Manage, 1–53 (2014)
8. Information security technology-Baseline for classified protection of information system. http://www.cspec.gov.cn/web/Upload/2011-04/file/zhengcefagui/201104140231219218854.pdf
9. Backup Methods. http://baike.baidu.com/view/6432240.htm?fr=aladdin
10. LAN Free and Server Free backup methods analysis. http://www.360doc.com/content/11/0309/10/5420793_99461431.shtml

Design and Performance Analysis of Utility Maximization-Based Cooperative MAC in Multi-rate WiFi Networks

Jiqiang Tang[1], Xiaoxiang Zou[(✉)], and Dongbin Wang[2]

[1] National Computer Network Emergency Response Technical
Team/Coordination Center of China, Beijing, China
{tangjq,zxx}@cert.org.cn
[2] National Engineering Laboratory for Mobile Network Security,
Beijing University of Posts and Telecommunications, Beijing, China
dbwang@bupt.edu.cn

Abstract. In this paper, a utility maximization-based cooperative MAC framework is developed for energy-constrained multi-rate WiFi networks over our previous work. A utility function represents the total payload transmission during the system lifetime is introduced to characterize the energy effectiveness. By means of regulating the cooperative probability to balance the energy consumption of high-rate nodes for their own transmissions and for forwarding transmissions of the source nodes they are willing to help, how to design a system utility maximization-based cooperative MAC is modeled as an optimization problem.

Keywords: Utility maximization · Cooperative MAC · Multi-rate WiFi networks

1 Introduction

As a novel MAC framework, cooperative communication is discussed frequently to improve the performance of nodes with low data rate. A detailed distributed MAC layer protocol named CoopMAC that deploys cooperation in a multi-rate WiFi network is described in [1]. In this protocol, the source node needs to discover the set of selected relays and select one helper to establish a cooperative mode to transmit its data by the use of a broadcast packet, while each chosen relay, upon receiving this packet, must respond to verify its availability as a relay. However, a node with a very low energy or heavy traffic usually dies out earlier than others, and CoopMAC does not consider the energy consumption distinction for nodes with different data rate.

In state-of-the-art research [2–4], when the goals of wireless network protocol design involves multiple targets, various indicators in the same multi-objective programming often cannot be achieved at the same time, which has been pointed out in previous researches [2, 4]. Specifically, optimum conditions of multiple indexes can sometimes be contradictory.

It is clear that energy consumption and bandwidth utilization are not synonymous. It is necessary to consider not only the cost of frame transmission, but of receiving, and

Y. Lu et al. (Eds.): ISCTCS 2014, CCIS 520, pp. 213–220, 2015.
DOI: 10.1007/978-3-662-47401-3_28

even of discarding it. Therefore, protocol designers must consider the proportions of different relays used by a source node in the protocol. Because the same node always serves as a relay for a source node, it has disproportionately high energy costs. Promiscuous mode operation, which is irrelevant to bandwidth utilization, also incurs some energy cost. However, energy is often treated as abstract commodity and subtle issues such as those suggested above are not addressed.

2 System Model

Before presenting details of the protocols, a system model is first set up. This model, along with several factors, is based on the assumptions that each node has an identical radio configuration and experiences the same propagation environment. The said factors include the transceiver power consumption, the energy consumption computation and the relation among rate, the power and the maximum transmission range.

To make the analysis tractable, we consider a single basic service set with n nodes of an IEEE 802.11b system. Similar to many other related works [1, 2], we only consider the uplink stream flows from terminal nodes to AP.

Definition 1. $\tilde{\mathbf{H}}^{(k)}$: the potential relay set for node k

$$\tilde{\mathbf{H}}^{(k)} = \left\{ h \left| \left[\frac{1}{R_{l(k,h)}} + \frac{1}{R_{l(h)}} \right]^{-1} > R_{l(k)}, h \in [1, n] \right. \right\} \tag{1}$$

Definition 2. $\mathbf{H}^{(k)}$: the optimal relay set for node k

If is not empty, let $R_{\text{coop}}^{(k)}$ be the largest average rate for two hop, then

$$\mathbf{H}^{(k)} = \left\{ h \left| \left[\frac{1}{R_{l(k,h)}} + \frac{1}{R_{l(h)}} \right]^{-1} = R_{\text{coop}}^{(k)}, h \in [1, n] \right. \right\} \tag{2}$$

Definition 3. $\mathbf{S}^{(k)}$: the source node set for node k to be a relay node.

$$\mathbf{S}^{(k)} = \left\{ s \left| \left[\frac{1}{R_{l(s,k)}} + \frac{1}{R_{l(k)}} \right]^{-1} = R_{\text{coop}}^{(s)}, s \in [1, n] \right. \right\} \tag{3}$$

Definition 4. q_k: cooperative probability vector;
Q: cooperative probability matrix.

For any transmission of node k ($k \in [1,n]$), cooperative probability q_{kh} is the probability that a node h belongs to $\mathbf{H}^{(k)}$ helps node k establish a two-hop transmission, where $h \in [1, n]$.

$$\boldsymbol{q}_k = (q_{k1}, \cdots, q_{kh}, \cdots, q_{kn}) \tag{4}$$

$$\boldsymbol{Q} = (\boldsymbol{q}_1, \cdots, \boldsymbol{q}_k, \cdots, \boldsymbol{q}_n)^{\mathrm{T}} \tag{5}$$

Where T represents matrix transpose operator; q_k is a vector with space of n matrices; and Q is a diagonal matrix with space of n × n matrices.

For l as any element of q_k or Q, q_{kl} is equal to 0, if l does not belongs to $\mathbf{H}^{(k)}$.

3 UM-CMAC: Utility Maximization-Based Cooperative MAC

3.1 Utility Function Definition

For an energy constrained wireless network system, it is the most meaningful to improve the throughput in the limited lifetime. Thus, q_k is defined as cooperative probability vector for a particular node k in a multi-rate WiFi network.

$$U_k(\boldsymbol{q}_k) = T_{\mathrm{sys}} \cdot S_k \tag{6}$$

Where T_{sys} denotes the system lifetime; S_k denotes the throughput of the node k; and $U_k(q_k)$ denotes the utility of the node k with cooperative probability vector.

To compute T_{sys}, we consider the duration between two successful transmissions of node k, which is denoted by ΔT. Due to the long-term fairness in WiFi networks [1], ΔT is not associated with node k. Therefore, ΔT can be formatted by S_k as $\Delta T = L/S_k$.

Let e_k be the total energy consumption in duration ΔT. Then, the lifetime of node k can be formulated as

$$T_k = \Delta T \cdot \frac{E_k}{e_k} = \frac{LE_k}{S_k e_k}, \; k \in [1, n] \tag{7}$$

The system lifetime is determined by the node with the minimized lifetime.

$$T_{\mathrm{sys}} = \min_{k \in [1,n]} \{T_k\} \tag{8}$$

According to the rule of utility maximization defined in [6], the utility function in this paper is expressed as with the system model.

$$\sum_{k=1}^{n} U_k(\boldsymbol{q}_k) = \left(\sum_{k=1}^{n} S_k\right) \cdot \min_{k \in [1,n]} \left\{\frac{LE_k}{S_k e_k}\right\} \tag{9}$$

Based on our previous work in [3], each node in a single hop WiFi network has the same throughput. The payload length is a constant, then

$$\sum_{k=1}^{n} U_k(\boldsymbol{q}_k) = nL \cdot \min_{k\in[1,n]} \left\{\frac{E_k}{e_k}\right\} \tag{10}$$

If the initial energy of each node is the same, the utility defined here is determined by the node with the largest energy consumption for the same payload length.

3.2 Proposed Cooperative MAC

Let $Q_{\text{opt}} = \arg \max_{Q}\{\sum_{k=1}^{n} U_k(\boldsymbol{q}_k)\}$ be the optimum cooperative probability matrix of node k. The key idea of UM-CMAC is to make the cooperative probability matrix be Q_{opt} over the CoopMAC in WiFi networks, which means that UM-CMAC maximizes the utility by a tradeoff between system throughput and lifetime.

In CoopMAC, the helper node can reject the request from a source node to start a cooperative communication. However, the original intention of CoopMAC is to make the throughput be optimum, and CoopMAC does not take energy consumption into account. For any node (given by s) belongs to $S^{(k)}$ in UM-CMAC receives a request of beginning a cooperation from node k, we define the cooperative response probability for node s launched by node k by a_{ks}, which indicates the probability that node s agrees to join in the transmission and serves as a helper node for node k.

Let $N_{\mathbf{H}^{(s)}}$ be the number of the best relay nodes in node s's candidate cooperative node set, and then the cooperative response probability vector of node k is

$$\begin{aligned}
\boldsymbol{a}_k &= (a_{k1}, \cdots, a_{ks}, \cdots, a_{kn}) \\
&= \left(\tilde{q}_{1k}N_{\mathbf{H}^{(1)}}, \cdots, \tilde{q}_{sk}N_{\mathbf{H}^{(s)}}, \cdots, \tilde{q}_{nk}N_{\mathbf{H}^{(n)}}\right), \forall k \in [1, n]
\end{aligned} \tag{11}$$

When each node obtains its cooperative response probability vector $\boldsymbol{a}_k$, the source node transfers a request for cooperation to any of its candidate helper node and appropriates response probability of cooperation, which decided to participate in the cooperation or reject the current source node transfers request in order to determine if source nodes using cooperative transmission mode of data transfer.

In order to avoid large overhead brought by a collision with long transmission, UM-CMAC adopts control frames sent before data transmission. The basic transmission mode in UM-CMAC uses RTS/CTS handshake, while the cooperative transmission mode uses RTS/HTS/CTS three–way handshake. This is depicted in Fig. 1.

When a source node reserves the channel, it will know whether there is at least one candidate helper from the cooperative table. If there is a helper, this source node will send a RTS (CoopRTS) to request to establish a cooperative transmission.

If the helper which the source node selected can successfully decode the RTS frame, it will query cooperative response probability and decide whether helps the source establish the cooperative transmission. If the helper node joins in the transmission, it will ready to send HTS will be sent out in a SIFS time by this probability.

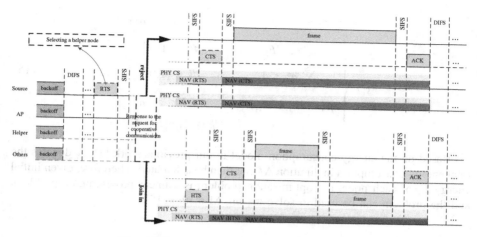

Fig. 1. The illustration of UM-CMAC protocol

3.3 The Programming Constraint Analysis

The utility function introduced is a function of the cooperative probability matrix within the system, so the goal for solving the utility maximization problem is to find the best cooperative probability matrix. UM-CMAC has the same rule of cooperative table update as Cooperative. Thus, for any node in the optimal relay node set, the probability of any other node selected to be a helper is the same.

$$q_{kh} \in \left[0, 1/N_{\mathbf{H}^{(k)}}\right], \forall k, h \in [1, n] \tag{12}$$

Moreover, according to the CoopMAC relay selection criteria, only a node belongs to the optimal relay node set of node k can serve as cooperative transmission node.

$$\sum_{h=1}^{n} q_{kh} \leq 1, \quad \forall k \in [1, n], \quad q_{kh} = 0, \quad \forall k \in [1, n] \, h \notin \mathbf{H}^{(k)} \tag{13}$$

Hence, to maximize the utility function $\sum_{k=1}^{n} U_k(\boldsymbol{q}_k)$ for a cooperative system is transformed to a min max problem.

$$\min_{Q} \max_{\forall k \in [1, n]} \left\{ \frac{e_k}{E_k} \right\} \quad s.t. \ (12) \ \text{and} \ (13) \tag{14}$$

Utilizing slack variable ξ, the formation 14 is equal to the following linear programming problem.

$$\min_{Q} \xi$$

$$s.t. \begin{cases} \xi \geq e_k/E_k, & \forall k \in [1, n] \\ \sum_{h=1}^{n} q_{kh} \leq 1, & \forall k \in [1, n] \\ q_{kh} \in \left[0, \, 1/N_{\mathbf{H}^{(k)}}\right], & \forall k, h \in [1, n] \\ q_{kh} = 0, & \forall k \in [1, n] \, h \notin \mathbf{H}^{(k)} \end{cases} \quad (15)$$

Based on the energy consumption model in our previous work [3], e_k denotes the total energy consumption in duration ΔT can then be calculated. Therefore, given initial energy E_k of each node, the optimization problem is a linear programming problem, and the problem can be used to solve the big M method [5].

4   Performance Evaluation

We developed an event-driven custom simulator to compare its performance with CoopMAC protocol as well as the 802.11b protocol. We use specify parameters of the widely used network interface card from Aironet company PC4800 series [5]. If not stated otherwise, the simulation is focused on the uplink and the other settings are the same as in [1]. Because of the length limit of this paper, a simple topology contains two nodes with an AP is considered, which is illustrated in Fig. 2.

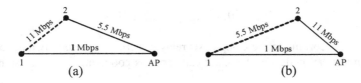

Fig. 2. Two topologies with two nodes in simulations

There is one element q_{12} in cooperative probability matrix is non-zero, so we only need to consider the interaction between cooperative probability q_{12} and system utility.

Note that, the system utility is influenced by q_{12}. When q_{12} increases, the utility increases first, but it decreases later. There is a maximum point of the system utility for each payload length setting, and this maximum point corresponds to the value of cooperative probability derived by formation 15.

Moreover, CoopMAC which is a comprehensive cooperative protocol and IEEE 802.11b which is a zero-cooperative protocol, where is equal to one and zero respectively, cannot realize the utility maximization. Hence, by adjusting the cooperative level, an optimal cooperative way will be found to establish the utility maximization. Furthermore, we should know there is no difference for the node 2 in topology (a) or in topology (b) in CoopMAC.

The interaction of cooperative probability and utility is provided in Fig. 3. We can see that two topologies are not equivalent for UM-CMAC even with the same payload and cooperative probability. Therefore, for the same source node, the relay node in these two scenarios needs to be distinguished in a cooperation enable system.

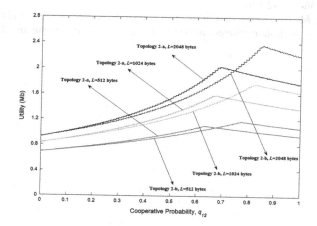

Fig. 3. The interaction of cooperative probability and utility

5 Conclusion and Future Work

This paper presented and discussed UM-CMAC, a utility maximization-based cooperative MAC builds on the IEEE 802.11 mechanisms. Special attention was paid to the safety of the protocol to the evaluation of its performance under realistic assumptions.

The proposed protocol is simple and backward compatible, yet it realizes a significant performance gain over the single relay based CoopMAC. It works for both the infrastructure mode and ad hoc mode of WiFi. Compared with CoopMAC and IEEE 802.11b, it enables a fully distributed yet robust cooperation using single relay. In our future work, we will analyze the performance of UM-CMAC in a mobile environment.

Acknowledgement. This work is supported by National Science and Technology Major Project of the Ministry of Science and Technology of China (2012BAH45B00).

References

1. Liu, P., Tao, Z., Narayanan, S., Korakis, T.: CoopMAC: a cooperative MAC for wireless LANs. IEEE J. Sel. Areas Commun. (JSAC) 25(2), 340–354 (2007)
2. Alhosainy, A. Kunz, T., Li Li: Robustness and stability of utility maximization algorithms for MANETs. In: 2014 13th Annual Mediterranean Ad Hoc Networking Workshop (MED-HOC-NET) (2014)

3. Tang, J.: 2012. Performance Analysis of the Cooperation at MAC Layer for Multi-rate Wireless Networks, Doctoral dissertation (2012)
4. Lee, J.-W., Chiang, M., Calderbank, A.R.: Jointly optimal congestion and medium access control based on network utility maximization. IEEE Commun. Lett. **10**(3), 216–218 (2006)
5. Mo, J., Walrand, J.: Fair end-to-end window-based congestion control. IEEE/ACM Trans. Netw. **8**(5), 556–567 (2000)
6. Zhou, A., Liu, M.: Cross-layer design for proportional delay differentiation and network utility maximization in multi-hop wireless networks. IEEE Trans. Wirel. Commun. **25**(1) (2012)

Advanced Persistent Threat Detection Method Research Based on Relevant Algorithms to Artificial Immune System

Bin Jia[1(⊠)], Zhaowen Lin[1,2], and Yan Ma[1]

[1] Network and Information Center, Institute of Network Technology,
Beijing University of Posts and Telecommunications, Beijing, China
{jb_qd2010,linzw,mayan}@bupt.edu.cn
[2] National Engineering Laboratory for Mobile Network Security
(No. [2013] 2685), Beijing, China

Abstract. In recent years, advanced persistent threat (APT) is a very popular high-end network attack pattern. Due to the strong concealment and latency, APT can successfully avoid general detection. The attacks usually were not found by the attacked targets when assault has been finished. Because current techniques used in computer and network security are not able to cope with the dynamic and increasingly complex nature of computer system and network security, it is hoped that we could find some biological enlightenment, including the use of immune-based system that will be able to meet this challenge. In this paper, we review the characteristics of APT, several existing algorithms of the artificial immune system (AIS), and analyze the disadvantages of these algorithms when they apply to anomaly behavior detection that has the characteristics of APT. Then we propose an improved algorithm idea of AIS to make some suggestions for future research work.

Keywords: Advanced persistent threat · Artificial immune system · Concealment · Latency · Many incremental memory antigens dynamic clonal selection algorithm

1 Introduction

The Internet has grown so successfully that it plays a crucial role in today's society and business. However, the Internet comes with important shortcomings because it is being threatened increasingly by network attack and infringement behavior, and has become a global problem, such as hacking. Network hackers have been launching malicious attack to the enterprise or individual computer users with ever-changing trick. As a result of these more elusive methods, so prevention is increasingly difficult. Advanced persistent threat (APT) is very popular high-end network attack pattern in recent years. APT marks the fundamental change of attack pattern compared with high risky hacking activity that usually aims at Internet. This threat pays close attention to the weakest link on the protective chain. In order to get critical assets, APT that targets some specific groups and individuals shall take particular system vulnerability and certain strategic users as aggressive targets. Due to the strong concealment and latency, APT can

Y. Lu et al. (Eds.): ISCTCS 2014, CCIS 520, pp. 221–228, 2015.
DOI: 10.1007/978-3-662-47401-3_29

successfully avoid general detection. The attacks usually were not found by the attacked targets when assault has been finished while the targets realized until it was too late. For example, the traditional network security system usually adopts white and black list method and signature-based detection way, however, the current APT takes more attack technique as breakthrough method based on the 0day vulnerability, and the method take the known vulnerability and virus as the main protective objective. Although malicious files and traffic passed the traditional security equipment inspection, the consequences of this doing are that the attacks what used 0day vulnerability cannot be identified effectively due to the defective detection methods. In addition, the conventional intrusion detection system would be divided into host-based intrusion detection system (IDS) and network-based IDS according to the monitored object, however, in the process of detection and prevention of APT, this distinction is no longer apparent.

To overcome the limitation of these issues that it brought about by the behavior of APT, many network security researchers have been working hard on developing new detection and defense methods and their related algorithms. In recent years, a series of algorithms of artificial immune system (AIS) have been applied to traditional IDS. However, these algorithms have some disadvantages for anomaly behavior detection that complies with the characteristics of APT of the computer network security domain. So there remain some open issues which have to be addressed in order to make the AIS a real-world problem solving [1]. In this paper, we proposed the algorithm idea of many incremental memory antigens dynamic clonal selection which is suitable for the anomaly behavior detection that has the characteristics of APT.

The remainder of this paper is organized as follows. Section 2 introduces the working mechanism of APT and several existing algorithms of AIS. Section 3 analyzes the disadvantages of these algorithms when they apply to anomaly behavior detection that has the characteristics of APT. Then, we propose the algorithm idea of many incremental memory antigens dynamic clonal selection on the applications of AIS for APT to make some suggestions for future research work in Sect. 4, and finally, Sect. 5 concludes this paper.

2 Background

2.1 The Working Mechanism of APT

With unceasing enhancement of the network attacking technology and its increasing complexity, these techniques have been being gradually evolved from single attack mode to cross-technological attack mode. The detection of APT becomes increasingly more difficult because of its extremely strong concealment and latency. Currently, the detection technology for the traditional computer network virus has made a large amount of research results in academia, and many of them have been turned into the industry products. But due to many differences that already exist between the working mechanism of detection and defense for APT and the detection mechanism for the traditional computer network virus, so the research for this technology is still at developing stage. The studies include the analysis based on graph theory, the distributed information gathering and collaborative correlation method based on big data and the strategy of network alarm event correlation and so on. The detection mechanism for the traditional computer network virus is illustrated in Fig. 1. As is shown in Fig. 2, the working mechanism of detection and defense for APT fully reflects the complexity of APT detection.

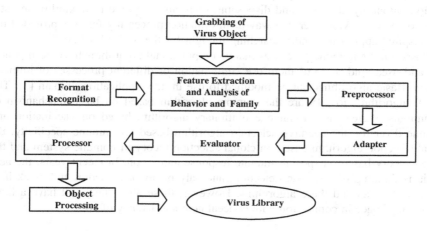

Fig. 1. Working mechanism of traditional virus detection

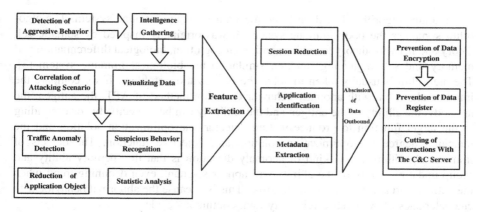

Fig. 2. Working mechanism of detection and defense for APT

2.2 AIS and a Series of Algorithms

The artificial immune system (AIS) is a highly complex, distributed, coordinated and self-adaptive system in bioinformatics. AIS can identify and eliminate adaptively the invaded foreign body of antigenicity. AIS can effectively maintain the stability of the environment within the body and prevent the next attack. From the perspective of system behavior, AIS shows certain similarities with IDS. And some characteristics of this system are relatively highly in line with the detection strategy of APT. Computer network security is very similar with biological immune system. They both maintain the security of the system in the dynamic environment. In this field, AIS should have anomaly detection capability to defend the unknown intrusion. Adaptability is also a necessary property of AIS that can learn the unknown intrusion and respond quickly to the learned intrusions. Other properties, such as self-learning, memorability, distributability, autonomy, diversity and disposability are also required to flexibility and stability for AIS [2]. Moreover, the way of information processing for AIS provided the new inspired approaches and researching thought for the research of APT.

Based on the immune processes many computational algorithms have been generated and used, and some of them use combination of different processes of immune system. Basic algorithms can be modified to use in new application domain [1]. The typical algorithms to AIS are the immune algorithm based on basic mechanism of the immune system, the immune evolutionary algorithm based on vaccination and immune diversity, the negative selection algorithm based on immune specificity, the clonal selection algorithm based on clonal selection theory in immune system and the danger theory based on special immune response and so on. In recent years, the academia is thinking of intrusion detection, anomaly behavior detection and black hole cover in APT around these algorithms. However, these algorithms still have a large researching space in connection with concealment and latency of APT.

3   Analysis and Comparison of Several Algorithms for AIS

The immune algorithm based on basic mechanism of the immune system. The algorithm simulates the body immune system. It was originally inspired by somatic cell theory and network theory to achieve antigen recognition, biological differentiation and memory and self regulating function similar to the biological immune system [3]. The algorithm is usually taken to solve the optimization problem. If we compare the immune algorithm with anomaly behavior detection method of APT, the antigen, the antibody, the affinity of the antigen and the antibody can be respectively corresponding to the target function to produce mature detector, the optimization solution and the matching degree the optimization solution and objective function. The defects of immune algorithm in this kind of anomaly detection is that the memory ability and group updating ability of the affinity will appear stagnant, even declining trend when the antigen and antibody continue to grow. This is because the abnormal behavior with characteristics of APT has a relatively long continuous cycle.

The immune evolutionary algorithm based on vaccination and immune diversity. This algorithm makes full use of the calculation model of evolutionary computation. The evolutionary computation has been applied widely as a directed random search optimization algorithm. Literature [2] presents a global evolution algorithm integrating the immune mechanism with evolution mechanism to prove that global convergence of the algorithm and further solve its degradation phenomenon arising from the existing algorithm. The convergence speed has improved significantly. The algorithm introduces the vaccine operator that has a good effect in practical application for solving the global invasive threat of APT. However, in anomaly detection of APT, the defect of this algorithm is that the algorithm cannot adjust the individual diversity of the single anomaly attack behavior. And it is based on the parent group, and cannot guarantee convergence in probability.

The negative selection algorithm based on immune specificity. Forrest [4] studies the negative selection algorithm for testing data changes to solve some problems in the field of computer network security. The negative selection process of AIS is a sophisticated anomaly detection method. With that the system monitor successfully abnormal changes in the network environment, the algorithm make the immune system to play an important role. The key of successful detection is that the system can distinguish between "self" and "non-self" information. The algorithm consists of three phases: defining self, generating detectors and monitoring the occurrence of anomalies [5]. For abnormal attack behavior of APT, there are two drawbacks to utilizing the negative selection algorithm, namely scalability and coverage, while these are the main barriers to its success as effective IDS. And there may be inherent problems with the computational efficiency of negative selection that can never be resolved. In addition, the anomaly detection system based on negative selection algorithm will have a lot of black holes. These black holes are non-self individuals which cannot be identified by all possible detectors [6]. The reasons of the black holes are mainly the matching criteria and internal pattern relationships of the self set [7].

The clonal selection algorithm based on clonal selection theory in immune system. This is an evolutionary algorithm which simulates the learning process of the immune system. The essence of which is to produce the variant solution group near optimal solution of each generation in the process of evolution according to the size of the affinity for cloning, which expands the scope of the search (i.e., increases the diversity of antibody). This doing helps to prevent prematurity of the evolution and to be limited to local minimum value for the search. Meanwhile it can accelerate the convergence speed by clonal selection. The existing disadvantage of this algorithm for the anomaly behavior detection to conform to the characteristics of APT is to inevitably produce degradation phenomenon when it provides evolutionary opportunities for the detectors population, such as the decline of the detector diversity and the affinity of antibodies (detectors) and the stagnation of detection rate (True, TP), etc.

The danger theory based on special immune response, Burgess advocated a different immunology theory called the danger theory [8]. Although this model is still controversial among immunologists, he considered this model to be more appropriate for AIS. Following this model, Burgess [9, 10] put the emphasis of AIS on an autonomous and distributed feedback and healing mechanism, triggered when a small amount of damage could be detected at an initial attacking stage. As shown in Kim et al. [11], the danger theory inspired that AIS was designed to adopt both the innate immune system and the adaptive immune system. However, the main idea of this theory is that AIS does not response to non-self but to danger. Similarly, not all of the abnormal behavior will be dangerous for the network in APT. Therefore, for the anomaly behavior detection of APT, the deficiency in the danger theory is that it is easy to produce false alarm rate, namely it is so-called danger, but in fact is the safe abnormal behavior.

Initialize Many Incremental Memory Antigens Dynamic Clonal Selection Algorithm
Create an initial immature detector population with random detectors;

Generation number = 1;
Do {
    If (Generation number = N)
       Select a new antigen cluster.

    Select 80% of self and non-self antigens from a chosen antigen cluster;
    //Reset Parameters
       Generation number++;
       Memory Detector Age++;
       Mature Detector Age++;
       Immature Detector Age++;

    Monitor Antigens
    {
      Monitor Antigens by Memory Detectors
        Check whether any memory detector detects any non-self antigen;
        Check whether any memory detector detects any self antigen;
        If (memory detector detects any self antigen)
          Delete this memory detector;
        Update memory detector population;

      Monitor Antigens by Mature Detectors

        Check whether any mature detector detects any non-self antigen;
        Check whether any mature detector detects any self antigen;
        Delete mature detectors that detect any self antigen;
        If (reach the certain activated threshold)
          Create new memory detectors;
        Old mature detectors are killed;

      Monitor Antigens by Immature Detectors
        Check whether any immature detector detects any self antigen;
        Delete any immature detector matching any self antigen;
        If (reach the tolerance time)
          Create new mature detectors;
    }

    If (immature detector population size + mature detector population size
      < non-memory detector population size)
      {
      Do {
        Generate a random detector;
        Add a random detector to an immature detector population;
        } Until (immature detector population size + mature detector population
size
          = non-memory detector population size);
      }
} While (generation Number < max Generation)

Fig. 3. Pseudo-code for many incremental memory antigens dynamic clonal selection algorithm

4   New Thoughts on the Applications of AIS in APT

Through above analysis, we can see that these algorithms about AIS have some shortcomings in the anomaly behavior detection of APT. Based on the dynamic clonal selection algorithm of AIS, combining with the characteristics of the strong conceal-ment and the long latent period in APT, and dynamic changing characteristic of net-work abnormal behavior in this environment, this paper presents the thought of many incremental memory antigens on the basis of the dynamic clonal selection algorithm according to the discovery of "dynamic immune memory" of the residual antigen theory in biology. And its purpose is to solve the anomaly behavior detection with characteristics of APT.

Kim has proposed the dynamic clonal selection algorithm in 2002 [12]. The pseudo code provides an overview of dynamic clonal selection algorithm [13]. The following pseudo code provides an overview of many incremental memory antigens dynamic clonal selection algorithm (Fig. 3).

On the basis of these algorithms above, to realize the dynamic clone selection of many incremental memory antigens, we design a set of operation, such as the replacement for many memory antigens, antigen memory population updating and the clone in accordance with antigen affinity, etc. The purpose of this doing is to effectively detect the network abnormal behavior with characteristics of APT. However, for pre-venting the useless memory detectors accumulation from reducing system efficiency, this algorithm still has relatively great room to improve.

5   Conclusions and Future Work

Network security is the key issue that affects the politics, the economy, the military and all aspects of ordinary people living in a country. In recent years, APT is a very popular topic and technical pattern in the field of network security. How to effectively detect and defense the network abnormal behavior of APT has became the researching focus in academia.

In this paper, we review the characteristics of APT, several existing algorithms of AIS, and analyze the disadvantages of these algorithms when they apply to anomaly behavior detection that has the characteristics of APT. Then we propose the algorithm idea of many incremental memory antigens dynamic clonal selection on the application of AIS for APT to make some suggestions for future researching work.

The preliminary results, though limited, we think that this approach holds promise and deserves the continuing investigation. For the future work, we will study how to use this improved algorithm idea to analyze and detect the actual network abnormal attack behavior with characteristics of APT.

Acknowledgements. This work was supported by the National High Technology Research and Development Program of China (863 Program) (No. 2013AA014702), Fundamental Research Funds for the Central Universities (2014PTB-00-04, 2014ZD03-03) and China Next Generation Internet Project (CNGI Project) (CNGI-12-02-027). In addition, the authors would like to thank the students in Information Network Center of BUPT for their valuable contribution to recom-mendations of this paper and the implementation of relevant projects.

References

1. Zheng, J., Chen, Y., Zhang, W.: A Survey of Artificial Immune Applications. Springer Science Business Media, New York (2010)
2. Dasgupta, D, Attoh-Okine, N.: Immunity based systems: a survey. In: IEEE International Conference (1997)
3. Hong, J., Lee, W., Lee, B., Lee, Y.: An efficient production algorithm for multihead surface mounting machines using the biological immune algorithm. Int. J. Fuzzy Syst. 2(1), 45–53 (2000)
4. Forrest, S., Perelson, A., Cherukuri, R.: Self-nonself discrimination in a computer[A]. In: Proceedings of 1994 IEEE Computer Society Symposium on Research in Security and Privacy[C], pp. 202–212. IEEE Computer Society, Los Almitos (1994)
5. Kim, J., Bentley, P.J., Aickelin, U., Greensmith, J., Tedesco, G., Twycross, J.: Immune system approaches to intrusion detection–a review. Nat. Comput. 6, 413–466 (2007)
6. Dhaeseleer, P.: An immunological approach to change detection: theoretical results [A]. In: Proceedings of the 9th IEEE Computer Security Foundations Workshop[C], pp. 132–143, Kenmare (1996)
7. Zhou, J., Dasgupta, D.: Revisiting negative selection algorithms [J]. Evol. Comput. 5(2), 223–251 (2007)
8. Matzinger, P.: Tolerance, danger, and the extended family. Annu. Rev. Immunol. 12, 991–1045 (1994)
9. Burgess, M.: Computer immunology. In: Proceeding of the Systems Administration Conference (LISA-98), pp. 283–297 (1998)
10. Burgess, M.: Evaluating cfegine's immunity model of site maintenance. In: Proceeding of the 2nd SANE System Administration Conference (USENIX/NLUUG) (2000)
11. Kim, J., Wilson, W.O., Aickelin, U., McLeod, J.: Cooperative automated worm response and detection immune algorithm (cardinal) inspired by t-cell immunity and tolerance. In: Jacob, C., Pilat, M.L., Bentley, P.J., Timmis, J.I. (eds.) ICARIS 2005. LNCS, vol. 3627, pp. 168–181. Springer, Heidelberg (2005)
12. Kim, J.,Bentley, P.J.: Towards an artificial immune system for network intrusion detection: an investigation of dynamic clonal selection [C]. In: Proceeding of the Congress on Evolutionary Computation, pp. 1015–1020. IEEE, Honolulu (2002)
13. Kim, J., Bentley, P.J.: Towards an Artificial Immune System for Network Intrusion Detection: an Investigation of Dynamic Clonal Selection

Human Mobility Simulation in Smart Energy Grid

Tianle Zhang[1,2(✉)], Lixin Liu[1,2], Shouyou Song[1,2], and Yuyu Yuan[1,2]

[1] Key Laboratory of Trustworthy Distributed Computing and Service (BUPT),
Ministry of Education, Beijing, China
[2] Beijing University of Posts and Telecommunications, Beijing 100876, China
{tlezhang, yuanyuyu}@bupt.edu.cn

Abstract. Smart grid is an emerging complex system of systems that continually provide distributed communication service to enable an efficient, optimal, reliable, secure energy transmission and distribution. Rapid growth in the number of Electric Vehicles (EVs) in use would have a significant impact on the capacity and efficiency of electric power network and thus post great challenges on the smart grid technology. The extent to which the scheduling can benefit the system depends greatly on the dynamic EV mobility pattern and levels of electricity usage of EVs. EV mobility simulation is useful in analyzing how charging scheduling works. In this paper, we focus on the need for human mobility model based simulation in smart grid to help validate the performance of charging scheduling of EVs in a distributed smart grid system. The mobility model simulates the driver's driving actions in micro domain such as steer, speed up and brake etc. to synthesize smooth, reasonable and realistic vehicle trajectory. The simulated EVs mobility can be configured to produce real world dynamic mobility pattern of a large scale of individual EVs in a certain fine grain. The charge scheduling algorithms are introduced in the simulation to validate the feasibility of the EV mobility model.

Keywords: Smart grid · Electric vehicle · Human mobility · Charge scheduling · State of charge

1 Introduction

In the last 10 years, Smart grids have gained the attention of the research community. Smart grid is an emerging complex system of systems that continually provide distributed communication service to enable an efficient, optimal, reliable, secure energy transmission and distribution [1].

With the smart-grid technologies, the electricity utility can manage load and help to schedule charging of EVs as much as possible outside of peak hours and feeding the electricity back into the grid in peak hours. The extent to which the scheduling can benefit the system depends greatly on the dynamic EV mobility pattern and levels of electricity usage of EVs. EV mobility simulation is useful in analyzing how charging scheduling works. In this paper, we focus on the need for human mobility model based simulation in smart grid to help validate the performance of charging scheduling of EVs in a distributed smart grid system. The mobility model simulates the driver's

© Springer-Verlag Berlin Heidelberg 2015
Y. Lu et al. (Eds.): ISCTCS 2014, CCIS 520, pp. 229–237, 2015.
DOI: 10.1007/978-3-662-47401-3_30

driving actions in micro domain such as steer, speed up and brake etc. to synthesize smooth, reasonable and realistic vehicle trajectory. The EV driver's behaviors such as parking, driving, traffic jamming, charging are introduced to the model. In the simulation, the EVs are auto-navigated to a verity of interest sites including workplace, home, markets, parking lots and charge stations etc. which are generated by an event-driven agenda based on common driver's daily activities on a regular base. The simulated EVs mobility can be configured to produce real world dynamic mobility pattern of a large scale of individual EVs in a certain fine grain.

In this paper, we fist studied the related work on EV trajectory generation to synthesize the real-world wide-scale mobility in a metropolitan area smart grid. Then we study the distributions of EVs and their energy consumption to show the pattern of usage. A human mobility model based simulation tools for smart grid is proposed. Finally we introduce several scheduling algorithms to EVs and compare the effect of EVs charging and recharging on the load of electricity network.

2   Related Work

With the rapid growth in the number of Electric Vehicles (EVs) in use, it is possible to facilitate the integration of EVs into power system. Mobile energy routing and exchanging (Grid-to-Vehicle, G2V) would have a significant impact on the electricity network capacity and quality. Large scale deployment and usage of EVs means the additional electricity needs for EVs which would amount to increasing percentage of country's electricity use and then has a great effect on the pattern of daily load curve. What's more, EVs are also some kind of mobile distributed power storage sources. EVs can feed electricity stored in their batteries back into the system when needed (Vehicle-to-Grid, V2G) to provide peak-shaving capacity. If well scheduled, the EVs can be a cost-effective measure of flattening the daily load curve and significantly reducing both generation and network investment needs. V2V(Vehicle to Vehicle) technology can enable specific EVs that is equipped with plenty energy storage to discharge power. Clearly, the EVs mobility and charging or discharge electricity activities are determined by the human mobility [2, 3], the scheduling is Human-mobility enabled. However the scheduler can help the EV owners to optimize the energy management and then impose a corresponding effect on the human mobility model in smart grid. Then understanding the human mobility and EV mobility patterns is a key challenge for the designs of routing protocols and scheduling schemes for smart grid networks.

For many years the researchers have assumed that the mobility of the devices forming such networks was totally unpredictable. In reality, this assumption is unrealistic since EVs are driven by people while auxiliary by the advanced information from the smart grid, whose mobility patterns usually depend on the user habits and operation habits [4]. Therefore, in order to better understand the opportunities offered by human mobility to enable optimized energy management and routing in smart grid, a human mobility model based simulation scheme is introduced to help validate the performance of scheduling of EVs in a distributed smart grid system. There is a lot of works on the mobility simulation of EV. In Alsace Auto 2.0, the objective is to optimize the impact of mobile EV charging on the grid by aggregating the load and storage capabilities of the

EV batteries and managing their charging patterns. SAVE (SAVE (Seine Aval Véhicule Électrique) is France's biggest trial program of all-electric mobility, ultimately involving around 100 EVs and around 150 charging spots. The travel demand simulation framework MATSim [5] is an agent based tool to simulate large scale traffic scenarios. However, none of the aforementioned studies has considered human mobility-enabled simulation scenarios in a wide area smart grid [6, 7].

3 Designs and Models

In this paper, we introduce the basic driver operations to post direct control to the mobility of EVs. This method can simulate the real physical moving action of vehicle and can synthesize smooth trajectory such as all kinds of reasonable curves instead of zigzag arbitrary trace as most current mobility models.

3.1 Driving Operation Based Human Mobility Modeling

We model the 3 basic mobility parameters. One is the speed V which is bounded to the current status of vehicle. The other is acceleration A which simulates the gas pedal and brake pedal of vehicle. The last parameter is the Wheel steering angle W which simulates the steering left or right process. The different combinations and time series of these key operations can describe almost all possible status and mobility of vehicle. Under the control of these parameters, the mobility status of EVs then can be modeled by an auto-machine of 3 basic stats shown in Fig. 1. This generated trajectory is in the same way as a real EV drives and is smooth and reasonable compared with zigzag arbitrary mobility model. The realistic trajectory is important to enable fine-grain simulation of mobility scenario such as short-range inter-vehicle communication, V2V charging etc. It will outcome a convincible encounter times and accurate mileage.

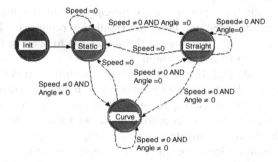

Fig. 1. Infinite status auto machine model of vehicle mobility process

3.2   Trajectory Synthesis Modeling

Based on the state machine of the mobility model, we calculate the time varied trajectory of EV according to dynamic operation of drivers on moving. At given time t, the position of EV at t + Δt (Δt is the time slot of refreshing) can be gotten by a parametric equation as following:

$$x' = x + v \cdot \Delta t \cos(\theta \cdot \pi/180) \tag{1}$$

$$y' = y + v \cdot \Delta t \cdot \sin(\theta \cdot \pi/180) \tag{2}$$

$$\theta' = \theta + \Delta t \cdot \omega \cdot 180/\pi \tag{3}$$

where, x' and y' is the coordinate of EV at next refresh time point. v is the time varied velocity of EV in pixel/slot(pixel is the screen unit and slot is the refreshing time slot). θ and α is the orientation angle of the EV and the steer wheel angle in degree (If the rotation of the ray is counterclockwise the angle has positive measure). θ' is the orientation angle at next time slot. ω is the angular velocity of EV in radians/s.

$$\omega = 2\pi/T = v/R$$

where L is the wheel base of EV (distance between front axle and rear axle) and R is the turning radius of EV.

$$R = L/\sin(\alpha \cdot \pi/180)$$

$$\theta' = \theta + \Delta t \cdot v \cdot \sin(\alpha \cdot \pi/180) \cdot 180/(L \cdot \pi) \tag{4}$$

$$v = \text{SimSpeed} \cdot \text{speed} \cdot y/x$$

where speed is the EV velocity in mile/hr. x is the space domain scale where 1 screen pixel stands for x miles(miles/pixel). y is the time domain scale where 1 screen redraw time slot interval stands for y hours(hr/slot). SimSpeed sands for the speed of simulation, the bigger the SimSpeed, the faster the simulation progresses. By adjusting the SimSpeed, we can control the progress of the simulation to achieve long term macro simulation and short term micro simulation.

According to formula (1,2,4), we can calculate the time varied trajectory of EV. Figure 2 shows the simulated trajectory controlled by mobility model. In (a) and (b), the EV steers left and right at fixed speed with steer angle α decreased from $15°$ to $5°$ continually. In (c), the EV steers right at fixed speed with steer angle α increased from $5°$ to $15°$ continually. In (d), EV fist steer right at low speed and then at high speed with the same steer operation. Under the same steer angle vary rate, the EV steer with different steer radius. In (e) the model use random speed and random steering angle $(-40° \sim 40°)$ and synthesizes reasonable and smooth trajectory as real world EV dose.

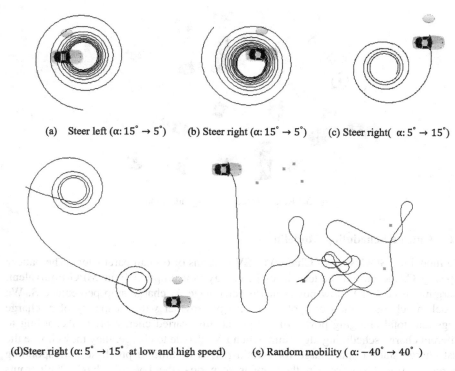

(a)   Steer left (α: 15° → 5°)   (b) Steer right (α: 15° → 5°)   (c) Steer right(α: 5° → 15°)

(d)Steer right (α: 5° → 15° at low and high speed)   (e) Random mobility (α: −40° → 40°)

Fig. 2. Synthesized trajectories of EV

3.3   Randomized Events Modeling

To make the charge scheduling more realistic, the simulation model introduces a randomized events generator. In real world, the EV may has a daily routs according to the driver's interests and agenda. EV may drive to the different interest sites such as work place, bank, school and home etc. and stay there for certain period accordingly. To simulation this procedure, we use a random function to generate randomized type of event at different geography location. Each EV is assigned to an agenda list which specifies when it should go to process what type of event at correspondent location. We generalize the traffic pattern of citizens according to the traffic density and transportation habits of different groups of drivers and get 6 typical transportation and travel related agenda templates (office worker, businessman, students, visitors, shopper) and 4 type of time related agenda templates (daytime and nighttime, weekday and weekend). The event site is randomly dropped on the map in a distributed way. The density and distribution of the events can be configured to reflect the difference in commercial and administrative prosperity of deferent areas (Fig. 3).

Fig. 3. Randomized daily agenda model

3.4   Charge Scheduling Modeling

We model the SOC(State of Charge) of EV in terms of 6 main parameters. The battery capacity C, the current battery level L, energy consumption E in MPG-Equivalent, charging speed P_EV, low power alarm percentage A, charge stop percentage S. We model the charge station or spot as an energy provider with a capacity of N charge plugs and total charging power of P_Spot at time varied energy price. According to different charge scheduling algorithm, when EVs decide to charge, they may choose the best charge station and charge for certain period of time to purchase corresponding charge energy. Moreover, in the regular scenarios, the EV may has a daily routs according to the driver's interests. EV may drive to and stop at the different interest sites (with different Geography Information System, GIS information) or park there for certain time. To enable simulating this daily process, we model the EV mobility by auto navigation procedures (in a smart grid network, an EV is installed an on-board unit, OBU, a GPS-based navigator. Therefore, from a digital map and GPS, the EV is aware of the locations of the charge station and event sites). The flow scheme is shown in Fig. 4.

In the real world, EVs have a daily traffic and certain mobility pattern. Smart EVs can schedule their charge time and site along their daily routine routes. To simulate these scenarios, the auto navigated EVs in the simulation are designed to be location sensitive and event driven in a time divided rolling robin, they repeatedly checks their surrounding and SOC in each time slot. EVs firstly check if they are plugged into a charge station, if so, they keep charging until they are fully charged or reach certain specified charge energy level. If EVs are not in charging, they check if they are engaged in processing interest events such as being at work or waiting in bank etc. If so, EVs just park there until they finish processing the event and resume their previous mobility. EVs keep sensing the GIS location of the interest event sites and the charging spots and calculate the distance and the estimated energy for arrival. If EVs find they are approaching the charging spots and they need purchase some energy, they will stop to charge. If not, EVs check if they approach some interest event sites and stop to process the events, if so. EVs keep checking the availability of the nearest charging

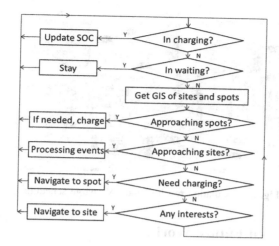

Fig. 4. Algorithm of EV auto navigation

spots based on SOC. If EVs need charging, they will make decision on the target charging spot according to assigned charging scheduling algorithms and navigate there. If EVs need not charge, they will navigate to certain event sites according to daily staff schedule. EVs repeat the above judgments and dispatch to enable simulate the smart charging in a realistic traffic environment.

We introduce 4 types of charging scheduling algorithms in the simulation. First is the SOC based charging schedule. EVs simply go to charge when they are in low power status, and charge fully or to designate energy level. The second algorithm is timer based charging. EVs charge at fixed time and fixed charge spot. The third is location based charging. EVs will stop at any charge spot if they pass by and purchase specified amount of energy. The last is service quality based charging. EVs choose the charge spot with best quality of service in term of availability, expected waiting time (when an EV arrives at an overloaded charge station, it is likely that the EV will wait for a long time before it is charged) and the price as well.

4   Simulation and Analysis

To evaluate and validate the simulation scheme of the EV mobility and charge scheduling progress, we set up a simulation scenario of a 10 miles × 10 miles urban area with 1000 EV nodes scattering homogeneously. We run the simulation with different deployment of charge stations and different charge scheduling algorithms. The total charging times of each charge stations are compared. By study the distribution and deviation of the utilization of the charge station, we can evaluate the feasibility of proposed planning and deployment of charging infrastructure. By study the SOC of EV we can analyze the impact of charging performance of different charge scheduling algorithms (Fig. 5).

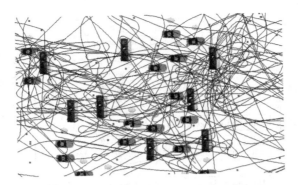

Fig. 5. Simulation result of the EV charge scheduling

5 Conclusion and Future Work

In this paper, we design and develop human mobility model based simulation tools for smart grid to help validate the performance of charging scheduling of EVs and the feasibility of charging infrastructure deployment in a smart grid system of a large scale of individual EVs. To achieve the realistic mobility of EV, we develop a human driving mobility model to simulate the driver's driving actions in micro domain such as steer, speed up and brake etc. and can synthesize smooth, reasonable and realistic vehicle trajectory. We further offer an event-driven agenda for EV to produce real world dynamic traffic pattern. By using the proposed simulation platform, simulation with different deployment of charge stations and different charge scheduling algorithms can be conducted, and the utilization of the charge station and charging performance of EVs can be compared and analyzed. We can evaluate the feasibility of proposed planning and deployment of charging infrastructure and the performance of proposed charge scheduling algorithms. In the further work, the mobility simulation can also provide distributed mobile scenarios for analysis of the 2-way communication connectivity [8] and demand response in smart grid. Moreover, we will study the impact of the human mobility on V2V charging in terms of contact and the inter-contact times. These metrics measure how long and how often two EVs come in contact.

Acknowledgement. This research was supported by "12nd Five-year Plan" for Sci & Tech Research of China (No. 2012BAH38X).

References

1. Boots, M., Thielens, D., Verheij, F.: International example developments in Smart Grids - Possibilities for application in the Netherlands, confidential report for the Dutch Government, KEMA Nederland B.V., Arnhem (2010)
2. Cacciapuoti, A.S., Calabrese, F., Caleffi, M., et al.: Human-mobility enabled networks in urban environments: is there any (mobile wireless) small world out there? Ad Hoc Netw. **10**, 1520–1531 (2012)

3. Gonzalez, M., Hidalgo, C., Barabasi, A.L.: Understanding individual human mobility patterns. Nature **453**(7196), 779–782 (2008). doi:10.1038/nature06958
4. Nor, J.K.: Art of charging electric vehicle batteries. In: WESCON 1993 Conference, California, USA, pp. 521–525 (1993)
5. (2008). http://www.matsim.org
6. Tang, J., Musolesi, M., Mascolo, C., Latora, V.: Temporal distance metrics for social network analysis. In: WOSN 2009, Proceedings of the 2nd ACM Workshop on Online Social Networks, pp. 31–36 (2009)
7. Leguay, J., Lindgren, A., Scott, J., Friedman, T., Crowcroft, J.: Opportunistic content distribution in an urban setting. In: CHANTS 2006: Proceedings of the 2006 SIGCOMM Workshop on Challenged Networks, pp. 205–212 (2006)
8. Hui, P., Crowcroft, J., Yoneki, E.: Bubble rap: social-based forwarding in delay tolerant networks. In: MobiHoc 2008: Proceedings of the 9th ACM International Symposium on Mobile Ad Hoc Networking and Computing, pp. 241–250 (2008)

Community Detection in Complex Networks: Algorithms and Analysis

Yuan Jie[1], Liu Zhishuai[1(✉)], and Xiaoyu Qiu[2]

[1] School of Information Engineering, Minzu University of China, Beijing, China
zhishuailiu@126.com
[2] Institute of Network and Education Technology,
Shandong University of Traditional Chinese Medicine, Jinan, China

Abstract. Community structure in networks indicates some meaningful groups or organizations in the real world. Various algorithms to detect community in complex networks were proposed. However, problems about how to judge the goodness and performance of algorithms are still open. This paper reviewed and analyzed the related work and algorithms for community detection, hoping to benefit researchers in related field.

Keywords: Community detection · Overlapping community · Scoring functions · Algorithm

1 Introduction

In real society, many relationships can be expressed as a complex network. For instance, in a school each student is a vertex in network, and there is an edge between two students if they share one class. The WWW is another example, every page can be seen as a vertex and if page A links to page B, then there is an edge between them. In fact networks are widely used in studies on social, biological, technological, and information subjects.

One of the most fundamentally characteristics in complex networks is the community structure, i.e. the groups in which vertices densely linked each other and sparsely linked to vertices beyond the group. Figure 1 from Ref. [1] displays a network with three communities. Communities, also called clusters or modules, are groups of vertices which probably share common properties and/or play similar roles within the network. Due to the important theoretical significance and application value, community structure research in complex network not only became the hot point in computer science but also attracted a large amount of researchers from physics, mathematics, biology and sociology fields.

2 Algorithms

Many algorithms have been proposed to detect communities in complex networks. They can be briefly classified in several types.

Y. Lu et al. (Eds.): ISCTCS 2014, CCIS 520, pp. 238–244, 2015.
DOI: 10.1007/978-3-662-47401-3_31

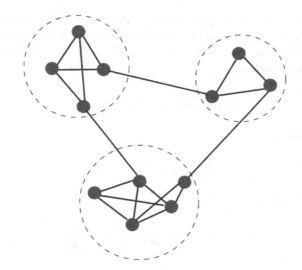

Fig. 1. A simple network with three communities, enclosed by the dashed circles.

2.1 Traditional Algorithms

Graph Partitioning. One of the earliest methods of community detection was proposed by Kernighan and Lin [2]. The Kernighan-Lin algorithm, stemmed from the partitioning thought, is still commonly used in nowadays, and often combined with other techniques. The strategy of KL algorithm is: initially parts a graph in subsets of vertices, such initial partition can be random or suggested by some information on the graph structure, and a quality function Q is introduced to measure the goodness of the partition; then move vertex in one subset to another or swap two vertices from different subsets so that Q has the maximal increase; for each iteration with positive and negative gains, the partition with the largest value of Q is the finally results.

However, in the progress of the KL algorithm only the best gain of Q is selected, that prone to get a locally optimal solution instead of globally optimal solution. Moreover, the biggest limitation of KL algorithm is the need of priori information, which means a bad initial partition usually leads to an unacceptable final result or convergence speed. The computational complexity of KL algorithm is $O(n^2\log n)$, where n is the number of vertices.

Hierarchical Clustering. Hierarchical clustering is another method to find communities in networks. The core thought of hierarchical clustering is identifying groups of vertices with high similarity. Basically there are two paths it can be classified:

- Agglomerative algorithm: starting from single vertex and merge the most similar ones iteratively. It is a bottom-up method.
- Divisive algorithms: in which networks are iteratively split into communities by removing edges link the least similar vertices pair. It is an up-down method.

Whether the agglomerative method or the divisive method, the important issue is how to define similarity. Various functions have been proposed to calculate the similarity, such as Euclidean distance, Manhattan distance and cosine similarity. Given a network/ graph in which vertices embedded into a n-dimensional Euclidean space, if the coordinates of two vertices are $A = (a_1, a_2, \ldots, a_n)$ and $B = (b_1, b_2, \ldots, b_n)$, then one could define the Euclidean distance

$$d_{AB}^E = \sum_{k=1}^{n} \sqrt{(a_k - b_k)^2},$$

(1)

the Manhattan distance

$$d_{AB}^M = \sum_{k=1}^{n} |a_k - b_k|,$$

(2)

and the cosine similarity

$$\rho_{AB} = \text{arccos} \frac{a \cdot b}{\sqrt{\sum_{k=1}^{n} a_k^2} \sqrt{\sum_{k=1}^{n} b_k^2}},$$

(3)

where $a \cdot b$ is the dot product of the vectors a and b. The variable ρ_{AB} is defined in the range $[0; \pi)$.

GN [3] and Fast-Newman [4] are both hierarchical algorithms. GN through a divisive method to get community structures: iteratively remove edges with the highest value of betweenness. As contrary, Fast-Newman is an agglomerative algorithm: it merges node clusters with the most gain or the least loss of modularity to ultimately find communities. A novel hierarchical algorithm [5], which based on density drop of subgraphs, has recently been proposed to output an optimal set of local communities automatically.

The advantages of hierarchical methods are that it can start without priori information or specific knowledge on the number of vertices. However, the weakness of the hierarchical algorithm include: fails to discriminate good from bad in many results it obtained; severely depends on the similarity measure adopted; always yields a hierarchical structure result whereas in many cases that is obviously wrong; dose not scale well so unable to apply in large networks.

Modularity Based Methods. Newman et al. [4] in 2004 proposed an algorithm in which they introduced a stopping criterion for the algorithm called Modularity Q. The Modularity function can be written as follows:

$$Q = \frac{1}{2m} \sum_{ij} (A_{ij} - P_{ij}) \delta(C_i, C_j),$$

(4)

where m is the number of vertices, A the adjacency matrix, P_{ij} the expected number of edges between vertices i and j in the null model, C_i indicate the community includes vertex i. The function $\delta(C_i, C_j) = 1$ if i and j are in one community, else $\delta(C_i, C_j) = 0$.

Interestingly, the Modularity Q itself has been studied thoroughly. A series of Modularity optimization based methods have been proposed, such as GA [6], MCD [7] and CGGC [8]. The latest methods include multi-level learning strategies algorithm [9] and path relinking technique [10].

However, recent research revealed that Modularity Q is inclined to find large communities, whereas networks in real world contain communities have very different size.

2.2 Algorithms for Overlapping Community Detection

Most of the algorithms mentioned above are at first designed to discover disjoint communities, i.e. vertices in networks belong to no more than 1 community. However, in natural networks it is common that one vertex belongs to several communities. For instance, a university professor has his own family, which can be seen as a community. In the same time he has colleague relationships with other professors in the same university, so he is a member of the faculty community as well. Moreover, members belong to multi communities usually play an important role in interaction between the corresponding communities. For these reasons, the issue of detecting overlapping communities has become quite popular in the last few years.

Clique Percolation Method. The most popular and famous method was proposed by Palla et al. [11], named Clique Percolation Method (CPM). In this method, the author used the term k-clique to indicate complete graph with k vertices. The algorithm is based on the assumption that the internal edges in a community are likely to form cliques due to their high density. Therefore, via searching adjacent cliques, one could detect communities, and the vertices in multi cliques can be seen as overlapping potions in communities. Empirical studies showed that small values of k (typically between 3 and 6) yield good results.

However, despite the conceptual simplicity, the weakness of CPM is that it assumes communities contain a large number of cliques, which is not always the case in real networks. On the other, if there are many cliques in networks, the algorithm may deliver trivial community structure: say the whole network as a community. One may argue that CPM algorithm are more like pattern matching rather than finding communities since they aim to find specific, localized structure in a network [12].

Link Clustering Based Algorithms. Another novel and promising approach to detect overlapping community has been recently suggested, i.e. determining clusters as sets of edges (or links) instead of vertices. Similar to vertices clustering, link clustering can intuitively deliver community as well. Moreover, link clustering-based methods have some intrinsic peculiarity. For example, it is easy to find overlapping structure, i.e. a node in the original graph is called overlapping if links connected to it are put in more than one cluster. Figure 2 shows a case of the benefit.

Many link-based algorithms were proposed. Evans et al. [13] projected a network into a weighted line graph, whose nodes are the links of the original graph,then community detection algorithms can be applied. Pasquale et al. [14] enhanced existing community detection algorithms by adding a pre-processing step in which edges are weighted. Sungsu Lim et al. [15] used the line graph as well as the original graph simultaneously to find overlapping structure.

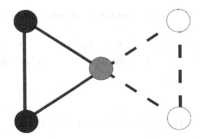

Fig. 2. Communities as sets of edges. In this figure, the graph has a natural division in two triangles, with the central vertex shared between them. If communities are identified by their internal edges, detecting the triangles and their overlapping vertex becomes easier than by using methods that group vertices.

The idea of clustering links is interesting. However, there are insufficient evidences to proof that it is better than grouping vertices, considering that these link-based methods also rely on an ambiguous definition of community [1].

Label Propagation Based Algorithms. In many situations, edges in complex networks indicate the information propagation among vertices. The generally results of the propagation are vertices in one community share the same information. Based on this thought, Raghavan et al. [16] proposed the Label Propagation based Algorithms (LPA). The strategy of LPA is: initially assign each vertex a unique label; each vertex update its label identifies to the label shows most times in its neighbor vertices at each iteration; the densely linked vertices will converge to the same label, which indicates the community structure. Some modified algorithms also have been proposed, such as COPRA [17], SLPA [18], etc.

The advantage of LPAs are no need of priori information, and the computational complexity of LPAs are O(m), where m is the number of edges in networks.

2.3 Alternative Algorithms

With decades of effort, many other interesting and promising algorithms have also been proposed. Statistical inference methods [19, 20] attracted plenty of attention for they usually give excellent results and they are mathematically principled. Against to single objective optimization, multi-optimization methods [21, 22] are under research now. Community detection in dynamic and/or delay-tolerant networks has also been studied [23, 24]. Finding communities in heterogeneous networks other than in homogeneous networks is a new approach in this area [25].

3 Scoring Functions

To define an algorithm good or bad, many scoring functions have been suggested. In fact, the Modularity Q by itself is a scoring function. In Ref. [26] a list of various commonly used scoring functions has been introduced. It is hard to say which function is better than others. Therefore, in this paper we selected four goodness metrics to introduce: density, clustering coefficient, conductance, and triangle participation ratio. Given a graph $G = (V, E)$ and a set of vertices $S \subseteq V$, let $ES = |\{(u, v) \in E \mid u, v \in S\}|$ be the number of edges in the subgraph induced by S. Let $OS = |\{(u, v) \mid u \in S, v \notin S\}|$ be the number of edges between the vertices in S and any vertex outside of S. A triplet is defined as a tuple of three nodes (u, v, w) where $(u, v), (v, w) \in E$. If $(u, w) \in E$, then the triplet is said to be closed, otherwise the triplet is open. A triplet is defined to be centered at a vertex, thus $(u, v, w) = (w, v, u)$, but $(u, v, w) \neq (v, u, w)$. We denote the set of closed and open triplets as Tc and To respectively. Given these notations, the goodness metrics for a community S are defined as follows:

- Density, $\dfrac{2|E_s|}{|S|(|S|-1)}$: the ratio of edges to the number of possible edges.

- Clustering coefficient, $\dfrac{|T_c|}{|T_c|+|T_o|}$: the ratio of closed triplets to all triplets.

- Conductance, $\dfrac{O_s}{2E_s+O_s}$: the fraction of edges that point outside the community.

- Triangle participation ratio, $\dfrac{|\{v \in T \mid T \in T_c\}|}{|S|}$: the fraction of nodes that belong to a triangle.

4   Conclusion

In this paper, we reviewed various algorithms ranging from traditional ones to the recently proposed ones. We analyzed the advantage and disadvantage for each algorithm/method. We also provided several commonly used scoring functions of algorithms.

As a result of substantial progress in recent years, it appears we now have an effective toolkit for studying community structure in networks. There is certainly still room for improvement in both the speed and sensitivity of community structure algorithms, and there are many interesting networked systems awaiting analysis using these methods.

References

1. Fortunato, S.: Community detection in graphs. Phys. Rep. **486**(3), 75–174 (2010)
2. Kernighan, B.W., Lin, S.: An efficient heuristic procedure for partitioning graphs. Bell Syst. Tech. J. **49**(2), 291–307 (1970)
3. Girvan, M., Newman, M.E.J.: Community structure in social and biological networks. Proc. Natl. Acad. Sci. **99**(12), 7821–7826 (2002)
4. Newman, M.E.J., Girvan, M.: Finding and evaluating community structure in networks. Phys. Rev. E **69**(2), 026113 (2004)
5. Qi, X., Tang, W., Wu, Y., et al.: Optimal local community detection in social networks based on density drop of subgraphs. Pattern Recogn. Lett. **36**, 46–53 (2014)

6. Guimera, R., Amaral, L.A.N.: Functional cartography of complex metabolic networks. Nature **433**(7028), 895–900 (2005)
7. Riedy, J., Bader, D. A., Meyerhenke, H.: Scalable multi-threaded community detection in social networks. In: 2012 IEEE 26th International Parallel and Distributed Processing Symposium Workshops & PhD Forum (IPDPSW), pp. 1619–1628. IEEE (2012)
8. Ovelgönne, M., Geyer-Schulz, A.: An ensemble learning strategy for graph clustering. Gr. Partitioning Gr. Clustering **588**, 187 (2012)
9. Ma, L., Gong, M., Liu, J., et al.: Multi-level learning based memetic algorithm for community detection. Appl. Soft Comput. **19**, 121–133 (2014)
10. Nascimento, M.C.V., Pitsoulis, L.: Community detection by modularity maximization using GRASP with path relinking. Comput. Oper. Res. **40**(12), 3121–3131 (2013)
11. Palla, G., Derényi, I., Farkas, I., et al.: Uncovering the overlapping community structure of complex networks in nature and society. Nature **435**(7043), 814–818 (2005)
12. Xie, J., Kelley, S., Szymanski, B.K.: Overlapping community detection in networks: The state-of-the-art and comparative study. ACM Comput. Surv. (CSUR) **45**(4), 43 (2013)
13. Evans, T.S., Lambiotte, R.: Line graphs, link partitions, and overlapping communities. Phys. Rev. E **80**(1), 016105 (2009)
14. De Meo, P., Ferrara, E., Fiumara, G., et al.: Enhancing community detection using a network weighting strategy. Inf. Sci. **222**, 648–668 (2013)
15. Lim, S., Ryu, S., Kwon, S., et al.: LinkSCAN*: overlapping community detection using the link-space transformation. In: 2014 IEEE 30th International Conference on Data Engineering (ICDE), pp. 292–303. IEEE (2014)
16. Raghavan, U.N., Albert, R., Kumara, S.: Near linear time algorithm to detect community structures in large-scale networks. Phys. Rev. E **76**(3), 036106 (2007)
17. Gregory, S.: Finding overlapping communities in networks by label propagation. New J. Phys. **12**(10), 103018 (2010)
18. Xie, J., Szymanski, B. K., Liu, X.: Slpa: uncovering overlapping communities in social networks via a speaker-listener interaction dynamic process. In: 2011 IEEE 11th International Conference on Data Mining Workshops (ICDMW), pp. 344–349. IEEE, (2011)
19. Newman, M.E.J.: Community detection and graph partitioning. EPL (Europhys. Lett.) **103**(2), 28003 (2013)
20. Arias-Castro, E., Verzelen, N.: Community detection in dense random networks. Ann. Stat. **42**(3), 940–969 (2014)
21. Shi, C., Yan, Z., Shi, Z., et al.: A fast multi-objective evolutionary algorithm based on a tree structure. Appl. Soft Comput. **10**(2), 468–480 (2010)
22. Shi, C., Kong, X., Fu, D., et al.: Multi-label classification based on multi-objective optimization. ACM Trans. Intell. Syst. Technol. (TIST) **5**(2), 35 (2014)
23. Bassett, D.S., Porter, M.A., Wymbs, N.F., et al.: Robust detection of dynamic community structure in networks. Chaos Interdisc. J. Nonlinear Sci. **23**(1), 013142 (2013)
24. Kim, C.M., Kang, I.S., Han, Y.H., et al.: A community detection scheme in delay-tolerant networks. In: Han, Y.-H., Park, D.-S., Jia, W., Yeo, S.-S. (eds.) Ubiquitous Information Technologies and Applications, pp. 745–751. Springer, Heidelburg (2013)
25. Shi, C., Kong, X., Huang, Y., et al.: HeteSim: a general framework for relevance measure in heterogeneous Networks. IEEE Trans. Knowl. Data Eng. **10**, 2479–2492 (2014)
26. Yang, J., Leskovec, J.: Defining and evaluating network communities based on ground-truth. In: Proceedings of the ACM SIGKDD Workshop on Mining Data Semantics, p. 3. ACM (2012)

Advanced Test Modelling and Execution Based on the International Standardized Techniques TTCN-3 and UTP

Axel Rennoch[✉], Marc-Florian Wendland, Andreas Hoffmann,
and Martin Schneider

Fraunhofer FOKUS, Kaiserin-Augusta-Allee 31,
10589 Berlin, Germany
{axel.rennoch,marc-florian.wendland,andreas.hoffmann,
martin.schneider}@fokus.fraunhofer.de

Abstract. In systems and service engineering testing is an important part to get confidence in quality and trust in security issues. Standardized testing techniques support the unique definition of abstract test models, configurations and behavior scenarios that can be executed automatically. This contribution presents the state of the art and future directions of two international standards for testing: the Testing and Test Control Notation (TTCN-3) from the European Telecommunication Standardization Institute (ETSI), and the UML testing profile (UTP) from the Open Management Group (OMG). Special emphasize is given to the translation from UTP to TTCN-3 test models, automated test execution using standard-compliant tool support and related examples from European projects.

Keywords: Test automation · Model-based test design · TTCN-3 · UML · UTP

1 Introduction

In the technical world of today testing is crucial for quality assurance, expensive (costs!) and time critical but only rarely practiced, often unsystematic and performed by hand, error-prone and even considered as uncool ("If you are a bad programmer you might be a tester.") or destructive.

The idea of advanced test modelling and execution is to have one abstract test technology for different kinds of tests, including distributed, platform-independent testing, integrated graphical test development, -documentation and analysis, and an adaptable, open test environment for test campaigns.

All areas of testing should be addressed, e.g. regression, conformance and functionality, interoperability, integration, security, load/stress testing and even monitoring and benchmarking shall be covered.

© Springer-Verlag Berlin Heidelberg 2015
Y. Lu et al. (Eds.): ISCTCS 2014, CCIS 520, pp. 245–252, 2015.
DOI: 10.1007/978-3-662-47401-3_32

2   Testing and Test Control Notation Version 3 (TTCN-3)

2.1   Concepts

TTCN-3 is the standardized test language and implementation published and maintained by the European Telecommunication Standardization Institute (ETSI) for formally defining test scenarios [4]. It has been designed purely for testing. TTCN-3 is both a specification technique and an implementation language. Abstract test definitions can be compiled into executable test programs written e.g. in Java, C or C ++. The specification is intended to be understood also by non-programmers. There are even different presentation formats available, e.g. for the text-based or graphical-oriented core notations. Most developers use the text-based notation that may be translated by some tools (e.g. TTworkbench [12]) into the graphical notation in order to illustrate e.g. test behavior steps or functions into a kind of well-known message sequence chart. A simple test case in textual notion as given in the following figure can be an input to the TTCN-3 based tester to communicate with a system under test (SUT) (Fig. 1).

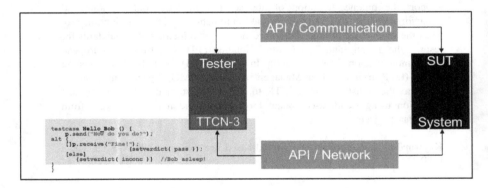

Fig. 1. Test execution using a TTCN-3 test system

In addition to the language notation, TTCN-3 technology provides much more: There is e.g. the standardized test system architecture with clearly defined interfaces and implementation rules for the primitives, but also various mapping rules for the integration of different data types or values specified with ASN.1, IDL or XML. Currently the standardized mapping from JSON to TTCN-3 is under development at ETSI and is planned to become the new part eleven of the TTCN-3 multipart standard in the 2015. A quick overview about the TTCN-3 types, programming constructs and predefined functions etc. is provided in the TTCN-3 Quick Reference Card that is freely available by BluKaktus [10].

2.2   TTCN-3 Major Use

TTCN-3 has a long history starting in 1992 with a first TTCN standard from ISO until it gains the great value and meaning of today, e.g. for the 3GPP mobile conformance center test specifications used by the Global Certification Forum [1]. The TTCN-3 technology is not restricted to telecom conformance testing and has a wide range of applicability, different communication paradigms and testing types. Actually it is used for multiple industrial domains that include telecom, automotive, medicine, finance, railways, avionics, etc. in both research and industry.

3 UML Testing Profile (UTP)

3.1 Concepts

The UTP Standard by the Object Management Group started in 2004 with its version 1.0, is currently published in its version 1.2 [9] from 2013, and is on the road to new version 2.0 that has been drafted and proposed in May 2014. UTP is based on UML version 2, and provides an industrial standard for (graphical) modeling of e.g. test architectures, behavior and data.

Its conceptual model includes and allows objects for test context, test cases, objectives, data, configuration, arbitration & verdicts, and logs. UTP offers a library with predefined types and values (to support e.g. ISO 25010 System and software quality model [7] or ISTQB test levels) and a mapping to TTCN-3.

3.2 UTP Major Use

Similar to TTCN-3, UTP offers domain-independent test modeling for dynamic testing approaches including test environments, test configurations, test case specifications (including test case derivation), test data specifications/values, test evaluation, i.e. managing and visualization of test results. It allows the integration of best practices such as keyword-driven testing, equivalence class testing, etc. and can be combined with other UML profiles (e.g., SysML, MARTE, SoaML) in order to support requirements traceability.

4 A Common View on TTCN-3 and UTP

It is not the intention of this paper to present or reflect the history or details of the various technical comparisons between TTCN-3 and UTP, since this exists for a long time and includes lots of excellent detailed work as given in [11] and [3] or [6]. In the industrial user perspective it appears that UTP has been developed after the establishment of TTCN-3 as kind of a derivate in some parts but UTP is on a much higher level of abstraction. UTP also tried to fill some gaps in TTCN-3 like the emphasis of the test environment and a generalization of some concepts that are present in TTCN-3 due to its historical root from earlier TTCN versions.

The integration of UTP and TTCN-3 focusses and allows the development of an efficient test platform fulfilling industrial testing requirements, ideally to execute high-level test models from UML testing profile.

As illustrated in Fig. 2, TTCN-3 is used in several domains as a binding link, i.e. a kind of middleware, between modelling and execution. Please note that there exist several tools to generate TTCN-3 code for test execution.

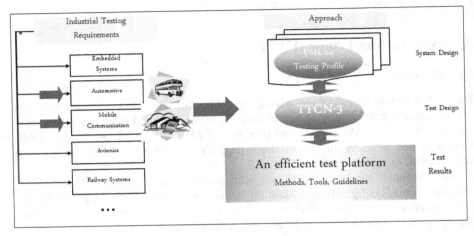

Fig. 2. Common approach using TTCN-3 and UTP

5   Tools and Applications

The acceptance of test techniques often depends on tools and experiences. Here we provide some well-known tools and applications, but also a short presentation of the European MIDAS project working for automated testing of Services architectures, available as a Software as a Service (SaaS) on a Cloud infrastructure. This project spans all activities including test generation, scheduling, execution, and arbitration and it relies on the standards TTCN-3 and UTP.

5.1   Industrial Perspective

First of all, the industrial application requires professional tool support and services. Today, there exist several high quality commercial tools on the market that include compilers/interpreters but also utilities with special focus on the e.g. generation of TTCN-3 code from high level model specifications. The following lists provide a selection retrieved from our knowledge and the TTCN-3 homepage at ETSI [4].

TTCN-3 Compilers and Interpreters

- Exhaustif/TTCN: compiler (C ++) produced by Métodos y Tecnología (MTP), Spain.
- OpenTTCN: interpreter (C, Java, C# interfaces) produced by OpenTTCN Ltd, Finland.
- Testcast: compiler (C/C ++, Java, C#) produced by ELVIOR, Estonia.

- Real Time Developer Studio: modelling tool including TTCN-3 compiler by PragmaDev, France.
- TAU Tester: compiler (C) by IBM.
- TTCN-3 Toolbox: compiler (C) by Danet Group, Germany.
- TTCN-3 Express: compiler (C#) by Fraunhofer FOKUS and Metarga GmbH, Germany.
- TTworkbench: compiler (C, Java) by Testing Technologies, Germany.

TTCN-3 Generators

- Qtronic by Conformiq OY, Finland, generate complete TTCN-3 test suites from e.g., UML, Java, or C# models.
- MaTeLo by All4Tec, France (TTCN-3 test suites from usage models specified using Markov chains).
- MOTES by ELVIOR, Estonia (from the state model of the SUT).

It is also possible to select one of the open source tools listed in the next section. However, customers need to carefully check the level of standard compliance, scope of the implementation and last but not least the professional vendor support from the tool provider. Under some circumstances (e.g. in standardization bodies) it is recommended to apply different tools in order to allow a wide distribution of the developed TTCN-3 scripts.

In the following, we summarize some short collection about the industrial usage of TTCN-3 technology:

Industrial use

Telecom industry

- Big telecom companies with hundreds of TTCN-3 engineers (e.g. Ericsson, Nokia, Siemens, Motorola) and a large distribution among SME.
- Standardization bodies: standardized test suites by ETSI, 3GPP (LTE!), OMA, TETRA and its members.
- IMS performance benchmark project by Intel, HP, BT, FOKUS, and others.
- Commercial test tool manufacturer like Spirent, Tektronix, Catapult, Nexus, R&S.
- Certification programs based on TTCN-3: e.g. WiMax forum.

Car communication systems

- Daimler, Volkswagen, SiemensVDO: edutainment bus system (test suite).
- Standardization groups like AUTOSAR and MOST cooperation, e.g. Car-to-car communication.

Other domains

- Medicine: SiemensMED (image processing), HL7 eHealth protocols (Interoperability).
- Power transmission and distribution: SiemensPTD (safe and reliable energy system).
- Financial data warehouse: International bank (functional /regression testing).
- Avionics: European Space Agency.
- Railways: Dutch railways (TT-Medal project [14]).

5.2   Research Perspective

From the researcher's viewpoint open source tools, free utilities and innovative research project results are of great value. The following provides a short selection of non-commercial tools listed due to our knowledge. Furthermore we provide a short introduction of an innovative framework for the integration of UTP and TTCN-3.

TTCN-3 Non-commercial tools

- LoongTesting testing platform including TTCN-3 compiler and integrated development environment by Information Processing Center of USTC, China.
- BBT TTCN-3 Compiler by BroadBit, Hungary.
- TRex by University of Göttingen that provides IDE functionality for TTCN-3 core notation, and support the assessment and automatic restructuring of TTCN-3 test suites (open-source Eclipse plug-in).
- T3doc by F. Engler and further developed by ETSI for generating HTML documentation via tagged TTCN-3 comments.
- Codec generator by IRISA as part of T3DevKit. It automatically generates a codec based on TTCN-3 type module(s), C ++ codec functions.
- T3DevLib by IRISA as part of T3DevKit. It allows the development or integration of Codec, SUT and Platform Adapter implementations written in C ++.
- Titan, a brand new Open source community project driven by Ericsson experts [13].

There are even more academic prototype/research tools, e.g. for guideline checking, quality analysis. Since there is not such big list of UTP research tools we like to put your attention to the Fokus!MBT framework [5] that allows some integration of the most important test development activities including automated test case synthesis and test execution (cp. Fig. 3).

5.3   The MIDAS Project

The European research project MIDAS [8] is developing a Cloud platform for automated testing of SOA services. For this purpose, model-based test generators, schedulers, and arbiters for functional and inference-driven testing, usage-based testing, and security testing are provided as services running on the MIDAS platform. The platform also provides dedicated services for test code generation and execution. To achieve this, all services rely on a UML profile that is based on UTP 1.2 with some advancement. Thus, all generator services generate models that are compliant to this MIDAS domain-specific language (DSL). The experiences with and the advancements of UTP 1.2 made in the MIDAS research project led to immediate contributions to the version 2 draft of UTP.

The test execution service of the MIDAS platform is completely based on TTCN-3 and corresponding compiler, plugins, and codecs are developed and gratefully provided by Testing Technologies IST GmbH. The model-based test cases compliant to the UTP-based MIDAS DSL are transformed to TTCN-3 and then executed against the service under test.

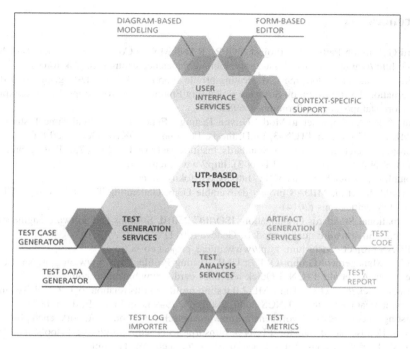

Fig. 3. Fokus!MBT

In 2015 the MIDAS project is in its third and last project year and thus, in its evaluation phase with the help of its pilots from the eHealth and the Logistics domain.

6 Outlook

TTCN-3 created a large international community with great expertise (see e.g. [15]), commercial and non-commercial tools. Today, TTCN-3 is established and well accepted for future usage. Most hand written scripts are easily, human readable description of test scenarios, free from programming issues, providing a transparent framework for end-customers that allows platform and tool vendor independence, with different presentation formats. The clear separation of testing issues allows writing of well-defined test configuration, data and behavior, as well as SUT specific adaptations and codecs.

UTP has been recognized by several communities but is still waiting for a larger field of application. The situation may change quickly in 2015 with the upcoming UTP version 2.

We thank our colleagues from the Fraunhofer FOKUS System Quality Testing team, the TTCN-3 and UTP communities, in particular our partners from the MIDAS consortium and our professional tool provider Testing Technology IST GmbH for the great work and cooperation, as well as the European Union's Seventh Framework Program (FP7-ICT-2012-8) under grant agreement no 318786 for their financial support.

References

1. 3rd Generation Partnership Project (3GPP), RAN5 Mobile Competence Center, Task force 160: http://www.3gpp.org/about-3gpp/mobile-competence-centre/mcc-task-forces
2. Ali, S., et al.: How does the UML testing profile support risk-based testing. In: 2014 IEEE International Symposium on Software Reliability Engineering Workshops. http://ieeexplore.ieee.org/stamp/stamp.jsp?arnumber=6983859
3. Dai, Z.-R.: An Approach to Model-Driven Testing – Functional and Real-Time Testing with UML 2.0, U2TP and TTCN-3, Ph.D. thesis, Fraunhofer FOKUS, Berlin (2006)
4. European Telecommunication Standards Institute (ETSI): ES 201 873: Testing and Test Control Notation, version 3 (TTCN-3). http://www.ttcn-3.org
5. Fraunhofer FOKUS: Fokus!MBT. http://www.fokusmbt.com
6. Herbold, S., et al: MIDAS project deliverable D3.6: Generating TTCN-3 from PIM UML SAUT Specifications (2014)
7. International Standards Organization: ISO/IEC 25010, Systems and software engineering - System and software quality models, Geneva (2011)
8. MIDAS project consortium. http://www.midas-project.eu
9. Object Management Group (OMG): UML Testing Profile. http://www.omg.org/spec/UTP
10. Rennoch, A., et al.: TTCN-3 Quick reference card. www.blukaktus.com
11. Schieferdecker, I., et al.: The UML 2.0 testing profile and its relation to TTCN-3. Testing of Communicating Systems. LNCS 2644, 2003, pp. 79–94. Springer, Berlin (2003)
12. Testing Technology: TTworkbench. http://testingtech.com/products/ttworkbench.php
13. Titan, Eclipse-based IDE for TTCN-3. https://projects.eclipse.org/projects/tools.titan
14. TT-Medal project consortium. https://itea3.org/project/tt-medal.html
15. TTCN-3 Bibliography: http://www.ttcn.de/bibliography

Understanding Human Goal Setting as a Means for Supporting Goal Oriented Requirements Engineering

Jørgen Bøegh(⊠)

Lemvig Gymnasium, Lemvig, Denmark
jorgen_boegh@yahoo.dk

Abstract. Identification of goals is notorious difficult. This paper analyses human goals from both psychological and biological viewpoints. The application of Maslows pyramid provides a hierarchical structure on human goals. The detailed understanding of human goals supports goal modeling in goal oriented requirements engineering.

Keywords: Goal identification · Requirement engineering · Human goals · Psychology · Hierarchical structure

1 Introduction

Goal Oriented Requirements Engineering is now established as an important part of the requirements engineering process. Some scholars even consider the goal oriented approach to be the requirements engineering community's most important contribution to software engineering. There is a large literature discussing the advantages of goals in requirements engineering. For example, [9] provides an extensive list of benefits: Goals ensure completeness of requirements, help to avoid irrelevant requirements, provide a reason for the requirements, provide a mechanism for structuring requirements, support analysis of alternative requirements, help managing conflicting requirements, separate stable from volatile information, and last but not least goals drive the identification of requirements.

Several goal oriented approaches have been developed. KAOS [10] and i* [17] are prominent examples of two quite different approaches. The KAOS method is a multi-paradigm framework that allows combination of different levels of expression and reasoning. It includes (semi)formal modeling, structuring and reasoning about goals, and supporting selection among the alternatives. The i* approach models how actors depend on each other for achieving their goals. The i* method is often used at a higher level of abstraction and earlier in the requirements process than the KAOS approach [6]. More comprehensive overviews of concepts and methods can be found in for example [11, 9, 15].

Goal identification is inherently difficult and neither KAOS nor i* solve the problem of identifying the basic goals. The literature also provides limited guidance. Guidelines are often general and of the form: Look for intentional keywords such as "purpose", "objective", "concern", "intent", "in order to", etc. in transcripts of

© Springer-Verlag Berlin Heidelberg 2015
Y. Lu et al. (Eds.): ISCTCS 2014, CCIS 520, pp. 253–259, 2015.
DOI: 10.1007/978-3-662-47401-3_33

interviews of people working in a company and look for company policies descriptions and company mission statements. These guidelines may provide some help, but they are not so easy to use in practice, especially for identifying high level goals. Furthermore, statements such as "improve productivity", "provide quality of service", "our employees are our most important resource" are vague. Goals must be made more explicit in order to be really useful.

Much human activity is based on goals. Goals are the tools with which people engage in volitional behavior. Each moment offers a myriad of possibilities for inter-action for each individual. Therefore people must decide which actions to take. These choices are based on goals.

2   The Nature of Goals

There are several definitions of a goal in the requirements engineering literature. For example, [9] defines a goal as "an objective that the system should achieve through cooperation of agents in the software-to-be and in the environment." In [1] goals are defined as "high-level objectives of the business, organization or system; they capture the reasons why a system is needed and guide decisions at various levels within the enterprise." Both definitions give a good intuition of the goal concept. For the purpose of this paper there is no need to enter a discussion of subtleties and pro and cons of different proposed definitions. The important objective is to obtain an under-standing of the nature of goals.

The goals in software engineering describe the purpose why the system must be build. The purpose of developing the system must be found outside the system itself – in the context in which the system will function. This is a major difference from human goals. People construct their own goals and do not necessarily depend on goals defined by others. However, we can identify goals of software systems by analyzing goals of human stakeholders.

Human goals are prescriptive statements of intent; they are desires for future states; they are higher-order entities that function as abstract, organizing structures and remain fairly stable over time. Goals can be considered as the mental representation of behaviors or behavioral outcomes that are associated with positive affect. They determine human actions. Most goals are linked to lower-level acts and skills and thus provide a reference point for cognition and action. Goal representations do not possess truth-conditions, but conditions of satisfaction. A goal cannot be true or false. How-ever, the goal-states as represented can either hold or not hold, or they can hold to various degrees.

3   The Psychology of Goals

Goals have been studies by psychologists for a number of years. There is even a specific branch of psychology called goal-setting theory, which was established about 30 years ago [12]. The aim of this theory is to understand how goals influence human performance. According to [12] there are four ways that goals influence performance of individuals. The four mechanisms are:

- Goals focus attention, effort, and action toward goal-relevant activities and away from goal-irrelevant activities.
- Goals serve as an energizer; higher goals induce greater effort, while low goals induce lesser effort.
- Goals affect persistence; high goals lead to greater persistence than do moderately difficult, easy, or vague goals.
- Goals activate cognitive knowledge and strategies that help people cope with the situation at hand; they motivate people to use existing abilities, pull stored task-relevant knowledge into awareness, and/or may motivate people to search for new knowledge.

However, there are situations where goals may have a negative effect. For example, when a goal is difficult and challenge the ability of a person, then the person will perform worse if the person considers the goal as a threat and not as a challenge, i.e. the situation is perceived as leading to failure with no available strategies to cope with it [5]. Focusing on failure seems to reduce a person's ability to finding an appropriate strategy for achieving a difficult goal, i.e. it creates a kind of tunnel vision.

Many human actions are clearly goal directed. However, there are other types of actions. Exploratory behavior is one example. During history of human life success has depended on the balance between trying out new ways of doing things and simply falling back to routine behavior. Noise in the decision process introduces an element of randomness in actions. Sometimes this explains why one action is chosen over another. Memory is also important in determining action choices. Finally, conditioned responding appears when people are faced with an uncertain or ambiguous situation. In this case people generally do what was successful before in similar situations, or they may even repeat previously made errors.

4 The Biology of Goals

Recently neurobiologists have also studied goals and how they lead to selecting actions. Their findings support the results obtained in psychology and confirm the basic nature of goals in human endeavor. Neurobiology is a means to obtain a deeper understanding of how human goals are represented and selected. Today neurobiology can to some extend explain observed psychological mechanisms.

To choose beneficial actions, the human brain applies a three layers architecture in the central nervous system [8, 14]. At the lowest level is an inherited, hard wired system, called the Pavlovian system. Hard wired means that it is built-in functions, and not something that is learned. This layer works very fast and takes care of some very basic behavior. The responses from the Pavlovian system can either be the avoidance or the approach of salient biological stimuli and cues associated to them. The rapid activation of these behavioral patterns has increased the fitness of the human being during evolution.

At the next level is a habitual, stimulus-driven system. The habitual system associates stimuli with responses that were rewarding in the past. Actions under habitual control are reflexive in nature, by virtue of their control by antecedent stimuli rather than their consequences.

At the highest level is an intentional, goal-directed system. The goal-directed system selects actions dependent on the match of anticipated action outcomes and current needs. This is called action-effect based actions. Actions under goal-directed control are performed with regard to their consequences. In other word, goals are represented as relations between actions and their consequences [2].

These three layers sometimes compete and sometimes cooperate with each other for making a decision about which course of action to take. However, the exact mechanisms connecting the three layers are not known today.

Two characteristics of goals are that actions are selected which are expected to produce desired results, and these actions are guided toward such goals by an interplay of prediction, control and monitoring. Neuroscience can now throw some light on the human decision process. Research reported in [7] indicates that the decision process comprises four steps:

(1) 'Early whether decisions': Decide whether to make any action at all. There could be three different reasons for making a decision:
(a) Routine processing of stimuli can fail to generate sufficient information to determine a response — for example, when selecting between two alternative actions in response to an ambiguous stimulus.
(b) A new reason for action can suddenly emerge, reflecting either a renewed basic need, such as hunger, or a new high-level desire, such as the desire to wave to a friend.
(c) A general drive to perform occasional voluntary actions would allow exploration of the behavioral landscape.
(2) 'What decisions': Select an appropriate goal. This decision has two forms:
(a) Select between goals (or tasks). Usually people have several simultaneous goals so it is necessary to schedule goals by selecting between them.
(b) Select between movements to achieve the goal. This involves choosing between alternative means to achieve the goal [3]. Most goals can be achieved in any of several ways, in part because of the redundancy that is built into the motor apparatus.
(3) 'Late whether decisions': Make a final predictive check and possible veto. The cost of the selected action might turn out to be high, it might be a poor means to achieve the selected goal, or the task or environment might have changed. Therefore a final check is performed before the motor system is committed.
(4) 'When decisions': Decide the timing of the action. The timing generally depends on coordinating the scheduling of other potential actions and routine processes. The timing of a specific action often depends on external circumstances and internal motivations rather than on any explicit 'when decision'.

The general thinking is that people define their goals, and when they act on these goals, they do so by making a conscious decision. Moreover, when they make a conscious decision to act it feels as if that conscious decision is the first and foremost cause of the act that follows. However, it turns out that actions are actually planned in the brain before they are consciously decided. It is possible to measure brain activity before decisions are consciously made. This fact questions whether or not humans have a free will to decide whatever they want. The impression that people are able to freely choose between different possible courses of action is fundamental to human mental life. However, it has been suggested that this subjective experience of freedom is no more than an illusion and that actions are initiated by unconscious mental processes long before the person become aware of his/her intention to act [4, 16].

For example, if a person wants to transport a vertical rod to either a high shelf or low shelf, then the person will grasp the rod at a low or high position, respectively, thereby facilitating the most convenient way of moving the rod [8]. This indicates that the activity is guided by the goal-directed system. However, the decision of where to grasp the rod is not an active, conscious decision. On the other hand, if a person wants to grasp and transport handled objects, such as a hammer or a screwdriver, then the person will grasp the objects according to their normal use in most cases, independent of the position of the shelf. These examples illustrate unconscious mental processes and show the subtle interplay between the habitual system and the goal-directed system.

5   A Hierarchical Structure for Human Goals

A possible approach to structure high-level personal goals is the Maslow pyramid [13]. The Maslow hierarchy of needs is an attempt to understand what motivates people; in other words, what are their basic goals. The original idea of the Maslow pyramid is that the most basic needs are at the bottom and needs at one level in the pyramid must be satisfied before a person will consider needs at the next, higher level. Although this hypothesis may not be true, the Maslow pyramid provides a good structure for understanding basic human goals. The Maslow pyramid is briefly outlined in the following:

Physiological Needs: These comprise the physical requirements for human survival. They are the most basic needs in the sense that if not satisfied then the human body cannot function properly. Hence the most basic human goals are related to access to air, food, drink, shelter (providing necessary protection from the elements), warmth, sex (maintaining an adequate birth rate), and sleep.

Safety Needs: When the physiological needs are met then goals related to safety, security, law, order and stability become important. These goals can be divided into personal safety (war, natural disasters, violence), financial safety (job security, insurance, reasonable accommodation), and health issues (accidents/illness and their adverse impacts).

Social Needs: The third level of goals relates to interpersonal relations and involves feelings of belongingness. This level comprises friendship, intimacy, and family. Humans need to feel a sense of belonging and acceptance among their social group, for example family, intimate partner, colleagues, friends, sports teams, professional organizations, religious groups, etc.

Esteem: The next level in the hierarchy is concerned with self-esteem, self-respect, achievement, mastery, independence, status, dominance, prestige, and managerial responsibility. Everybody wants to feel respected, accepted and valued by others. Maslow distinguishes between two types of esteem needs. The first type is the need for respect from others such as a need for status, recognition, fame, prestige, and attention. The second type manifests itself as the need for self-respect, including a need for strength, competence, mastery, self-confidence, independence, and freedom.

Self-Actualization: This is the highest level in the pyramid. It is about realizing personal potential, self-fulfillment, seeking personal growth and peak experiences. This level of goals refers to what a person's full potential is and the realization of that potential. It covers a broad range of goals, for example to become a perfect employee, to create a beautiful piece of art, to make a new invention, etc.

Although about 70 years old, the Maslow pyramid is still widely recognized as a cornerstone of modern psychology. In recent years some researchers have put forward some change proposals to the hierarchy, for example to place social needs closer to the bottom of the pyramid. It seems that human behavior has gradually changed in the direction to seek human contact and social interaction. However, a discussion of these issues is outside the scope of this paper.

6   Conclusion

This paper provides insight into the nature of human goals. In particular, it provides a hierarchical structure of goals defined by the Maslow pyramid, a well-established framework from psychology.

Using this understanding gives the requirements engineer a starting point for identifying the highest level goals, thereby providing a theoretical sound approach for developing a goal model from the top down perspective by asking "how" questions. This should of course be combined with a bottom up approach asking "why" questions whereby a more complete goal model can be developed.

There are other types of goals that must be considered when developing a goal model for a system. This includes goals for groups of people as well as organizational goals. Such goals should also be understood in detail in order to obtain a complete goal model.

References

1. Anton, A.I.: Goal-based requirements analysis. In: Proceedings of the Second International Conference on Requirements Engineering, pp. 136–144 (1996)
2. Balleine, B.W., O'Doherty, J.P.: Human and rodent homologies in action control: corticostriatal determinants of goal-directed and habitual action. Neuropsychopharmacol. Rev. **35**, 48–69 (2010)
3. Cisek, P., Kalaska, J.F.: Neural correlates of reaching decisions in dorsal premotor cortex: specification of multiple direction choices and final selection of action. Neuron **45**, 801–814 (2005)

4. Dijksterhuis, A., Aarts, H.: Goals, attention, and (un)consciousness. Annu. Rev. Psychol. **61**, 467–490 (2010)
5. Drach-Zahavya, A., Erez, M.: Challenge versus threat effects on the goal–performance relationship. Organ. Behav. Hum. Decis. Process. **88**, 667–682 (2002)
6. Edirisuriya, A., Zdravkovic, J.: Goal support towards business processes modelling. In: International Conference on Innovations in Information Technology, pp. 208–212 (2008)
7. Haggard, P.: Human volition: towards a neuroscience of will. Nat. Rev. Neurosci. **9**, 934–946 (2008)
8. Herbort, O., Butz, M.V.: Habitual and goal-directed factors in (everyday) object handling. Exp. Brain Res. **213**(4), 371–382 (2011)
9. van Lamsweerde, A.: Goal-oriented requirements engineering: a guided tour. In: Proceedings RE 2001 5th IEEE International Symposium on Requirements Engineering, Toronto, pp. 249–263 August 2001
10. van Lamsweerde, A., Letier, E.: From object orientation to goal orientation: a paradigm shift for requirements engineering. In: Wirsing, M., Knapp, A., Balsamo, S. (eds.) RISSEF 2002. LNCS, vol. 2941, pp. 325–340. Springer, Heidelberg (2004)
11. Lapouchnian, A.: Goal-Oriented Requirements Engineering: An Overview of the Current Research, Research Report, University of Toronto (2005)
12. Locke, E.A., Latham, G.P.: New directions in goal-setting theory. Curr. Dir. Psychol. Sci. **15** (5), 265–268 (2006)
13. Maslow, A.H.: A theory of human motivation. Psychol. Rev. **50**, 370–396 (1943)
14. Rigoli, F., Pavone, E.F., Pezzulo, G.: Interaction of goal-directed and Pavlovian systems in aversive domains. In: Proceedings of the CogSci 2011, pp. 3211–3216, Boston (2011)
15. Sen, A.M., Hemachandran, K.: Goal oriented requirement engineering: a literature survey. Assam Univ. J. Sci. Technol.: Phys. Sci. Technol. **6**(2), 16–25 (2010)
16. Soon, C.S., Brass, M., Heinze, H.-J., Haynes, J.-D.: Unconscious determinants of free decisions in the human brain. Nat. Neurosci. **11**, 543–545 (2008)
17. Yu, E.: Towards modeling and reasoning support for early-phase requirements engineering. In: Proceedings RE-97 - 3rd International Symposium on Requirements Engineering, Annapolis, pp. 226–235 (1997)

The Improvement and Implementation of iSLIP Algorithm Based on FPGA

Zeng Guang[1(✉)], Yao Lin[1], Zhao Ming[2], and Ma Yilan[1]

[1] School of Computer and Communication Engineering, University of Science and Technology Beijing (USTB), Beijing 100083, People's Republic of China
ustbzg2012@163.com
[2] Hotan Teachers College, Xinjiang 848000, People's Republic of China
Xjzhaoming8898@163.com

Abstract. High-efficiency scheduling algorithm ensures the high throughput rate of switching network and high utilization rate of bandwidth. In order to reduce the communication time delay and BER (Bit Error Rate) of data transmission, we improve the iSLIP scheduling algorithm and achieve a better performance of high speed switching system by using less FPGA resources.

Keywords: Scheduling · iSLIP · FPGA · Performance

1 Introduction

The purpose of scheduling algorithm is to complete matching input ports and output ports of a switching network in order to realize non-blocking switching of the data frame. High-efficiency scheduling algorithm can greatly reduce the waste of resources caused by competition, thus improving the rate of throughput and bandwidth utilization of a switching network and reducing the communication time delay and BER [1].

In this article, we use the virtual output queues (VOQ) model in the input buffer of switching based on the FPGA network switching platform. The internal switching network structure is a combined input and crossbar queues (CICQ) with high-efficiency. On this platform, two major indicators measuring scheduling algorithm performance are bandwidth utilization and time delay. Based on the two indicators, we conduct a comparative analysis of characteristics of two common switching algorithms, RRM and iSLIP. Then, we make an improvement on iSLIP and finally realize high-efficiency performance of switching algorithm.

The rest of the paper is organized as follows: common switching algorithms are introduced in Sect. 2; Methods to improve the scheduling algorithm and scheduling architecture are presented in Sect. 3; Verification of the switching platform based on FPGA is described in Sect. 4; Conclusion remarks are given in Sect. 5.

2 Common Scheduling Algorithms

2.1 RRM Scheduling Algorithm

RRM (Round Robin Matching), known as time slice rotation algorithm, is a scheduling algorithm widely used in the network system [2]. The basic principle of RRM

Y. Lu et al. (Eds.): ISCTCS 2014, CCIS 520, pp. 260–266, 2015.
DOI: 10.1007/978-3-662-47401-3_34

scheduling algorithm is based on assigning a number of time slices to a certain scheduling process [3]. The scheduling scheme of RRM is shown in Fig. 1 [4].

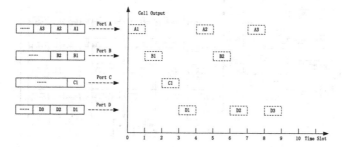

Fig. 1. RRM scheduling algorithm

The advantage of RRM scheduling algorithm is its simpleness. It is relatively easy to implement in hardware and can reach 100 % throughput under the uniform traffic; however, under the non-uniform traffic mode, its performance will be reduced greatly [5].

2.2 ISLIP Scheduling Algorithm

iSLIP scheduling algorithm was proposed by Nick McKeow, Stanford university [7]. It is then improved as ESLIP algorithm, which has been used in routing of Cisco GSR12000 series [1]. The scheduling process is shown in Fig. 2:

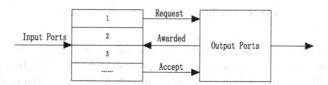

Fig. 2. Scheduling process of iSLIP scheduling algorithm

3 The Improvement of ISLIP Scheduling Algorithm

3.1 Switching Structure

This system adopts the VOQ + Buffered Crossbar exchange structure, namely common CICQ [8]. Its switching structure is shown in Fig. 3.

3.2 Algorithm

iSLIP scheduling algorithm has the best performance in terms of equity and priority control; however, due to the its complexity in implementation, measure should be taken

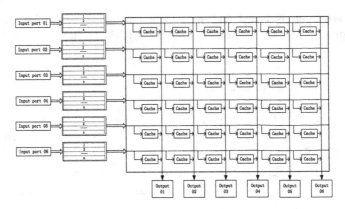

Fig. 3. CICQ switching structure

to further improve it. The improved iSLIP scheduling algorithm block diagram is shown in Fig. 4:

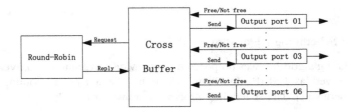

Fig. 4. The block diagram of improve iSLIP

The improved iSLIP scheduling algorithm is shown in Fig. 5:

The improvement can greatly simplify the process of iSLIP scheduling algorithm. It can facilitate the successful implementation on FPGA while maintains iSLIP scheduling algorithm's advantages in terms of equity and priority control. In addition, combined with the rotary mechanism of RRM scheduling algorithm, data sending is no longer constrained by the sending priority completely. This can avoid the situation where high priority input ports keep sending data while low priority ports keeps waiting to send data, which in turn can avoid the overflow of the cache from the low priority input ports.

4 Simulation and Implementation Analysis

4.1 Simulation Analysis

According to the modified iSLIP scheduling algorithms in Sect. 3, we conduct an iSLIP arbitrator function simulation. The waveform is shown in the Fig. 6:

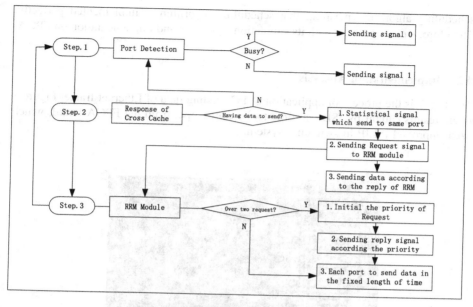

Fig. 5. The improve algorithm of iSLIP

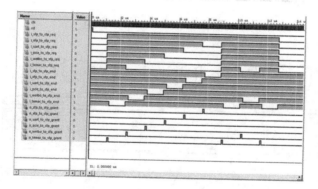

Fig. 6. Simulation waveform of improved iSLIP

We can see from the above Fig. 6 that when the SFP, XFP, PCIE, UART, TEMAC, WEIBO ports have sent the request signals to the destination output port SFP (i_xx_to_sfp_req), according to the priority order of rotary mechanism, it is the TE-MAC port's request that is responded first (namely o_temac_to_sfp_grant is high level). After TEMAC port has sent a complete frame of data to the SFP, a low level of signal indicating the completion of transmission is produced (namely i_te-mac_to_sfp_end is low level), which is used to inform iSLIP arbitrator that port SFP is idle and available for next data transmission from WEIBO port, shown as in Fig. 7. The rest can be done in the same manner. What we can conclude from the simulation waveform is that it is completely in line with the expected situation of improved iSLIP scheduling algorithm, meaning that scheduling algorithm is implemented perfectly. Therefore, we can proceed with its simulation, synthesis and implementation on FPGA.

4.2 Implementation Analysis

The Fig. 7 is the process of application of PC sending data of Ethernet frame. Figure 8 is the results caught by ISE real-time tools, Chipscope, from the FPGA board, which used improved iSLIP in switching system:

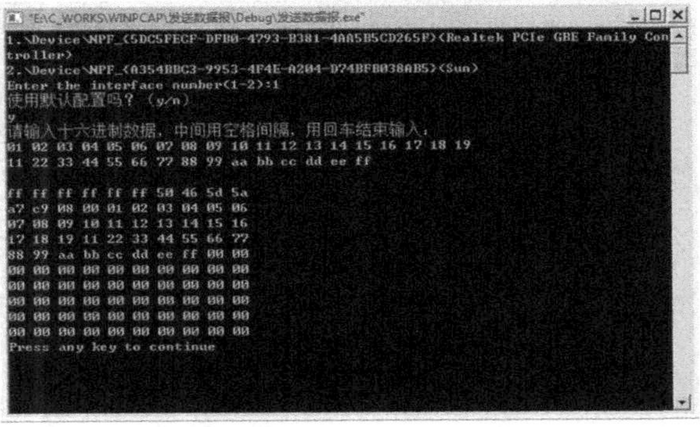

Fig. 7. PC sends the source data

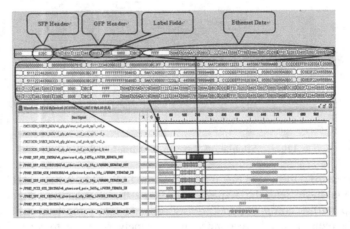

Fig. 8. Switch data in FPGA board caught by Chipscope

Figures 9 and 10 show FPGA resources utilization before and after the improvement of scheduling algorithm. Through comparison between the selected data in the cells with red border, we can see clearly that the improved scheduling algorithm can use less resources of FPGA to realize efficient switching.

Device Utilization Summary (estimated values)				[-]
Logic Utilization	Used	Available	Utilization	
Number of Slice Registers	10968	316800	3%	
Number of Slice LUTs	8246	158400	5%	
Number of fully used LUT-FF pairs	6800	14898	46%	
Number of bonded IOBs	109	440	25%	
Number of Block RAM/FIFO	68	516	13%	
Number of BUFG/BUFGCTRLs	15	32	46%	

Fig. 9. FPGA resources utilization before Improved

Device Utilization Summary (estimated values)				[-]
Logic Utilization	Used	Available	Utilization	
Number of Slice Registers	10968	316800	3%	
Number of Slice LUTs	8246	158400	5%	
Number of fully used LUT-FF pairs	4316	14898	28%	
Number of bonded IOBs	92	440	20%	
Number of Block RAM/FIFO	59	516	11%	
Number of BUFG/BUFGCTRLs	15	32	46%	

Fig. 10. FPGA resources utilization of improved iSLIP

5 Conclusion

In this paper, we combine the rotary mechanism of RRM scheduling algorithm with iSLIP scheduling algorithm to integrate the advantages of RRM scheduling algorithm with iSLIP scheduling algorithm, so as to improve iSLIP scheduling algorithm. We also apply it to the second level node cache of the output scheduling and apply RR_LQD scheduling algorithm to the first level of VOQ queue scheduling. Ultimately, we successfully realize the non-blocking switching exchange system with high-performance.

Through an analysis of the simulation and test results of verification on FPGA, we can conclude that the proposed scheme and the improved strategy can use less FPGA resources to achieve a better performance of high speed switching system, and the whole system can operate stably and accurately based on the FPGA experiment platform.

Acknowledgement. This research is supported by the Fundamental Research Funds for the Central Universities (No.FRF-TP-14-046A2), and also supported by the National Natural Science Foundation of P. R. China (No.61102060).

References

1. Teng, X.: Research of scheduling mechanism and wireless bandwidth allocation mechanism of on-board switching in Spatial Information Networks. National University of Defense Technology, November 18, 2009 (In Chinese)
2. Yoshigoe, K., Christensen, K., Jacob, A.: The RR/RR CICQ switch: hardware design for 10-Gbps link speed. In: IEEE International Performance, Computing and Communications Conference Proceedings, pp. 481–485 (2003)

3. Sun, H., Zhang, D., Zhang, S.: Implementation of round robin scheduling algorithm based on FPGA. J. Electron. Inf. Technol. **25**(8), 1143–1147 (2003). (In Chinese)
4. Lei, C.: The Design and Simulation of Data Exchange System on Fibre Channel Switch. Huazhong University of Science & Technology, January 11, 2011 (In Chinese)
5. Shin, E.S., Mooney, V.J., Riley, G.F.: Round-robin arbiter design and generation. In: Proceedings of the International Symposium on System Synthesis, pp. 243–248 (2002)
6. Lai-xin, P., Zi, Y., Wen-dong, Z., Chang, T.: A novel scheduling algorithm based on longest queue detecting for CICQ switching fabrics. J. Electron. Inf. Technol. **17**(6), 1457–1462 (2010). (In Chinese)
7. Mekkittikul, A., Mekeown, N.: A practical scheduling algorithm to achieve 100% through put in input-queued switches. In: Proceedings of IEEE Information, San Francisco, pp. 792–799, April 1998
8. Javidi, T., Magill, R., Hrabik, T.: A high-through put scheduling algorithm for a buffered crossbar switch fabric. In: ICC2001, pp. 555–557 (2001)

The Optimization Design of High Q Microwave Photonic Filters Based on Cascade Fiber Bragg Gratings

Gao Huimin[⊠] and Zeng Guang

School of Computer and Communication Engineering, University of Science and Technology Beijing (USTB), Beijing 100083, China
78141055@qq.com

Abstract. Quality factor is one of the most important indicators of measuring microwave photonic filter performance and the optimization of microwave photonic filter has been a change area recently. In this paper, a novel one order infinite response microwave photonic filter (OO-IIRMPF) model is built, and the structure of Fiber Bragg Gratings (FBGs) with the erbium doped fiber pair is proposed. By simulating the amplitude response and optimizing the parameters, the conclusion that the infinite quality factor can be realized theoretically is obtained, and the condition is that the product of the weighting coefficients of feedback loops should be equal to 1. Moreover, the infinite impulse response (IIR) filter cascade system and finite impulse response (FIR) filter cascade system are constructed and compared to find the best filter parameters. The microwave photonic filter with high Q value designed in this paper has the virtue of simple structure and lower cost.

Keywords: Microwave photonic filters · High Q value · Fiber bragg gratings · IIR · FIR

1 Introduction

Taking advantages of low dissipation, large bandwidth, light weight and strong resistance to electromagnetic interference, microwave photonic technology has attracted the attention of the researchers in wireless and optical fiber communication field around the world quickly. Applying this technology to the traditional microwave signal processing field and using microwave filter based on optical fiber and optical devices have important theoretical and potential economic value [1].

Currently, the implementations of the high Q filter scheme are mainly based on active infinite impulse response (IIR) filter, and the research of filter frequency selectivity is poor [2, 3]. In order to improve the performance of frequency selective filter and enhance the high Q value, the structure of erbium doped fiber with FBGs pair based on one order infinite response microwave photonic filter (OO-IIRMPF) model is proposed in this paper. Based on the model designed in this paper, a high quality system with infinite impulse response (IIR) filter and finite impulse response (FIR) filter cascade are built.

The rest of this paper is organized as follows. Section 2 introduces the basic principle of microwave photonic filter, including the analyses of the free spectral range (FSR) and

© Springer-Verlag Berlin Heidelberg 2015
Y. Lu et al. (Eds.): ISCTCS 2014, CCIS 520, pp. 267–273, 2015.
DOI: 10.1007/978-3-662-47401-3_35

the high quality factor. The OO-IIRMPF model which based on the erbium doped fiber with the FBGs pair is designed in Sect. 3. The IIR filter cascade system and FIR filter cascade system are presented in Sect. 4. Conclusion remarks are given in Sect. 5.

2 Basic Principle of Microwave Photonic Filter

As an important device in the microwave photonics, microwave photonic filter, is essential to the microwave photonic signal processing technology, and been applied widely in areas such as the radar and Radio Over Fiber (ROF) system. The frequency response of filter is cyclical, and this cycle is defined as the free spectral range (FSR) of filter. The response of filter is decided by two important factors, one is the weight (a_n), which determines the shape of the filter transfer function, and the other one is the delay unit ($n\tau$), which determines the free spectral range. The relationship between these two factors can be expressed as [4, 5]:

$$FSR = \frac{1}{\tau},\tag{1}$$

For a specific filter amplitude-frequency response, the frequency selective characteristics can be represented by the quality factor (i.e., Q value), which can be defined as the ratio of the filter FSR and 3 dB bandwidth [5]:

$$Q = \frac{FSR}{\Delta f},\tag{2}$$

The value of the quality factor is related to the number of the tap. If the tap number N > 10, the change of the quality factor is proportional to the change of the number of tap, which means that the more tap number, the higher quality factor. Moreover, the FIR type microwave photonic filter's structure is simple and increasing the number of tap can improve the quality factor of the system, but that is at the expense of the complexity and cost of the system structure. Meanwhile, the IIR type microwave photonic filter, which can form a feedback loop by using a variety of simple structure, can implement a large number of tap, and the cost is relatively low, which is more conducive to the application of actual system [5, 6].

By cascading FIR and IIR, their respective advantages can be accessed, and shortcomings can be made up. Then the simple structure and low cost microwave photonic filter with high Q value can be realized, which will be described in the subsequent sections through theoretical derivation and experimental verification.

3 Theoretical Model

The theoretical model of OO-IIRMPF is constructed as Fig. 1, where 'a' is the weighting coefficient of the branch, and 'T', 'b' and 'g' are denoted as the delay, the coefficients, the gain of the feedback loop respectively.

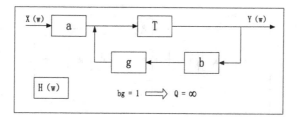

Fig. 1. The theoretical model of OO-IIRMPF [5]

According to the paper [5–7], we can conclude that when the product of the coefficient and gain of OO-IIRMPF loop is equal to 1, the unlimited tap can be got, which means the maximum quality factor (Q value) is maximal. And combined with the filter transfer function expression, it can be seen that when the pole of filter transfer function is reached to 1, the quality factor (Q value) of filter can reach infinity in theoretically.

3.1   The OO-IIRMPF Model Based on Erbium Doped Fiber with FBGs Pair

So far we have derived the condition of obtaining the high Q value of microwave photonic filter, and then we will discuss the OO-IIRMPF structure based on the erbium doped fiber with FBGs pair.

A kind of OO-IIRMPF structure based on erbium doped fiber with FBGs pair is given as Fig. 2.

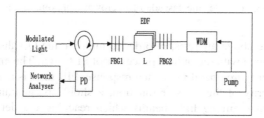

Fig. 2. OO-IIRMPF structure with FBGs pair [5]

This structure adopts a pair of FBGs. The modulated optical signals are put into the FBGs pair connected by the erbium doped fiber. Some of optical signals are reflected by FBG1, and the other parts are reflected by FBG2 after being amplified, which then are put into FBG1 again. Part of output signal is formed the tap of impulse response, the rest is recycled being put into the erbium doped fiber with FBGs pair. Consequently, the signals are amplified and reflect transmitted constantly and effectively by a pair of FBGs, and form a large number of taps. Then, the signal flow obtained from the structure can be described as Fig. 3 [7].

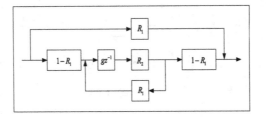

Fig. 3. Signal flow of OO-IIRMPF

3.2   Cascade Model of Microwave Photonic Filter

According to the derivation of J. Capmany [4], we can know that the optical incoherent is the premise of optical cascade equal to electrical cascade. Assume the transfer functions of two incoherent optical microwave photonic filters before being cascaded are $H(\omega)$ and $G(\omega)$, and electrical transmission functions are $H_f(\Omega)$ and $G_f(\Omega)$. Then, the optical signal processors of the two filters which have been cascaded constitute the microwave photonics filter shown in Fig. 4 [5, 8].

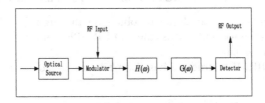

Fig. 4. After the cascade of microwave photonic filter

According to the above analysis, in order to improve the Q value, the FBG based on IIR filter is cascaded with the optical processer of FIR filter. The effect of IIR filter is to realize the smaller narrowband frequency response. FIR filter is used to double FSR. To ensure the linearity of the transfer function, it should be guaranteed that there is no optical interference among light beams which reaching the detector through the optical path.

4   Simulation and Analysis

The experimental equipment is shown in Fig. 5. The FIR filter is cascaded behind the active IIR filter, which is used to realize the frequency response of two-way signals. The structure is a non-equilibrium Mach-Zed Interferometer (UMZI) structure, which is consisted by two optical combiner with the coefficient ratio 50:50. The UMZI arms have a certain length difference, and the lower arm is longer. The length difference can be control by inserting an adjustable optical delay line (OVDL) on one arm, and the delay time is T_2. When the length difference of the arms reaches $l_{oc}/2$, $T_2 = T_1/2$, and

$FSR_2 = 2FSR_1$. At this time, the pass-band center frequency of the FIR filter is aligned to one of two adjacent peaks of IIR filter. Meanwhile, the stop-band center frequency of FIR filters is aligned to the other peak. In this way, the FSR and Q value are both doubled after the filters are cascaded [8, 9].

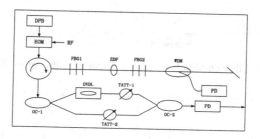

Fig. 5. Experimental apparatus to get high Q value [5]

The parameters setting of the first simulation model are as follows: $R1 = 0.5$, $R2 = 0.5$, when $g = 1, 2, 7$, the different amplitude frequency responses of the filter can be got shown in Fig. 6.

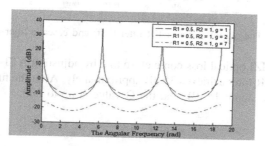

Fig. 6. Filter amplitude-frequency response influence by gain

As can be seen from the Fig. 6, when the gain is 2, get a depth of about 50 dB narrow frequency response, and increase or decrease the gain of erbium-doped fiber, not only the bandwidth, filter depth is small.

The parameters setting of the second simulation model are as follows: $g = 2, R_2 = 1$, FBG1 reflectivity is increased from 0.2 to 0.8 and $g = 2, R_1 = 0.5$, and FBG2 reflectivity is increased from 0.3 to 1. The different filter amplitude-frequency responses are shown in Fig. 7.

In Fig. 7, when the reflectance is equal to 0.5, the product of three factors is 1. Moreover, the bandwidth of the filter is narrowest, the depth is greatest, and then the maximum Q value is got.

Contrasting to the theoretical curve, the experimental IIR filter response curve and cascade filter response curve is shown in Fig. 8.

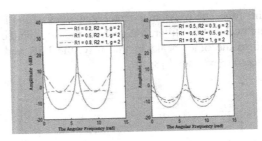

Fig. 7. Filter amplitude-frequency response influence by R1/R2

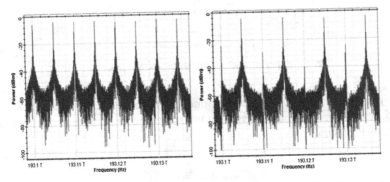

Fig. 8. The output curve of IIR filter (left) and cascade filter (right)

Making the UMZI optical loss come close to 1 by adjusting ATT-1 and ATT-2, the rejection ratio of FIR filter achieves 35 dB approximately. After the filters are cascaded, the rejection ratio is about 18 dB, and the Q value is up to 800.

5   Conclusion

In this paper, the basic theory of microwave photonic filter is comprehensively analysis. Starting from the basic theory of the digital filter, the microwave photonic filter transfer function is deduced. Besides, and the microwave photonic filter tap response and the high quality factor characteristic are detailed, and the interaction intuitive analysis of the multiple characteristic parameters of microwave photonic filters is proposed. Constructing the OO-IIRMPF theoretic model, and according to the signal transmission flow and the general transfer function expression obtained by the principle of automatic control, it is concluded that when the product of the weighted coefficients of the feedback loop is 1, the infinite quality factor can be got theoretically.

Moreover, based on the IIR and FIR cascading, a filter scheme with low cost and high Q value is present and verified by experiments.

Acknowledgement. This research is supported by the Fundamental Research Funds for the Central Universities (No.FRF-TP-09-015A), and also supported by the National Natural Science Foundation of P. R. China (No.61272507, No.61102060).

References

1. Capmany, J., Pastor, D., Ortega, B.: Experimental demonstration of tunability and transfer function reconfiguration in fiber optic microwave filters composed of linearly chirped fiber-grating fed by laser array. Electron. Lett. **34**(23), 2262–2264 (1998)
2. Marti, J., Ramos, F., Laming, R.I.: Photonic microwave filter employing multi-mode optical sources and wide band chirped fiber gratings. Electron. Lett. **34**(18), 1760–1761 (1998)
3. Leng, J.S., Lai, Y.C., Zhang, W., Williams, J.A.R.: A new method for microwave generation and data transmission using DFB laser based on fiber Bragg gratings. IEEE Photonics Technol. Lett. **18**(16), 1729–1731 (2006)
4. Capmany, J., Ortega, B., Pastor, D.: A tutorial on microwave photonic filters. J. Light Wave Technol. **24**(1), 201–229 (2006)
5. Chunhui, Q.: Study on Microwave Photonic Filter and Generator Based on Fiber Bragg Grating. Jiaotong University, Beijing (2012)
6. Minasian, R.A.: Photonic signal processing of microwave signals. IEEE Trans. Microw. Theory Tech. **54**(2), 832–846 (2006)
7. Zeng, F., Wang, J., Yao, J.: All-optical microwave band pass filter with negative coefficients based on a phase modulator and linearly chirped fiber bragg gratings. Opt. Lett. **30**(17), 2203–2205 (2005)
8. Pastor, D., Ortega, B., Capmany, J., Sales, S., Martinez, A., Munoz, P.: Optical microwave filter based on spectral slicing by use of arrayed waveguide gratings. Opt. Lett. **28**(19), 1802–1804 (2003)
9. Capmany, J., Pastor, D., Ortega, B.: Efficient side lobe suppression by source power apodization in fiber optic microwave filters composed of linearly chirped fiber grating by laser array. Electron. Lett. **35**(8), 640–642 (1999)

The Implementation of GFP Protocol Based on EOS in FPGA

Ma Yilan[1(✉)], Yao Lin[1], Zeng Guang[1], and Matturdi Bardi[2]

[1] School of Computer and Communication Engineering, University of Science and Technology Beijing (USTB), Beijing 100083, China
g20128302@xs.ustb.edu.cn
[2] School of Mathematics and Information, Hotan Teachers College, Xinjiang 848000, China
matturdibardi@163.com

Abstract. Through a comparative analysis of three encapsulation technology related to the EOS, namely LAPS, PPP, GFP, this paper discusses the advantages of the encapsulated Ethernet data by GFP protocol and the implementation of the Ethernet frame GFP mapping into SDH protocols based on Xilinx's Virtex-6 FPGA.

Keywords: EOS · GFP · Encapsulation · FPGA

1 Introduction

SDH refers to a transmission system, known as synchronous digital system. It is composed of some SDH network elements (NE), synchronizing and multiplexing information transmission on the fiber, satellite or microwave. The EOS (Ethernet over SDH) is a technology that directly encapsulates local data into Ethernet frames according to a certain Ethernet encapsulation, packages simply and then maps it into SDH frame that can be transmitted between the SDH equipment. By SDH transmission lines, it achieves point-to-point transfer. Simply put, the purpose of EOS is to provide an efficient service features to support data on the existing SDH platforms [1].

The Ethernet data has characteristics of burst and variable length. It is greatly different from SDH frame, which demands strict synchronization. So it needs to introduce an appropriate adaptation protocol of data link to complete Ethernet data encapsulation to realize the SDH frame mappings. Currently, there are three kinds of link adaptation protocol that can complete Ethernet data encapsulation, namely PPP (point to point protocol), LAPS (link access procedure SDH) and GFP (Generic Framing Procedure). The latter, as an advanced common protocols and technology in data adaptation, can adapt a variety of high-level customer data transparently. Its flexible frame delimited, un-fixed frame length and other characteristics [2] has greatly improved the efficiency of data transmission and switching. As GFP over SDH technology is relatively mature with a higher degree of standardization, it is currently the most promising data encapsulation protocol of Ethernet services.

The rest of the paper is organized as follow: principle of GFP protocol is introduced in Sect. 2; the advantage of GFP compared with other link layer protocols of adaptation

© Springer-Verlag Berlin Heidelberg 2015
Y. Lu et al. (Eds.): ISCTCS 2014, CCIS 520, pp. 274–280, 2015.
DOI: 10.1007/978-3-662-47401-3_36

is presented in Sect. 3; implementation of GFP encapsulate protocols on FPGA board is described in Sect. 4; conclusion remarks are given in Sect. 5.

2 The Principle of GFP Protocol

GFP, as the name implies, is a universal mapping technology of grouping fixed-length or variable-length data to unify the adaptation process and transmitting the data in a variety of high-speed physical channels. According to the standard of GFP, it defines two modes: one is transparent mapping mode, the other is the frame-mapping mode. The former aims at block code data flow model, mainly for data stream of Fiber Channel, FICON and ESCON interfaces, the latter targets at the PDU data streaming mode, usually for data stream of IP, MPLS and Ethernet. We focus on introducing the latter briefly for terminal data attributes based on our system test platform.

GFP defines two types frame structure: the client frame and the management of frame. Their structures including GFP core header and GFP payload area, as shown in Fig. 1.

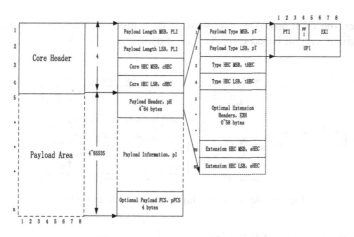

Fig. 1. GFP frame structure [3]

3 The Advantages of GFP Protocol

At present, three commonly used link layer adaptation protocols are: PPP/HDLC (Point to Point/High-Level Data Link Control), LAPS (Link Access Procedure-SDH), GFP (Generic Framing Procedure). The advantages and disadvantages of these three are shown in Fig. 2.

Based on the above chart, it can be seen that GFP has good adaptive ability and high efficiency on the fixed-length or variable-length data encapsulation. It is more advantageous to the data processing in the process of switching. Considering the current physical properties of the system platform, GFP protocol will be the best

Protocol	General	Advantage	Disadvantage
PPP/HDLC	Provide point to point link data trasmission	Smaller encapsulation resource, simple implementation and wide application	Have problem of filling effect and safe hidden trouble
LAPS	Similar to the HDLC protocol, to encapsulate the IEEE802.3 Ethernet frame	Simplifies the PPP/HDLC and higher encapsulation efficiency	Based on the delimited synchronously, still not solve the flaw of HDLC
GFP	An advanced data signal adaptation, mapping technology	Carry variety business, higher boundary search efficient and good ability of error correction	Implementation is more complicated

Fig. 2. The advantages and disadvantages of three protocols [1, 2, 4, 5]

choice. But not all traditional GFP protocol fields are suitable for this system, it is needed to improve or perfect the related fields to bring this system more superiority. This will be introduced in the next section.

4   Implementation of GFP Protocol

In this paper, the GFP protocol is implemented on the experimental platform of high-speed switching system based on FPGA as shown in the Fig. 3.

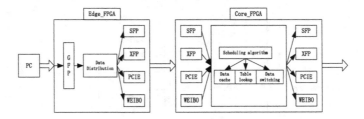

Fig. 3. Design of the high-speed switching system

4.1   Encapsulation of GFP Protocol

This system uses the GFP encapsulation strategy shown in the Fig. 4.

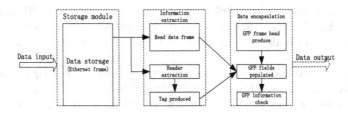

Fig. 4. GFP encapsulation process

Input data of Ethernet is stored in a register first. It will copy the data frame header and send it to the corresponding module of information extraction while reading the data frame. After generating the label fields' information, it will output complete data frame and the label field to data encapsulation module together. Then, the data encapsulation module will count data frames and the label fields. Thus, GFP frame header will be produced. Finally, GFP frame format, the corresponding GFP frame header, the label field, data frame information and other content will be calibrated and checked in accordance with Fig. 1. Verilog is encoded according to the encapsulation process. We get the RTL diagram shown in Fig. 5.

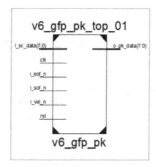

Fig. 5. RTL of GFP encapsulation

The simulation waveform of Ethernet data with GFP encapsulation is show in Fig. 6.

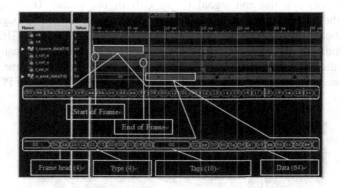

Fig. 6. The simulation waveform of GFP

In simulation, the length of the first Ethernet data frame is 64 bytes, and the value of the first two bytes of the core of header portion from the graph marked is (0056) 16 = 86. Again, through the GFP frame format shown in Fig. 1, we can know that after the encapsulation of GFP's, its total length (86 bytes) is the sum of the core header

(4 bytes), the type region (4 bytes), the extension field (10 bytes), the data field (64 bytes) and the check field (4 bytes). So we can verify the header portion of the core of the simulation result is correct. By contrast with the original Ethernet frame, we can find that the type of the subsequent extraction, domain fields, extension fields, data fields, etc. are consistent with our expectation. It shows that GFP encapsulation module test is success, and the next step of building systems can be proceed.

4.2   GFP Protocol Implementation on Board

The process of Ethernet data frames from PC to the source FPGA board system is shown in Fig. 7.

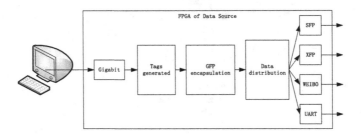

Fig. 7. Procedure of data source on FPGA board

According to the above data processing, we can code by Verilog and simulate to the whole data source FPGA board system. The results are shown in the following Fig. 8.

From Fig. 8, we can see the valid signal of the frame (i_gfp_val) between the start signal (i_gfp_sof) and the end signal (i_gfp_eof) of the frame. This signal corresponding to the GFP encapsulated data (i_gfp_data) is under the control signal, which exactly distributed data to the corresponding port of XFP, SFP, UART, PCIE, WEIBO, TEMAC. It indicates that the data source function of FPGA board is basically realized. The Fig. 9 is the process of application of PC sending data of Ethernet frame. Figure 10 is the real-time results got by ISE real-time tools, Chipscope, from the FPGA board.

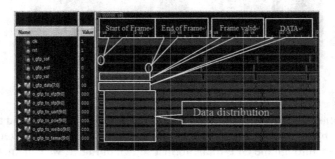

Fig. 8. Simulation waveform of distributed data

Fig. 9. PC sends the source data

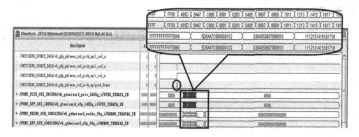

Fig. 10. Real-time data in FPGA board caught by Chipscope

From the above, we can see that good_frame is at a highly active level, meaning the received data frame is a complete and effective one. An analysis of the Chipscope results shows that it is consistent with the simulation results of Fig. 7. And the data of sender from the light mouth and the electric mouth are consistent with encapsulated GFP data. In addition, compared the source data from PC with the data caught by Chipscope, the data contents are consistent. This suggests that the data source FPGA board runs normally, and the function is implemented successfully.

5 Conclusion

We use EOS technology to directly pack Ethernet frame transmitted in the local network into GFP frame and map the GFP frame into SDH frame that can be transmitted between the SDH equipment to achieve the point-to-point transmission on the SDH transmission lines. The simpleness of GFP protocol ensures that this process can be carried out efficiently.

Combining with the switching system based on the technology of EOS, this paper shows the full implementation of the GFP and demonstrates the application and the implementation process of GFP protocol in detail, which finally obtains good results.

Acknowledgement. This research is supported by the Fundamental Research Funds for the Central Universities (No. FRF-TP-14-046A2), and also supported by the National Natural Science Foundation of P. R. China (No. 61170225).

References

1. Xiaoyan, L.: GFP protocol for Ethernet services on SDH application research and logic implementation. Northwestern Poly Technical University, March 2004 (in Chinese)
2. Rong, S.: GFP protocol structure characteristics and the key technology. Opt. Commun. Technol. **03**, 17–23 (2003). (in Chinese)
3. ITU-T G.7041 standard. http://www.itu.int/
4. Kai, D.: GFP protocol implementation based on FPGA. J. Electron. Compon. World **11**, 46–49 (2004). (in Chinese)
5. Ruiqin, S.: The structure and characteristics of GFP frame agreement. Jiangsu Commun. Technol. **6**, 22–24 (2003). (in Chinese)

An Improving Algorithm for Combined Input-Crosspoint-Queued Switches

Ling Xu[✉], Yueyun Chen, and Zheng Gong

School of Computer and Communication Engineering,
University of Science and Technology Beijing (USTB), Beijing, China
cqxling@163.com

Abstract. In recent years, combined input-cross-point-queued (*CICQ*) switch is a research hotspot on switches. *CICQ* is a switch fabric with buffers in cross-points. Although the existing round-robin algorithms of *CICQ* switch can achieve 100 % throughput under uniform traffic, the throughput have poor performance when the traffic model is non-uniform. In this paper, we proposed a load balancing algorithm based on round-robin algorithm ($LB - RR$). The proposed $LB - RR$ algorithm can make any of the non-uniform traffic to uniform. The simulations show that the $LB - RR$ can achieve the throughput nearly 100 % for any traffic model.

Keywords: *CICQ* · Round-robin algorithm · Load balancing algorithm · Throughput · Traffic model

1 Introduction

In the past decade, the input-queued switched architectures have been become the main research hotspot in high-speed switching. But the input-queued switch have head-of-line blocking (HOL), its throughput rate can only reach 58.6 % [1]. So many researchers began to focus on the research on the output queue, the output-queued switch architectures have 100 % throughput, through its throughput is very high, the internal rate of switch structure is also required very high, the memory bandwidth is the sum of all input port bandwidth, which limits its extensibility [2].

In view of the advantages and disadvantages of the input queue and the output queue, Nabeshima put forward the combined Input-cross-point-queued switch architectures. *CICQ* switch use virtual output queue (*VOQ*) [3] in each input port, and each intersection set up a buffer, in a time slot, each intersection buffer allows a read and a write operation, So *CICQ* don't need internal speedup and has a better scalability. Each input port corresponding to a scheduler in order to solve the problem of input contention, so we can decide to send a cell in the head of a *VOQ* into corresponding scheduler, as well as the output port, so *CICQ* switch need $2N$ schedulers.

Recently, attracted by the promising scalability of *CICQ* switches, lots of useful ideas and algorithms ware proposed and the research is still on the way. In general, those scheduling algorithms trying to provide the switch: (1) low complexity; (2) small cross-point buffer size; (3) nice throughput, can be reduced as the following two styles [4].

© Springer-Verlag Berlin Heidelberg 2015
Y. Lu et al. (Eds.): ISCTCS 2014, CCIS 520, pp. 281–287, 2015.
DOI: 10.1007/978-3-662-47401-3_37

The first type of schedulers is round-robin algorithm [5]. In [6], a round-robin algorithm was introduced. It described three steps of the round-robin algorithm. In [4], it introduced an efficient round-robin algorithm for *CICQ*, each input arbiter is associated with dual round-robin pointers, by this algorithm, *CICQ* switch can achieve the throughput nearly 100 % and low overage delay under uniform and a broad class of non-uniform traffic patterns. In [7], this paper proposed a scheduling algorithm based on the frame, it can change frame size dynamically according to the size of each *VOQ*. So it has certain adaptability. The second type of schedulers is weight-based algorithm, this algorithm typically use the length of *VOQ* queue or the delay of the head cell as weights, and find the most weight queue to scheduling in each time slot, for example, LQF-RR [8] and OCF-OCF [9] algorithms are based on weight, these algorithms can get close to 100 % throughput rate in uniform traffic model. All the above algorithms about round-robin can solve the problem of throughput in uniform traffic model. However, it solved the mis-sequencing problem of the original load-balancing switch in [10]. So we propose *LB − RR* algorithm to solve the throughput of *CICQ* in non-uniform traffic model.

The rest of the paper is organized as follows. Section 2 introduces the system model. Section 3 describes *LB − RR* algorithm and the address structure of cell. Section 4 introduces uniform traffic and non-uniform traffic, including simulation. Finally, Sect. 5 summarizes this paper.

2   System Model

The switch structure consists of five elements: input ports, the first *VOQ* queue, the load balance, the second *VOQ* queue, output ports and the switch core interconnecting the second *VOQ* queue and the output ports, each second *VOQ* queue has a round-robin scheduler. Here we define the fixed size packet as a cell, and the basic time unit of the switch structure for a cell scheduling is called a time slot, cell arrival process obey the Bernoulli distribution.

We define the following notations in this paper:

1. In each slot, cells arriving at input port i and destined for output j are first stored in the corresponding FIFO buffer which is called "virtual output queue", denoted by $VOQ_{i,j}$.
2. After cells through load balancing structure, the address of cell will be changed, denoted by $VOQ_{i,k}$.
3. The number of cells into input port i is denoted by λ_i.
4. The switch core uses $N \times N$ cross-point buffer, each cross-point buffer has only one cell room, the cross-point buffers are denoted by $XPB_{i,k}$.
5. The number of cells in $VOQ_{i,j}$ queue is denoted by λ_i, so we can get a equation (Fig. 1):

$$\lambda_i = \sum_{j=1}^{N} \lambda_{i,j} \tag{1}$$

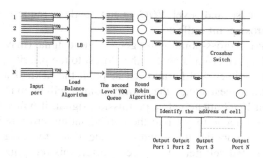

Fig. 1. The three structure of combined input-cross-point-queued switches

In each time slot, at most a cell can arrive at each input, and when the cell get into the input port (the first level) buffer structure, judging by the load balance structure, when the number of cells is uniform, the load balance don't need deal with these cells, but when the number of cells is non-uniform, the load balance will deal them by using the load-balance algorithm. Finally, these cells will be transferred to the corresponding second VOQ queue and the corresponding cross-point buffer by using round-robin algorithm.

3   The LB-RR Algorithm

The steps of the $LB-RR$ algorithm are as follows:

1. The cell gets into the corresponding input port, denoted by λ_i.
2. These cells in the VOQ queue put into the load balance, consider two cases:
   (1) If these cells in this queue is uniform, the load balance won't deal with them, they will be directly sent to the next level buffer queue.
   (2) If these cells in this queue is non-uniform, the load balance will detect the number of each VOQ queue respectively, and then sum the number of these cells in same $VOQ_{i,j}$ queue, finally to get average, if the number of cells in $VOQ_{i,j}$ less than the average, these cells which the other VOQ queue more than the average, put the last queue until the number of cell reach the average number. If the number of cell in $VOQ_{i,j}$ more than the average, this $VOQ_{i,j}$ will be distributed the extra cells to other queue, by this way to achieve the best degree of uniformity. Note the address of these cells which assigned to other VOQ queue will be changed, form the front (i, j) into (i, k), k denote the address that the cell will be assigned to the new VOQ queue corresponding to the destination address, and these cells will be assigned to the new c queue which have a higher priority in the queue.
3. All of these cells are deposit to the next level buffer queue.
4. The approximate uniform queue use the round-robin algorithm, the round-robin algorithm are as follows [6]:

(1) Request: The second level *VOQ* queue sends a request signal to a corresponding cross-point buffer.
(2) Permission: If a cross-point buffer get a request signal (may be greater than 1), it will send a permission signal to the closest to the priority pointer of the *VOQ* queue. This pointer will be allowed to point the next. If a cross-point buffer doesn't get a request signal, the priority pointer will be in the original position.
(3) Accept: If a *VOQ* queue gets a permission signal, it will select the cell in the head of *VOQ* queue to get into the corresponding cross-point buffer.
5. The output port also applies the round-robin algorithm to select cell form crossbar buffer. When selected cell get into the recognizer, this recognizer will identify the original address of cell, if the address of these cells is different, they will be send to the corresponding output port, or these cells having the same output port address will be sent to the buffer in the recognizer.

For example, it shows the state of the pointer when the time slot is $(i - 1)$. A *CICQ* have five input ports and five output port, according to the round-robin algorithm, a cell in the head of $VOQ_{1,3}$ is sent to the cross-point buffers (Fig. 2).

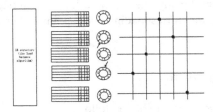

Fig. 2. The state of input point using the round-robin algorithm in the $(i - 1)$ time slot.

When the time slot is t. $VOQ_{1,4}$ receives the permission signal, a cell at head of $VOQ_{1,4}$ is sent to the $XPB_{1,4}$, other input port have the same process (Fig. 3).

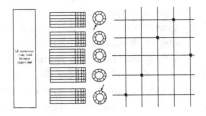

Fig. 3. The state of point using the round-robin algorithm in the i time slot

4 Traffic Model and Simulation Analysis

1. The Uniform Traffic Model
This section using uniform traffic model are the permissible flow model, the input port and output port are not overload.

The arrival process of each input port are assumed to obey the Bernoulli independent distribution, each *VOQ* queue have the same load. *LB − RR* algorithm is only on the basis of the RR algorithm increases a load balance structure, *LB − RR* algorithm don't work under the uniform flow, so the throughput of *CICQ* using the *LB − RR* algorithm equal to the throughput of *CICQ* using the RR algorithm.

The throughput of *CICQ* using *LB − RR* algorithm is as follow:

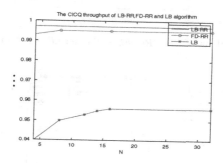

Fig. 4. The *CICQ* throughput of the *LB − RR*, *FD − RR* and *LB* algorithm

Based on the analysis of the simulation above, when we don't consider delay, it shows the *LB − RR* algorithm is superior to the *FD − RR* algorithm in Fig. 4. According to the Fig. 4, the *CICQ* throughput of just using LB algorithm is the most small. So the *LB − RR* algorithm is better under the uniform traffic model.

2. The Non-Uniform Traffic Model

We consider two non-uniform flow model, there are hot-spot flow model and Diagonal flow model. Firstly, we introduce these two models.

(1) The Hot-spot Traffic Model

The arrival process of cell obeys the Bernoulli distributed when the system model use the Hot-spot traffic model, this model define a parameter $w \in [0, 1]$, the load in each *VOQ* queue of the *CICQ* structure is defined by

$$\lambda_{i,j} = \begin{cases} \rho(w + \frac{1-w}{N}), & i = j \\ \rho\frac{1-w}{N}, & i \neq j \end{cases} \tag{2}$$

When $w = 0 \lambda_{i,j} = \frac{\rho}{N}$. It is a uniform Bernoulli process. When $w = 1$, the load arriving at the i input port concentrate on the $VOQ_{i,i}$ (Fig. 5).

(2) The Diagonal traffic model

The arrival process of cell obeys the Bernoulli distributed when the system model uses the Diagonal traffic model traffic model, but the arriving cell is not uniform distributed on the $VOQ_{i,j}$, it obeys (Fig. 6):

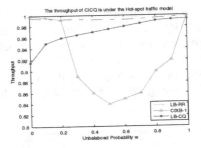

Fig. 5. The *CICQ* throughput of *LB − RR*, *FD − RR* and *LB − CQ* under the Hot-spot traffic

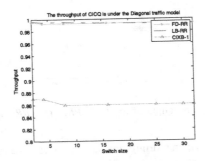

Fig. 6. The *CICQ* throughput of *LB − RR*, *FD − RR* and *CIXB − 1* under the diagonal traffic

$$\lambda_{i,j} = \begin{cases} \frac{2}{3}\lambda_i & j = i \\ \frac{1}{3}\lambda_i & j = (i + 1) \bmod N \\ 0 & \text{else} \end{cases} \qquad (3)$$

5 Conclusions

In order to improve the performance of the *CICQ* switch with one-cell cross-point buffers under non-uniform, this paper put forward a *LB − RR* algorithm, this algorithm consists of two parts, one part is *LB* algorithm, other part are Round-Robin algorithm. The *LB − RR* algorithm makes the non-uniform flow traffic to uniform. According to simulation results, the *LB − RR* algorithm gets a very good performance on different traffic models.

Acknowledgement. This research is supported by the National Natural Science Foundation of China under Grant No. 61272506, No. 61102060.

References

1. Hluchyj, M.G., Karol, M.J.: Queueing in high-performance packet switching. IEEE J. Sel. Areas Commun. **6**(9), 1587–1597 (1988)
2. Zheng, Y., Gao, W.: A dual round-robin algorithm for combined input-crosspoint-queued switches. Comput. Commun. Netw. **2**, 755–759 (2005)
3. Tamir, Y., Frazier, G.L.: Dynamically-Allocated multi-queue buffer for VLSI communication switches. IEEE Trans. Comput. **41**(6), 725–737 (1992)
4. Zheng, Y., Shao, C.: An efficient round-robin algorithm for combined input-crosspoint-queued switches. In: IEEE International Conference on Networking and Services, (ICAS/ICNS) (2005)
5. Rojas-Cessa, R., Oki, E., Jing, Z., Chao, H.J.: CIXB-1: combined input-one-cell-crosspoint buffered switch, In: Proceedings of the Workshop on High Performance Switching and Routing, pp. 324–329 May 2001
6. Fei, L., Bing, L., Leilei, Z.: Design and Implementation of Buffered Crossbar Scheduling Algorithm with Round Robin Scheduling. Comput. Sci. **40**(6A) (2013)
7. Rojas-Cessa, R., Oki, E., Jing, Z., Chao, H.J.: CIXB-1: combined input-one-cell-crosspoint buffered switch. In: Proceedings of the Workshop on High performance Switching and Routing (HPSR 2001), pp. 324–329, May 2001
8. Javidi, T., Magil, R.B., Hrabik, T.: A high-throughput scheduling algorithm for a buffered crossbar switch fabric. In: Proceedings of the IEEE International Conference on Communications (ICC 2001), pp. 1586–1591, June 2001
9. Nabeshima, M.: Performance evaluation of a combined input-and-crosspoint-queued switch. IEICE Trans. Commun. **E83-B**(3), 737–741 (2000)
10. Cai, Y., Wang, X., Gong, W., Towsley, D.: A study on the performance of a three-stage load-balancing switch. IEEE/ACM Trans. Netw. **22**(1), 52–65 (2014)

A New Network Coding Scheme in Two-relay OFDMA Networks

Hui Zhao[✉], Yueyun Chen, and Xiaopan Yuan

School of Computer and Communication Engineering,
University of Science and Technology Beijing (USTB),
Beijing 100083, People's Republic of China
zhemail@126.com

Abstract. In orthogonal frequency division multiple access (OFDMA) networks, relay nodes utilize network coding for the received information to improve spectrum efficiency. However, network coding spreads may result in some errors. These bit errors along the relay's transmission, which results in high BER in receivers. To solve the error spread problem, we propose a new coding algorithm called dualism network coding (DNC) algorithm to cripple the spread of error effectively for 2-relay networks. In the proposed algorithm, relay node reuse the bit decoded from the received information for the network coding of next slot. The simulation results show that the proposed algorithm is effective to solve the problem of error propagation effectively.

Keywords: Network coding · Error propagation · Coding algorithm

1 Introduction

With the wide application of wireless communication technology, the traditional local area network couldn't satisfy people's needs, so the wireless network appeared and developed rapidly. With the emerging of wireless standards have took the orthogonal frequency division multiplexing access (OFDMA) technology as an important kind of broadband wireless access technology, such as 802.16 [1]. Due to the limited of spectrum resources, many researchers combined the OFDMA with network coding [2–4], so that improve the spectrum efficiency further. Network coding realized the collaboration between the various nodes to achieve the multiple hop transmission, the scheme of covering most of the services for mobile users is particularly important [5].

The advantage of network coding in wireless network has been researched in some articles [6, 7] which improves the performance of the system significantly through the integration of network coding with other advanced technology in wireless network [8]. About two relay network coding algorithms in OFDMA network also have some research [9, 10], but the coding algorithm has a weakness that is At the expense of time cost, and the re-initialization segment isn't very good at BER performance, temporarily called the existing coding algorithm in the article. This paper proposes a new algorithm can solve the error propagation problem very well.

© Springer-Verlag Berlin Heidelberg 2015
Y. Lu et al. (Eds.): ISCTCS 2014, CCIS 520, pp. 288–294, 2015.
DOI: 10.1007/978-3-662-47401-3_38

2 The Model Two Relay Network Coding

Two relay OFDMA networks coding model as shown in Fig. 1(a) the user A and B forward message through two base stations in traditional way that needs four sub carriers, but it can reduce the number of sub-carrier by using network coding (Fig. 2(b)) who will improve the spectrum efficiency and power efficiency. But there will be some error propagation. For this kind of situation there are some paper had studied the solutions to solve it. But the solutions are all at the cost of time, during the segmentation process that the more to initialize the better BER performance when the corresponding time overhead will also increase. In this paper, we proposed a new encoding algorithm based on this network model, this algorithm can avoid the problem of reinitializes in the process of information transmission and has a better performance.

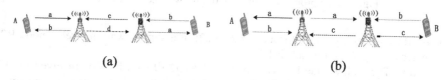

(a)   (b)

Fig. 1. Network model for two-relay OFDMA networks

3 Network Encoding and Decoding Algorithm

3.1 Network Coding Algorithm

In the two relay OFDMA network system, suppose that each transmission time between two nodes is a time slot (TS). Denote TR1 as the data that relay nodes to transmit and denote $x_j(n)$ as the received data for relay node R1 or R2 from node j (j = A, B, R1, R2) at the nth TS. Also denote temp as the intermediate variable which is to decode the data at the last time slot and as code element in the next time slot, RA(n), RB (n) as the nth received data for user A and B, define a1, a2,...,a_N and b1, b2,...,b_N as the data which two users will to send. If the users send N bits that coding algorithm need N + 2 time slots, specific encoding process as shown in Fig. 2.

Suppose that there are two users A and B which have five bits need to be transmitted through two relay, the specific process of encoding:

1. The first TS1, two relay R1 and R2 have no information transmission since there is no any information. Just two client users send information bit a1, b1, respectively.
2. The second TS2, two users will sent information bit a2, b2 to the adjacent relay, the relay R1, R2 received information bits a1, b1 from user A and B.
3. The third TS3, two users will sent information bit a3, b3 to the adjacent relay where relay R1 and R2 will start coding arithmetic that encode a1, b1 and a2, b2 which received inTS1, TS2 respectively. That is a2 ⊕ b1 ⊕ a1, b2 ⊕ a1 ⊕ b1, respectively.
4. The fourth TS4, R1 decode b2 ⊕ a1 ⊕ b1 that received in TS3 that is b2 ⊕ a1 ⊕ b1 ⊕ a1 ⊕ b1, decoding b2 as the next coded element then the relay

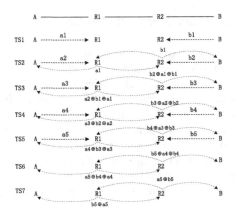

Fig. 2. The proposed coding algorithm with network coding

node R1 transfer encoding for a3 ⊕ b2 ⊕ a2; in a similar way, the relay node R2 transfer coding for b3 ⊕ a2 ⊕ b2.

5. The fifth TS5, relay node R1 will decode b3 ⊕ a2 ⊕ b2 which be received in the TS3, namely b3 ⊕ a2 ⊕ b2 ⊕ a2 ⊕ b2 that decoding b3 as the next encoding element then the relay node R1 transfer encoding for a4 ⊕ b3 ⊕ a3; By the same token, the relay node R2 transfer encoding for b4 ⊕ a3 ⊕ b3.

6. In the same way, the sixth time slot TS6, relay node R1, R2 transfer encoding for a5 ⊕ b4 ⊕ a4, b5 ⊕ a4 ⊕ b4, respectively.

The detailed coding procedure is described as Table 1.

Table 1. Network coding algorithm

```
Algorithm: Network coding
1. if n=2
     T_R1(n)=X_A(n-1);
     T_R2(n)=X_B(n-1);
2. else if n=3
     T_R1(n)=X_A(n-1)⊕X_R2(n-1)⊕X_A(n-2);
     T_R2(n)=X_B(n-1)⊕X_R1(n-1)⊕X_B(n-2);
3. else if n=4:N+1
     temp_R1=X_R2(n-1)⊕X_A(n-3)⊕R_A(n-1);
     T_R1(n)=X_A(n-1)⊕temp_R1⊕X_A(n-2);
     temp_R1=X_R1(n-1)⊕X_B(n-3)⊕R_B(n-1);
     T_R2(n)=X_B(n-1)⊕temp_R2⊕X_B(n-2);
4. else n=N+2
     temp_R1=X_R2(n-1)⊕X_A(n-3)⊕R_A(n-1);
     T_R1(n)=X_A(n-2)⊕temp_R1;
     temp_R1=X_R1(n-1)⊕X_B(n-3)⊕R_B(n-1);
     T_R2(n)=X_B(n-2)⊕temp_R2;
5. end if;
```

3.2   Network Decoding Algorithm

Users A, B received the information from relay node R1, R2, then can decoding them according to the previous related information the process as shown in Table 2.

Table 2. The process of decoding

Receive	0	b1	b2	b3	b4	b5
解码⊕	a1	a2⊕a1	a3⊕a2	a4⊕a3	a5⊕a4	a5
A	a1	a2⊕b1⊕a1	a3⊕b2⊕a2	a4⊕b3⊕a3	a5⊕b4⊕a4	b5⊕a5
B	b1	b2⊕a1⊕b1	b3⊕a2⊕b2	b4⊕a3⊕b3	b5⊕a4⊕b4	a5⊕b5
解码⊕		b2⊕b1	b3⊕b2	b4⊕b3	b5⊕b4	b5
Receive	0	a1	a2	a3	a4	a5

The detailed decoding procedure is described as Table 3.

Table 3. Network decoding

```
Algorithm2: Network decoding
1. for n=1:N-1
          RA(n)=TR1(n) ⊕ an+1 ⊕ an;
          RB(n)=TR2(n) ⊕ bn+1 ⊕ bn;
2. else if n=N
          RA(n)=TR1(n) ⊕ an;
          RB(n)=TR2(n) ⊕ bn;
5. end if;
```

3.3   Network Coding Error Propagation Problem

The proposed algorithm can effectively cripple the spread problem of the error which will disappear after a limited transmission because of offset each other which will instead of a block of initialization. The process analysis of error propagation shows in Table 4.

Table 4. The process of error diffusion

Receive		0	b1	b2	b3	b4	b5
A	a1	a2	a3	a4	a5		
R1		a1	a2⊕b1⊕a1	a3⊕b2⊕a2	a4⊕b3⊕a3	a5⊕b4⊕a4	b5⊕a5
R2		b1	b2⊕a1⊕b1	b3⊕a2⊕b2	b4⊕a3⊕b3	b5⊕a4⊕b4	a5⊕b5
B	b1	b2	b3	b4	b5		
Receive		0	a1	a2	a3	a4	a5

There are two cases about error link, the link of AR1, BR2 and R1R2. The first case as shown in table within the line between the user and relay node link to produce the error, assuming that a2 happened the error in the process of transmission to the R1 then b1 will not be able to correct decoding, thus in the following process of propagation, the receiver decodes the a2, b2 will go wrong, due to the correlation of coding in the next time slot this error will be offset, so the next time slot error will not continue to spread. The second case as shown on the dotted line in the table where produce error between the relay node link, assuming a1 to R2 produces error in the process, the decoding information b2, b3 will produce errors for user A on the receiving end, in the same way the decoding information a1, a3, a4 are wrong for user B, but the next time slot the a5, b5 decoding is correct, the error in this time slot will cancel each other.

4   Result and Analysis

We use the simulation method to observe the end-to-end BER performance in terms of each link. In order to compared the BER performance with the existing coding algorithm, we generated $N = 10^6$ bits randomly as the user A and B transmission of data, Denote N as the number of bits in each group data packet and n can only be selected from 10^6 bits. The simulation values for n are from $\{10, 20, 40, 50, 100, 160, 200\}$. Denote the BER of AR_1, R_1R_2 links as P_{eA}, P_{eR} and P_{eB}, respectively. When $P_{eA} = P_{eB} = P_{eR} = 10^{-4}$ the result of BER performance comparison as Fig. 3 which include no coding, coding and my coding algorithm is proposed in this paper where the end-to-end BER for user j can be expressed as Eq. (1).

$$BER_j = \frac{\sum_{i=1}^{\frac{10^6}{n}} err_j(i)}{10^6} \tag{1}$$

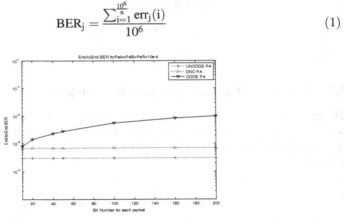

Fig. 3. BER performance for algorithm with $P_{eA} = P_{eB} = P_{eR} = 10^{-4}$

We can see that with network coding, wherever the error occurred that error message will be broadcast to two directions, so the error will be generated in both terminals. But the performance of the proposed algorithm will not change with the change of n, namely the algorithm does not produce serious error propagation problem.

Then we fixed the BER of the middle link and changed the BER of two terminal link, the end-to-end BER performance as Fig. 4 shows the average BER of the two users when $P_{eR} = 10^{-3}$.

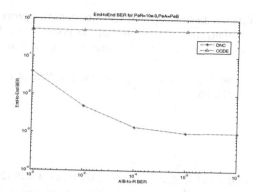

Fig. 4. BER performance for the coded and un-coded algorithms with $P_{eR} = 10^{-3}$

We can see from the figure, the performance of the existing coding algorithm is seriousness, but it is better for proposed coding algorithm than existing algorithm.

Finally we fixed BER of the link between user and relay nodes, changed the BER of the middle link. Figure 5 shows that the BER performance of three kinds of method.

We can see the existing coding algorithm of BER is also seriousness shown in Fig. 5, and with the increase of P_{eR} we can see the end-to-end BER of the proposed coding algorithm is better and better.

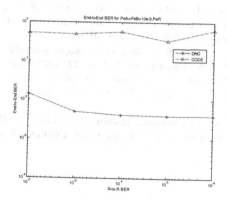

Fig. 5. BER performance for the coded and un-coded algorithms in terms of P_{eR}

Above all, through comparing the BER performance of various circumstances, the proposed coding algorithm performance had a very big enhancement than existing coding algorithm.

5 Conclusion

In the two OFDMA relay networks realize network coding algorithm scheme by the collaboration of the relay to improve spectrum efficiency. We proposed algorithm had a better enhancement than existing coding scheme on the BER performance which can not to segment and initialize. In this paper in terms of complex processing of algorithm is a little higher than initialization algorithm, but the price for the base station is not significantly affected and it can meet the real-time demand of data service.

Acknowledgement. This work is supported by the National Natural Science Foundation of China under Grant No. 61272506, No.61170225.

References

1. Air Interface for Fixed Wireless Access Systems, IEEE Std.802.16 (2004)
2. Zhang, X., Li, B.: Network-coding-aware dynamic subcarrier assignment in OFDMA-based wireless networks. IEEE Trans. Veh. Technol. **60**, 4609–4619 (2011)
3. Katti, S., Rahul, H., Hu, W., Katabi, D., Medard, M., Crowcroft, J.: XORs in the air: practical wireless network coding. IEEE/ACM Trans. Network. **16**(3), 497–510 (2008)
4. Xu, H., Li, B.: XOR-assisted cooperative diversity in OFDMA wireless networks: optimization framework and approximation algorithms. In: IEEE Communications Society Subject Matter Ecperts, pp. 2141–2149 (2009)
5. Oyman, O., et al.: Multihop relaying for broadband wireless mesh networks: from theory to practice. IEEE Commun. Mag. **45**, 116–122 (2007)
6. Keshavarz-Haddad, A., Riedi, R.H.: Bounds on the benefit of network coding for wireless multicast and unicast. IEEE Trans. Mob. Comput. **13**(1), 102–115 (2014)
7. Sengupta, S., et al.: An analysis of wireless network coding for unicast sessions: the case for coding-aware routing. In: 26th IEEE International Conference on Computer Communications, INFOCOM 2007, pp. 1028–1036 (2007)
8. Tang, B., Ye, B., Lu, S., Guo, S.: Coding-aware proportional-fair scheduling in OFDMA relay networks. IEEE Trans. Parallel Distrib. Syst. **24**, 1727–1739 (2013)
9. Zhao, H., llow, J.: Network coding in two-relay OFDMA networks using re-initialized transmission scheme. In: 8th Annual Communication Networks and Services Research Conference, pp 23–28 (2010)
10. Kim, B.-G., Lee, J.-W.: Opportunistic resource scheduling for OFDMA networks with network coding at relay stations. IEEE Trans. Wirel. Commun. **11**(1), 210–221 (2012)

RAMID: A Novel Risk Assessment Model of Information Dissemination on Social Network

Hongzhou Sha[1,3], Xiaoqian Li[2(✉)], Qingyun Liu[3], Zhou Zhou[3],
Liang Zhang[2], and Lidong Wang[2]

[1] Beijing University of Posts and Telecommunications, Beijing, China
buptss@bupt.edu.cn
[2] National Computer Network Emergency Response Technical Team,
Beijing, China
xiaoqianli@bjtu.edu.cn, zl@isc.org.cn, wld@cert.org.cn
[3] Institute of Information Engineering Chinese Academy of Sciences,
Beijing, China
{liuqingyun,zhouzhou}@iie.ac.cn

Abstract. In recent years, a large number of social applications created new challenges to inhibit the spread of false information. And how to evaluate the threats of the false information dissemination remains one of the major concerns in the Internet security issues. Existing schemes focused on the operational safety of information systems and ignored the importance of assessment of false information dissemination. In this paper, we propose a novel method to evaluate the threat of false information dissemination. By analyzing social network application's structure and the information transmission mode, it proposed a risk assessment model for the false information dissemination. With this model, it is easy to evaluate and estimate the level of risks in social applications. Experiment verifies the effectiveness and correctness of this model in providing security recommendations and finding the most dangerous risk point.

Keywords: Network security · Risk assessment model · Analytic hierarchy process · Social application

1 Introduction

In recent years, social applications have become one of the most important platforms for people to post and share information [1]. However, they also provide new ways for the transmission of false information [2], which has a widely impact in other fields, such as privacy protection [3], authentication [4], security assessment and data access control [5]. For instance, on April 24, 2013, the hacker stole the Twitter account of Associated Press and released false news which claim that the White House has suffered two bombing attacks and the U.S. President Obama was injured in the blast. Affected by the wide spread of the false information, the U.S., stocks fluctuate significantly while the Dow fell 140 points in two minutes. Therefore, it is an urgent task to quantify or estimate the risks of false information dissemination in social applications.

© Springer-Verlag Berlin Heidelberg 2015
Y. Lu et al. (Eds.): ISCTCS 2014, CCIS 520, pp. 295–303, 2015.
DOI: 10.1007/978-3-662-47401-3_39

To address this issue, lots of traditional risk assessment methods [6] have been proposed. They work well for the traditional information systems. However, they cannot be applied for the social applications [7] because the introduction of social networking elements has a tremendous impact on the dissemination of false information. In fact, it is a new topic for the risk assessment of false information dissemination in social network application where little progress has been made.

In this paper, we propose a novel assessment model named by RAMID (Risk Assessment Model of Information Dissemination) in order to estimate the risks of social applications. More precisely, it first analyzes the security requirements caused by the dissemination of false information and compare it with other traditional threats. Then, it puts forward an assessment model of information dissemination for the social application, and finally gives out the corresponding quantitative calculation. In this way, it is easy for people to quantify the risks of information transmission and compare the risks between different network applications. Experimental results indicate the correctness and effectiveness of this evaluation method.

2   Related Work

The general network security assessment methods can be divided into two categories: artificial assessment and automatic evaluation. Artificial assessment usually carries out questionnaires, and depends on experts' advice. It is simple, effective, and has a wide range of assessment objectives. But, it is easy to introduce subjective factors, which may lead to a different result of the same application's evaluation by different people. Automatic methods evaluate the object by taking a method which automatically identifies vulnerabilities or attack. It is automatic, repeatable and easy to control, and it can be accepted by people much more easily compared to the manual evaluation. Therefore, there are many works based on the automatic evaluation method. For instance, Shen Zhiwei et al. [8] analyzes the spread of false information, and gives out safety recommendations for different situations. But it did not make the analysis of actual network applications. Feng Deng et al. [9] reviewed the assessment model, evaluation criteria, assessment methods and assessment tools in the area of information security assessment. But their risk evaluation is mainly based on the vulnerability scanning technology.

In summary, the traditional risk assessment methods [10] focused on the assessment of threats in the operating system. Thus, it usually takes the attacks and weaknesses log as its source of data. However, the threat introduced by false information dissemination differs from before [11]. And the traditional network security assessment in this aspect is neither universal nor feasible. In this paper, we propose a social application-oriented information dissemination risk assessment model, give the corresponding quantitative calculation method, and verify the correctness and effectiveness based on the analysis of real instance.

Table 1. Threats and security requirements

Threats	Security requirement					
	Confidentiality	Integrity	Reliability	Audibility	Repudiation	Controllability
System threat	√	√	√	√	√	√
Communication threat	√	√	√	√	×	×
Application threat	√	√	√	√	√	√
Performance threat	×	×	√	√	×	×
Correctness of design	√	×	√	√	×	×
False information	×	×	×	√	√	√

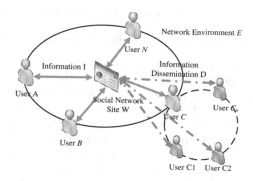

Fig. 1. The transmission mode of information of social network application

3   Risk Assessment of False Information Dissemination

Social network applications may generate different information from normal web applications. In this section, we start from the analysis of the security requirements for the threats of information dissemination, then discuss the social information dissemination model and finally the structure of the information transmission risk. A hierarchical risk assessment model of false information dissemination is carried out by using of system decomposition technique. And people may evaluate the threats of false information dissemination faced by such application based on the risk items involved in the information dissemination process.

3.1   The Analysis of Security Requirements

People in different areas may have different requirements and emphases for the network system. Traditional network security risk assessment focused on the threat to the operation of software system [12]; while the threat introduced by false information dissemination is related to the trust [13]. The correspondence between the security requirements and threats is shown in Table 1. It is obvious that the risk assessment of false information dissemination has some special security needs. For example, its requirement for confidentiality, integrity and availability are not obvious, but it has a higher requirement for the reliability, controllability and non-repudiation.

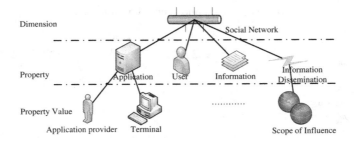

Fig. 2. The transmission mode of information of social network application

3.2   Information Dissemination Model of Social Network

Figure 1 shows the information dissemination model of social network applications. In Fig. 1, W represents social networking site which is the beginning or ending places for information dissemination; $A - N$ represents different user of social network application who is the provider and consumer of information; the $C_1 - C_n$ represents the user's followers are disseminators of and consumer of information; I represents the information which users publish; D represents the dissemination process; E represents the network environment which is the place where the dissemination process of information occurs.

Figure 1 indicates that in a network environment E, the elements of social applications include social application site W, users $U = A, B, \ldots, N$, information I and information dissemination D. In social applications, the dissemination process of false information is produced by the above four elements.

3.3   Risk Assessment Model of Information Dissemination

We first give out two related concepts before the introducing of the risk assessment model of information dissemination.

Definition 1 (Information Dissemination Risk). The likelihood of adverse effects on the Internet user due to the content the transmission of the information is called as information dissemination risk.

Definition 2 (Risk Network of False Information Dissemination). We define it as a relation network, which expresses the risks of false information dissemination based on the visit relationship. It is formally defined as $G = \{V, E\}$, where V represents the set of social network nodes, E represents a set of directed edges. $V = \{V_i | F, R\}$ where V_i is the i_{th} network node whose risk is described by F, R. F represents the functional value of V_i, which in other words means the losses suffered by losing node V_i. R represents the total risk of V_i. $R = \{R_i | G, W\}$ where G represents the possibility of spreading false information through vertex V_i. W represents the safety impact of vertex V_i. It is typically used in this way $R = G * W$[12]. Besides, $E = \{E_i | U_s, U_e, \rho\}$, where U_s represents the starting point of the edge, U_e represents the end of a directed edge, and ρ represents the probability of passing information risk.

Table 2. The weight and structure of the risk assessment model RAMID

Dimension	Property	Weight	Property value	Weight
Website	Application provider	0.5	Types of application provider	1
	Access terminal	0.5	Support platform of application	1
User	User identity	0.7	User authentication	0.5
			IP address hiding technology usage	0.5
	User relationship	0.3	User contact tightness	1
Information	Information relevance	0.3	Information relevance degree	1
	Information audibility	0.7	Information post audibility	0.4
			Information repost audibility	0.3
			Comment audibility	0.3
Dissemination process	Transmission of information	0.6	Information access method	0.4
			Direction of the information flow	0.3
			Communication method	0.3
	Dissemination effectiveness	0.4	Total number of users	0.5
			Number of daily active users	0.5

On the basis of related definitions given above, the social network application is decomposed into three levels: dimension, property and property value. And Fig. 2 proposes a hierarchical risk assessment model using system decomposition technique. The threats of false information dissemination for each social application can be evaluated based on the risk items involved in the information dissemination process. As shown in Fig. 2, a top-down hierarchical order are dimension, property and property value.

In order to facilitate comparison and quantitative calculations, Table 2 shows the structure of the detailed evaluation model. Among them, the second and third indicators characterize the impact of various elements on the spread of false information. They are from four dimensions that are social networking sites, users, information and information dissemination process. And Sect. 3.4 will further discuss the weights of each indicator.

3.4 Determining the Weights of Evaluation Indicators

Weight is a magnitude which is used to evaluate the relative importance of various factors in a form of comparison. It reflects the influence degree of various factors to the assessment target. Let a judge object decompose into n judge factors: $u_1, u_2, u_3, ..., u_n$. The relative weight of each assessment criteria for the evaluation object is: $w_1, w_2, ..., w_n$, and they constitute the weight vector $W = \{w_1, w_2, ..., w_n\}^T$. The following two steps are adopted to determine the relative weights of several factors under a certain level by using pairwise comparison judgment matrix and consistency test method.

(1) Construct pairwise comparison, judgment matrix of all levels. The decision maker compares each two factors, and establishes the judgment matrix: $A = a_{ij\,n*n}$, where a_{ij} denotes the relative importance of factor u_i and u_j.

(2) Consistency check. Root method is used to calculate the relative weights. The elements of the matrix A is multiplied by row; calculate the n_{th} root of the result (the order of matrix A: n); and normalize the root vector into

vector W; calculate the maximum eigenvalue of matrix $\lambda_{max} = \sum_{i=1}^{n} \frac{(Aw)_i}{nw_i}$, where $(Aw)_i$ represents the i_{th} element of Aw. Calculate the consistency index CI: $CI = \frac{\lambda_{max}-n}{n-1}$, where n is the order of the matrix A. Calculate the consistency ratio: $CR = \frac{CI}{RI}$ For $n = 1, 2, ..., 9$, Satty [14] gives out the value of RI. And the consistency of judgment matrix is acceptable when $CR < 0.10$, otherwise the matrix should be reviewed in order to be accepted. For example, the judgment matrix A of information Auditability is shown in Table 3. $\lambda_{max} = 3.0016, CI = 0.0008, CR = 0.0014 < 0.10$. The weights are rounded to be reserved with a decimal. And the weights of each evaluation index as shown in Table 2.

Table 3. Pairwise comparison judgement matrix of information auditability

Information audibility	Post	Repost	Comment	Weight
Post	1	4:3	4:3	0.4
Repost	3:4	1	9:08	0.312
Comment	3:4	8:09	1	0.288

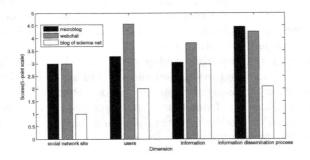

Fig. 3. The histogram of risk profile of typical applications

4   The Experiment of Risk Assessment

In order to verify the correctness of the risk assessment model, this section analyzes some typical social applications with the risk assessment model.

4.1   The Evaluation and Verification

Two typical social applications are selected in our experiment: (1) Sina Microblog; (2) Tencent Webchat. Both applications own some features such as convenience of message delivery, introduction of a new mode of interaction. And they have become the most widely used social network applications. The analysis of these two applications has great practical significance and certain representation. The risk profile among microbiology, webchat and traditional application

Table 4. Risk item scores of typical application

Dimension	Risk item score		
	Sina weibo	Tencent webchat	Blog of sciencenet
Type of application	1	1	1
Support platform of application	5	5	1
User authentication	2.4	3.8	2.1
Use of hiding techniques	1	1	1
Tightness degree of user contact	3	4	3
Information relevance degree	5	1	1
Information post audibility	1	5	5
Information repost audibility	3	5	1
Comment audibility	3	5	5
Information access method	5	5	1
Direction of the information flow	5	5	5
Communication method	3	3	3
Total number of users	5	5	1
Number of daily active users	4	3	1

(Web of Science blog) of each dimension are listed in Table 4. Among them, the scores of the user authentication are estimated by the calculation of 100 randomly selected users. In order to provide appropriate security suggestions, risks of the three applications are compared together in four dimensions as shown in Fig. 3. The data source of Fig. 3 includes the data in Table 4 and the weight given above.

As shown in Table 4 and Fig. 3, compared to traditional applications, social applications has greater potential risk in the false information dissemination. The major causes of the risk are the rapid development of mobile terminal for social network applications, the significant increase of the number of anonymous users, the forwarding feature allows faster dissemination of information and so on.

Figure 3 presents the comparison of the scores of Microblog and Webchat. As it illustrates, Webchat creates more risks than Microblog in the dimension of users and information content, where the main risk comes from the user authentication and information auditability. And Microblog produce more risks than webchat in the dimension of information dissemination process, since Microblog is more likely to spread false information further with a large number of daily active users. Moreover, their risk scores are not far-off from the dimension of websites.

4.2   Comparison with Traditional Assessment Method

In this section, it illustrates the comparison with traditional assessment methods from the perspective of the evaluation effectiveness and safety recommendations.

Effectiveness of Assessment. In the evaluation process, the traditional methods usually consider the security threats of the system operation, and simply add the risk of different vulnerability together. Compared with traditional methods, this novel method focuses on the analysis of the threat in social applications introduced by false information dissemination. With full consideration of the impact of risk dissemination, it is more accurate than traditional methods. In addition, the visual representation of the assessment results avoids the loss of information caused by calculating risk by simple superposition method.

Safety Recommendations. In the field of risk assessment, the premise of developing safety recommendations is to figure out which vulnerability with the greatest impact [12]. In the aspect of comparison between different risks, traditional methods over-rely on experts' advice, which makes the risk of specific applications not comparable. In our model, with the introduction of some objective risk items, it is much more convenient for an evaluator to compare different applications, identify the most risky points, and further analyze the most dangerous risk point. It also provides reliable evidence to develop security recommendations. Therefore, it is better than the traditional assessment method.

5   Conclusion

In this paper, we present an evaluation method constitute by the evaluation model and three levels of evaluation indicators. In the future, we will further analyze the false information dissemination in social applications, and introduce more cases to improve this model.

Acknowledgment. This work was supported by The National Science and Technology Support Program (Grant No. 2012BAH46B02); the National Natural Science Foundation (Grant No. 61402464,61402474).

References

1. Yan, M.X.G.: Electric systems analysis (2004)
2. Li, Y., Liu, J.: Mechanism and improvement of direct anonymous attestation scheme [j]. J. Henan Univ. (Nat. Sci.) **37**(2), 195–197 (2007)
3. Cohen, J.E.: DRM and privacy. Commun. ACM **46**(4), 46–49 (2003)
4. Das, M.L., Saxena, A., Gulati, V.P.: A dynamic id-based remote user authentication scheme. IEEE Trans. Consum. Electron. **50**(2), 629–631 (2004)
5. Yu, S., Wang, C., Ren, K., Lou, W.: Achieving secure, scalable, and fine-grained data access control in cloud computing. In: 2010 Proceedings IEEE INFOCOM, pp. 1–9. IEEE (2010)
6. Budak, C., Agrawal, D., El Abbadi, A.: Limiting the spread of misinformation in social networks. In: Proceedings of the 20th international conference on World wide web, pp. 665–674. ACM (2011)
7. Bass, T.: Intrusion detection systems and multisensor data fusion. Commun. ACM **43**(4), 99–105 (2000)

8. Shen, Z., Zhang, B., Li, F.: Research of internet governance based on harmful information propagation model (2010)

9. Feng, D.G., Zhang, Y., Zhang, Y.Q.: Survey of information security risk assessment. J. China Inst. Commun. **25**(7), 10–18 (2004)

10. Zhang, T., Hu, M.Z., Yun, X.C., Zhang, Y.Z.: Research on computer network security analysis model. J. China Inst. Commun. **26**(12), 100–109 (2005)

11. Joshi, J.B., Aref, W.G., Ghafoor, A., Spafford, E.H.: Security models for web-based applications. Commun. ACM **44**(2), 38–44 (2001)

12. Zhang, Y.Z., Fang, B.X., Chi, Y., Yun, X.C.: Risk propagation model for assessing network information systems. J. Softw. **18**(1), 137–145 (2007)

13. Le, K., Jiwu, J., Yuewu, W.: The trust expansion and control in social network service. J. Comput. Res. Dev. **47**(9), 1611–1621 (2010)

14. Saaty, T.L.: How to make a decision: the analytic hierarchy process. Eur. J. Oper. Res. **48**(1), 9–26 (1990)

An Active Approach for Automatic Rule Discovery in Rule-Based Monitoring Systems

Chao Ding[1,2], Mingxia Zeng[2], Kui Wang[2], Polo Pei[3],
Zhongzhi Luan[1,2(✉)], and Depei Qian[1,2]

[1] Beijing Municipal Key Laboratory of Network Technology,
Beihang University, Beijing, China
super.d.scse@gmail.com,
zhongzhi.luan@jsi.buaa.edu.cn, depeiq@buaa.edu.cn
[2] Sino-German Joint Software Institute, Beihang University, Beijing, China
{zengguagua91,wangkui890325}@163.com
[3] Tencent Corporation, Shenzhen, China
polopei@tencent.com

Abstract. In large-scale cloud service datacenters, there always have a monitoring center in charge of the health status of all system components. When faults occur, it should react rapidly and notify managers to avoid further lose. The most popular solution for fault detection in enterprise environments is rule-based detection. And to our knowledge, there exists a limitation for the existing rule-based solution that rules are always configured by managers relying on experiences, which is wildly inaccurate and wastes lots of labor. We present a methodology that can discover monitoring rules automatically and accurately in this paper. And through our experiment, we demonstrate it correct and effective.

Keywords: Fault diagnose · Fault analysis · Rule analysis

1 Introduction

In the emerging cloud computing era, enterprise data centers host a plethora of web services and applications, including those for e-Commerce, distributed multimedia, and social networks, which jointly serve many aspects of our daily lives and business. For such applications, the lack of availability, reliability, or responsiveness can lead to extensive financial loss. When faults occur, such as server breaking down or hijacking, the monitoring center should react quickly and throw some anomaly alarming to managers to avoid further failure. However, the increasing size and complexity of enterprise applications, together with the large scale data centers in which they operate, make anomaly management highly challenging.

Anomaly and fault detection have been well studied in computer system domain. For example, the work in [7] models the web-based system into a weighted graph and applies graph mining techniques to monitor the graph sequences for failure detection. Magpie [2] uses the stochastic context free grammar to model and monitor requests' control flow across multiple machines for the purpose of detecting component failures and localizing performance bottlenecks. The Pinpoint project [3], which is similar to

© Springer-Verlag Berlin Heidelberg 2015
Y. Lu et al. (Eds.): ISCTCS 2014, CCIS 520, pp. 304–310, 2015.
DOI: 10.1007/978-3-662-47401-3_40

Magpie, proposes two statistical methods to analyze the request path shapes and component interactions to detect failures in the web-based systems. However, to the existing enterprise systems, the most important factor for monitoring is simply effective. And rule-based monitoring system can just meet the needs. Actually, there exist many large-scale cloud service providers, such as Tencent and Alibaba, using rule-based monitoring solution.

However, the biggest letdown of rule-based solutions is the rules are always configured by managers relying on experiences, which is wildly inaccurate and wastes lots of labor. In this paper, we propose an approach that can discover monitoring rules automatically and accurately. Through our experiment, we prove that our method can generate monitoring rules which are more sophisticated and accurate than the artificial rules.

The rest of the paper is organized as follows. In Sect. 2, we give a description of problem background and identification problem we are going to solve. Sections 3, 4 give the detailed methodology of our methodology, followed by experimental results in Sect. 4.2. In the last Sect. 5, we conclude our work.

2 Problem Statement

2.1 Background

In monitoring centers, monitoring endpoints are usually deployed for application-level components (business components), but not for functional components such as routing nodes and data nodes. Our interest is to ensure healthy operation of application-level components in general. What's more, one specific application-level component always has many monitoring dimensions, which comprise variety of monitoring items. And monitoring center monitors all the monitoring items based on some rules named fault alarming rules, which are the main targets we study. Most large-scale cloud service providers, such as Alibaba and Tencent, are using fault alarming solutions based on rules. And there are two kinds of alarming rules: one is threshold rules and the other is volatility rules. The threshold rule limits bounds of monitoring value and the volatility rule limits stability and fluctuation degree of status curve.

To those monitoring centers, the biggest problem they are facing is all the monitoring rules is set up by manpower. As a result, there appeared three issues:

Unsophisticated. Usually administrators assign one threshold rule and one volatility rule to a monitoring item, which is unreasonable because the status curve is always disordered and complicated.

Inaccurate. The artificial rules only depend on experiences of rule-makers. However, when services and businesses become larger, the normal status of system components become more complex too.

Labor-intensive. Along with the burst growing of cloud services, the man power involved in monitoring configuration and management is also increasing rapidly.

In this paper, we propose a method of automatic rule configuration by mining regularities of historical monitoring data.

2.2   Assumption

We consider that one monitoring item should show similar state pattern during a time-cycle. The rationality is that the components' performance is related to business needs. Business needs tend to follow a pattern during each time-cycle, so that the components' performance should also follow a pattern accordingly. Our methodology is based on periodic character of monitoring value. The following content details our method in two aspects: auto configuration for threshold rules and auto configuration for volatility rules.

3   Methodology

The threshold rule limits bounds of status value which has a Max threshold and a Min threshold. And the volatility rule limits stability and fluctuation degree of status curve. Our method can not only configure the rules automatically, but also configure it more precisely. And the only difference between solutions for threshold rules and volatility rules is that threshold solution can analyze the monitoring value x_j^i (i represent one specific day and j represent one unique sample point of the day i), while for volatility solution, we should quantity "volatility" first as $v_j^i = \frac{x_j^i - x_{j-5}^i}{x_j^i}$. And in the following content, we take threshold rule as example, analyzing data of x_j^i.

We define a set of variables as follows: let T denotes a time-cycle and T_i could be a sub time period during T. σ_i is the max threshold and min threshold for each T_i. $R_{threshold}$ is the threshold rule constituted by tuple $<T_i, \sigma_i>$. Our goal is to compute $R_{threshold}$ by analyzing historical monitoring data.

3.1   Step 1: Generate Value Ranges

The monitoring curve should show periodic regular patterns related to specific businesses. Therefore, although the monitoring value of a same sample point during different time-cycles cannot be identical, it should fluctuate in a limited range. By computing the ranges of all sample points of specific monitoring item, we can get two fluctuation range curves (Max and Min), through which we can judge whether the monitoring item plays well (normal condition) or not. As we can see in Fig. 1, the curves in grey are the fluctuation range curves of the monitoring curve in one time-cycle. We assume the time-cycle is one day for convenience.

Let Y_j represent the data of the same sample point during one time cycle of N days. And $Y_j = \{x_j^i | 1 \leq i \leq N\}$, j represents an unique sample point. We use Kolmogorov-Smirnov testing to judge whether Y_j fits normal distribution $N(\mu, \sigma^2)$. If Y_j fits normal distribution, then we can get $P\{|X - \mu| < 3\sigma\} = 99.73\%$. We call 3σ as limiting error, and almost all the X values are in the interval centered with μ with the radius of 3σ. If Y_j doesn't fit normal distribution, we assign the threshold range as $[\mu - 3\sigma, \mu + 3\sigma]$.

Repeat this to all the sample points x_j^i, we will get the threshold ranges of specific monitoring item, just as what we can see in Fig. 1.

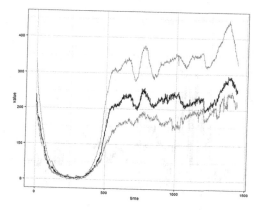

Fig. 1. Status curve ranges

3.2   Step 2: Convergent Rules

Through Step1, we get the normal range curve of all sampling points during one time-cycle through which we can assign each point a unique threshold rule, which form the $R_{threshold}$ finally. However, in real enterprise environments, there may be too many threshold rules for one monitoring item, which will put pressure on alarm analyzing system and also hard to manage and view. Therefore, we need to aggregate those fluctuation rates into different clusters (cluster analysis), so as to use one threshold rule for one cluster instead of various rules, but costing some fluctuation precision.

The fluctuation rate be $\gamma = \frac{Max_j - \mu}{\mu}$ or $\gamma = \frac{\mu - Min_j}{\mu}$. Then we use cluster analysis [9] method to cluster rate γ. There have lots of cluster analysis algorithms, such as the basic k-means [8], affinity propagation [6], k-means ++ [1], etc. In our methodology, we use the k-means ++ algorithm. We will skip implementation details of K-means ++ in this paper since readers can find it in [1]. By designating cluster numbers at first, we aggregate γ into some intervals, and take the cluster center γ_{center} as unified fluctuation rate. For example, in Fig. 2, there have three clusters divided by solid lines in grey, and the dashed grey lines are the cluster centers respectively.

3.3   Step 3: Generate Time-Period Based Rules

Our goal is to find $R_{threshold}$ constituted with tuple $< T_i, \sigma_i >$, in which T_i represents a time period. Time boundary of T_i can be found by projecting clusters to the timeline. However, the fluctuation rate curve always fluctuate severely near the cluster boundary, which make it hard to determine the related time boundary. So we use curve fitting [5] method to fit the discrete γ points first and then calculate the intersections of fitting curve and cluster boundaries to get T_i. There have so many curve fitting algorithms including polynomial fitting, Bayesian curve fitting [4], etc. We use polynomial fitting in our method because it's simple and effective as we don't need high precision. Through ten order fitting, we can get a smooth fitting curve as in Fig. 3.

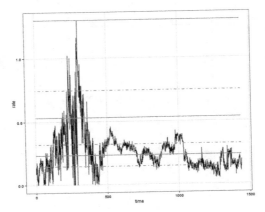

Fig. 2. Clusters of fluctuation rate

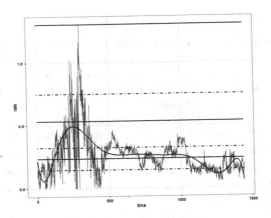

Fig. 3. Curve fitting result

4 Evaluation

4.1 Dataset

Our experiment is based on real data collected from one of the Tencent monitoring systems. We collected outburst anomaly alarms on June 1st, 2014 and July 30th, 2014, denoted as X_a, X_b, X_c. There are two kinds of anomalies: The real anomalies affirmed by monitoring managers; the fake anomalies caused by inaccurate rules or other reasons. And we know all the real anomalies and fake anomalies for X_a, X_b, X_c.. And it is sure that all possible anomalies in system are all include in.

There have two standards to judge the auto configuration solution, one is correctness and the other is effectiveness. The correctness means that the anomalies found by our method should cover all real anomalies in system. The effectiveness means that auto configuration rules should boundary more reasonable than the artificial rules.

4.2   Experiment Result

In Table 1, we list anomalies detected by artificial rules of $X_a, X_b, X_c.$, let "man-anomalies" represent these anomalies. Also, we list the anomaly detection result using rules generated by our methodology denoted as "auto-anomalies".

We can see from Table 1:

Table 1. The manual vs. auto anomaly detection result

Dataset			
X_a	man-anomalies	real anomalies	fake anomalies
	30	1	29
	auto-anomalies	real anomalies	fake anomalies
	9	1	8
X_b	man-anomalies	real anomalies	fake anomalies
	40	2	38
	auto-anomalies	real anomalies	fake anomalies
	7	2	5
X_c	man-anomalies	real anomalies	fake anomalies
	120	15	105
	auto-anomalies	real anomalies	fake anomalies
	41	15	26

1. The fake anomalies found by auto configuration rules are much less than those found by manual rules.
2. The real anomalies found by the two kinds of rules are totally identical.

The first one demonstrates the effectiveness of our method and the second one demonstrates the correctness of our method. So we can draw a conclusion that the rules generated by our methodology can not only guarantee checking out all real anomalies, but also make the monitoring rules more sophisticated and accurate. And the most importantly, we generate the monitoring rules automatically which can save a lot of labor and time in enterprise systems.

5   Conclusion

In this paper we present a methodology for automatic rule discovery in the rule-based monitoring systems. By analyzing the historical status data of monitoring items, our approach can abstract regularities in it and configure the threshold rules and volatility rules respectively in three steps. Our experiment results based on real data sets demonstrated that our method can automatically generate monitoring rules which are more sophisticated and accurate than the artificial ones.

Acknowledgment. This work is supported by the National Key Technology R&D Program (Grant NO. 2012BAH17FOI) and NSFC-NSF International Cooperation Project (Grant NO. 61361126011).

References

1. Arthur, D., Vassilvitskii, S.: k-means ++: the advantages of careful seeding. In: Proceedings of the Eighteenth Annual ACM-SIAM Symposium on Discrete Algorithms, pp. 1027–1035. Society for Industrial and Applied Mathematics (2007)
2. Barham, P., Isaacs, R., Mortier, R., Narayanan, D.: Magpie: online modelling and performance-aware systems. In: HotOS, pp. 85–90 (2003)
3. Chen, M.Y., Kiciman, E., Fratkin, E., Fox, A., Brewer, E.: Pinpoint: problem determination in large, dynamic internet services. In: DSN 2002 Proceedings.of the 2002 International Conference on Dependable Systems and Networks, pp. 595–604. IEEE (2002)
4. Denison, D., Mallick, B., Smith, A.: Automatic bayesian curve fitting. J. R. Stat. Soc.: Series B (Stat. Methodol.) **60**(2), 333–350 (1998)
5. Foundation, W.: Curve fitting. http://en.wikipedia.org/wiki/Curvefitting
6. Frey, B.J., Dueck, D.: Clustering by passing messages between data points. Science **315** (5814), 972–976 (2007)
7. Id´e, T., Kashima, H.: Eigenspace-based anomaly detection in computer systems. In: Proceedings of the Tenth ACM SIGKDD International Conference on Knowledge Discovery and Data Mining, pp. 440–449. ACM (2004)
8. Kanungo, T., Mount, D.M., Netanyahu, N.S., Piatko, C.D., Silverman, R., Wu, A.Y.: An efficient k-means clustering algorithm: analysis and implementation. IEEE Trans. Pattern Anal Mach. Intell. **24**(7), 881–892 (2002)
9. Tan, P.-N., Steinbach, M., Kumar, V.: Cluster analysis: basic concepts and algorithms. In: Tan, P.-N., Steinbach, M., Kumar, V. (eds.) Introduction to Data Mining, pp. 487–568. Addison-Wesley, New York (2006)

Memory Centric Hardware Prefetching in Multi-core Processors

Danfeng Zhu[1], Rui Wang[1(✉)], Zhongzhi Luan[1], Depei Qian[1],
Han Zhang[2], and Jihong Cai[2]

[1] School of Computer Science and Engineering, Beihang University,
Beijing, China
{Danfeng.zhu, wangrui, zhongzhi.luan,
depeiq}@buaa.edu.cn
[2] Science and Technology on Special System Simulation Laboratory,
Beijing Simulation Center, Beijing, China

Abstract. Hardware prefetching is widely employed in modern processors. It has been proved that prefetching can significantly improve application's performance unless it exhibits sparse locality. Nevertheless, prefetching may result in performance degradation in CMP systems as it issues many off-chip memory requests. In this paper, we propose MCPref, a prefetching mechanism that is sensitive to the load of memory bus. Unlike traditional prefetching mechanism, MCPref opens when memory bus is starve and halts when memory bus is busy. Simulation results show that our non-feedback prefetcher design is effective in the scenario of multi-core architecture.

Keywords: Hardware prefetching · Memory scheduling · Multi-core

1 Introduction

As an effective memory latency tolerance mechanism, hardware prefetching is widely employed in modern processors [1–4]. By loading several cache lines ahead of current requested block, hardware prefetching can effectively reduce cache misses that might occur in the future. Prior work [5] shows that prefetching can significantly improve single application's performance unless it exhibits sparse locality. Nevertheless, prefetching may result in performance degradation in CMP systems, for it produces much more off-chip memory requests.

Figure 1 shows the prefetching benefits we observed in an IBM x3650 multicore server during the growth of workloads. In this observation, all the duplicated benchmarks threads share memory system, especially the last level cache and memory controller. We can see that all the benchmarks benefit from prefetching when the workload is light while suffer from prefetching when workload is heavy. Since the result are the average value of 32 times running and the standard deviations of the speedup value are rather low, we can conclude that the prefetching becomes ineffective when the memory system is overloaded. Memory access requests introduced by prefetching increase the risk of overloading memory system. We also notice that prefetching performs better in four workloads than one workload for some benchmarks.

© Springer-Verlag Berlin Heidelberg 2015
Y. Lu et al. (Eds.): ISCTCS 2014, CCIS 520, pp. 311–321, 2015.
DOI: 10.1007/978-3-662-47401-3_41

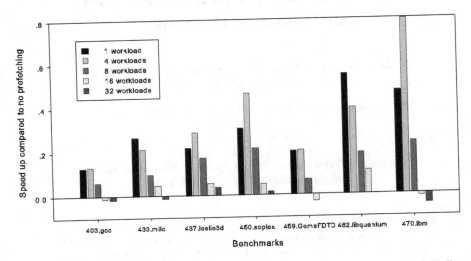

Fig. 1. Prefetching benefits in modern multi-core server against various amount of duplicated workloads with several benchmarks in CPU 2006.

We think that it is mainly because some common used data (like dynamic link libraries) of some threads are prefetched by the former threads. In our experiment, we can only open and halt the prefetching manually in the BIOS. However, we need to switch the prefetch controller state when the extra memory requests generated by prefetching contend with normally memory requests.

We need to detailed analysis the contention source. The main contentions are the following:

(1) Prefetching operations may increase the load of memory bus, and delay normal request when memory bus is busy;
(2) When prefetching requests are responded, the prefetched data may evict valid cache lines;
(3) When some cache lines are evicted due to prefetching, they may have to be written back to main memory, which will increase the load of memory bus.

Prior works address these problems by introducing feedback mechanisms [7–11]. For example, 810 give priorities to prefetching requests according to feedback information of prefetching accuracy, and [6, 7] adjust prefetching stride with feedback information of evicted cache lines or response time of memory accesses.

These work use feedback since they overestimate the *benefits* of prefetching when determining whether or not to enable prefetching or whether or not to issue prefetching operations. Metrics such as prefetching accuracy and prefetching coverage dominate memory scheduling decisions in the memory controller.

Meanwhile, we observe the follows insights:

(1) If memory system is overloaded, even effective prefetching should be discarded. In read buffer of memory controller, prefetching requests at most have equal priorities with normal memory requests; and in cache, prefetched data at most is equally important with the data that is already in cache.

(2) If memory system is idle, even invalid prefetching can be allowed.

(3) Prefetching accuracy is not as important as memory access load produced by prefetching. So, only when memory system is not busy, prefetching accuracy makes sense. When we determine whether to issue a prefetching operation, prefetching accuracy and fairness are not the most important factors.

Feedback is a prediction-based mechanism. Events in the past are imprecise when used to predict future, and feedback information takes too many CPU cycles to make decisions.

We propose SMEP, a non-feedback prefetching mechanism, which can address the side effect of prefetching such as memory overload and cache pollution. SMEP is a memory controller centric prefetching method that makes full utilization of memory bandwidth. In the SMEP, memory controller monitors memory bus status, if memory bus is idle or page mode requests are needed, it triggers appropriate prefetching operations buffered in prefetcher.

The contributions of this paper are as follows:

(1) We propose a directly memory efficient prefetching method which can avoid the extra memory access load;

(2) The proposed prefetching method can significantly reduce the possibility of evicting valid cache lines without introducing much extra storage space within CPU;

(3) The proposed method can greatly reduce the second round memory access requests caused by the write back of evicted dirty cache lines.

2 Related Works

2.1 Prefetching in Modern Processors

In Intel Pentium4 processor, hardware prefetching is associated with L2 cache, and it can get two cache lines ahead of the current data requested [1]. IBM Power6 has two levels prefetch engine, L1 prefetcher and L2 prefetcher [3]. L1 prefetcher normally gets two cache lines ahead of the current cache lines being requested, and L2 prefetcher can get up to 24 cache lines ahead of the current location. The prefetching will terminate at the end of a DRAM page.

2.2 Prefetching Scheduling

Srinivasan et al. [7] propose a memory load-aware prefetching mechanism which use memory access latency monitor to learn the current memory load status. If latency increases, prefetcher will reduce prefetching operations or completely be closed to avoid memory contention with normal memory accesses. However, the memory accessing latency comprises not only the queuing time in memory controller, but also DRAM time constraints. Long latency does not necessarily mean queue congestion. Therefore, the feedback mechanism cannot get accurate information about memory bandwidth usage, and there is time lag between the feedback information and the real memory accessing status.

Reference [9] gives priorities to prefetching operations and common memory accesses in memory controller according to prefetching accuracy. They have several hardware additions to record prefetching information and evaluate the benefits of prefetching operations. If the prefetching is accurate, the prefetching operations will be equally treated with normal operations; otherwise they will be posterior to the normal operations or even be discarded. Reference [13] propose to issue prefetching operations according to the layout of prefetched data in DRAM memory, to make full use of page mode and bank parallel access. This method does not consider co-scheduling of normal memory requests and prefetching requests.

Reference [11] observes that simply prioritizing accurate prefetches and de-prioritizing inaccurate ones is not applicable to all types of applications. This paper uses a demand boosting mechanism to guarantee the response time of normal memory accesses, and extends PAR-BS policy [12] to be aware of prefetching accurancy when batching memory accesses. Its scheduling policy depends on the feedback of prefetching accuracy and applications' performance degradation.

References [14, 15] propose to flexibly schedule write back requests by extending the control scope of memory controller. The *Virtual Write Queue* in memory controller in 14 monitors memory bus status, and triggers write back operations from last level cache as needed. These works do not involve prefetching. Inspired by these works, we propose to extend the control scope of memory controller to prefetching engine, and schedule prefetching operations according to memory bus status.

3   Non-feedback Hardware Prefetching

In SMEP we assume that hardware prefetching engine issues prefetching requests when cache miss occurs(prefetch-on-miss),we will talk other patterns (like prefetch-on-hit) in the following sections.

The main idea of SMEP is as follows:

(1) Prefetcher provides candidate prefetching addresses according to cache miss status,
(2) Prefetcher stores these addresses in candidate queues, which are visible to memory controller.
(3) Memory controller monitors the status of memory bus, and issues prefetching operations,
    (a) the read operations in prefetching candidate queue can form a series of page mode read and bank parallel read.
    (b) read operations are not enough to maintain a certain length of read sequence before memory bus is switched to write, and the prefetching candidate queue has more read operations;
    (c) there is no operations to be sent to memory bus.

(4) Memory controller efficiently schedules write back operations of LRU cache lines when some cache lines can form a page mode write burst.

Our prefetching algorithm cooperates with memory access algorithm. We assume that the memory access algorithm is PAR-BS [12]. The process of non-feedback prefetching is as follows:

(1) When cache miss happens, let i denote the missed cache block address, the prefetcher takes k as stride and puts n cache blocks i + k, i + 2 k, i + 3 k, ..., i + nk into candidate prefetching queue Q1 (Where, n is the depth of prefetching, k and n are configurable. We set k = 1 and n = 2 in this paper). Assuming that the number of requests that prefetcher can buffer is L. If the length of Q1 exceeds L, the earlier candidate prefetching requests will be discarded.
(2) Sort the candidate requests in Q1 by row number and send the candidate prefetching request list to Memory Controller.
(3) Memory Controller inserts candidate prefetching requests into memory access queue according to the current condition of memory bus by following rules:
   (i)   If there are requests that have the same addresses as current accessing row in candidate prefetching request list, then insert these addresses into memory access queue after that row. Memory access rules should be hold here. If memory access algorithm has specified the upper bound of page mode access, the excessive prefetching requests will be discarded.
   (ii) If requests in memory access queue cannot access all banks in parallel, but there are requests that access the idle banks in candidate prefetching request list, then insert these requests behind the banks in execution. According to memory access algorithm, if the accessed banks in parallel exceeds the upper bound, other prefetching requests will be discarded.
   (iii) If read requests do not reach the read/write switching threshold (read/write switching occupies long bus time, so Memory Controller schedules as much read/write requests as possible before switching), then find the row that are most requested from candidate prefetching list and insert the requests that access this row into memory access queue to fill the read request queue.
   (iv) Let t denote the life time of a candidate memory access request and discard overtime prefetching requests in Memory Controller every interval of t.
(4) Check the length of memory access queue in Memory Controller, if the length exceeds preset threshold then discard all prefetching requests and clear Q1. Repeat From 2).

There are several caveats for this approach. First is the time to generate candidate prefetching queue, the algorithm above starts calculation when cache miss happens. However, it can also be triggered by other events such as cache hit.

Second is the algorithm to generate candidate prefetching queue. It varies with stride k and depth n. Besides, it depends on the length of the queue.

Last is the way to deal with effective prefetching requests. Effective prefetching may be inefficient. If memory bus is overloaded, even precise prefetching should not be executed. Therefore, we must be sure that prefetching won't overload memory access scheduling before carrying out the effective prefetching requests. We check the length of remaining prefetching request queue to determine the memory access load. The value of remaining length is preset and can be configured according to hardware environment.

The advantages of our prefetching method are as follows:

(1) It avoids overloading memory bus by scheduling prefetching operation according to memory access queue.
(2) It does not need any feedback mechanism. The aforementioned feedback mechanisms have latencies and are inaccurate.
(3) It can achieve approximate effect without accurate prefetching.

As discussed above, the architecture of non-feedback prefetcher is illustrated in Fig. 2.

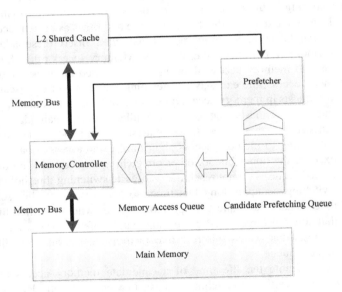

Fig. 2. Architecture of non-feedback prefetcher.

4   Evaluation

4.1   Simulation Methodology

We use a cycle accurate x86 CMP simulator for our evaluation. Table 1 shows the baseline configuration of each core (Table 2).

We use the SPEC CPU 2006 benchmarks for experimental evaluation. Each benchmark was compiled using ICC (Intel C Com-piler) or IFORT (Intel Fortran Compiler) with the -O3 option and was run with the reference input set for 200 million representat ive x86 in-structions as selected by Pinpoints [23].

Table 1. Baseline configuration of each core

Execution core	Out of order; 15 stages; decode/retire up to 4 instructions, issue/execute up to 8 microinstructions, 256-entry reorder buffer; 32-entry load-store queue
Front end	Fetch up to 2 branches; 4 K-entry BTB; 64 K-entry gshare,64 K-entry PAs, 64 K-entry selector hybrid branch predictor
On-chip caches	L1 I and D: 32 KB, 4-way, 2-cycle, 1 read and 1 write ports;Unified L2: 512 KB (1 MB for 1-core), 8-way, 8-bank,15-cycle, 1 read/write port; 64 B line size for all caches
Prefetcher	Stream prefetcher with 32 streams, prefetch degree of 1, cache line prefetch distance (lookahead) of 64

Table 2. Shared resource configuration for single-, 4-,and 8-core CMPs

DRAM controller	On-chip, demand-first FR-FCFS scheduling policy;1 controller for 1-, 4-, 8-core CMP (also 2 for 8-core); 64, 128, 256-entry L2 MSHR and MRB for 1-, 4-, 8-core
DRAM and bus	DDR3 1333 MHz [14], 16 B-wide data bus per controller; Latency: 15-15-15 ns (tRP,tRCD,CL), BL = 4;Latency: 15-15-15 ns (tRP,tRCD,CL), BL = 4; 8 DRAM banks, 4 KB row buffer per bank

The parameters of prefetching in our evaluation are in Table 3.

Table 3. Parameters

Prefetch degree	1
Prefetch stripe	1
Prefetcher Buffer size	16
Memory Controller buffer size	256
Max page mode access number	8
Max bank parallel access number	8
Min reads before bus turn to write	16

We choose 25 benchmarks from the integer and floating-point test suite of SPEC CPU2006. To test the scalability of our prefetcher, we run the benchmarks under 4-core, 8-core and 16-core architecture respectively. We take average memory access time as our performance metric. It is calculated by following formula:

L1 cache hit rate*L1 cache access time + L1 cache miss rate*L2 cache hit rate*(L1 cache access time +L2 cache access time) + L1 cache miss rate*L2cache miss rate*(L1 cache access time + L2 cache access time +main memory access time).

Note that memory access time is measured in clock cycles. We set L1 cache access time as 3 clock cycles, L2 cache access time as 12 clock cycles and main memory access time as 335 clock cycles. We compare our prefetcher with the one that is widely implemented in modern CPUs.

4.2   Result

The experimental results are shown in Figs. 3, 4, 5 and 6.

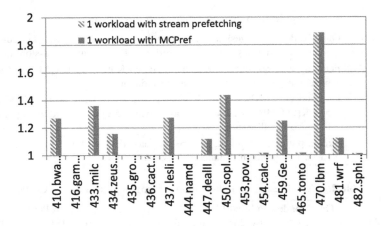

Fig. 3. Speedup of MCPref against stream prefetching under 1-core architecture.

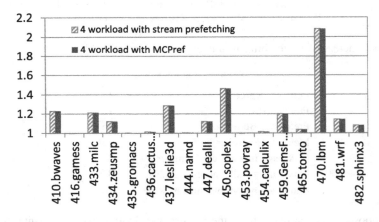

Fig. 4. Speedup of MCPref against stream prefetching under 4-core architecture.

The optimization results under 1-core and 4-core architecture can be classified in two cases: (1) gamess, gromacs, namd and povray eliminate the side effects cause by too much prefetching; (2) The performance improvements of other benchmarks are negligible. Most of them maintain their performance after optimization.

The optimization results under 8-core architecture can be classified in three cases: (1) the performance of bwaves, milc, leslie3d, soplex, GemsFDTD and lbm has significant improvement; (2) gamess, gromacs, namd and povray eliminate the side effects cause by too much prefetching; (3) The performance improvements of other benchmarks are negligible.

We classify the optimization results under 16-core architecture in three cases: (1) Compared with 4-core and 8-core architecture, the performance benefit of bwaves, milc, leslie3d, soplex, GemsFDTD and lbm are more significant although the overall

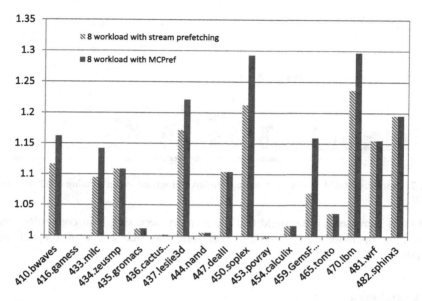

Fig. 5. Speedup of MCPref against stream prefetching under 8-core architecture.

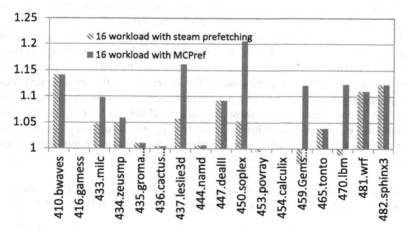

Fig. 6. Speedup of MCPref against stream prefetching under 16-core architecture.

speedup from prefetching is lower than that in 8-core situation; (2) MCPref eliminates the side effects on gamess, gromacs, namd and povray cause by too much prefetching; (3) The performance improvements of other benchmarks are negligible. Although the geometric average speedup of MCPref over naïve prefetching is 2.7 %, MCPref avoid the performance degradation when the memory is congesting. It also provide at most over 11 % performance improvement (Fig. 7).

We also test the performance of a group of sensitive programs in a 2-core processor when we allocate different amount of workload copies. We observed that when

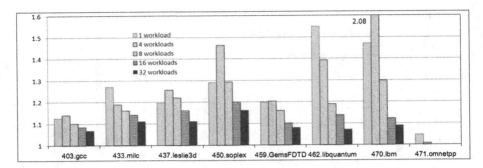

Fig. 7. Speedup of SMPref on prefetching sensitive programs when running 1-32 workloads

workloads increase to a threshold that the memory accessing is in congestion, many prefetching operations are throttled. Therefore, the side effect of prefetching is postponed.

5 Conclusion

The research of processor architecture has entered the era of multicore. The competition of limited resource among processor cores is the bottleneck of memory access, which makes it more difficult to solve the problem of "memory wall".

In this paper, we propose a memory centric prefetching that prefetches data blocks into cache as long as memory bus is not busy. We introduce a new design philosophy of hardware prefetcher. The prefetching operation is determined by the state of memory bus rather than the prefetching efficiency. We develop a multicore oriented memory access optimization simulator to test the performance of non-feedback hardware prefetcher. The experimental results show that non-feedback prefetching mechanism can avoid the side effects of prefetching caused by aggressive memory requests. So we believe that our prefetching design is effective in the scenario of multicore/manycore architecture.

Acknowledgement. This research is supported by 863 Program of China under grant 2012AA010902, by the NSF of China under grant 61133004, 61073011, and 61202425.

References

1. Hinton, G., Sager, D., Upton, M., Boggs, D., Carmean, D., Kyker, A., Roussel, P.: The microarchitecture of the pentium 4 processor. Intel Technol. J. (**Q1**) (2001)
2. Sinharoy, B., Kalla, R.N., Tendler, J.M., Eickemeyer, R.J., Joyner, J.B.: POWER5 system microarchitecture. IBM J. Res. Dev. **49**(4/5), 505–521 (2005)
3. Le, H.Q., Starke, W.J., Fields, J.S., Connell, F.O., Nguyen, D.Q., Ronchetti, B.J., Sauer, W. M., Schwarz, E.M., Waden, M.T.: IBM power6 microarchitecture. IBM J. Res. Dev. **51**, 639–662 (2007)

4. Doweck, J.: Inside Intel Core microarchitecture and smart memory access. White paper, Intel Research Website (2006). http://download.intel.com/technology/architecture/sma.pdf
5. VanderWiel, S., Lilja, D.J.: Data prefetch mechanisms. ACM Comput. Surv. 32(2), 174–199 (2000)
6. Zhuang, X., Lee, H.-H.: Reducing cache pollution via dynamic data prefetch filtering. IEEE Trans. Comput. 56(1), 18–31 (2007). (water)
7. Srinivasan, S.: Prefetching vs. the memory system: optimizations for multicore server platforms. Ph.D. thesis, University of Maryland, Dept. of Electrical & Computer Engineering (2007)
8. Srinath, S., Mutlu, O., Kim, H., Patt, Y.N.: Feedback directed prefetching: improving the performance and bandwidth-efficiency of hardware prefetchers. In: Proceedings of the 13th International Symposium on High-Performance Computer Architecture (HPCA), Phoenix, AZ, pp. 63–74, February 2007
9. Lee, C.J., Mutlu, O., Narasiman, V., Patt, Y.N.: Prefetch-aware DRAM controllers. In: Proceedings of the 41st International Symposium on Microarchitecture (MICRO), Lake Como, Italy, pp. 200–209, November 2008
10. Ebrahimi, E., et al.: Coordinated control of multiple prefetchers in multi-core systems. In: MICRO-42 (2009)
11. Ebrahimi, E., Lee, C.J., Mutlu, O., Patt, Y.N.: Prefetch-aware shared resource management for multi-core systems. In: Proceedings of the 38th International Symposium on Computer Architecture (ISCA), San Jose, CA, June 2011
12. Mutlu, O., Moscibroda, T.: Parallelism-aware batch scheduling: enhancing both performance and fairness of shared DRAM systems. In: Proceedings of the 35th International Symposium on Computer Architecture (ISCA), Beijing, China, pp. 63–74, June 2008
13. Lee, C.J., Narasiman, V., Mutlu, O., Patt, Y.N.: Improving memory bank-level parallelism in the presence of prefetching. In: Proceedings of the 42nd International Symposium on Microarchitecture (MICRO), New York, NY, pp. 327–336, December 2009
14. Stuecheli, J., Kaseridis, D., Daly, D., Hunter, H., John, L.K.: The virtual write queue: coordinating DRAM and last-level cache policies. In: The 37th Interenational Symposium on Computer Architecture, June 2010
15. Lee, C.J., Narasiman, V., Ebrahimi, E., Mutlu, O., Patt, Y.N.: DRAM-aware last-level cache writeback: reducing write-caused interference in memory systems. HPS Technical report, TR-HPS-2010–002, April 2010
16. Casmira, J.P., Kaeli, D.R.: Modeling cache pollution. Int. J. Model. Simul. 19(2), 132–138 (1998)
17. Jain, P., Devadas, S., Rudolph, L.: Controlling cache pollution in prefetching with software-assisted cache replacement. Technical report TR-CSG-462, Massachusetts Institute of Technology (2001)
18. Megiddo, N., Modha, D.: ARC: a self-tuning, low overhead replacement cache. In: Proceedings the 2nd USENIX Conference on File and Storage Technologies, San Francisco, pp. 115–130, 31 March–2 April 2003
19. Wu, C.J., Jaleel, A., Martonosi, M., Steely, S.C., Emer Jr., J.: PACMan: prefetch-aware cache management for high performance caching. In: Proceedings of the 44th International Symposium on Microarchitecture (MICRO) (2011)

Performance-Aware Based Correlated Datasets Replication Strategy

Lin Ye, Zhongzhi Luan[✉], and Hailong Yang

Sino-German Joint Software Institute, Beihang University, Beijing, China
{lin.ye,Zhongzhi.luan,Hailong.yang}@jsi.buaa.edu.cn

Abstract. Performance-aware based correlated datasets replication strategy (PCDRS) has been put forward to solve the issue of how to place datasets at a wide area distributed environment to support researchers on interdisciplinary scientific research. The issue is addressed from three parts. First of all, we gave out the replica number based on the performance requirement of the datasets. Secondly, according to the performance of the datanode, we determined the location for placing the datasets replica. Thirdly, we distinguished data from hot and cold to control the number of replicas elastically. The strategy has been put into tests on a HDFS cluster. The result shows that our strategy is performance effective in maintaining the reliability of datasets and promoting the access performance of the cluster.

Keywords: Correlated data · Performance-aware · Elastic replica management

1 Introduction

In the interdisciplinary collaboration of Qinghai Lake oriented biodiversity conservation and ecological system evolution research, scientific data resources usually come from multi-sources, which are commonly heterogeneous. The data resources may include such as video data and remote sensing image data in GB scale and may also include such as GPS data in KB scale. The data quantity is so big that the output of data can achieve terabytes. These data generally has significant relationship of time and space coupled and interrelated, namely time-space correlation. According to this property, the interdisciplinary correlation of the whole datasets in research needs to be analyzed. It may affect the results of the research greatly if lacking the aspect of data. So the problem of maintaining the reliability and availability of the datasets has been brought out.

In this paper, we address the problem of maintaining the reliability and availability of time-space correlated datasets for interdisciplinary collaboration of research. In particular, we propose Performance-aware Based Correlated Datasets Replication Strategy (PCDRS). First of all, a probability model is built to determine the relationship between replica number and reliability. The minimal number of replicas [1] that meets the system requirement of reliability can be calculated based on this model. Then, according to the performance parameters of datanode and the Queueing Theory [2], the blocking probability of datanodes is figured out to determine where to place replicas. Thirdly, an elastic replication strategy is presented to adjust the datasets availability and

Y. Lu et al. (Eds.): ISCTCS 2014, CCIS 520, pp. 322–327, 2015.
DOI: 10.1007/978-3-662-47401-3_42

storage availability based on the user access model. At last, PCDRS is implemented and evaluated in HDFS.

2 Performance-Aware Replication Strategy

The purpose of this paper is to design a performance-aware based correlated datasets replication strategy that seeks to calculate the minimal number of replicas to satisfy the need for reliability and determine where to place these replicas. Additionally, PCDRS dynamically adapts to the changes in data access patterns and data popularity. In this section, we first describe the model that capture the relationship between replica number and reliability [3], and then present the method to determine the places that hold these replicas and the elastic replication strategy.

2.1 Replica Number

We assume that datasets D has S files $D = \{F_1, F_s \ldots F_S\}$, D has been divided into N blocks, $D = \{d_1, \ldots d_i, \ldots d_N\}$, $F_s = \{d_p \ldots d_q\}$, all the N blocks are stored in M datanodes $DN = \{DN_1, \ldots DN_j, DN_M\}$, block d_i has attribute tuple $d_i = (s_i, r_i, t_i)$, s_i, r_i, t_i respectively represents block size, replica number, response time requirement. Datanode has attribute tuple $DN_j = (s_j, bw_j, a_j)$, s_j, bw_j, a_j are storage capacity, bandwidth, and reliability of DN_j. As for the issue of datanode reliability [4], it is usually generalized as the issue of failure probability of the entire data storage system. Through the statistics of historical records of failure can give out the average failure probability f of the system. Then the reliability of datanode can be depicted as $a_i = 1 - f$.

As we mentioned in Sect. 2, if datasets D is reliable, it needs all the blocks to be reliable. As for block d_i, there must be one of r_i blocks reliable, in other words, the datanode that store the exact replica must work fine. Then the unreliability of d_i is f^{r_i}, that means all the datanodes that store the r_i blocks are in failure. At the beginning, to meet the reliability requirement, all the data blocks' replica number is the same r. Then every data block's unreliable probability is f^r [5].

In this paper, we do not consider many replicas stored in one datanode, the failure of the datanode leads to all the replicas it stored unavailable. The datasets D's unreliable probability [3] is $P(\overline{D}) = P(\overline{d_1} \cup \overline{d_2} \cup \ldots \cup \overline{d_N})$, $P(\overline{D}) = \sum_{i=1}^{N} (-1)^{i+1} C_N^i f^{r_i}$, then the reliability of D is

$$a = 1 - \sum_{i=1}^{N} (-1)^{i+1} C_N^i f^{r_i} \tag{1}$$

So for a given system reliability parameter A, it only needs to satisfy $a \geq A$. According to formula (2), we can work out the minimal number of replica number that reaches the reliability requirement.

$$a = 1 - \sum_{i=1}^{N} (-1)^{i+1} C_N^i f^{ri} \geq A \tag{2}$$

2.2 Data Distinguish

Under the condition of ensure the reliability of the datasets, we distinguish data between hot and cold and elastically adjust the number of replicas for the relevant data blocks.

So-called hot data is the data that receives high concurrent access. The replicas that exist can hardly afford to offer qualified service. We have defined 3 kinds of hot data [6].

1. If every replica of F_s has a high concurrent access request, exceeding the threshold, it is definitely hot data. As shown in formula (3), $\sum dc_i/r_i$ is the average concurrent access number. dc_M is the concurrent access threshold of F_s. The replica number of F_s has to be increased to decrease the average concurrent access number to less than dc_M.

$$dc_i/r_i > dc_M \tag{3}$$

2. If not every replica of F_s has a high concurrent access request, but only some replicas have a high concurrent access number. Then F_s is still hot data. In formula (4), d_M is the concurrent access threshold of a replica.

$$\exists i \in [1, q - p], dc_i/r_i > d_M \tag{4}$$

3. The concurrent access number is limited. Assume that N_j blocks stored in DN_j. $DN_j = \{d_{j1}, d_{j2}, \ldots d_{jN_j}\}$. None replicas in DN_j has a high concurrent access request, but the whole concurrent access number of all replicas has exceed the concurrent access threshold c_j of DN_j. The replica that has the highest access number must be migrated to other datanode.

2.3 Replica Placement

The resources in datanode are finite, so the quantity of concurrent access that it can provide is also limited. So it gives a priority to consider placing replicas on datanode that has lower blocking probability. We use $M/G/c_j/c_j$ model [7] to get the blocking probability of DN_j. The model is backed up by the following parameters.

The concurrent access up bound c_j. It can be calculated by considering the requirement of response time for replica and the finite bandwidth. The parameter c_j can be figured out by formula (5).

$$\sum_{i=1}^{c_j} \frac{s_i}{t_i} \leq bw_j \tag{5}$$

The access rate p_j. It can be calculated by using the access historical records to get the average access frequency in time window T.

The average service time st_j. Referred to the temporal locality, the next access coming may visit the same block. So we also use the access historical records to get the average service time in time window T. $1/st_j$ represents the average complete rate of service.

The blocking probability B_j. When DN_j receives a service request, it will provide service at average time st_j, the service number at most up to c_j, other access request will be rejected. So DN_j can be modeled as $M/G/c_j/c_j$ system with access rate p_j and complete rate of service $1/st_j$, the blocking probability can be calculated by formula (6).

$$B_j = \frac{(p_j st_j)^{c_j}}{c_j!} \left[\sum_{k=0}^{c_j} \frac{(p_j st_j)^k}{k!} \right]^{-1} \tag{6}$$

In general, (4) pays adequate attention to the main parameters that DN_j receives a access request. The lower the blocking probability, the more service the datanode can provide. The replica created should be placed there.

3   Experiment and Analysis

3.1   Experiment Environment

HDFS is a cluster system that can store large scale data in distributed environment [8]. We evaluated PBCDRS in a HDFS cluster [9] with 1 namenode as servo node and 12 datanodes. These 13 servers are IBM Blade HS22, divided into 3 rack3. The namenode has 2 Intel Xeon E5520 CPUs of 2.26 GHz, 12 GB Memory, 250 GB SATA disk. The datanodes have an Intel Xeon E5420 CPU of 2.50 GBHz, 8G memory, 250 GB SATA disk. These nodes are connected with Gigabit Ethernet network. The topology of the cluster is shown in Fig. 1.

3.2   Performance Analysis

Under the system failure rate f = 0.1, the number of blocks that datasets divided into 5, 8, 10, 15, we can see that different replica number has different effect on the reliability. The relationship between reliability and the block number that datasets divided is shown is Fig. 2. Obviously, the more the replica number, the more blocks the datasets can be divided under the same reliability. When the replica number comes to 3, the reliability seems to be 1. More replicas have little marginal increment.

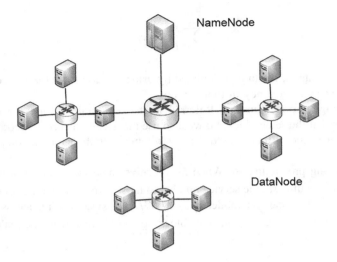

Fig. 1. Topology of experiment cluster

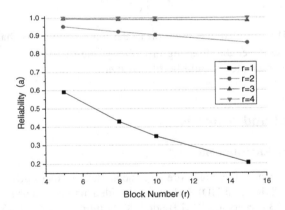

Fig. 2. The relationship between reliability and block number

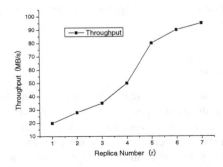

Fig. 3. The relationship between system throughput and replica number

Figure 3 tells us that more replicas can provide more chance for users to access data. The throughput is greatly increased. When the replica number reaches a specific value, the marginal benefit for replicas that newly created increases less and less. Obviously, the system keeps load balance.

4   Conclusion

In this paper, we present, design and implement PBCDRS, a strategy that can maintain the reliability of datasets, and can find a reasonable position to place the replica, and can elastically adjust the number of replicas based on the user access model. Our proposed strategy not only satisfies the requirement of datasets reliability, but also maintains the load balance; also, it improves the user access performance by increase replica and saves the storage capacity by deleting the useless replicas.

Acknowledgment. This work is supported by the National Key Technology R&D Program (Grant NO. 2012BAH17FOl) and NSFC-NSF International Cooperation Project (Grant NO. 61361126011).

References

1. Cidon, A., et al.: Copysets: reducing the frequency of data loss in cloud storage. In: USENIX Annual Technical Conference, Citeseer (2013)
2. Lazowska, E.D., Zahorjan, J., Graham, G.S., Sevcik, K.C.: Quantitative System Performance: Computer System Analysis Using Queueing Network Models. Prentice-Hall Inc., Upper Saddle River (1984)
3. Qingsong, W., et al.: CDRM: a cost-effective dynamic replication management scheme for cloud storage cluster. In: 2010 IEEE International Conference on Cluster Computing (CLUSTER) (2010)
4. Bhagwan, R., Savage, S., Voelker, G.M.: Understanding availability. In: Kaashoek, M., Stoica, I. (eds.) IPTPS 2003. LNCS, vol. 2735, pp. 256–267. Springer, Heidelberg (2003)
5. Rodrigues, R., Zhou, T.H.: High availability in DHTs: erasure coding vs. replication. In: van Renesse, R. (ed.) IPTPS 2005. LNCS, vol. 3640, pp. 226–239. Springer, Heidelberg (2005)
6. Zhendong, C., et al.: ERMS: an elastic replication management system for HDFS. In: 2012 IEEE International Conference on Cluster Computing Workshops (CLUSTER WORK-SHOPS) (2012)
7. Leung, Y.-W., Hou, R.-T.: Assignment of movies to heterogeneous video servers. IEEE Trans. Syst. Man Cybern. A Syst. Humans 35(5), 665–681 (2005)
8. Sammer, E.: Hadoop Operations. O'Reilly Media Inc., Sebastopol (2013)
9. HDFS Users Guide. hadoop.apache.org/docs/current/hadoop-project-dist/hadoop-hdfs/Hdfs UserGuide.html

Monitoring Social Events on Sina Weibo

Xi Zhang[(⊠)], Guanhong Jiang, and Yuan Su

Key Laboratory of Trustworthy Distributed Computing and Service,
Ministry of Education, School of Computer Science,
Beijing University of Posts and Telecommunications, Beijing 100876, China
zhangx@bupt.edu.cn, jguanhong@126.com,
aisolver@gmail.com

Abstract. Public opinion from social network has proved to play important roles in usual life. How to extract them massive data from social network and social media has attract a lot research efforts. This paper addresses several key issues in the design and implementation of an event monitoring system based on social network. Our proposed system aims at extracting and mining social events from social network, and foucuses on: (1) Collecting data from weibo; (2) Extracting event information such as time and location; (3) Modeling and displaying. We describe the main architecture and processing flow of the system in detail.

1 Introduction

In the past decade, online social networks have become ubiquitous in our life. With the development of the social media, information dissemination capabilities of traditional media constantly undermined by the Internet, while the amazing ability of social network to create content and information dissemination capabilities make itself growing more and more important. The traditional medias, like radio, television, newspapers, magazines gradually gave way to the social media because of their ability to communicate is limited, and the news area is narrow. When people are connected by a network, it becomes possible for them to influence each other's behaviors and decisions, e.g., whether to adopt a political opinion or a product. Such influences occur through information diffusion on social networks. Public Opinion among the community is a collection of emotions reflection in a certain range of time and in a certain area for social events or social phenomena. People's cognition, emotion, attitude and behavior for an event are reflected in the process of the retweeting and commenting one after another. Public opinion from social network has proved to play important roles in usual life, and even decisive roles in some situations, such as the Arab spring. Therefore, monitoring social events on social network and collecting the public opinion is important to government,corporations and even for individual users. In this paper, we address the key issues in design and implementation of a social event monitoring system for sina weibo. After crawling data from sina weibo, our proposed system can extract, analyze, store and show the social events, according to the users' requirements.

Y. Lu et al. (Eds.): ISCTCS 2014, CCIS 520, pp. 328–335, 2015.
DOI: 10.1007/978-3-662-47401-3_43

2   Related Works

In this section, we briefly discuss the existing event monitoring systems based on social networks. The public opinion research on network began in 2005, and has achieved explosive growth in 2009. The relevant papers in CNKI had risen from 348 to 1202 during the two years between 2009 and 2011. After years of research accumulation on public opinion monitoring [1, 2], we can find some excellent case studies and practical systems home or abroad. Oil prices Knew is a system based on social networks using big data analysis techniques to forecast oil price. On the basis of a large number of microblog data acquisition (acquired approximately 2.32 million microblog messages), and tracking opinion leaders (by finding 700 people out of 16 million), it can forecast the change in the oil price by a success rate of over 95 %. The website "twitinfo", which is constructed by Massachusetts Institute of Technology, is a platform aimed to collect information, and to static the time and the location of the event, and then do some statistical visualization process. YingJi system is a platform for public opinion monitoring and guidance on microblog, which can monitor real time messages, provide accurate alarm and deep analysis. There are many companies dedicated to the commercialization of public opinion system, which also made great contribution to public opinion research. However, most of prior work focused on community, forum and blog, and the microblog is harder to monitor because of it generates messages with high volume and velocity. Our work focused on sina weibo, and provides more efficient monitoring services because data are crawled according to user's need.

3   Event Monitoring System Model

As mentioned in the previous section, our system aims to deal with three demands, information collection, data analysis and results display. And we designed two separate subsystems to meet the demands. The first part is designed to collect, store and analyze information, and the second part is for displaying. The two parts share a common database, through which the extracted information is sent to the display part. And the two separate parts can work separately, i.e., if one part stops working, the other part can still work in some extent.

3.1   Information Collection and Analysis

To achieve our goal to collect information from sina weibo precisely, we designed a process of information collecting in detail shown in Fig. 1.

We can conclude from the diagram above that the main part of our information collection system is information collecting, information analyzing and information storage. And the most important issues that we should deal with are what kind of information to collect, how to log in the microblog system and how to analyze it and get the required information.

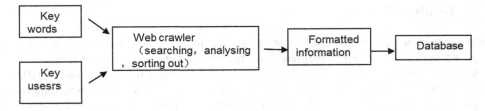

Fig. 1. Information collection and analysis

3.1.1 The Design of Collection

Microblog contains vast amounts of information, which makes information processing difficult to accomplish. How much information to collect could fall into a big dilemma, that is, excessive amount of information could result in low efficiency in the system. While a small amount of information could lead to absence of representative and inaccurate conclusions.

To explain our collection design, we should first introduce the power-law distribution. The power-low distribution is a result of Matthew Effect, which means the strong will be stronger, and the weak will be weaker. We can find this kind of phenomenon everywhere in nature or in our normal life. The strong wolf in the wind will be stronger, and only the several strongest ones can own and enjoy enough food. And there are little billionaires in the world, but they own the most wealth in our world. In the world of social network, the power-law distribution also works, e.g., The celebrity is minority in weibo, but they catch the most followers. This gives us a revelation that we can keep our concentration on users with high impact, and mainly monitoring only a few people can bring us a large amount of information. It inspires our collection design as follows:

Key Words->Sensitive Microblogs->Key People->Sensitive Microblogs

Key Words are the words we set to determine what kind of information to collect. When searching them, we can get the relevant content. Then we look for those who has posted or reposted the content, and follow them with our monitoring account. Therefore, their recent microblog can display in our profile afterwards. This information can satisfy our needs with high probability. In this way, we achieve our goal—less content with more information.

3.1.2 Microblog Login Simulation

Using API methods to collect information is convenient and could get structural data, however, it is expensive since sina charged a lot for this service. Otherwise, the API interfaces are prohibited significantly. Hence we choose the login simulation method., which are studied through "wireshark" capture. For the security of the users' information, Sina microblog take strict measures for authentication. Currently, Sina Weibo uses sha1 and base64 encryption algorithm, and it takes sha1's iterative encryption to encrypt password. Figure 2 shows how http packets be transferred during the entire Sina Weibo login process.

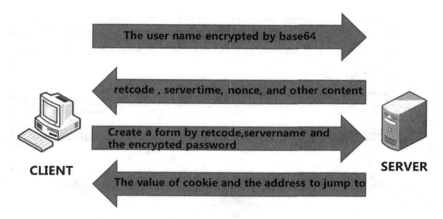

Fig. 2. The login process

The login process is explained as follows:

- Clients use base64 algorithm to encrypt the user name, and send it to the server by using GET method;
- If success, the server will send back a form that contains the return code "retcode", server uptime "servertime", random number "nonce" and other content, which is transmitted for subsequent use, a return code of 0 indicates that the transfer was successful;
- The clients use "servertime", "nonce", and other numbers that are given by the server before and the password which is encrypted by sha1 algorithm to create transport value, and send it to the server;
- The value returned by the server sets a cookie, and the clients save it to a designated place for the next use, usually valid for 5–7 days. And the server returns an address to jump to, and then the microblog login succeeds.

3.1.3   Analysis

Now we can login the microblog and get the required content. Then how can we get the information from the content which contains lots of useless information? The Regular expression [3–5] is the answer. It is a single string used to describe or match a set of syntactic rules in line with the string. In many text editors or other tools, the regular expressions are often used to retrieve or replace those texts that match a pattern.

The method we used is the web information extraction technology that is based on the principle of visual analysis. The page we want to extract the information usually have certain characteristics in the visual style, generally there will be some relatively clear delimiter between information we want to extract with other information. According to this method, we can achieve the purpose of information extraction. Html elements can be divided into simple objects (such as <url> \ <hr>, etc.), container objects (such as <table>) and grouped objects to extract the information by different categories and different levels.

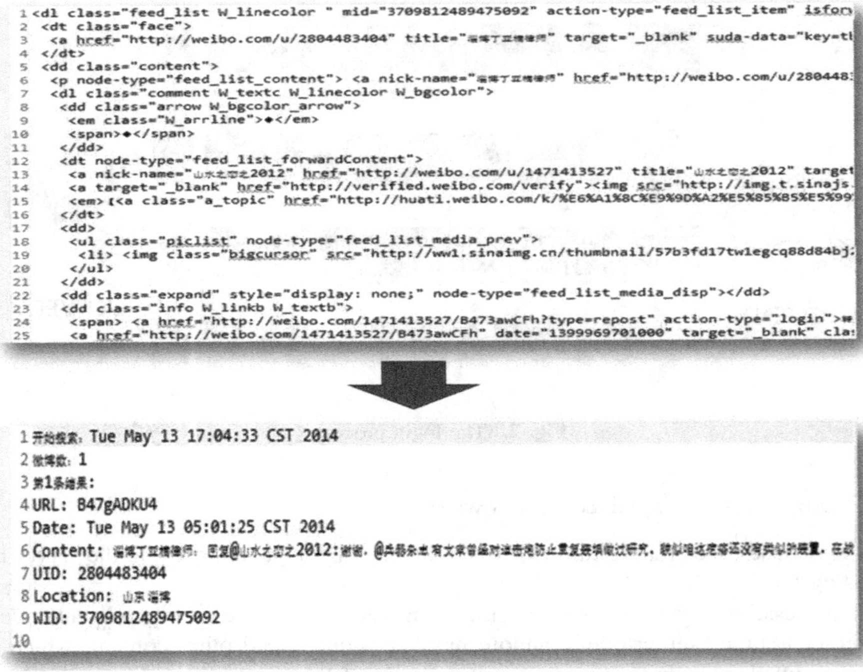

Fig. 3. Information extraction

Figure 3 shows the information we get after extracting.

And in our model, expect the content, the most important information we should pay attention to is the time and the location. Sometimes, the time of a content may give us even more information than the content: why the content gets popular suddenly, who is the first people that find the topic interesting, and what is the source of the topic. And we can also find out which topic is going to be the most popular one in an area, which can give us more time to prepare for it. And the location is more complicated, a piece of microblog can contain three kind of information, the place that the event occurred, the place where the people who published the microblog is, and the location the people registered. We collected both of time and location information, which can help researchers to discover useful information that may help them in their research.

3.2 Information Display

Nowadays researches on the social network tend to solve problems and find answers according to a well-designed visual system, which should be friendly for user interaction, and be able to store user information and manage their authority. So we make full use of some mature systems and new techniques for data visualization.

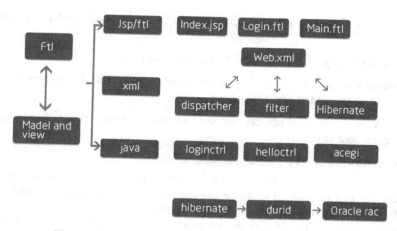

Fig. 4. The construction of the information display system

We use hibernate [6] to help us to operate database, and spring MVC to help us to construct our foreground frame. And we use spring frame to take the two parts together, send data between them. Here Fig. 4 can help us explain that our system really looks like:

3.2.1   The Construction of the Foreground

Then we will introduce our display subsystem and some important functions. Easyui is the basement of our foreground part. It is a set of UI plugins based on JQuery. Makin full use of it can help a lot in creating a feature-rich and beautiful UI interface. We make use of its layout, panel and tree. And we insert "ztree" in it to display the content in by a structure of menu tree."Easyui" is used for layout, and "ztree" is used to organize the content.

Based on the structure we have designed, the most important part is the data visualization. Information visualization makes use of computer support, interactive, and visual representation of abstract data to enhance user awareness of these abstract information which do not have the physical attributes and space characteristics. And its main task is to observe the abstract information. Our information visualization objects is mainly statistics, which can use one or several data tables to express. Each row of the table represents a value of the recording observation and each column represents a property. The data table is composed by S piece of data records, and each record contains 2 elements. Namely $Fi = (fi1, fi2)$, $I = 1, 2..., S$. The most common Parallel Coordinates is used for visualization in our system.

3.2.2   The Database Operation Module

Hibernate is a mature object-relational mapping framework which package JDBC object lightly. To comprehend hibernate, we first explain the following key words:

Transaction: The application to specify atomic units of the object, which is single-threaded, short-lived. It abstracts the application from the underlying isolate specific

JDBC, JTA or CORBA transaction. In a word, it is the basic unit to operate the database.

TransactionFactory: A factory used to generate Transaction.

ConnectionProvider: A factory to generate JDBC connection. It separates our other functions from the underlying Datasource.

Session: A single-threaded objects that used for interoperate between the application and the persistent store,

SessionFactory: A factory used to generate Session.

Before we make use of hibernate, we should configure two kinds of files first. Hibernate.cfg.xml file is used to define the connection with the database. And *.hbm. xml files is used for mapping the data in the database.

Besides, we should configure the Datasource, including the database connection parameters and the parameters for druid. And we use Person.java for mapping the form of the database. And we use PersonDao.java to package the operation of the database, which can greatly simply our coding. And druid is used to manage the database connections and encrypt the database connection parameters.

3.2.3   The Control Module

The control module is the core of our system. The "DispatcherServlet" module of the "Spring" frame sends "url" to the control module to deal with. The main functions of the control module includes: (1) The processing logic of the url request; (2) Make use of Persondao.java to operate the data in database; (3) Return the class "Modeland-View" which contains return parameters and the name of jsp file.

3.2.4   The Login and Access Control Module

Acegi is another interesting part of our system. It is used to control the authority of the users. Acegi intercepted login request by AuthenticationProcessingFilter to get Principal and Credential information. The process includes:

- Verify the username and password. To verify them, acegi calls the Filter authentication manager AuthenticatiomManager. AuthenticatiomManager itself does not have authentication function. It is actually a verification controller, which is used to manage the process and manner of verification. AuthenticatiomManager achieve verification by calling the provider, a manager may have more than one provider, but as long as there is a validated provider, manager considers the validation is successful. In this part, we should understand two points: first, provider can be configured, because acegi is based on spring; second, AuthenticatiomManager can be rewritten, and you can change the manager controller as your wish.
- Verify by provider. Provider is the real authentication module, and determines the authentication mode. Acegi provider currently provides several authentication methods, such as, dao, jaas, cas, x509, ldap, After verification provider will return the authentication objects.
- AuthenticationProcessingFilter saves the objects in the ContextHolder. Then the authentication section ends.

3.2.5   The Process of the System

We have introduced the whole system, then the whole process that how a request turns to be a required information is explained here. Firstly, the system gets a "url" request, and it will be sent to the configuration file Web.xml. If it is an illegal request, the filter will find it, and tackle the problem. Otherwise, the dispatcher will send it to the control module according to the information that we have written in Web.xml. And then the control module will deal with it. If it is a request for data from database, the control module will call **dao.java to get data from the database with the help of Hibernate. After some calculations, the control module will send the processed data and the name of a jsp file which is used to display the data to our foreground module by the class ModelandView.

4   Conclusion

In this paper, we address how to design and implement an event monitoring system based on sina weibo. Our proposed system could extract required social events, and display them to users. We also explains some key techniques, such as the login simulation process and the data processing module. Our system is efficient in collecting and storing data and could monitor events as users' need.

Acknowledgements. This work was supported by State Key Development Program of Basic Research of China (No. 2013CB329605), the Natural Science Foundation of China (No. 61300014), and also by the Fundamental Research Funds for the Central Universities [2013RC0301].

References

1. Jure, L., Andreas, K., Carlos, G., et al.: Cost-effective outbreak detection in networks. In: Proceedings of the 13th ACM SIGKDD International Conference on Knowledge Discovery and Data Mining, San Jose, CA, USA, pp. 420–429 (2007)
2. Lee, C.-H., Chien, T.-F., Yang, H.-C.: An automatic topic ranking approach for event detection on microblogging messages. In: 2011 IEEE International Conference on Systems Man and Cybernetics SMC 2011 Anchorage AK, USA, pp. 1358–1363 (2011)
3. Fayyad, U., The, K.D.D.: Process for extracting useful knowledge from volumes of data. Commun. ACM **11**, 27–34 (1996). doi:10.1145/240455.240464
4. Raggett, D., Hors, A.L.: HTML 4.01 Specification.W3C Recommendation (1999)
5. Hors, A.L., Wilson, C.: Document Object Model (DOM) Level 2 HTML Specification (Version 1.0). W3C Working Draft (2000)
6. Hibernate persistence framework. http://www.hibernate.org/. Accessed 15 June 2013

Information Integration of Heterogeneous Employment Service Information of College Graduates

Yibo Xie and Zhongzhi Luan[✉]

Sino-German Joint Software Institute, Beihang University, Bejing, China
{yibo.xie,zhongzhi.luan}@jsi.buaa.edu.cn

Abstract. There are various university employment service systems that provide useful information for graduates built by different employment service agencies and universities. However, due to the heterogeneous data models and structures, the information of these systems cannot be shared, which makes it impossible to satisfy the need of personnel flow. After analyzing these problems, we design a distributed heterogeneous information integration system, which can solve the problem effectively, and therefore provides a transparent environment for the users.

Keywords: Heterogeneity · Information integration · Mediator

1 Introduction

Nowadays, more and more university and college career service centers have built employment service information systems with the rapid development of information technology. Since these systems developed individually, the data models and structures of them are not consistent and standard; thus the employment information is decentralized managed and cannot be shared among these systems. It has become the bottleneck of employment service information development. After analyzing the details of the problem, we implement a distributed heterogeneous information integration system. This system integrates heterogeneous data sources from various employment service systems and provides users a transparent platform.

2 Information Integration

The core task of information integration is to integrate distributed heterogeneous data sources, allowing users to access these data sources transparently. Integration means to maintain data consistency in all the data sources and improve the efficiency of information sharing. Transparency means users do not need to know they access data from heterogeneous data sources. The system we designed to tackle this problem is called Information Integration System, which provides users with a unified data source access interface and performs user's access requests to the data sources. The Information Integration System model is shown in Fig. 1.

© Springer-Verlag Berlin Heidelberg 2015
Y. Lu et al. (Eds.): ISCTCS 2014, CCIS 520, pp. 336–341, 2015.
DOI: 10.1007/978-3-662-47401-3_44

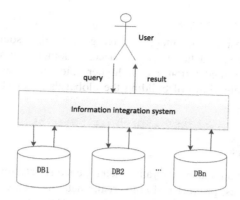

Fig. 1. The Information Integration System model

3 The Challenges of Information Integration System

The major challenges in heterogeneous information integration system include how to effectively solve the heterogeneity of distributed information, how to achieve the transparency users access, and how to maintain the autonomy of local systems.

3.1 Heterogeneity

Heterogeneity refers to the data resource of the Information Integration System with multiple types of formats. It occurs at different levels. The bottom layer of heterogeneity is different hardware platform, operating system and network protocol; and the higher layer is different programming languages, data models, and different understanding and description of a same concept.

3.2 Transparency

Transparency is associated with the degree of system solving heterogeneity, which determines the functionality and ease of the information integration system. It contains platform transparency, system transparency and data sources transparency.

3.3 Autonomy

Autonomy means a data source is independent from other data sources, and is also independent from the information integrated system.

4 Architectures of Information Integration

In the area of information integration, there already exist a lot of mature architectures. The most commonly used architectures are federation, mediation and data warehouse [3], which solve the data-sharing problem and provide decision support in various environment.

4.1   Federation

Federation is the easiest way to integrate heterogeneous data sources. Although data sources are independent, a data source can access another data source through data transforming interface. Federation has a higher integration degree and less user involvement, but the algorithm of building the global data model is complicated and has a poor scalability.

4.2   Data Warehouse

The strategy of data warehouse integrating heterogeneous data sources is to copy data from these data sources, pretreat and convert the data according to a centralized and unified view, and store them in the data warehouse. The data warehouse looks like a common database to users. It is easy to control and manage information using a data warehouse. The disadvantage is that the data warehouse increases the complexity and reduces the reliability of the system.

4.3   Mediator

Mediator integration is a software component [7]. Mediator does not store data. A user's query will be translated into one or more queries to the local data sources. Then, mediator handles the responses from the local data sources together and returns the user the final result. Mediator integration focuses on processing and optimizing the global query. It can integrate data sources which are not in the form of database and has a good query performance and strong autonomy. The drawback of mediator is that it is usually read-only while federation integration supports read-write. In our system, we adopt mediator.

5   Mapping Language

Mapping language specifies the relationship of sources with the view. Since the mediator has to decide which data to retrieve from sources and how to combine them into the unified view, the data integration system need to specify the correspondence between the local schemas of sources and the global schema [4] . The mapping languages mainly fall into two categories: Global As View (GAV) and Local As View (LAV) [1, 2].

5.1   Global As View (GAV)

In GAV, the global schema is described in terms of the local schemas [6]. A query (view) V over the combined schemas of the sources specifies the contents of each relation R in the global schema g [2]. So in GAV we can describe the correspondence between the local schemas and the global schema through a set of mappings of the form:

$$Vi \rightarrow I\ (Ri)$$

One for each relation Ri of the global schema. I(Ri) is the identity query over Ri [5].

Advantages. Since GAV mappings describe how the global database can be constructed from the local databases, a query in the global schema can be translated to corresponding queries in the local schemas through view unfolding [8, 10]. So the query result is simple.

Disadvantages. In GAV, how data from multiple sources are combined to form global relation tuples need to be specified by a mapping. Therefore GAV-based systems cannot add a source independently of other sources. When adding a new source to the system, we must modify the corresponding mappings.

5.2   Local As View(LAV)

While in GAV the global schema is described in terms of the local schemas, LAV expresses each local schema as a function of the global schema [6]. For each local schema in the system, LAV describes which data of the global database are present in the source [2]. In LAV, we can describe the correspondence between the local schemas and the global schema through a set of mapping of the form

$$I\ (Ri) \rightarrow Ui$$

One for every relation Ri in the local schemas, where Ui is a query in the global schema and I is the identity query [5].

Advantages. Additional source can be added to a LAV-based system independently since each source's mappings do not relate to each other in the system.

Disadvantages. First, a local schema cannot be modeled by the global schema if the local schema has information the global schema doesn't have. Second, the query answers cannot be obtained as easy as GAV [10].

For the simplicity of query answering, we use GAV mappings.

6 System Implementation

To solve the heterogeneity of graduates' information, we propose a distributed information integration architecture as shown in Fig. 2. The architecture is divided into application layer, mediator layer, wrapper layer and data source layer.

The system implements the transparency for the user's operations. Users access data on the global schema and they will not realize the heterogeneity of the local data sources. Application layer parses the user's request and describes it in xml format based on the global schema, and then passes it to mediator layer [1].

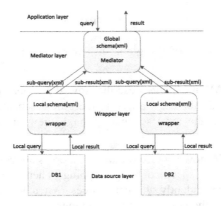

Fig. 2. Information Integration Architecture

Mediator layer accepts the request of a user, handles it and returns r the result to application laye. Mediator layer uses GAV mappings to describe the relationship between the global schema and the local schemas. Upon receiving a request from application layer, mediator translates the user's query into one or more sub-querys on the local schemas depending on GAV mappings, passes them to wrapper layer. After wrapper layer gets the sub-results from the local sources, mediator integrates them into final result according GAV mappings, then returns it to application layer [9].

Wrapper layer uses a distributed architecture since data sources are distributed. Wrapper can wrap the data sources in a unified data model so that the system can describe the relationship between the global schema and local schemas in GAV. We use xml to describe the data sources [1]. When a wrapper gets a sub-operation from mediator layer, it translates the sub-operation to the local operation which the local schema can operate. Then the wrapper describes the sub-result using xml and returns it to mediator layer.

7   Conclusions

In order to tackle the problem of different data structure and format of various employment service systems, the paper proposes a distributed heterogeneous information integration system. The system describes query of the global schema and local schemas in xml, and uses GAV mappings to describe the relationship between the global schema and local schemas. It solves the heterogeneity problem in a certain level and provides a transparent environment.

By now, the system has to modify the global schema when adding a new local schema. We will improve the mapping mode between the global schema and local schemas so as to make the system more scalable in the future.

Acknowledgment. This work is supported by the National Key Technology R&D Program (Grant NO. 2012BAH17FOl) and NSFC-NSF International Cooperation Project (Grant NO. 61361126011).

References

1. Halevy, A., Rajaraman, A., Ordille, J.: Data integration: the teenage years[C]. In: Proceedings of the 32nd International Conference on Very Large Data Bases. VLDB Endowment, pp. 9–16 (2006)
2. Katsis, Y., Papakonstantinou, Y.: View-based data integration[M]. In: Liu, L., Tamer özsu, M. (eds.) Encyclopedia of Database Systems, pp. 3332–3339. Springer US, New york (2009)
3. Hull, R.: Managing semantic heterogeneity in databases: a theoretical prospective[C]. In: Proceedings of the Sixteenth ACM SIGACT-SIGMOD-SIGART Symposium on Principles of Database Systems, pp. 51–61. ACM (1997)
4. Levy, A., Rajaraman, A., Ordille, J.: Querying heterogeneous information sources using source descriptions[J]. (1996)
5. Doan, A.H., Halevy, A.Y.: Semantic integration research in the database community: a brief survey[J]. AI magazine 26(1), 83 (2005)
6. Lenzerini, M.: Data integration: a theoretical perspective[C]. In: Proceedings of the Twenty-first ACM SIGMOD-SIGACT-SIGART Symposium on Principles of Database Systems, pp. 233–246. ACM (2002)
7. Garcia-Molina, H., Papakonstantinou, Y., Quass, D., et al.: The TSIMMIS approach to mediation: data models and languages[J]. J. intell. inf. syst. 8(2), 117–132 (1997)
8. Ullman, J.D.: Information integration using logical views[M] Database Theory—ICDT 1997, pp. 19–40. Springer, Heidelberg (1997)
9. Kossmann, D.: The state of the art in distributed query processing[J]. ACM Comput. Surv. (CSUR) 32(4), 422–469 (2000)
10. Calì, A., Calvanese, D., De Giacomo, G., et al.: Data integration under integrity constraints [M] Seminal Contributions to Information Systems Engineering, pp. 335–352. Springer, Berlin Heidelberg (2013)

Find Behaviors of Network Evasion and Protocol Obfuscation Using Traffic Measurement

Quan Bai[1,2], Gang Xiong[1(✉)], and Yong Zhao[1]

[1] Institute of Information Engineering,
Chinese Academy of Sciences, Beijing, China
{baiquan,xionggang,zhaoyong}@iie.ac.cn
[2] University of Chinese Academy of Sciences, Beijing, China

Abstract. With the development of computer network, security has become more and more important. Intrusion Detection Systems (IDS) and firewalls have been used to detect and block malicious applications and specific protocols. As a result, some malicious applications begin to mimic common application protocol or obfuscate themselves to get rid of detection, which is called Network Evasion. Evasion hazards the Internet security seriously. So it is necessary to find a method to detect behavior of network evasion and protocol obfuscation. In this paper, we analyzed and listed some common network evasion techniques and protocol obfuscation examples. We proposed a method based on measurement and statistics to find protocol obfuscation behavior. We took web crawler as an example. We measured massive of traffic in the real high speed network, found the differences of statistical characteristics between Google web crawlers and the private web crawlers. A model was proposed to detect obfuscation of web crawlers. With this model, we found some web crawlers with the behavior of protocol obfuscation. And we think this method is useful to discover and verify other behaviors of network evasion and protocol obfuscation.

Keywords: Network evasion · Protocol obfuscation · Traffic measurement · Statistics · Web crawler

1 Introduction

With the ongoing evolution of networking technologies, network security technologies has become more and more important to respond to ever more complex issues and malicious behaviors. Intrusion Detection Systems (IDS) and firewalls have been used to detect and block malicious applications and specific protocols. As a result, some malicious applications begin to mimic common application protocol or obfuscate themselves to get rid of detection, which is called Network Evasion.

In network security, evasion is bypassing an information security device in order to deliver an exploit, attack, or other form of malware to a target network or system, without detection. Network Evasions are typically used to counter network-based intrusion detection and prevention systems (IPS, IDS) but can also be used to by-pass

© Springer-Verlag Berlin Heidelberg 2015
Y. Lu et al. (Eds.): ISCTCS 2014, CCIS 520, pp. 342–349, 2015.
DOI: 10.1007/978-3-662-47401-3_45

firewalls. Various advanced and targeted evasion attacks have been known since the mid-1990s [1, 2].

Protocol obfuscation is just one method of Network Evasions. IDS systems and firewalls detect and block malicious applications using protocol identification techniques. For example some firewalls will not let the ICMP protocol to get through, which leads to the failure when ping a PC inside the firewall. So malicious applications begin to mimic common application protocol or obfuscate themselves to get rid of detection. It is often used in P2P applications such as eMule and BitTorrent [3, 4].

In normal case, a firewall can detect and block malicious applications and let common application protocol get through, as is shown in Fig. 1.

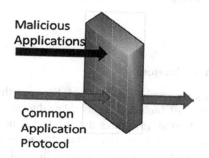

Fig. 1. Normal case

However, if a malicious application obfuscates itself to look like a common application protocol, it will get through the firewall, as is shown in Fig. 2.

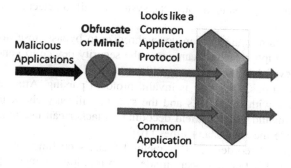

Fig. 2. Protocol obfuscation

Evasion and Protocol obfuscation hazard the Internet security seriously. So it is necessary to find a method to detect behavior of network evasion and protocol obfuscation.

In this paper, we analyzed and listed some common network evasion techniques and protocol obfuscation examples. We proposed a method based on measurement and statistical characteristics to find protocol obfuscation behavior. At last we took web crawler as an example. We measured massive of traffic in the real high speed network, found the differences of statistical characteristics between Google web crawlers and the private web crawlers. A model was proposed to detect obfuscation of web crawlers. With this model, we found some web crawlers with the behavior of protocol obfuscation. And we think this method is useful to discover and verify other behaviors of network evasion and protocol obfuscation.

The rest of the paper is organized as follows. Sect. 2 reviews the related work. Sect. 3 lists some protocol obfuscation examples. Sect. 4 proposes a method based on measurement and statistics. In Sect. 5 we take web crawler as an example to show that method based on measurement and statistics is useful to find behaviors of network evasion and protocol obfuscation. Finally, Sect. 6 concludes our work.

2   Related Work

2.1   Network Evasion Techniques

Network evasion methods are used in the network between the origin and destination hosts; in some cases this will include actions taken by an attacker to modify their outgoing traffic. Hernacki B et al. [5] thinks the attacker of network evasion desires to perform some action that they want security administrators to remain ignorant of, or to take some action that network controls, such as a firewall or IPS, would normally prevent. They classified evasion techniques into five major categories based on how they function.

Tunneling. The main idea is to disguise their traffic as another, different type of traffic. The second type of traffic, which is called tunnel, is usually a common application protocol which can cross some barrier, while the original traffic may not [6, 7].

Flooding. The main idea is to cause the system to fail to detect a subsequent attack. Like DDoS.

Desynchronization. Attacker can desynchronize to bypass, insertion, induced discard, and state corruption, which can cause the security device to generate a different view of higher-level data than the target [8].

Encoding variations. One way is invalid protocol parsing. Attacker can construct one HTTP request with two URLs and the system will only check the first one [9]. Another way is invalid protocol field decoding. Attacker can use unknown encoding methods or encode message many times [10].

Segmentation and reordering. This method focuses on limitations in the sensors' ability to handle traffic that has been divided into multiple segments [8].

2.2   Protocol Obfuscation

Bonfiglio et al. [11] presents that Skype traffic obfuscates VoIP protocol, as both proprietary and encrypted protocol. First they use the statistical properties of the message content to fingerprint Skype's message framing; and then, statistical characteristics in flow features such as packet arrival rate and packet lengths are identified using Naive Bayesian techniques. Hjelmvik E et al. [12] presents that BitTorrent's MSE protocol and Skype can be identified by fingerprinting statistically measurable properties of TCP and UDP sessions. Bar-Yanai R et al. [13] proposes a statistical classifier which is based on a combination of k-means and k-nearest neighbor geometrical classifiers. It is shown to be very robust to obfuscated traffic such as Skype and encrypted BitTorrent.

3   Protocol Obfuscation Examples

Besides BitTorrent and Skype there are many other examples of protocol obfuscation.

FTE (Format-Transforming Encryption) Proxy. The core idea of this technique is to morph or shape encrypted data into regular expression. It works by transforming encrypted data in words of a specific language based on a regular expression [14]. The principle is shown in Fig. 3.

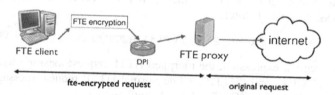

Fig. 3. FTE proxy principle

SkypeMorph. SkypeMorph [15] disguises communication between the bridge and the client as a Skype video call. Once the bridge receives the call, the client innocuously drops the call and uses the channel to send the obfuscated Tor messages. As shown in Fig. 4.

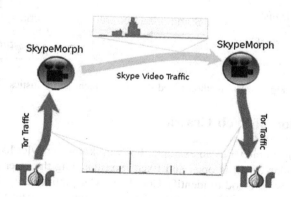

Fig. 4. SkypeMorph principle

Dust. All packets of Dust consist entirely of encrypted or random single-use bytes. Dust conversation therefore consists of two in-band packets: one intro packet, and one data.

Telex. In Telex, a new cryptographic scheme based on elliptic curves for tagging TLS handshakes such that the tag is visible to a Telex station.

4   Method Based on Measurement and Statistics

Reviewing the related works we can see statistical methods are proved to be effective when dealing with behavior of protocol obfuscation. Although a malicious application may obfuscate itself as a common protocol, it cannot get all the characteristics of the common protocol, especially the general characteristics of message structure in statistics.

Take FTE as an example: although it can morph HTTP protocol using a regular expression, it cannot get the characteristics of fields of HTTP request message. One regular expression is like below:

"^GET\\ \\/([a-zA-Z0-9\\.\\/]*) HTTP/1\\.1\\r\\n\\r\\n$"

Using this regular expression, the morphed HTTP request message will only have key words like "GET" and "HTTP", while normal HTTP request message will also have fields like "FROM", "HOST", "User Agent" and so on.

So our approach is that, firstly we measure the traffic of a certain common application protocol in real network; and secondly we do statistics on message structure to summarize general characteristics; finally those who declare as common application protocol but do not match the general characteristics are recognized as behaviors of network evasion and protocol obfuscation.

The method based on measurement and statistics is shown in Fig. 5.

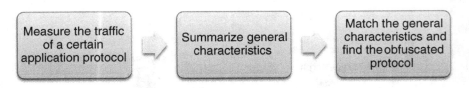

Fig. 5. The method based on measurement and statistics

5   Obfuscation of Web Crawler

We analyze Google crawler as an example. For well-known crawler like Google, it has its own User-Agent which is open and fixed. So, matching the User-Agent field is a simple and effective method to identify Google crawler preliminarily. Furthermore, IP addresses can also be another evidence of Google crawler, because Google crawler programs are running in several distributed machines and their IP addresses are open and fixed.

According to our idea, we began with matching User-Agent to do statistics with massive of Google crawlers traffic in the real network; then we filtered them with the IP addresses of Google crawlers. With these "real" Google crawlers, we found out the statistical characteristics of fields' information and the order of them. The fields we choose include: (1) *Request Method*, (2) *Host*, (3) *Connection*, (4) *Accept*, (5) *From*, (6) *User-Agent*, (7) *Referer*, (8) *Accept-Language*, (9) *Accept-Encoding*, (10) *Cookie*, (11) *X-Forward-For*.

We do the statistics with the order of each field of crawlers from Google IP, and we find the general order of them:

Host→Connection→Accept→From→User-Agent→Accept-Encoding.

And the statistical characteristics of fields' information is shown in Table 1.

Table 1. Statistical characteristics of fields' information of Google crawler

Field	Most general characteristics	Percentage
Request method	GET	99.79 %
Host	(uncertain)	*
Connection	Keep-Alive	99.60 %
Accept	*/*	94.71 %
From	googlebot(at)googlebot.com	95.21 %
User-Agent	(User-Agent of Google)	*
Referer	(NULL)	98.89 %
Accept-Language	(NULL)	99.15 %
Accept-Encoding	gzip, deflate	98.62 %.
Cookie	(NULL)	99.27 %
X-Forward-For	(NULL except for Googlebot-Image/1.0)	99.47 %

They are above 95 % flows of Google crawler which follow the above order.

According to these characteristics, we formalize a model to detect HTTP message. Using this model, we can filter out the obfuscated ones of Google crawlers. The structure of obfuscated web crawler detection model is shown in Fig. 6.

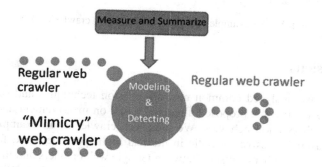

Fig. 6. The structure of obfuscated web crawler detection

The typical Google crawler packet is shown in Fig. 7. We can see the order of each field and the information of each field is just matching what we find using measurement and statistics.

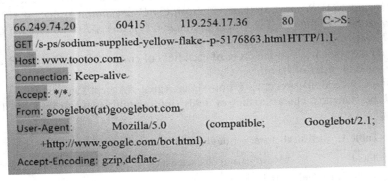

Fig. 7. An example of typical crawler packet

However, we also found some messages which are different from the above ones. These flows only have fields like User-Agent and Host which are the necessary information to be recognized as flow of crawler. But their IP addresses are not Google IP at all. They are the obfuscated web crawler found by our detection model. An example of typical obfuscated crawler packet is shown in Fig. 8.

```
119.78.219.62        13165        74.125.128.106        80    C->S.
GET
      /sorry/?continue=http://www.google.ca/search%3Fnewwindow%3D1%26site%3
      D%26start%3D1%26num%3D100%26source%3Dhp%26q%3Dinurl:/iwebssns/
      %2520%2520%2520affluent HTTP/1.1.
User-Agent:          Mozilla/5.0          (compatible;          Googlebot/2.1;
      +http://www.google.com/bot.html).
Host: www.google.com.
```

Fig. 8. An example of typical "obfuscated" crawler packet

6 Conclusions

In this paper, we analyzed common network evasion techniques and some protocol obfuscation examples. We proposed a method based on measurement and statistics to find protocol obfuscation behavior. We took web crawler as an example to test our idea. We measured massive of traffic in the real high speed network, found the differences of statistical characteristics between Google web crawlers and the private web crawlers. A model is proposed to detect obfuscation of web crawlers. With this model, we successfully found some web crawlers with the behavior of protocol obfuscation. And we think this method is useful to discover and verify other behaviors of network evasion and protocol obfuscation.

Acknowledgements. This work is supported by the National Science and Technology Support Program (No. 2012BAH46B02, No. 2012BAH45B01); the National High Technology Research and Development Program (863 Program) of China (No. 2011AA010703); the Strategic Priority Research Program of the Chinese Academy of Sciences (No. XDA06030200).

References

1. Cohen, F.: Managing network security—Part 14: 50 ways to defeat your intrusion detection system. Netw. Secur. **1997**(12), 11–14 (1997)
2. Vidal, J.M., Castro, J.D.M., Orozco, A.L.S., et al.: Evolutions of evasion techniques against network intrusion detection systems. In: ICIT 2013 The 6th International conference on Information Technology (2013)
3. Khan, H., Khayam, S.A., Rajarajan, M., et al.: Wirespeed, privacy-preserving P2P traffic detection on commodity switches. (under submission, 2013)
4. Puangpronpitag, S., Chuachan, T., Pawara, P.: Classifying peer-to-peer traffic using protocol hierarchy. In: 2014 International Conference on Computer and Information Sciences (ICCOINS), pp. 1–6. IEEE (2014)
5. Hernacki, B., Bennett, J., Hoagland, J.: An overview of network evasion methods. Inf. Secur. Tech. Rep. **10**(3), 140–149 (2005)
6. Rostami-Hesarsorkh, S., Jacobsen, M.: Detecting encrypted tunneling traffic: U.S. Patent 8,856,910, 2014 October 7
7. Winter, P.: Enhancing Censorship Resistance in the Tor Anonymity Network (2014)
8. Ptacek, T.H., Newsham, T.N.: Insertion, evasion, and denial of service: eluding network intrusion detection. Technical report, Secure Networks, January 1998
9. Vigna, G., Robertson, W., Balzarotti, D.: Testing network-based intrusion detection signatures using mutant exploits. In: Proceedings of the 11th ACM Conference on Computer and Communications Security, pp. 21–30. ACM (2004)
10. Roelker, D.J.: HTTP IDS evasions revisited. Sourcefire Inc. (2003)
11. Bonfiglio, D., Mellia, M., Meo, M., et al.: Revealing skype traffic: when randomness plays with you. ACM SIGCOMM Comput. Commun. Rev. **37**(4), 37–48 (2007). ACM
12. Hjelmvik, E., John, W.: Breaking and improving protocol obfuscation. Technical report 123751, Chalmers University of Technology (2010)
13. Bar - Yanai, R., Langberg, M., Peleg, D., Roditty, L.: Realtime classification for encrypted traffic. In: Festa, P. (ed.) SEA 2010. LNCS, vol. 6049, pp. 373–385. Springer, Heidelberg (2010)
14. Dyer, K.P., Coull, S.E., Ristenpart, T., et al.: Format-transforming encryption: more than meets the DPI. IACR Cryptology ePrint Arch. **2012**, 494 (2012)
15. Moghaddam, H.M., Li, B., Derakhshani, M., et al.: SkypeMorph: protocol obfuscation for Tor bridges. In: Proceedings of the 2012 ACM Conference on Computer and Communications Security, pp. 97–108. ACM (2012)

Research of eID Mobile Identity Authentication Method

Xu Wu[1,2,3], Yue Fan[1,2(✉)], Xi Zhang[1,2], and Jin Xu[1,2]

[1] Key Laboratory of Trustworthy Distributed Computing and Service (BUPT),
Ministry of Education, Beijing, China
[2] School of Computer Science, Beijing University of Posts
and Telecommunications, Beijing, China
{wux,zhangx,xujin59545,ly_fanyue}@bupt.edu.cn
[3] Beijing University of Posts and Telecommunications Library, Beijing, China

Abstract. In the new era of big data, existing mobile identity authentication methods lack universal protection for user privacy, which causes user privacy leaking happened frequently. Based on electronic identity (eID), this paper proposes a mobile identity authentication method. Using near field communication (NFC) technology to integrate eID into the application system's authentication process, this paper designs and implements the eID authentication procedure. This method guarantees user identity authentication safe and reliable as well as protects users' privacy validly on mobile terminals. Experiment shows it's a universal and effective solution.

Keywords: Mobile identity authentication · eID · NFC

1 Introduction

In the era of big data, users are enjoying the personalized network services; meanwhile, they are facing an increasingly threaten of personal privacy, this posed a dilemma. In September 2014, WooYun.org, an open vulnerability reporting platform, revealed two technical vulnerabilities of Ctrip.com. During the mobile wireless product development process, Ctrip.com opened the debugging ports of the user payment service interface. It made the log files can be arbitrarily accessed, which contained cardholder's name and ID number, bank card category and number, CVV code and other privacy information [1]. Also In September 2014, many Hollywood stars' private photos were leaked and trafficked by hackers maliciously [2]. Due to weak passwords was used while accessing the iCloud service, hackers can easily launched targeted violence guessing attacked, what's more, hackers got directly access to all private information once user uploaded. The ultimate reason for the leakage of user privacy, despite vulnerabilities in mobile product development, or users' omission, or hackers' attack, is lack of a secure and effective mobile identity authentication method. As the only valid and authoritative identity proof of remote user, electronic identity (eID) can not only ensure the authenticity of personal identity, but also effectively avoid the leakage risk of user identity information, which been reserved in network service provider. In order to realize the mobile Identity authentication method, this paper uses near field

© Springer-Verlag Berlin Heidelberg 2015
Y. Lu et al. (Eds.): ISCTCS 2014, CCIS 520, pp. 350–358, 2015.
DOI: 10.1007/978-3-662-47401-3_46

communication (NFC) technology to read and transmit eID information safely and efficiently, and researches on the eID authentication process. It's anonymous in front-end and real-name in back-end, and gives an effective way to protect user privacy.

2 Related Work

Currently, mobile identity authentication method contains traditional password, dynamic password, etc. But they all exist user privacy leakage problem. Traditional password is easy to be cracked and memorized, and it's easy to be intercepted by network sniffer over transmission. Dynamic password, such as Short Message Service (SMS) verification code, can effectively ensure security of user identity by using a new password each time. But once mobile device been lost or theft, it's hard to guarantee the authenticity and legality of identity authentication. Which means user's privacy will be exposed. An effective user identity authentication method is badly requisite on mobile terminals.

In the Internet era, in order to solve the trustworthy authentication of user identity, eID came into being. Research and development on eID is earlier in foreign countries. As one of the countries which early spread eID card, Belgium conducted a nationwide promotion of eID in September 2004 [3], and the eID card can be used for both official proof of identity and electronic signature. In November 2010, the German government began distributing new German ID card equipped with a contactless chip [4], with three distinct functions: first, as Network ID which verifies the identity of the card holder in the Internet; second, electronic signature; third, electronic passports. Additionally, the government has also freely provided AusweisApp [5] (for Desktop Applications) and MONA (Mobile usage of the new German identity card) (for Mobile Applications) [6] served as clients for citizens, which further popularizes the use of German ID card. The clients have been used to achieve necessary communication and encryption protocols and play bridge role between the ID card and eID service systems. In April 2011, the White House released NSTIC (National for Strategy trusted identity in cyberspace), and planned to build safe, efficient and convenient Identity Solutions for individuals and organizations [7]. France has currently applied electronic ID to the entire country, it's of a high standardization phase, and the secure and reliable French electronic ID has been mainly used for authentication and electronic signature both in the field of e-commerce and e-government [8]. As electronic ID has played a more and more important role in user authentication for the Internet community, applications for electronic ID will continue to increase, and the development potential of electronic ID in the field of mobile authentication will also widely be concerned by various countries.

The existing domestic eID terminal carriers interact with personal computer (PC) by USB ports, but mobile devices have few USB ports. The information exchangement between mobile devices are mainly through short-range wireless communication means, Infrared, Bluetooth, radio frequency identification (RFID) and NFC are included. Infrared implements data transmission point to point with low costs, but requires that equipments reach direction alignment without intermediate obstacles. Bluetooth has the advantage of far transmission distance, high transmission speed and high security with respect to the Infrared, but needs larger power; RFID identifies specific goals through radio signals, then reads and writes the relevant data. The communication process is easy to control with high recognition speed [9], large data capacity and long life. NFC has evolved by RFID, as NFC uses unique signal attenuation technique [10], compared with RFID, the characteristics of NFC include close distance, high bandwidth and low energy consumption; moreover, NFC provides a faster connection, data transmission and less costly communication means in contrast with Bluetooth, thus NFC is more suitable for exchanging sensitive information.

In short, traditional mobile user authentication methods can't effectively protect user's private information, neither can it ensure the authenticity of user's identity. The solution that combines eID authentication with NFC technology [11] to achieve mobile identity authentication, will be a new idea.

3   Mobile Authentication Framework Based on eID

Different from traditional identity cards, eID is used for remotely verifying real identity of users through the network. eID system has relied on the national citizen identity information database of Public Security Ministry which covers 1.3 billion population, and has generated a set of unique network identifiers and digital certificates. From the design principle, eID is just a string of network identifier, which does not contain any user identity information; from the management ideas, eID is established and managed by unified organization. Under the premise of ensuring the authenticity of personal identity, eID can effectively prevent disclosure of personal information. The mobile eID authentication method in this study includes five parts: NFC-based eID card, eID Mobile Client (eMC), eID Unified Authentication Service System (eUASS), Application Foreground after interfaces transformation (AF), and Application Background Server (ABS). The overall framework of eID mobile authentication framework is shown in Fig. 1.

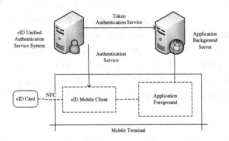

Fig. 1. Overall framework of eID mobile authentication

3.1   NFC-Based eID Card

As traditional eID terminal carriers are used through USB ports, they don't apply to mobile devices. This paper designs a new eID terminal carrier based on NFC technology, which interacts with mobile terminal in non-contact way. The eID card mainly consists of Subscriber Identity Module (SIM) module, CPU encryption chip using specific cipher algorithms, NFC chip, NFC antenna and other necessary physical hardwares. The SIM module stores unique personal eID certificate, private keys and PIN code. To ensure safe usage of eID card, when users try to use their eID cards for authentication, they are required to enter PIN codes; besides, CPU encryption chip is used for encryption before information transmission for the sake of safety and reliability in interaction process; furthermore, NFC chip is the communication unit with mobile terminals. The components of eID card coordinate and jointly realize the various functions of the eID card. eID requires real-time network authentication, which effectively enables eID unique, privacy-protective and credible.

3.2 eID Mobile Client (EMC)

As the communication bridge between eID card, mobile terminal, eUASS and AF, eMC has many functions, mainly include receiving eID requests issued by AF; reading effective information in eID card; proxy authentication of eID information by the secure session channel established with eUASS; receiving verification results fed back by eUASS and returning the results to AF afterwards.

3.3 eID Unified Authentication Service System (EUASS)

eUASS mainly provides identity authentication service and validation verification service for network operation token.

1. eID Authentication service. eUASS receives eID authentication requests from eMC, then verifies the validation of eID information, and lastly returns results to eMC.
2. Token verification service. eUASS receives validation verification request of token from ABS, returns token verification results back to ABS.

3.4 Application Foreground (AF)

To support for eID application, AF needs related interface transformation. eID-Login way will be added to log module. When users choose to login application systems in eID-Login way, AF issues a request to eMC for verifying eID information, and then waits for the verification results to be fed back.

On this basis, logical interface to receive and judge verification results of eID information also need to be added for AF. The verification results include two kinds of situations: successful and failed, for the former situation, the verification result contains a network operation token generated by eUASS, the legitimacy of the token will be validated later by ABS which play a role of proxy; for the latter case, AF will refuse user to access the application system.

3.5   Application Background Server (ABS)

ABS is served to process service logic for all kinds of requests from AF, which provides proxy validation interface of token. ABS interacts with eUASS, and executes corresponding business logic according to token validation results.

4   Mobile Identity Authentication Process

In order to achieve complete, trusted and secure eID mobile identity authentication, the operation process of eID mobile identity authentication have been designed into 9 steps, as shown in Fig. 2 as below.

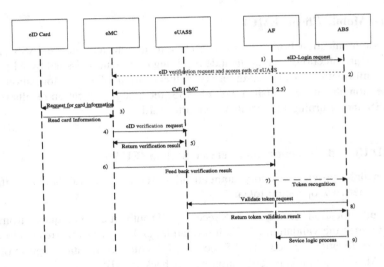

Fig. 2. eID mobile identity authentication process

3. User chooses eID-Login way to login application system, AF initiates the eID-Login request to ABS.
4. ABS forwards user's login request, access path of eUASS and application system identifier to AF. Among them, application system identifier refers to a unique sequence number identifies an application system. Later AF turns to eMC interface according to login request type shown as the 2.5) step in Fig. 2.
5. eMC prompts user to put eID card close to mobile device. After verifying PIN code successfully, eMC obtains effective information from eID card through communication between eID card and NFC unit in mobile device.
6. eMC sends eID information and application system identifier to eUASS.
7. eUASS verifies the validity of eID information. If the eID information is authentic, eUASS computes a network operating token according to time stamp, eID information and application system identifier, and returns the token to eMC. If eID information is illegal, eUASS feeds back corresponding error codes to eMC.

8. eMC returns verification result of eID information back to AF in accordance with application system identifier.
9. AF performs the logical operation of next step on the basis of verification result received in step 6).If the result is positive, AF obtains a token from it, and then move on to step 8); if the result is negative, ABS refused user to access AF, the authentication process will come to an end.
10. ABS communicates with eUASS for validity verification of token.
11. If token has been verified to be valid, user will login application system successfully by the username binded with eID information; if token has been verified to be invalid, ABS refuses access of application system from user, and requires user for verification of eID information again.

5   Technical Implementation of eID Mobile Identity Authentication

5.1   Implementation of eMC

eMC has three modules as follows:

1. eID information reading module
eMC implements read and write operations of information in the eID card by calling API functions included in packages such as android.nfc and android.nfc.tech.

2. PIN code verification and modification module
eMC requires users to enter PIN code before reading the certificate information from eID card. If user enters wrong PIN code five times in succession, the function of eID card will be locked by eMC. In addition, user can also modify PIN code.

3. eID information verification module
eMC submits eID information obtained through eID information reading module to eUASS for verification. Https protocol is used to guarantee secure and credible communication between eMC and eUASS. The process of feeding back verification results to AF is performed afterwards.

5.2   Implementation of eUASS

eUASS offers two interfaces to be accessed. For one thing, eUASS verifies the legality of eID authentication application, check out whether the application is supported in the service range of eUASS. For another, eUASS verifies the validity of token, then feeds back verification results.

5.3   Interface Modification of AF

On the one hand, AF needs to provide eID-Login way for user to access the application system, the eID-Login button redirects to the access path of eUASS. On the other hand, AF offers token application interface, which requests eUASS to issue token.

5.4   Interface Modification of ABS

1. Token analysis interface. Analyze token value from the verification results.
2. Proxy authentication of token. ABS delivers token parsed out to eUASS, receives authentication results of token from eUASS.

6   Experiment Analysis

Beijing University of Posts and Telecommunications Online Learning Platform System is selected as the experiment scene of eID mobile identity authentication method. It's a platform that provides professional courses learning and community communication. The main functions include online video courses, online exercise, online evaluation, results query, and community communication. Users not only can learn network video courses and perform online evaluation, but also can interact with others in the learning community.

The login interface of Online Learning Platform home has provided eID-Login way, as shown in Fig. 3.

Fig. 3. The login interface of Online Learning Platform home

User chooses eID-Login way to log on to Online Learning Platform, the system automatically jumps to eMC interface. eMC receives request of eID verification, the main interface of eMC is shown in Fig. 4. Before obtaining the information in the eID card, eMC requires user to enter PIN code, PIN code authentication interface is shown in Fig. 5.

Fig. 4. eID authentication interface of eMC

Fig. 5. PIN code authentication interface

Fig. 6. The main interface after successful login

AF automatically jumps to the main interface which user have logined successfully, as shown in Fig. 6.

The experiment shows the process of accessing Online Learning Platform on mobile terminal by eID-Login way, and achieves foreground anonymous and background real-name. The whole operation process is simple and quick, demonstrates the validity of the eID mobile identity authentication method.

7   Conclusions

In order to solve user privacy protection problem effectively in the age of big data, this paper designs and implements eID mobile identity authentication method. The method combines NFC technology with eID skillfully. The advantages of NFC include low energy consumption, high efficiency and secure communication, furthermore, eID is privacy-protective and highly trustworthy. So we give full play to the advantages of NFC and eID to implement real-time authentication process. On the premise of ensuring identity authenticity, the method can effectively prevent personal privacy information leakage. The experiment proves that it is a universal and efficient solution for mobile identity authentication. Besides, it lays a good foundation for the application of eID in the nationwide.

Acknowledgements. This study was both supported by the Major Research Plan of the National Natural Science Foundation of China [91124002], National Culture Support Foundation Project of China [2013BAH43F01], and National High Technology Research and Development Program of China (863 Program) No. 2012AA01A404.

References

1. Zhu, Z.X.: Secure payment log of Ctrip could be downloaded, which led to a large number of users bank card information leakage (cardholder's ID number, bank card number, CVV code and bank card Bin). 10 October 2013. http://www.wooyun.org/bugs/wooyun-2010-054302
2. The editorial department of Shaanxi channel for people's daily. The indecent photos of Hollywood actresses have been leaked, which again sounds the privacy leakage alarm. 04 September 2014. http://sn.people.com.cn/n/2014/0904/c349214-22214088.html
3. De Cock, D., Wolf, C., Preneel, B.: The Belgian electronic identity card (overview) [C]. Sicherheit, February 20–22, 2006, Magdeburg. 2006: 298-301
4. Poller, A., Waldmann, U., Vowé, S., et al.: Electronic identity cards for user authentication-promise and practice [J]. IEEE Secur. Priv. **10**(1), 46–54 (2012)
5. Bundesamt für Sicherheit in der Informationstechnik (BSI). Ausweisapp2, 10 November 2014. https://www.ausweisapp.bund.de/informieren
6. Horsch, M.: Mobile Authentication Using the New German Identity Card. Darmstadt University of Technology, Darmstadt (2011)
7. Grant, J.A.: The National Strategy for Trusted Identities in Cyberspace (NSTIC): enhancing online choice, efficiency, security, and privacy through standards. IEEE Internet Comput. **15**(6), 80–84 (2011)
8. Naumann, I., Hogben, G.: Privacy features of European eID card specifications. Network Secur. **2008**(8), 9–13 (2008)
9. Michahelles, F., Thiesse, F., Schmidt, A., et al.: Pervasive RFID and near field communication technology. Pervasive Comput. IEEE **6**(3), 94–96 (2007)
10. Curran, K., Millar, A., Mc, G.C.: Near field communication [J]. Int. J. Electr. Comput. Eng. (IJECE) **2**(3), 371–382 (2012)
11. Kostakos, V., O'Neill, E.: NFC on mobile phones: issues, lessons and future research. In: Proceedings of the Fifth IEEE International Conference on Pervasive Computing and Communications Workshops, pp. 367–370 (2007)

Reaching Critical Mass: The Effect of Adding New Content on Website Visitors and User Registration

Krishna Moniz[1]([✉]) and Yuyu Yuan[2]

[1] University of Montana, Missoula, MT, USA
krishnamoniz@live.nl
[2] Beijing University of Posts and Telecommunications, Beijing, China

Abstract. This examines the effect that new content has on virtual community. The advice given to creators of virtual communities tend to be anecdotal and lacks statistical underpinning. Website creators are frequently advices to continuously add new content as this will spur interest in the website and lead to more users signing up and participant. This study analyses real life data gathered over a two year period to prove that new content does indeed attract more visitors and user registrations, but that it does not increase user participation.

Keywords: Virtual community · Critical mass · Website · Online · Content · Visitors · Analytics · User behavior · Internet

1 Introduction

New virtual communities, or websites requiring registered user base, generally aim for the attaining critical mass. The creators of the new website are willing to radically the content, user experience, registration process and even the purpose of the website if it means that the resulting site is more likely to attain critical mass (Schiffman 2008; Loj 2007). This is understandable as such website only become profitable, and thus sustainable, after reaching a critical mass. Well-known examples include Reddit.com, Ebay.com and Facebook.com. But, the history of the internet is also filled with many unknown websites and services that just did not gather enough users. Online ventures such as Sprouter, Google Wave, iTunes' Ping, and Walmart's The Hub. These ventures all failed spectacularly despite providing innovative technology, an active user base and a lot of investment capital.

The critical mass is the point at which a website undergoes a phase change. Prior to this change the website will limp along and requires active support and endorsement from its creators. Failure is very likely. Following the change, the website garners a large enough cluster of active participants to fuel its own growth, which often times becomes exponential. The resulting website is very likely to become self-sustaining, although it may still collapse due to stagnation. We can look to sites as Friendster and Myspace for examples of that.

This concept of critical mass can be explained by using the percolation theory, which describes the rapid transition between stable phases once a specific phase passes

© Springer-Verlag Berlin Heidelberg 2015
Y. Lu et al. (Eds.): ISCTCS 2014, CCIS 520, pp. 359–369, 2015.
DOI: 10.1007/978-3-662-47401-3_47

a critical point called the percolation probability. The theory was used by to describe the formation of stable ice-shelves in the Artic (Golden et al. 1998). Applying these lessons to Computer Science, allows us to explain the rapid phase change websites undergo once they've reached critical mass (Westland 2010).

Westland shows that there are more factors at play than the much touted installed base of total users. A major contributor to reaching critical mass is increasing the desire to join the network, rather than just getting them to sign up. The realization that if users perceive some use from the site, but do not join, they will likely reconsider at a later period, i.e. once the site has reached critical mass. This in itself describes part of the exponential growth in user base following the critical mass point. A steady stream of active users will do more to push the website towards critical mass than large inactive user base.

In a similar vein we can look at rise of paywalls in among news providers. Is it better to provide content free of charge and charge advertisers for the privilege to sit next to that content (Rysman 2009; Chandra 2009), or are we better off charging consumers directly for content? The switch to paywalls has been popular among some online content providers; examples include the economist, the New York Times and Slate+ . However, research shows that a paywall tends to result in less diverse group of visitors. This may be advantageous depending on your target audience. Higher income groups tend to have no problem with paywall content, thus a site with a paywall leads to wealthier clientele. Or it may hurt your chances of success. Younger visitors tend to opt out of websites with a paywall, thus resulting in an older, less trendy, clientele (Chiou and Tucker 2013). Once again the best choice lies in creating a website setup that increases the desire to join the network.

In this paper we look at one possible way of increasing the desire to join the network. Specifically, we determine if a regular addition of new content, containing a clear call to action leads to more registered users, or if it primarily affects already registered users. We also study the effect that the number active registered users have on the website visitors (includes registered users and unregistered visitors).

The paper details a single experiment in which we compare the number of users with latent desire to join a virtual community, user base of the community (i.e. users that have already joined) and the effect that improving the quality of the website via the addition of new content has on both of these. According to Westland, the desire to join the network is major factor to reaching critical mass. As such, identifying the effect that new content has on the desire to join a network, would greatly aid in the creation of a successful virtual community.

2 Literature Review

As our research focuses on increasing the desire to join the network. The network in the Westland's case refers to a virtual community. A generic description of the virtual community, which predates the commercial internet (Harris and Gerich 1996) is Social aggregations that emerge from the Net[work] when enough people carry on those public discussions long enough, with sufficient human feeling, to form webs of person relationships in cyberspace (Rheingold 1993).

This requires the creation of an online personality or what we currently call a user account. How much this user account represents the actual person/user controlling the account differs depending on the type of community. Some communities require detailed information of the user, including offline verification of identity, while others allow for completely anonymous accounts. An example this can be 4chan, where each reply in a discussion is posted by a unique automatically generated anonymous account. The community prides itself on having no link between user and user account.

In this study we focus on a single type of community namely a transaction community. This from a 1996 classification of virtual communities which consist of interest communities, relationship communities, fantasy communities, and transaction communities (Armstrong and Hagel 1996). The transaction community functions as a platform to connect users wishing to conduct a business transaction. The only required information is therefore the contact information of the participating users.

Making the assumption that a better websites make for an increase in desire to join the network, we studied factors that contribute to the quality website. The Website Assessment Index (WAI) rates a website on several factors that contribute to the quality of the site (Miranda and Bañegil 2004). These factors are:

- *Accessibility*

  Accessibility concerns the ease with which visitors (registered users or not) can find the website and recognize whether or not the website would be useful to them. The accessibility also includes Search Engine Optimization (SEO) and Search Engine Marketing (SEM). As these are marketing methods aimed at attracting more visitors to the website (Hernández et al. 2009).
- *Speed*

  Speed is the expected loading time for a webpage. The inverse correlation between loading time and user satisfaction is well-known (Hoffman and Novak 1996).
- *Navigability*

  Navigability refers to the usability of the website and how quickly a visitor can find the information or interaction that he/she is looking for.
- *Content-Quality*

  Content Quality concerns the usefulness of the information provided by website. It is rather wide field and can cover static content written by the website, and interactions between visitors of the website.

In this study we intermittently improve the quality of the website by creating additional content. The content includes a call-to-action, which entices the user to actively participate. The expectation is that this should improve the quality of the website and result not just in more active engagement by registered users, but increase the number of visitors or the desire to join the network.

3 Experiment and Methodology

3.1 Environment and Setup

Our experiment concerns the website www.freelance.sr (Poeran 2011). The website is a *transaction community* which has not yet reached critical mass. The website focuses on job application in small local market, with a labour force of about 200.000 people (Algemeen Burea voor de Statistiek/Censuskantoor 2013).

The website is the online market leader and faces no major local competitors. Prior to the study period, a conscious effort was made to maximize the quality of the website. The accessibility was given serious concern, with active SEO and SEM efforts. The website loading speed was carefully monitored and the site itself was overhauled to maximize loading speed. The user interface design of the website was review to simplify navigation and make it easy for users to find the necessary content. However, as the studied website concerns a transaction community, we expected the content to be user generated and thus the initial version of the site had a limited amount of content.

A short assessment of the website indicates high accessibility, with freelance.sr being the top result for local job application searches on Google; high speed, being a primarily a text website with a high amount of static content; high navigability, with the homepage and most content pages containing clear and simple instructions; low content quality, with the expectation that most content is user generated and the low user base (below critical mass) and small market leads to a limited supply of actual content.

Given the above assessment we can identify a clear point of improvement, namely the content quality and directly measure the effect that the improvement of the content (the addition of new job applications) will have on the visitors to the website.

The effect of new content, in the form of new job applications was studied for two years, namely from January 2012 to December 2014. Over the study period, we exercise limited constraint over changing the aspects website assessment not related to user content. This gives us sufficient confidence that the effects on the user base and the visitors were primarily the result of the addition of additional content.

Furthermore, the nature of the content, job applications, allow for direct analysis of the result. The job application is only available for a limited time. Any interaction between users, must take place within that limited time. Each job application follows a similar format, limiting interactions to a single application page. Obfuscated contact information of kept all communication between the users on the website where it could recorded for future analysis.

The experiment defines three entities:

1. (Unique) **Visitors.** These are people with the *desire to join the network*. The visit the website, know of its existence, but not necessarily members of the virtual community.
2. (Registered) **Users.** These are people who have joined the virtual community. Basically, the user base. They are members who count towards the critical mass.
   Users can be *job-providers* who can post jobs; or *job-applicants* who can interact with jobs.
3. **Jobs.** The job is a description of a job and the opportunity for users to apply for to do the job. The job can be read by visitors and users, but only job-applicants (a type of user) can interact with the job. Interaction (with the job) is only possible in the period between posting a job and closing a job.

The experiment defines three events:

1. **Posting a Job.** This is creation of new content. The job is posted by a job-provider (a type of user). The job can be read by visitors and users, but only job-applicants (a type of user) can interact with the job. A job can be posted at any time.
2. **Closing a Job.** All posted jobs are automatically closed after a predefined period (10 or 21 days). Once a job is closed, interaction with the job is impossible. At this point the job-provider can hire one of the applicants for the job.
3. **Registering a User.** This is when a visitor registers himself as a member of a virtual community, thus becoming a user. A user can register at any time. Prior to reaching critical mass, registration tends to happen slowly. Rapid increase in registration rates is a characteristic of reaching critical mass (Westland 2010). It is important to note that the website in our experiment has not reached critical mass.

The experiment defines two interactions:

1. **Replying to a Job.** This allows the user to post a comment on the application or ask a question to the job provider. A user can reply as many times as he wants. The job-provider who created the job can reply to the user's comment.
2. **Applying for a Job.** This allows the user to indicate that he wishes to be hired for this job. A user can apply only once.

The relationship between the entities, events and interactions are shown in Fig. 1.

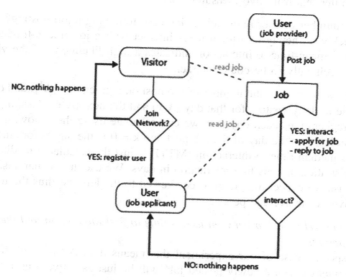

Fig. 1. Relationship between entities

3.2   Hypotheses

Now that we have defined the environment and what we are monitoring, we can hypothesize expected reaction of the entities to the given events. We expect that the specific case of freelance.sr will follow the general behaviour as given in the following hypotheses:

H1: Adding new content increases the desire to join the network

In the specific case of our experiment this means that: If someone posts a job (adds new content), the number of visitors (people with the desire to join the network) will increase noticeably.

We can infer this from a single measurement:

- Does the number of visitors on a given day correlate with the number of jobs post on the previous 48 h?

To determine this, we take the number of job post on a given day ($\Delta^1 j$) and compare it to the change in daily visitors for that day ($\Delta^1 v$) and the next ($\Delta^2 v$).

Assuming that the number of visitor is v, we can calculate using the following formula:

Note that $k = 1$ is the day of the job post and $k = 0$ is the day before the job post.

H2: There is a relationship between useful content and the size of the user base.

In the specific case of our experiment this means that: A visitor (someone with the desire to join the network) is more likely to register as a user (join the network /increase the size of the user base) if someone posts a job (provides useful new content).

We can infer this from two measurements:

- Does the number of user registrations increase following a job posting?
- How quickly do newly registered users interact with a job (mean-time-to-interaction)? Low mean-time-to-interaction indicates a high likelihood of the visitor registering specifically so he could interact.

To determine this, we take the number of job post on a given day ($\Delta^1 j$) and compare it to the change in daily visitors for that day ($\Delta^1 r$) and the next ($\Delta^2 r$). Assuming that the number of registrations each day is r, we can calculate using the following formula:

Note that $k = 1$ is the day of the job post and $k = 0$ is the day before the job post.

A user's median-time-to-interaction (MTTI) is just the calculated median between the user registration and his first interaction in days. We use the median instead of the mean, because we expect the graph to be skewed to the left and thus the mean is not representative of the average person.

H3: there is no relationship between user's time to first interaction and the frequency of his interactions

In the specific case of our experiment this means that: A visitor who joins specifically to interact with a newly posted job, will be just as active a user as one who joined for other reasons.

This can be inferred from a single measurement:

- Is there correlation between a user's median-time-to-interaction and the frequency of his interactions?

A user's interaction frequency is the average number of daily interactions since registration.

4 Results and Analysis

For H1, we calculate the number of job post on a given day $(\Delta^1 j)$ and compare it to the change in daily visitors for that day $(\Delta^1 v)$ and the next $(\Delta^2 v)$. The results for this are given in Table 1.

Table 1. Mean and std. dev. of Δv

Increase in number of job post events $(\Delta^1 j)$	Number of occurrences	Mean $(\bar{x_1})$ change in visitors for that day $(\Delta^1 v)$	Mean $(\bar{x_2})$ change in visitors for the next day $(\Delta^2 v)$	Standard deviation (σ_1) of change in visitors for that day $(\Delta^1 v)$	Standard deviation (σ_2) of change in visitors for the next day $(\Delta^2 v)$
0	764	0.086650	0.121951	0.790331	0.840608
1	118	0.789934	0.659389	1.137964	1.070795
2	29	1.118544	0.980043	1.718204	1.275526
3	13	0.803684	0.819302	1.216454	1.272822
4	4	1.179752	0.800433	0.874899	0.985485
5	2	0.290153	2.767715	0.172604	2.364398

Using a standard t-test we can determine if there is a significant difference between days with a job posting and days without a job posting. We can clearly see from the results that the inclusion of at least one job posting significantly (significance level of $\alpha = 0.1$) increases the number of visitors (desire to join the network).

In the case of 5 new job postings on single day, the results are no longer significant. We contribute that to the low number of event occurrence (only 2 data points) and do not consider it indicative of any relationship between the variables Table 2.

Table 2. Standard t-test for change in visitors for that day

$\Delta^1 j$	$\bar{x_1}$	90 % Confidence Interval		Sig. (2-tailed)
		Lower $\bar{x_1}$	Upper $\bar{x_1}$	
0	0.086650	0.0396	0.1337	–
1	0.789934	0.6162	0.9636	0.000
2	1.118544	0.5758	1.6613	0.002
3	0.803684	0.2024	1.405	0.035
4	1.179752	0.1503	2.2092	0.074
5	0.290153	−0.4804	1.0607	0.253

A similar test for the 2nd day value gives us more or less the same results, i.e. there is a significant difference between days with a job posting and days without a job posting. However, the increase in visitors is less extreme than on the first day. This indicates that the increase in the desire to join the network jumps up and peaks right after the addition of new content. Expectedly, the desire decays as time goes on.

Once again, the low number of event occurrence (in the case of 4 and 5 new job postings), lead to results that cannot be considered significant Table 3.

Table 3. Standard t-test for change in visitors for the next day

$\Delta^1 j$	$\bar{x}_2$	90 % Confidence Interval		Sig. (2-tailed)
		Lower $\bar{x}_2$	Upper $\bar{x}_2$	
0	0.121951	0.0719	0.172	–
1	0.659389	0.496	0.8228	0.000
2	0.980043	0.5771	1.383	0.000
3	0.819302	0.1901	1.4485	0.039
4	0.800433	−0.3592	1.96	0.203
5	2.767715	−7.7881	13.3236	0.346

Once again, the low number of event occurrence (in the case of 4 and 5 new job postings), lead to results that cannot be considered significant.

For H2, we calculate the number of job post on a given day ($\Delta^1 j$) and compare it to the change in daily registrations for that day ($\Delta^1 r$) and the next ($\Delta^2 r$). The results for this are given in Table 4.

Table 4. Mean and std. dev. of Δr

Increase in number of job post events ($\Delta^1 j$)	Number of occurrences	Mean ($\bar{x}_1$) change in registrations for that day ($\Delta^1 r$)	Mean ($\bar{x}_2$) change in registrations for the next day ($\Delta^2 r$)	Standard deviation (σ_1) of change in registrations for that day ($\Delta^1 r$)	Standard deviation (σ_2) of change in registrations for the next day ($\Delta^2 r$)
0	764	0.290092	0.346697	1.484218	1.570856
1	118	0.869894	1.146739	1.929406	2.992118
2	29	1.531478	1.038855	2.892257	1.945597
3	13	0.625427	0.374043	0.945299	0.721516
4	4	3.916667	0.287500	2.266912	0.337577
5	2	0.318182	1.500000	0.964237	0.707107

Once again, a standard t-test can determine if there is a significant difference between days with a job posting and days without a job posting. We can clearly see from the results that the inclusion of at least one job posting significantly (significance level of $\alpha = 0.1$) increases the number of actual registrations Table 5.

Table 5. Standard t-test for change in registrations for that day

$\Delta^1 j$	$\bar{x}_1$	90 % Confidence Interval		Sig. (2-tailed)
		Lower $\bar{x}_1$	Upper $\bar{x}_1$	
0	0.290092	.2049	.3830	–
1	0.869894	.5754	1.1644	0.000
2	1.531478	.6178	2.4451	0.008
3	0.625427	.1581	1.0927	0.034
4	3.916667	1.2492	6.5841	0.041
5	0.318182	−3.9866	4.6230	0.722

Once again, the low number of event occurrence (in the case of 4 and 5 new job postings), lead to results that cannot be considered significant. The two day effect is the same. A notable difference between the visitors (desire to join) and the actual registrations, is that the effect is stronger if for actual registrations on the second day. This makes sense, as new content may entice people to "check the site", but only register if they return more frequently Table 6.

Table 6. Standard t-test for change in registrations for the next day

$\Delta^1 j$	$\bar{x}_2$	90 % Confidence Interval		Sig. (2-tailed)
		Lower $\bar{x}_2$	Upper $\bar{x}_2$	
0	0.346697	.2418	.4300	–
1	1.146739	.6901	1.6034	0.000
2	1.038855	.4586	1.7112	0.006
3	0.374043	.0174	.7307	0.086
4	0.287500	−.1097	.6847	0.187
5	1.500000	−1.6569	4.6569	0.205

We also look at how quickly users start interacting once they've registered. The median resulted in MTTI is **0** days. This indicates that the average user tends to make his first interaction a right after registration. As expected the distribution is skewed to the left, showing a large concentration of users who interact immediately and a long tail of users who interact much later. In fact the *mean* time to interaction is a full month and a half.

The results are visible in Table 7 and Fig. 2 distribution of user time-to-interaction.

For H3 we look at the relationship between a user's time to first interaction and the frequency of his interactions. We compared the two using Pearson's product-moment

Table 7. Mean and media time to interaction

Number of active users	785
Mean	45.5 days
Median	0 days

correlation coefficient. The resulting coefficient of 0.077 shows that there is no correlation between the two. The lack of correlation is visible in showing that the majority of user interact infrequently regardless of how soon they started their first interaction (Fig. 3).

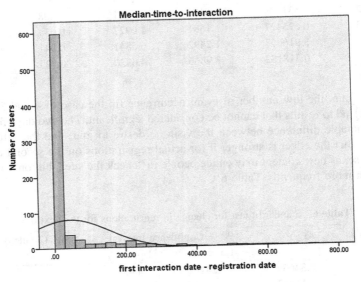

Fig. 2. Distribution of user time-to-interaction

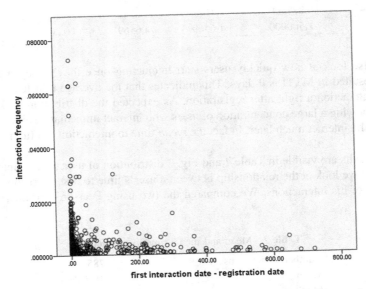

Fig. 3. Relationship between time-to-interaction and frequency of interactions

5   Conclusion

From the results in this study, we can conclude that the addition of new content positively effects a virtual community's chances of success. The data clearly shows that both the desire to join the network and the actual registrations of the website noticeably increase the immediate period following the placement of new content.

We've also showed that a majority of users start interacting immediately after registering in the community. However, these is no qualitative difference between these users and users who wait a long while before interacting. The general result is that both users interact just as often.

This study adds statistical support for the common sense approach of "content is king" that most website entrepreneurs have. Frequent addition of useful content is a clear contributor a starting website's goal of reaching critical mass.

A special thanks to Navin Poeran for allowing us the use of website statistics for this analysis.

References

Algemeen Burea voor de Statistiek / Censuskantoor, Census 8 Landelijke Resulaten Volume I. Paramaribo: Algemeen Burea voor de Statistiek (2013)

Armstrong, A., Hagel, J.: The real value of on-line communities. Harvard Bus. Rev. **74**, 134–141 (1996)

Chandra, A.: Targeted Advertising: the role of subscriber characteristics in media merkets. J. Ind. Econ. **57**, 58–84 (2009)

Chiou, L., Tucker, C.: Paywalls and the demand for news. Inf. Econ. Policy **25**, 61–69 (2013)

Golden, K.M., Ackley, S.F., Lyte, V.I.: The percolation phase transition in sea ice. Science **282**, 2238–2241 (1998)

Harris, S.R., Gerich, E.: Retiring the NSFNET backbone service: chronicling the end of an era. ConneXions **10** (1996)

Hernández, B., Jiménez, J., Martín, J.: Key website factors in e-business strategy. Int. J. Inf. Manag. **29**, 362–371 (2009)

Hoffman, D.L., Novak, T.P.: Marketing in hypermedia computer mediated environments. J. Mark. **60**, 50–68 (1996)

Loj, E.: Reaching online critical mass (2007). http://www.eugeneloj.com/: http://www.eugeneloj.com/2007/02/online_critical.html

Miranda, F.J., Bañegil, T.M.: Quantitative evaluation of commercial websites. Int. J. Inf. Manag. **24**, 313–328 (2004)

Poeran, N.: Freelance.sr (2011). http://www.freelance.sr

Rheingold, H.: The Virtual Community: Homesteading on the Electronic Frontier. Addison-Wesley, Reading (1993)

Rysman, M.: The economics of a two-sided markets. J. Econ. Perspect. **23**, 125–144 (2009)

Schiffman, B.: In Praise of Friendster, 9 May 2008. http://www.wired.com: http://www.wired.com/2008/05/friendster-inpr/

Westland, C.: Critical mass and willingness to pay for social networks. Electron. Commer. Res. Appl. **9**, 6–19 (2010)

A Method to Build and Expand the Domain Dictionary Automatically Based on WordNet

Xu Wu[1,2,3], Weiyi Zhang[1,2(✉)], Xi Zhang[1,2], and Jin Xu[1,2]

[1] Key Laboratory of Trustworthy Distributed Computing and Service (BUPT),
Ministry of Education, Beijing, China
{wux,zhangx,xujin59545}@bupt.edu.cn
[2] School of Computer Science, Beijing University of Posts
and Telecommunications, Beijing, China
jessie-chagnwy@hotmail.com
[3] Beijing University of Posts and Telecommunications Library, Beijing, China

Abstract. Domain dictionary plays an increasingly important role in information processing, natural language processing, etc. However, the process of establishing a domain dictionary is tedious, strenuous, and has a high degree of human intervention. This paper proposes a method of building and expending a computer terminology dictionary based on semantic dictionary WordNet. By analysis of the structure of WordNet and the relationships between the concept nodes in it, meanwhile collecting informations and integrating to a computer jargon set, build a tree structure primary domain dictionary by purning non-computer domain nodes and eliminating rings in WordNet. Then analyze of sematic of new terminology to insert it in an appropriate position in primary domain dictionary, thus enable automatic extension. Experiments and analysis show that this method can effectively build and automatically extend a computer professional domain dictionary.

Keywords: Domain dictionary · Wordnet · Automatic expansion · Semantic analysis

1 Introduction

In the areas of information processing technology, domain dictionary acts as a more and more important role and has important applications in various field such as natural language processing, parsing, and semantic search. Although the traditional general-purpose dictionary which has been developed through a long period of study is more mature, it lacks depth and breadth, which causes that its effect of application in specific field is not that satisfied. For different applications, the terms have obvious characteristics in the field, which requires information description and query tool can identify areas that information belongs, and precisely express the semantic information the terms want to convey. In view of this, domain dictionary, an information technology tools, has come into being. The basic elements of domain dictionary are words or terms extracted and refined from the professional field corpus, which can reflect the characteristics of specific areas. At the same time, collect as much the terms semantic

© Springer-Verlag Berlin Heidelberg 2015
Y. Lu et al. (Eds.): ISCTCS 2014, CCIS 520, pp. 370–381, 2015.
DOI: 10.1007/978-3-662-47401-3_48

information as possible, establish and improve the semantic system, build a domain dictionary contains rich semantic information which can better adapt to the specific fields. Based on this, this paper designs a domain dictionary construction and automatic extension method based on WordNet, and rich in semantic information in the computer domain dictionary and realize automatic expansion with the new term.

2 Related Works

As early as in 1990, Kyo C. Kang has described the effects of domain analysis in software reuse, and uses domain dictionary which consisted of domain terminologies in the domain model of his technical report [1]. As can be seen, the domain terminology constitute an important part of domain dictionary. The current domain term extraction method is mainly divided into the following three kinds [2]:

1. Rule based method, which is dependent on linguists' language knowledge to describe term characteristics by constructing rule base. The advantage of this kind of method is the high recall and high precision in information retrieval. However, the artificial domain dictionary construction not only needs a great amount of work which causes high cost, but also lacks of timeliness, so automatic domain dictionary construction gradually becomes the focus of current research. Such as Lee proposed a method does not depend on the dictionary while used SVM classification to extract term, but the recall rate is low [3].
2. Dictionary based method, namely uses professional terminology set to extract domain terms, mainly for term selection and new terms found according to information professional dictionary. Jing Zhang uses this method to implements term extraction through web dictionary [4]. However, this kind of method also rely on manual.
3. Statistical based method, that is, uses word co-occurrence phenomena and correlation analysis to get domain concepts. It only needs a domain specific raw corpus without semantic annotation, such as Turney's using genetic algorithm and machine learning algorithm to extract domain term from texts [5], Witte's extracting terms by using the naive Bayes technology to train the discrete eigenvalue of phrases [6], Myunggwon's using Wikipedia to complete domain terminology extraction [7]. This method is suitable for handling large text, but because lacks of syntax and semantic analysis, it cannot guarantee the accuracy.

As can be seen, the single term extraction method always has some shortages, so the current study used a combination of approaches, such as, Lin He implements term selection through the distribution and active degree of the candidate term [8], Leihan Zhang uses PATTree model combining with C-Value to choose candidate term [9], and Qing Tang proposes an ontology term extraction method based on term component extension [10]. This paper proposes an improved method of term extraction based on the dictionary, using the generic semantic dictionary combining with dictionary of professional terms to avoid artificial intervention in the process of constructing. Among them, the general semantic dictionary introduces WordNet, which constructs a "word network" according to the meaning of a word and can be seen as a shallow semantic dictionary. Although WordNet is not a strict upper ontology, it contains concept node, relations and attributes, all of which are indispensable elements of domain dictionary construction, or more, ontology. WordNet interlinks not just word forms-strings of letters-but specific senses of words. It contains lexical relations such as synonymy, antonymy, hyponymy, meronymy, morphological relations, among which the basic semantic relations are synonymy, and synonym sets are the basic building units of WordNet [11]. From the cognitive point of view, the noun is the main form of the concept, so the noun is the main part of the domain dictionary studied in this paper, and the research object of this article is limited to the noun WordNet network.

Semantic similarity is used to measure the degree of similarity between semantic contents or meanings of documents or terms, and it is an important way to expand domain terminology. WordNet Similarity is a Perl module that implements a variety of semantic similarity and relatedness measures based on information found in the lexical database WordNet. In particular, it supports the measures of Resnik, which defines that one criterion of similarity between two concepts is "the extent to which they share information in common" [12]; Jiang-Conrath, which synthesizes edge- and node- based techniques by restoring network edges to their dominant role in similarity computations, and using corpus statistics as a secondary, corrective factor, etc. These methods have different advantages, computer domain terms combining with what this paper will realize one of algorithm to implement dictionary expansion.

3 Process and Algorithm Design

In this paper, the designing idea is to divide building and expanding process into two steps: firstly, construction, which in simple words is to use WordNet and computer jargon set together building a primary domain dictionary. Secondly, expansion, which means to add new terms into the computer domain dictionary. The idea is shown in Fig. 1.

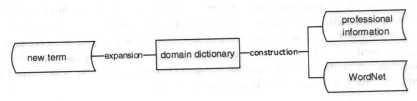

Fig. 1. The framework of domain dictionary construction

As is shown above, the construction process of primary domain dictionary mainly depends on the noun network of WordNet. With the help of computer professional information, the network can form into a dictionary with the semantic structure of the noun network in WordNet which contains a number of domain terms and the relationship between them. On the other side, through getting the keywords and calculating the similarity between the keywords and the terms in primary domain dictionary, the expansion process can add new term into domain dictionary automatically and keep the original semantic structure of it. The design of construction and expansion will be shown as follows.

3.1 Design of Domain Dictionary Construction

Domain dictionary construction is intended to form a tree-structured domain dictionary which contains multiple domain terminology and their semantic relations, that is, the primary domain dictionary. This paper use nouns in WordNet as a basis for constructing domain dictionary, after extracting noun structure, eliminating rings, marking and pruning the unnecessary nodes, thus complete the initial formation of a tree-structured domain dictionary with WordNet semantic structure. The construction process is shown as follows.

As is shown in Fig. 2, construction process is divided into the following 5 steps:

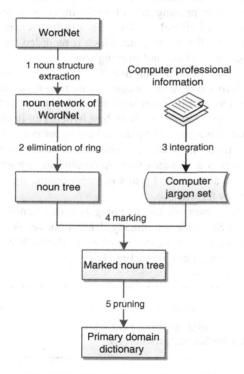

Fig. 2. Domain dictionary construction

1. Noun structure extraction. That is, to extract nouns form WordNet and build a noun network. Noun network contains the node and the relationships between them, the node in this paper is defined as SenNode, which shown in Fig. 3.

   Among them, SenNodeID represents the concept node's number which uses the id in WordNet directly, hypernmy represents its upper node, hyponyms represents its

SenNode
- SenNodeID: String
- hypernym: SenNode
- hyponyms: List<SenNode>
- sensenode: List<String>
- sense: String
- inilevel: int
- level: int
- freq: double
- remain: boolean

Fig. 3. Class diagram of SenNode

lower nodes list, sensenode is the vocabulary list of the concept node, sense represents its meaning. At the same time, in order to ensure the accuracy of the similarity calculation after pruning, recording the initial node level in WordNet and the level after pruning by initlevel and level. Freq is the average frequency of all the lexical in the vocabulary list of the node, which is recorded for elimination of ring. Remain is recorded for marking and pruning step.

2. Elimination of ring, and set up a noun tree. The WordNet allows one concept node has more than one hypernym, which means the noun network still has several rings and this will bring a lot of trouble in similarity calculation. In this case, this paper uses the weights as the selection criteria of best hypernym. In other words, the node who has the maximum weight will be the unique hypernym. The calculation of the weight will be discussed in Sect. 3.3. This step can eliminate the ring in noun network and turn it into a tree structure. According to characteristics set of noun structure in WordNet and results by lots of experiments, the tree structure named OwlTree is defined as follows:

Wherein, sensenodes represents the mapping between SenNodeID and SenNode, and SenNodeID and SenNode are already defined above. Ws represents the mapping between SenNodeID and vocabulary of its SenNode. Note that a concept node usually contains more than one word Fig. 4.

OwlTree
- sensenodes: HashMap<String, SenNode>
- ws: HashMap<String, List<String>>

Fig. 4. Class diagram of OwlTree

3. Integration, which means to integrate computer professional information and construct a computer jargon set. The noun in WordNet covers most of the common vocabulary in English, so there is need to screen out the domain terminology. The steps are: construct a computer jargon set, mark and prune the nodes which are note in it, so that reconstruct the noun tree. This paper selects "Microsoft Press Computer User's Dictionary" to extract terminologies and definitions from it and integrate

them into a computer jargon set. The following work is to label and prune the nodes does not belong to the computer jargon set.

4. Marking, that is to mark the nodes which are in the computer jargon set. In a tree structure, if the node A is deleted, its hyponyms should become the hyponyms of A's hypernym. This process forms a marked noun tree.
5. Pruning, that is to say, prune the unmarked nodes. At this point, a tree-structured primary domain dictionary which contains several domain terms is constructed.

3.2   Design of Domain Dictionary Expansion

Domain dictionary automatic expansion refers to that when a new term appears, the process to join it into domain dictionary. For the expansion method, this paper uses similarity calculation to add new term into dictionary. Since the new term does not exist in the domain dictionary and cannot directly be used to calculate the similarity, there is need

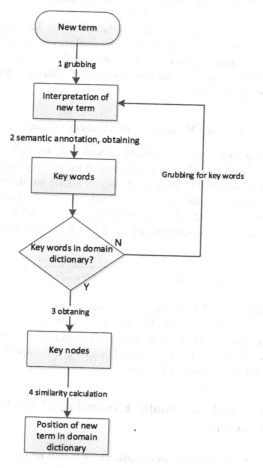

Fig. 5. Domain dictionary expansion

to be turn new term into other words that exist in the domain dictionary. In this paper, these terms become keywords, and get keywords by acquiring new term's interpretation and semantic annotation. The automatic expansion process is shown as follows.

As is shown in Fig. 5, the automatic expansion process is divided into the following 4 steps.

1. Grubbing the new term's interpretation. When new terms appears, firstly obtaining its definitions through the internet.
2. Semantic annotation and obtaining. Get the semantic annotation of the interpretation in step1, thus obtain the key words. This paper uses the important nouns in the interpretation as the key words.
3. Determine whether the keyword is in the domain dictionary. If in, identify key nodes, which are the nodes between the node of keyword and the keywords' parent node. If not, find the keyword's interpretation, repeat the first step and reduce the weight of the new keywords in the following similarity calculation, until there is enough keywords in the domain dictionary.
4. Similarity calculation. Computing the similarity of the keywords and key nodes found in step 3, get every key nodes' average similarity with every keywords. Take the key nodes of the highest average similarity, put the new term as the key node's hyponym and add it into the domain dictionary. Thus complete the automatic extension of domain dictionary.

3.3   The Calculation of the Weights of the Concept Node

In elimination of ring step, which described in Sect. 3.1, to each node who has more than one hypernyms, need to calculate the weight of every hypernym. In this paper, the weight of a node is determined by both frequency of all the words in the vocabulary list and the level of the node: the higher the frequency, the greater the weight; the smaller the level, the greater the weight. The adjustment factor α is used to adjust the weight of the frequency and the level. Above all, the weight calculation formula is as follows:

$$weight_{new} = \frac{freq_{new}}{freq_{new} + freq_{temp}} \times \alpha + \frac{level_{new}}{level_{new} + level_{temp}} \times (1 - \alpha) \qquad (1)$$

As is described in Sect. 3.1, freq represents the average frequency of all the lexical in the vocabulary list of a SenNodes. The frequency is relatively large, and the level is not in the same magnitude of it. Even using adjustment factor α, the weight of frequency is still much larger than that of level. Therefore, this paper uses the form of ratio to set frequency and level into the 0-1 range.

4   Construction and Automatic Expansion of the Computer Domain Dictionary

Construction and automatic extension of this chapter will realize the computer domain dictionary.

4.1 Construction of a Primary Domain Dictionary Based on WordNet

The construction process needs to access and obtain the noun concept nodes and hyponymy relations between them in WordNet. This paper uses JWI (the MIT Java Wordnet Interface), a Java library for interfacing with Wordnet, to access WordNet and complete noun structure extraction, elimination of rings, marking and pruning non-computer nodes.

1. Extract nouns form WordNet and build a noun network. This paper uses the depth first search manner, obtaining noun network in WordNet by recursive searching the hyponyms of the initial noun node entity in WordNet until all the noun nodes are traversed. Key codes of noun structure extraction are as follows:

```
//assuming that newnode is the current node while Sen-
node is its hypernym.
For newnode := Hyponym_first To Hyponym_last{
    Sennode.hyponym.add(newnode);
    Newnode.hypernym := newnode;
    newnode.sensenode:= newnode.Synset.getWords()
    newnode.sense := newnode.Synset.getGloss();
    OwlTree.addSenNode(newnode);
/}
```

2. Elimination of ring, and set up a noun tree. This paper uses the depth first method as traversal way to get noun structure in WordNet. As a result, when travailing to a node (say newnode), if newnode is already in OwlTree, it must have multiple hypernyms because it has been travailed by another hypernym. Then, there is need to calculate the weight of newnode's every hypernyms using the formula presented in Sect. 3.3, which uses the frequency of all the words in the vocabulary list, the level of the node, and adjustment factor α. In WordNet/dict there is a file named cnlist, in which all word's frequency in WordNet are recorded. So directly use this file can acquire frequency information. The level is recorded in SenNode. Through times of test, this paper selects 0.7 as the value of factor α.

3. Mark the nodes which are in the computer jargon set. This paper uses computer jargon set as a professional dictionary to mark the domain terms. Uses depth first manner to iterate through all the nodes in the noun tree. When iterating the node, scans all the words in the vocabulary list (sensenode) of the node and find out whether they are in the computer jargon set. If one word of the node's sensenode exists in computer jargon set, the node remains, and the "remain" flag of the node is true; otherwise, the flag remains false.

4. Prune the unmarked nodes. Uses depth first manner to iterate through all the nodes in the noun tree. If the node has the "remain" flag, it is retained; otherwise, prune it from the noun tree, and delete the relationship between the deleting node and its hypernym and hyponyms while set up relationship between its hypernym and hyponyms.

4.2   Expansion of Computer Domain Dictionary

The previous section has established a primary domain dictionary, while the expansion of new term will be implemented in this section. Based on the expansion process in Sect. 3.2, automatic expansion process of domain dictionary are as follows.

1. Get new term's interpretation. When new terms appear, firstly get the definition through the network resources such as Google dictionary, Wikipedia, etc
2. Use semantic annotation to get the keyword. The majority interpretations consist of one or two sentences. This paper uses ltp-cloud [13] to get the semantic annotation of these sentences through its API, then obtain the keywords. Note that the keywords are nouns that are meaningful.
3. If the keyword is not in the domain dictionary, treat the keyword as a new term to acquire its interpretation, semantic annotation, key words of the keyword and reduce the weight of these key-keywords in the following calculation. In order to reduce the number of iterations and enables new terms to join the domain dictionary accurately, the number of keywords is set to 5, and the weight adjustment factor is 0.8, namely for each key words not in the domain dictionary, their weight of keywords take 0.8.
4. Computing the similarity of the key words and key nodes. The key words acquired through step 1-3 are all in the domain dictionary, thus can utilize tree structure to calculate the similarity. According to the similarity calculation methods for WordNet in JWS, this paper design and implement RestLink algorithm. The key node whose average similarity with key nodes is the highest becomes the new term's hypernym.

The following takes Wi-Fi as an example and expounds its process of joining domain dictionary. First of all, gets its explanation through the Wikipedia. The explanation is as follows:

Wi-Fi, also spelled Wifi or WiFi, is a local area wireless technology that allows an electronic device to exchange data or connect to the internet using 2.4 GHz UHF and 5 GHz SHF ISM radio bands.

Part of the semantic annotation results in LTP-cloud are as follows:

```
<word id="0" cont="Wi-Fi" pos="ws" ne="O" parent="5" relate="ATT" />
<word id="1" cont="," pos="wp" ne="O" parent="0" relate="WP"
/>
<word id="2" cont="also" pos="v" ne="O" parent="5" re-
late="ATT">
    <arg id="0" type="A0" beg="0" end="1" />
    <arg id="1" type="A1" beg="3" end="3" />
</word>
<word id="3" cont="spelled" pos="ws" ne="O" parent="2" relate="VOB" />
<word id="4" cont="Wifi" pos="ws" ne="O" parent="5" relate="ATT" />
<word id="5" cont="or" pos="n" ne="O" parent="6" relate="ATT" />
<word id="6" cont="WiFi" pos="ws" ne="O" parent="8" relate="SBV" />
<word id="7" cont="," pos="wp" ne="O" parent="6" relate="WP" />
<word id="8" cont="is" pos="v" ne="O" parent="-1" relate="HED">
<arg id="0" type="A0" beg="0" end="7" />
<arg id="1" type="A1" beg="9" end="9" />
</word>
```

The terms are: or, a, area, technology, an, to, or, to, UHF, radio. Among them, or, a, an, to are all stop words and not useful. Therefore, key words: area, technology, UHF, radio. Area, technology and radio is in the computer jargon set, while UHF not. So there is also need to acquire keywords of UHF and reduce their weight. The UHF keyword are high, frequency and band. After calculation, the six key words and the {local area network, LAN} node have the highest average similarity. Therefore, the new term Wi-Fi is placed as the hyponym of {local area network, LAN}.

5 Experimental Results and Analysis

Based on the "Microsoft Press Computer User's Dictionary", this paper build a computer jargon set, and uses 1127 terms to construct a primary domain dictionary. Part of the structure shown in Fig. 6.

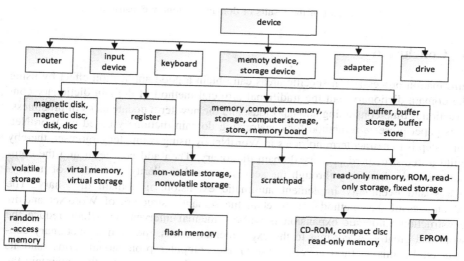

Fig. 6. Part of the primary domain dictionary

Figure 6 shows part of the relations of the SenNode device and its lower nodes, which represented by an arrow pointing from hypernym to hyponyms. As can be seen, the build process in this paper can generate a domain dictionary covers most of the field of computer jargon and semantic structure.

In this paper, screened 100 new areas popular computer science term, which extend into the primary areas of dictionaries. Part of the structure shown in Fig. 7.

Figure 7 shows the semantic structure of SenNode computer network and its hyponymys. Among them, Wi-Fi, Token-Ring, FDDI, CSMA-CD are the new terms expanded into. As can be seen, this method makes new terms correctly join into domain dictionary, and realize expanding automatically.

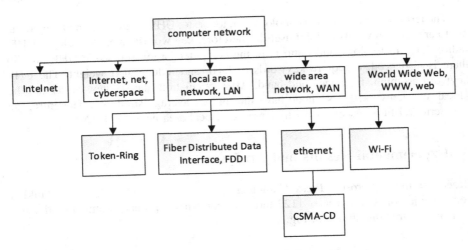

Fig. 7. Part of the results of domain dictionary expansion

6 Conclusion

Information processing in specific areas can obtain a good application effect by using the domain dictionary, but the traditional artificial method of domain dictionary construction is time-consuming and laborious, and the new term update lacks of timeliness. This paper presents a method for constructing domain dictionary based on WordNet. First step is to extract terminologies in WordNet by using computer jargon set, thereby build a tree-structured primary domain dictionary. Then add new term into the computer domain dictionary through the acquisition and similarity calculation of its keywords and eventually implement automatic extension of domain dictionary. The advantages of this method are to retain the semantic structure of WordNet and its construction automatic expansion is without manual intervention, which reduce the workload greatly. According to the experimental results, the domain dictionary constructed by this method covers most of the computer professional terms, and its expansion process can join new terms into the dictionary correctly thus maintain the semantic structure of the domain dictionary.

Acknowledgements. This work was supported by the Major Research Plan of the National Natural Science Foundation of China [91124002] and National Culture Support Foundation Project of China [2013BAH43F01].

References

1. Kang, K.C., Cohen, S.G., Hess, J.A., et al.: Feature-oriented Domain Analysis (FODA) feasibility study Software Engineering Institute, Carnegie-Mellon University, Pittsburgh, PA (1990)

2. Yan, Q., Zhang, H.: The research progress of chinese domain-term automatic extraction methods. Comput. Know. Technol. **28**, 044 (2014)
3. Lee, C.-M., Huang, C.-K., Tang (Fayuan), K.-M., Chen, K.-H.: Iterative machine-learning chinese term extraction. In: Chen, H.-H., Chowdhury, G. (eds.) ICADL 2012. LNCS, vol. 7634, pp. 309–312. Springer, Heidelberg (2012)
4. Jing, Z.: A thesis submitted in fulfillment of the requirements for the degree of master of engineering . Jiangsu University of Science and Technology (2012)
5. Turney P.: Learning to Extract Keyphrases from Text (1999)
6. Witten, I.H., Paynter G.W., Frank, E., et al.: KEA: practical automatic keyphrase extraction. In: Proceedings of the Fourth ACM Conference on Digital Libraries, pp. 254–255. ACM (1999)
7. Hwang, M., Kim, J., Gim, J., et al.: Domain terminology collection for semantic interpretation of sensor network data. Int. J. Distrib. Sens. Netw. **2014**, 9 (2014)
8. Leihan, Z., Lv, X., Zhuo, L., et al.: Research on extraction methods for domain ontology terminology. J. China Soc. Sci. Tech. Inf. **33**(2), 167–174 (2014)
9. Lin, H.: Domain ontology terminology extraction based on integrated strategy method. J. China Soc. Sci. Tech. Inf. **31**(8), 798–804 (2012)
10. Qing, T., Lv, X., Zhuo, L., et al.: Research on domain ontology term extraction. New Technol. Libr. Inf. Serv. **001**, 43–50 (2014)
11. Miller, G.A., Beckwith, R., Fellbaum, C., et al.: Introduction to wordnet: an on-line lexical database. Int. J. Lexicogr. **3**(4), 235–244 (1990)
12. Resnik, P.: Using Information Content to Evaluate Semantic Similarity in a Taxonomy (1995). cmp-lg/9511007
13. Language Technology Platform. http://www.ltp-cloud.com/

Research on Modeling of Software Automatic Test

Jincui Yang[1,2(✉)], Yuyu Yuan[1,2], and Tianle Zhang[2,3]

[1] School of Software Engineering, Beijing University of Posts
and Telecommunications, Beijing, China
[2] Key Laboratory of Trustworthy Distributed Computing and Service (BUPT),
Ministry of Education, Beijing, China
{jincuiyang,yuanyuyu,tlezhang}@bupt.edu.cn
[3] School of Computer Science, Beijing University of Posts
and Telecommunications, Beijing, China

Abstract. Software testing is important activity in software development life cycle, automatic test can cut down cost of manual testing and to increase reliability of it. Many approaches have been proposed for automatic test techniques, but research on automatic test architecture and modeling is very little, software automatic test lacks explicitly formal description. This paper firstly proposed an architecture model of automatic test. Based on the architecture model, this paper proposed the process model and dynamic model of automatic test. The architecture model described the relationship of two kinds of elements in automatic test, the process model defined the detail flow of automatic test process, and the dynamic model refined automatic test process in iterative perspective.

Keywords: Automatic test · Architecture · Process model · Dynamic model

1 Introduction

Software testing is important activity in software development life cycle, automatic test can cut down cost of manual testing and to increase reliability of it. At present, more and more software companies begin to attach importance to automatic test, many approaches have been proposed for automatic test techniques, but research on automatic test architecture and modeling is very little, current researches on software automatic test remain at non formalization stage, which is usually used non formalized diagram and text, interfaces existed between components cannot be described. Software automatic test lacks explicitly formal description. This paper will research on modeling of software automatic test.

The remainder of this paper is organized as follows: In Sect. 2, we introduce the related works about software architecture model, software test process and Rational Unified Process (RUP) framework, these works will be referenced in automatic test model. In Sect. 3, we propose three types of automatic test model, the architecture model, the process model and the dynamic model. Finally, in Sect. 4, we give simple summary.

© Springer-Verlag Berlin Heidelberg 2015
Y. Lu et al. (Eds.): ISCTCS 2014, CCIS 520, pp. 382–388, 2015.
DOI: 10.1007/978-3-662-47401-3_49

2   Related Works

For describe software automatic test architecture, software architecture formal method will be referenced. At present, there are a lot of software architecture description language [1, 2], the more common are: ACME language, Wright language, C2 language, UniCon language, Darwin language. Through the analysis and comparison of these formal languages, this paper focused on the ACME language [3], and draw on the advantages of other language forms.

ACME is an architecture exchange language proposed by Carnegie Mellon University's David Garlan. ACME uses seven types of design elements to describe the architecture of a system, seven design elements are the components, connectors, ports, roles, systems, representations and representations map, the most basic elements of software architecture description is components, connectors, and the systems.

Software testing is a process rather than a single activity. This process starts from test planning then designing test cases, preparing for execution and evaluating status till the test closure. According to GB/T 15532-2008 [4], we can divide the activities within the fundamental test process into the following basic steps: test planning, test design, test execution and test summary. Automatic test has its own characteristics, but the test process should uniformity to the fundamental process.

The Rational Unified Process (RUP) is an iterative software development process framework created by the Rational Software Corporation [5]. The RUP has determined a project life-cycle consisting of four phases. These phases allow the process to be presented at a high level in a similar way to how a 'waterfall'-styled project might be presented, although in essence the key to the process lies in the iterations of development that lie within all of the phases. Also, each phase has one key objective and milestone at the end that denotes the objective being accomplished. Software testing process should adapt this kind of development model.

3   The Automatic Test Model

For modeling of software automatic test, first of all, we need analysis the base elements contained in software automatic test process, and classify these elements.

Though analysis and discussion, we think it is more reasonable classifying the automatic test elements according to work products and activities. We defined automatic test elements into components and connectors, the following were their definitions:

- Components

The work products related to testing activities in the process of automatic test. For example: test plan, test requirement.

- Connectors

The testing activities included in the process of automatic test. For example: making test plan, designing test case.

3.1   Architecture Model

The automatic test is mainly composed of components and connectors. By analyzing the dependence relationship between components and connectors in respect of structure and behavior, we got the basic architecture model of automatic test, as shown in Fig. 1.

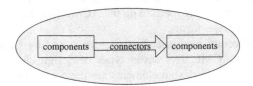

Fig. 1. Architecture model

The automatic test architecture model described the base elements and their relationship. Components are the work products in the process of automatic test, connectors are the testing activities included in the process of automatic test. Components and connects are not a one-to-one relationship, the input of a connector may be some components, output of a connector may be some other components too.

Components in the process of automatic test includes: code and documents, test requirement specification, test plan, test case specification, test scenario specification, test environment specification, test script, test environment, test result data, bug record, bug analysis report, test result data analysis report, test process report and test summary report.

Connectors in the process of automatic test includes: analyzing test requirement, making test plan, designing test case, designing test scenario, designing test environment, developing test script, establishing test environment, executing test, catching result data, analyzing test result, analyzing bug, analyzing test process, summarizing test process and result.

3.2   Process Model

The automatic test process includes a series of activities, different organizations perform these activities may have very different methods. Some organizations may very formal implementation of all these activities, while others may optionally perform certain activities. Establishment the standard automatic test process model will provide a reference to test teams. Software test team can be based on the standard model, according to the actual requirement of business development, customize their own automatic test process.

Based on ISO/IEC 9126 [6–9] and GB/T 15532-2008 [4], through the detailed analysis, we got the automatic test process model, as shown in Fig. 2.

Similar to the fundamental test process, the automatic test process model contains four stages too, they are: test planning, test design, test execution and test summary.

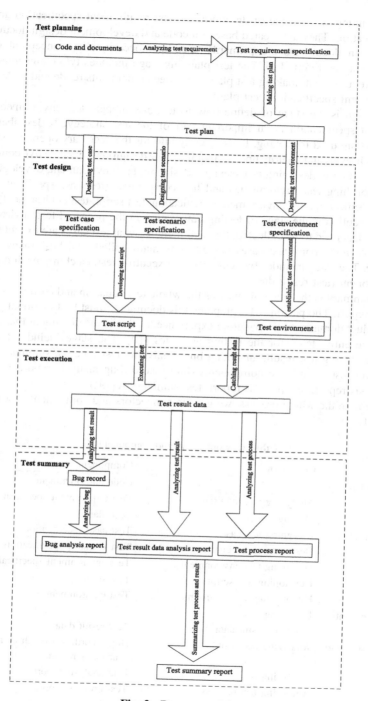

Fig. 2. Process model

Test planning is the stage of definition the test requirement specification and test plan specification. They are created based on code and development design documents. System design documents are primarily used and occasionally, conceptual design documents may be referred to. The test planning stage includes two connectors (analyzing test requirement, making test plan) and three components (code and documents, test requirement specification, test plan).

Test design is the stage of define how to test and prepare test environment. Test environment specification is an important part of the test strategy. It describes what environment are used for testing. It also clearly informs the necessary operating systems and OS patch levels and security updates required. The design stage include five connectors (designing test case, designing test scenario, designing test environment, developing test script, establishing test environment) and five components (test case specification, test scenario specification, test environment specification, test script, test environment).

Test execution is the stage of testing automation in the prepared test environment. Test result data need to be collected, this will include, what test cases are executed, how long it took, how many test cases passed, how many failed, and how many are not executable. The stage includes two connectors (executing test, catching result data) and one component (test result data).

Test summary is the stage of analysis the whole test situation and carries on the test summary report. The person, who prepares this document, must be functionally strong in the product domain, with very good experience, as this is the document that is going to drive the entire team for the testing activities [10]. The stage includes four connectors (analyzing test result, analyzing bug, analyzing test process, summarizing test process and result) and five components (bug record, bug analysis report, test result data analysis report, test process report, test summary report).

Summarize the whole process, we got the connectors and components list as show in Table 1.

Table 1. Connectors and components list

Stage	Connector	Component
Test planning		Code and document
	Analyzing test requirement	Test requirement specification
	Making test plan	Test plan
Test design	Designing test case	Test case specification
	Designing test scenario	Test scenario specification
	Designing test environment	Test environment specification
	Developing test script	Test script
	Establishing test environment	Test environment
Test execution	Executing test	
	Catching result data	Test result data
Test summary	Analyzing test result	Bug record, test result data analysis report
	Analyzing bug	Bug analysis report,
	Analyzing test process	Test process report,
	Summarizing test process and result	Test summary report

3.3   Dynamic Model

At present, the software development process transform from the waterfall development model to the RUP iterative development model, which requires the software testing process to adapt this kind of development model, test process needs to be further decomposed in each phase of software development process, an iteration is a complete testing process cycle.

According to the RUP software process model, by researching the workflow of the automatic test process, we get the dynamic model of automatic test, as shown in Fig. 3.

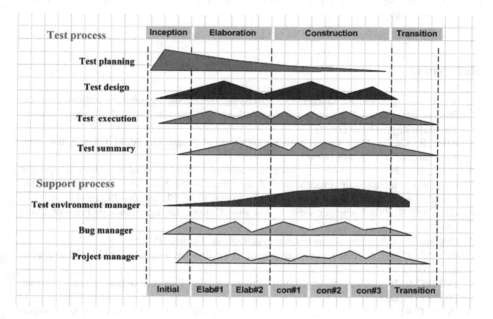

Fig. 3. Dynamic model

Automatic test process can be described using two-dimensional coordinate, the horizontal axis represents time and shows the lifecycle aspects of the software developing process, the vertical axis represents workflows, which group activities logically by nature.

The automatic test process contains seven core workflows, divided into four core test process workflows (test planning, test design, test execution, test summary) and three core support workflows (test environment manager, bug manager and project manager).

The graph shows how the emphasis varies over time. In the inception phase, we spend more time on test planning, and in later iterations we spend more time on test execution and test summary.

4 Summary

This paper researched on modeling of software automatic test, provided three kinds of automatic test model. Architecture model describe the relationship of two kinds of elements (components and connections) in automatic test. Process model define the detail flow of the automatic test process. Dynamic model refines automatic test process in iterative perspective.

Acknowledgements. This paper is supported by The National Natural Science Foundation of China (Grant No. 91118002) and "Eleventh Five-year Plan" for Sci & Tech Research of China (No. 2012BAH38X).

References

1. Allen, R., Douence, R., Garlan, D.: Specifying dynamism in software architectures. In: Proceedings of the Workshop on Foundations of Component-Based Systems, Zurich, Switzerland, pp.11–22 (1997)
2. Allen, R., Garlan, D.: A formal basis for architectural connection. ACM Trans. Softw. Eng. Methodol. **6**(3), 213–249 (1997)
3. Allen, R., Garlan, D., Ivers, J.: Formal modeling and analysis of the HLA component integration standard. In: Proceedings of the Sixth ACM SIGSOFT Symposium on the Foundations of Software Engineering, Lake Buena Vista, FL, pp. 70–79 (1998)
4. GB/T 15532-2008 Computer software test specification. Beijing: Standards Press of China (2008)
5. October 2014. http://en.wikipedia.org/wiki/Rational_Unified_Process
6. ISO/IEC 9126-1: Software engineering-Product quality-Part 1: Quality model. Geneva: ISO/IEC (2001)
7. ISO/IEC 9126-2: Software engineering-Product quality-Part 2: External metrics. Geneva: ISO/IEC (2003)
8. ISO/IEC 9126-3: Software engineering-Product quality-Part 3: Internal metrics. Geneva: ISO/IEC (2002)
9. ISO/IEC 9126-4: Software engineering-Product quality-Part 4: Quality in use metrics. Geneva: ISO/IEC (2001)
10. October 2014. http://en.wikipedia.org/wiki/Test_strategy

The Design and Implementation of APK eBooks Online Generation System Based on FBReader

Xu Wu[1,2,3], Jiada Shi[1,2(✉)], and Xiaqing Xie[3]

[1] Key Laboratory of Trustworthy Distributed Computing and Service (BUPT),
Ministry of Education, Beijing, China
[2] School of Computer Science,
Beijing University of Posts and Telecommunications, Beijing, China
jiada8866@126.com
[3] Beijing University of Posts and Telecommunications Library, Beijing, China
{wux,xiexiaqing}@bupt.edu.cn

Abstract. Users can easily upload custom books and complete e-book production online through automatically generating APK eBooks. Rich the e-books service of library, providing a new way for the library to built eBooks warehouse, but also to provide readers with a new service of making a custom APK eBook. Designed and implementated of APK eBooks Online Generation System based on FBReader with Android compilation mechanism and Ant, FBReader and other open source software. Solved the key technical issues, such as the production of eBook template, automated APK generation and signature conflicts during packaging process. After testing, the system is stable, simple to operate, and has a good interactive interface. The original uploaded file format types needs further expanded. In digital libraries and mobile reading and other fields have good application prospects.

Keywords: APK ebooks · Online Generation · Open source software · Mobile reading

1 Introduction

With the rapid development of modern information science and technology, the public reading way also is undergoing new changes. The appearance of online media, e-books, smart phones and other new digital media brought the traditional reading to a broader space and extend mobile reading this new way of reading.

In the context of mobile reading, in order to meet the immediate and moving needs of readers, the library should be adapted to the new situation, and focus on the service model optimization, improve and extend the e-book services continuously. At the same time the library should also enrich their own e-book collections, solid service infrastructure [1].

To this end, this paper analyzes the Android compilation mechanism, proposed the design of APK eBooks Online Generation System based on FBReader, use the APK eBooks as the carrier of the contents, to personalized custom eBook online production.

© Springer-Verlag Berlin Heidelberg 2015
Y. Lu et al. (Eds.): ISCTCS 2014, CCIS 520, pp. 389–400, 2015.
DOI: 10.1007/978-3-662-47401-3_50

Finally, download the APK by scanning the QR code, achieve rapid acquisition and sharing of e-books. On the one hand the use of the popular APK e-book as a carrier can enhance the fun of reading, students can convert the published articles or the learning materials they uploaded into e-books so that they can be more convenient to use the phone to read the e-books. This is a new service to provide students with a method of making a custom APK eBook. On the other hand extended the way to build an e-book warehouse of the library. Attract teachers and students to upload excellent article and high-quality academic papers by implementing online quickly generate eBook. Processed into e-books to form various features topics e-book warehouse and enhance the future competitiveness of the library.

2 Requirements Analysis and Technique Solution

2.1 Requirements Analysis

As the main object of mobile reading, e-books with its convenient, easy to store, large information density, paperless, environmental protection, can add bookmarks when reading, powerful information retrieval capabilities and other characteristics are widely loved by readers, more and more people read through the e-books [1]. According to the "Eleventh National Reading Survey" shows that in 2013 41.9 % of the Chinese nationals had experience of phone reading, compared with 31.2 % in 2012 increased by 10.7 percentage points, of which 2013 national per capita of adult reading e-books 2.48, an increase of 0.13 over 2012 of 2.35 [2]. Thus, the use of mobile phone to read e-books are from fashion to normal life.

But with the development of network technology and the abundant resources, users no longer satisfy the limit content of e-books. There is an increasing need of making custom personalized e-book. Such as libraries want to make the outstanding papers or sections of new books into e-books, making use of the advantages of the e-book to fully display these outstanding works. Students want to convert their favorite learning materials or articles into e-books, can more easily use mobile phones for reading. The current practice of making custom personalized e-books is very complicated [3]. Use the popular office software to edit the content of e-books, such as WPS Office or Microsoft Office. Then use specialized software to convert your own text into a corresponding e-book format after editing is completed. At home and abroad, there are many websites providing online services to convert e-book format, such as 2epub.com [4] docdroid.net [5]. After the conversion is complete users still need to manually download from the website and then copy to a particular directory of proprietary e-book reading software to read. Even with online conversion service of e-book format, making a custom e-books still need to go through a series of complicated steps.

The convenient of e-book reading and the tediousness of e-books generation made a tremendous contrast, so we need an equally convenient mobile e-book production to solve this conflict.

2.2 Technique Solution

Considering intelligent mobile terminals equipped with Android system emerge from a multitude of intelligent mobile terminal platform with its open-source nature, good man-machine interface, a large number of applications and powerful transaction processing capabilities [6]. More and more users use the Android software to reading, so we can combine the Android reading software program (APK format) with the concept of e-book, forming a new e-book format which is the APK e-book. Packaged into APK e-book has the following advantages.

(a) APK e-books are easy to install. User can download and install directly, eliminating the tedious matters, such like copying files.
(b) APK eBook which in general have been integrated flip effect, navigation, etc., can be read without using external tools.
(c) Each APK e-books installed on Android mobile terminal is an icon, user clicks, which is convenient for user to click and unload.

These advantages can effectively simplify the tedious steps to convert the e-book format, and manually copy files to fixed directory of e-book reader.

Based on the above analysis, using a mobile phone for mobile reading has become people's normal life, e-book is a good carrier of reading content, has been received by more and more users. If we can take advantage of B/S structure, which operate from anywhere without having to install any special software, and use Web development technology to implement online generated APK e-book, make full use of the advantages of APK e-books, and offer more convenient method for mobile phone users to download, can allow users to customize and get personalized e-book more easily and quickly. It can meet the needs of library to spread high-quality original articles and provide a new way for library to build library of e-books, also can provide students with a new service to generate custom e-book online.

3 The Detailed Design of the Application System

3.1 The Process Design of the System

If you are developing the Android application in Eclipse, Eclipse outputs an .apk file automatically to the bin folder of the project, so you do not have to do anything extra to generate the .apk. When in a non-Eclipse environment to achieve APK online automated generation, the workflow of Android compiling and publishing is shown in Fig. 1.

The Android Asset Packaging Tool (aapt) takes your application resource files, such as the AndroidManifest.xml file and the XML files for your Activities, and compiles them. An R.java is also produced so you can reference your resources from your Java code.

The aidl tool converts any .aidl interfaces that you have into Java interfaces.

All of your Java code, including the R.java and .aidl files, are compiled by the Java compiler and .class files are output.

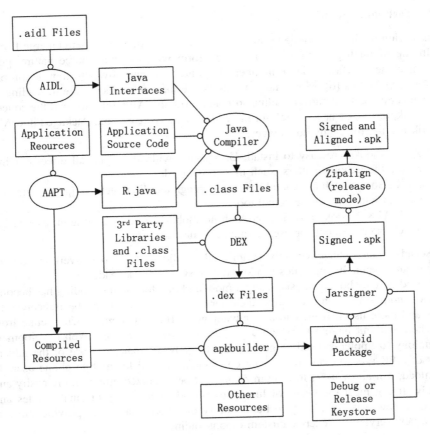

Fig. 1. The flowchart of Android compilation and release

The dex tool converts the .class files to Dalvik byte code. Any 3rd party libraries and .class files that you have included in your project are also converted into .dex files so that they can be packaged into the final .apk file.

All non-compiled resources (such as images), compiled resources, and the.dex files are sent to the apkbuilder tool to be packaged into an .apk file.

Once the .apk is built, it must be signed with either a debug or release key before it can be installed to a device.

Finally, if the application is being signed in release mode, you must align the .apk with the zipalign tool. Aligning the final .apk decreases memory usage when the application is running on a device.

According to the Android compilation and release process, in order to generate the user upload documents online into APK e-books online, the application system implementation process is as follows:

(a) Prepare the application source code. FBReader is free, fast and highly customizable e-book reader for devices running Android OS. By this moment (August

2014) FBReader was downloaded from Google Play to more than 10 million devices. Highly customizable. Choose colors, fonts, page turning animations, dictionaries, bookmarks, etc. to make reading as convenient as you want. Supports popular ebook formats: ePub, fb2, mobi, rtf, html, plain text, and a lot of other formats [7]. By considering that the system is based on FBReader to customize APK eBook template.

(b) Pick out the source files need to customize from the source code, and replace the keywords of source files based on parameters the user input on a web page.

(c) Then in a non-Eclipse environment to achieve source code automatically compiling, APK generation, signature and optimization. Apache Ant is a Java library and command-line tool whose mission is to drive processes described in build files as targets and extension points dependent upon each other. The main known usage of Ant is the build of Java applications. Ant supplies a number of built-in tasks allowing to compile, assemble, test and run Java applications. Ant can also be used effectively to build non Java applications, for instance C or C++ applications. More generally, Ant can be used to pilot any type of process which can be described in terms of targets and tasks [8]. Ant can play a good role to achieve source code automatically compiling, APK generation, signature and optimization.

(d) Finally generate download link, and generate QR code based on the download link to facilitate mobile phone users to download. ZXing ("zebra crossing") is an open-source, multi-format 1D/2D barcode image processing library implemented in Java, with ports to other languages [9]. Therefore, in order to organically integrate the link generation module into the system, the system uses ZXing to generate a QR code.

3.2 The Structural Design of the System

Based on the process design, the overall framework of application system is shown in Fig. 2.

Basically the system has the following three function module.

1. FBReader Edit Module. FBReader edit module is mainly composed of file upload module, book information module and EPUB conversion/edit module
The file upload module is used to upload files or pictures which will be generated into APK e-book.

The book information module is used to collect the information of user custom books. When uploading files, the file upload module automatically selected files that accord the transformation format in the user's local directory. When users do not upload any files and move to the next step operation, the file upload module prompts the user have not upload the original file. And the file upload module shows a progress bar for uploads to present a user-friendly interactive interface.

The EPUB conversion/edit module is used to convert doc files user uploads into EPUB format, and edit the converted EPUB files according to the information the book information module collected.

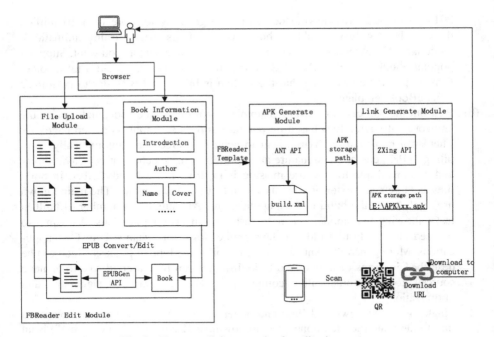

Fig. 2. The overall framework of application system

2. APK Generate Module. This module will store files user uploads to e-book template customization directory and use the book information user fills out to replace the corresponding keywords in the template source file and finally compile and generate the APK e-book installation files.
3. Link Generate Module. This module provides users with two types of download after APK e-books generated. One way is to directly generate URL link, the user can click on the download link to download APK directly to the computer. Another way is to convert a download link to QR code for smartphone users to download.

4   The Implementation of the System

4.1   FBReader Edit Module

This paper modify the FBReader which the source size is about 20 M into the APK e-book template which the size of about 4 M, so that can reduce the time of automatically compile and generate an e-book about 10 s, and the size of the generated APK e-book is about 700 k. In view of the FBReader reader two custom still need the following:

1. Implement the personalized custom book name. Because the name displays in the mobile phone after FBReader be installed is defined in the file AndroidManifest.xml located in the Android project root directory, we can change the name of generated APK to the custom name as long as replace the project name defined in this source. The implementation of the method is to create a temporary file, such like

AndroidManifest.xml.template, then marked the special field that will be modified in this file. For example, replace the value of "android:label" with "ANDROID_ APP_NAME" in "<activity android:lbel="ANDROID_APP_NAME">". Using HashMap to store the value that will be replaced, and calling the method named installFullPathTemplate to cover the source file. The first parameter is the path of the new temporary file AndroidManifest.xml. The second parameter is the source file that want to be generated. The third parameter is the Map object that has the replace information. The key code is as follows:

```
keywords.key ← ANDROID_APP_NAME
keywords.value ← project name
out ← temporary file
in ← generated file
while (line ← one line of in) and (line is not null)
   if keywords is not null
   then
      for i ← 1 to n
         do replace the key and value of keyword i
```

2. Implement the personalized custom book content. After the installation of APK e-book is completed, it should be the custom book uploaded by user when user clicks APP icon. But when FBReader first loaded, it will call the method getHelpFile () in BookUtil.java to open the help file. Based on this mechanism of FBReader, the paper implement the function that FBReader will open a custom books uploaded by user in the reading for the first time by add a custom method getUserUploadFile() in BookUtil.java. The key code of method getUserUploadFile() is as follows:

```
GET-USER-UPLOADFILE()
   p ← "data/book/mybook.epub"
   srcFile ← createFileByPath(p)
   if srcFile is exist
      then bookDir ← getBookFolderFromSDCard()
      if length[bookDir] > 1
         then destPath ← bookDir + "/mybook.epub"
            copy the upload file to the SD card to solve
Chinese garbage problem
            return upload file
         else return default file
      else return FBReader help documentation
```

Copy the books stored in the assets directory to the book directory in memory card books, there are two reasons:
(a) FBReader does not support Chinese file name in assets directory, if there is a Chinese filename in assets folder, will get an error in compilation phase.
(b) FBReader can't display the cover which belongs to the books in the assets directory, but can only display the content.

4.2 APK Generate Module

Users through the browser to upload a custom book files and fill out the book information, after modifying the FBReader source code by FBReader edit module, has been able to compile the source code file that contains user-defined books and book information. The system will transmit the source files to APK generate module, by calling the Android SDK Tools to automatically complete the compilation of source code, APK generation and signature and optimization.

In this paper, using Ant to complete the compilation of source code, APK generation, signature and optimization in background automatically. Ant is composed of built-in tasks and optional tasks. Ant needs a file named build.xml at runtime, by calling the target tree, it can perform a variety of task. The implementation of APK generate module is added the packaged signature-related target in the build.xml file, by calling the Ant API to perform the zipalign target in the build.xml building file to complete automatically the generation of a signed APK.

Duplicate signature problems may arise when many people use the packaging process in the system. The solution is to set up the package name in AndroidManifest. xml file with random package name, such like "com.ebook.book123abc". The final package name must begin with a letter, there will be a compilation error if with the beginning of the figure.

4.3 Link Generate Module

After APK generate module completing the compilation of source code, APK generation and signature and optimization, system needs to generate the corresponding QR code based on the APK e-book download path, so that users do not need to download the APK to their computer and then transferred to the phone, but by scanning the QR code to the download the APK directly to mobile phones and other mobile terminals. This system uses the ZXing library to output the QR code based on the APK e-book download path. The implementation code is as follows.

```
downloadFilePath ← getRootDir()
content ← downloadFilePath
if content is not null
   then encoding
   store QR image into file
   return the file of QR image
else return error message
```

5 Implementation Effects

Users through the browser to access this system, it first displays content upload interface. As shown in Fig. 3.

In this step, the system provides a file upload function, allowing users to upload the original file that will be made into APK e-books. When uploading files, the system

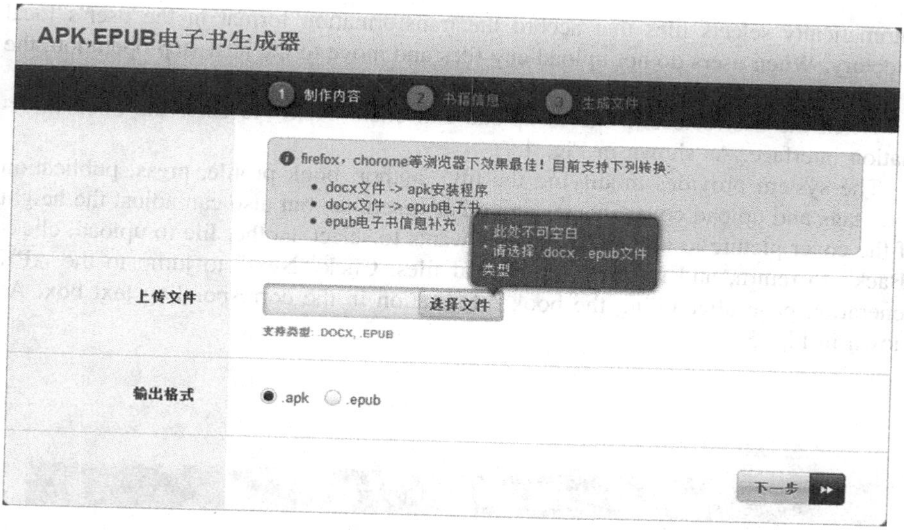

Fig. 3. Content upload interface

Fig. 4. Book information interface

automatically selects files that accord the transformation format in the user's local directory. When users do not upload any files and move to the next step operation, the system prompts the user have not upload the original file.

When the user selects a file to upload and click "Next" to enter the book information interface. As shown in Fig. 4.

The system provides modifying the title, author, book profile, press, publication date, tags and upload cover images and other functions, but also can adjust the height of the cover picture to upload. If the user wants to select another file to upload, clicks "Back" to return, and re-select the upload files. Click "Next" to jump to the APK generation page after filling the book information in the corresponding text box. As shown in Fig. 5.

Fig. 5. APK generation interface

Figure 5 shows the finally generated file types and download methods. Where users can scan QR code through mobile phones and other mobile terminal, download and install directly. Users can also by clicking on the "download to your PC" to save the generated files to their computer. Clicking "Continue" button to return to the content upload interface, to start a new APK e-book production.

Every APK e-book installed on the Android mobile terminal is a single icon, user can read easily by clicking to enter the e-book. The main functions of the installed APK e-book: book content can be selected, copied, shared, added to bookmarks; there is a wealth of custom settings; support for multiple flip effect, night reading mode, the screen orientation settings, display book chapters, book search, font scaling and other functions. Some features shown in Fig. 6.

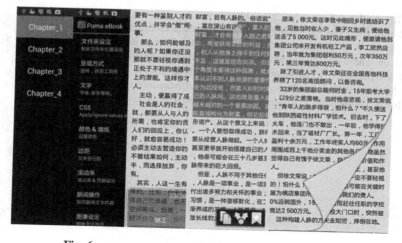

Fig. 6. some screenshots of the generated APK e-book

6   Conclusion

This paper designs and implements an APK eBooks Online Generation System Based on FBReader to meet the actual needs, and introduce the design ideas, implementation and final implementation effects systematically. The system can generate a user's favorite book into an APK e-book which is a separate application. It's convenient to read and manage, and eliminating the tedious process of installing the reader and convert e-book format, and then import the e-book into the reader.

In terms of the content of the e-book and copyright, in order to avoid infringement issues that may occur, the system can be deployed on systems with EID authentication, making the system-generated e-books have credibility and traceability, to provide an effective solution for possible infringement problems.

In future work, we must further expand the user upload file format, and continue to optimize the conversion efficiency, reduce execution response time and bring readers a better user experience and improve the level and quality of the library service.

Acknowledgements. This study is supported by the National High Technology Research and Development Program of China (863 Program) No. 2012AA01A404 and the 2013 Educational Reform Program of Beijing University of Posts and Telecommunications.

References

1. Yuxiang, Yang: Study on the e-book service of public library under environment of mobile reading. J. Libr. Inf. Sci. Agric. **26**(6), 164–167 (2014)
2. Chinapublish: National Reading Survey[EB/OL] (2014). http://www.chuban.cc/ztjj/yddc/2014yd/. 12 September 2014
3. Lei, Xia: Making EPUB ebook with INDESIGN. China Sci. Technol. Inf. **1**, 98–99 (2014)

4. EPUB[EB/OL], 4 September 2014. http://www.2epub.com/
5. docdroid[EB/OL], 4 September 2014. http://www.docdroid.net/
6. Kefeng, W.: The Design and Implementation of Information Push and Management System Based on Android. Dalian University of Technology, Dalian (2012)
7. FBReader[EB/OL], 16 September 2014. http://fbreader.org/
8. Apache Ant[EB/OL], 25 September 2014. http://ant.apache.org/
9. GitHub. ZXing[EB/OL], 10 September 2014. https://github.com/zxing/zxing

Domain-Specific Semantic Retrieval of Institutional Repository Based on Query Extension

Xu Wu[1,2,3], Pengchong Li[1,2(✉)], Jin Xu[1], and Xiaqing Xie[3]

[1] Key Laboratory of Trustworthy Distributed Computing and Service (BUPT),
Ministry of Education, Beijing 100876, China
{wux, xujin59545}@bupt.edu.cn,
tripple_x@sina.com
[2] School of Computer Science, Beijing University of Posts
and Telecommunications, Beijing, China
[3] Beijing University of Posts and Telecommunications Library, Beijing, China
xiexiaqing@bupt.edu.cn

Abstract. Researchers have found that most institutional repositories are still using the retrieval technology based on keywords, but because the information resource of which they contain are abundant and highly specialized, such retrieval techniques often can not satisfy the users. This paper designs and implements a Domain-Specific Semantic Retrieval of Institutional Repository, using semantic dictionary WordNet to perform word sense disambiguation and Extension, and the results obtained by filtering the domain dictionary, and take advantage of the open source Lucene search engine tools to complete the document retrieval. Experimental results show that there is improvement in terms of coverage and precision.

Keywords: Query extension · Institutional repository · Domain · Semantic retrieval · Wordnet · Lucene

1 Introduction

Under the promotion of Open Access Scholarly Information Campaign, Institutional Repository (Hereinafter referred to as IR), as a new way of academic communication, the "green channel" of the Open Access Campaign and the power engine of knowledge and information society, gradually become the focus of attention of domestic foreign academics, university libraries, research institution libraries, along with the changes in the traditional academic information exchange system [1].

2 Related Works

Research of some of the well-known universities (Beijing University of Posts and Telecommunications, Beijing University, Tsinghua University, University of Calgary, Hong Kong University of Science and Technology, etc.) have found that the Information Retrieval of their IR is still Retrieval based on keyword matching technology,

© Springer-Verlag Berlin Heidelberg 2015
Y. Lu et al. (Eds.): ISCTCS 2014, CCIS 520, pp. 401–411, 2015.
DOI: 10.1007/978-3-662-47401-3_51

that is, each time to retrieve only get article contains keywords entered by the user. However, search results of this traditional retrieval methods depends entirely on the keywords user input. Silverstein et al. study shows that the average length of English Query is 2.35 word [2]. The research by Huijia Yu about Sogou search engine user query logs in February 2006, pointed out that in Chinese, the queries that their key words less than three take up 93.15 % of the total number of queries, and the average length of query is 1.85 words [3]. GWFURNAS's early study in 1987 has pointed out the above problems, that however selection of keywords is, the term coverage ratio of users expressed intent is still very small [4]. Thus, during the search process, the user search needs search engine got is few. However, in natural language, there are many synonyms and synonyms, and there are a lot of polysemy. In the meantime, difference of custom in expression results in dissimilar representations may describe the same thing or the same representations may describe different things. This results in that the search engines can not accurately understand the user's intent to retrieve.

To solve the problem, the query Extension technique appears [5]. Query Extension technique add the words semantically related to the original query keywords to the original query in a way of logical "or" to get a more detailed search query and then use the new query to search the documents. This technique improves the recall and precision of information retrieval and solves the long-term problem of query and retrieve intent mismatch. By analyzing the user retrieve habit and digging their retrieve intent it compensate for the defect of insufficient query information [6]. But the traditional query Extension technique does not take the polysemy problem into account in the process of word extension. Lyons has pointed out in 1995, that almost certainly whether now or any time there has never been a natural language that one word corresponds to exactly one sense [7]. Query extension to some extent eased the problem of inconsistent statements caused by synonyms and improve the retrieval recall, but for the polysemy problem it may be counterproductive and somehow reduce the precision. Therefore, before the procedure of query extension, word sense disambiguation (WSD) needs to be done to choose the right sense for the words to be expanded. WSD is based on semantic similarity calculation. The similarity calculation method proposed by Jiang [8] in 1997, which combines the classification structure and vocabulary corpus statistics, is considered to be an effective similarity calculation method.

3 Mentality of Designing

This paper designs and implements a domain-specific institutional retrieval method based on query expansion. Use the domain dictionary to filter out the unnecessary extended word to further improve the precision. The retrieval system contains two main module, Document processing module and User search module. The function of the system design is shown in Fig. 1.

3.1 Document Processing Module

The main function of Document processing module is creating indexes for the documents of institutional repository. This module contains 3 sub-modules including

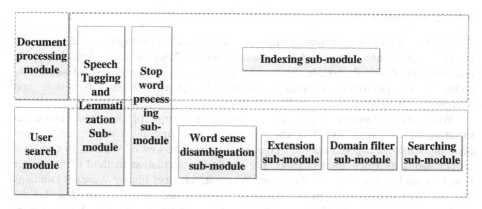

Fig. 1. Function of the system design

Speech tagging and lemmatization sub-module, Stop word processing sub-module and Indexing sub-module (Speech tagging and lemmatization sub-module and Stop word processing sub-module are common sub-modules between Document processing module and User search module).

Speech tagging and lemmatization sub-module is responsible for the document part of speech annotation and the transformation from the original words in the document to its lemma. The language of the semantic retrieval system is English. There are separators between English words, thus it does not need the word segmentation process. However, English words has different forms, such as singular and plural nouns, verb tenses and so on. The words need to be normalized. There are two main word normalization method, Lemmatization and Stemming. Lemmatization transforms the words to get their normal form, whereas Stemming reduces the words to get their stem of root-form [9]. Although both of them can achieve the purpose of effectively unifying the word form, they is big difference between them. By comparing the principle of the two methods, we can see that the Stemming mainly by means of reducing suffix of word to get the stem, while the Lemmatization always get the lemma by transformation of the word endings. Comparison shows that Stemming has a main defect, the result acquired by a simple manner of reduction may not be what we wanted or even a meaningful word. Therefore, we choose the Lemmatization method. Currently there are already a number of tools which has implement the Lemmatization such as European Languages Lemmatizer, CST's Lemmatiser, WMTrans Lemmatizer, orphAdorner, Norm, Standford CoreNLP, NLTK and the like.

Stop word processing sub-module is in charge of removing stop words from the documents. There are many functional words in natural language, which have no real meaning. The functional words such as "a", "an", "the", "that", help describe nouns and express concepts in the text. On one hand, these words appear more frequently in the document, taking up a lot of disk space. On the other hand, because of the universality of these words, almost every document more or less contains these words, and thus they have no positive effect on distinguishing two different documents. Therefore, we have to remove these stop words before indexing.

Indexing sub-module is responsible for creating indexes for the documents.

3.2 User Search Module

The main function of User search module is to extend the user query, and return the search results to user. This module contains 6 sub-modules including Speech tagging and lemmatization sub-module, Stop word processing sub-module, Word sense disambiguation sub-module, Extension sub-module, Domain filter sub-module and Searching sub-module.

Word sense disambiguation sub-module is in charge of determine the exact meaning of the word. WSD is the process of resolving the meaning of a word unambiguously in a given natural language context. The key of WSD is to choose a proper similarity calculation method. The similarity calculation method of this paper based on the English semantic dictionary Wordnet, the label library Wordnet Domains and the Wordnet copus Semcor. Wordnet is established and maintained under the guidance of George A Miller, professor of cognitive psychology laboratory at Princeton University [10]. Wordnet entries are grouped according to the meaning, and each group is known as synset. Synset contains a brief explain to distinguish different semantic relationships between different synsets. There are a number of relationships between synsets such as hyponymy relation, part-whole relation, synonymy relation, antonym relation and so on. Wordnet Domains is an extension of Wordnet, and it add one of more subject domain labels for each synset [11]. The domain set used in Wordnet Domains has been extracted from the Dewey Decimal Classification and in order to ensure completeness the mapping has been computed. Currently, the latest Wordnet Domains contains a total number of 168 domain labels, among which 45 are basic domain. There are some words in Wordnet that cannot be classified as one of the above domains, Wordnet Domains classified it as factotum. Semcor is a semantic annotation copus for Wordnet. It provides examples for each synset in Wordnet. The original corpus of semcor is extract from Brown corpus, using a variety of tools for the automatic syntax and semantics annotation, and finally is proofread manually.

Extension sub-module extend new words according to the query words meanings acquired by Word sense disambiguation sub-module.

Domain filter sub-module further determine the word which has the highest similarity with the original query word to get the final extension word. Since the retrieval system is specific to computer domain, we use computer science dictionary to filter the pre-extended word to get the final extended word in the proper domain.

Search sub-module transforms the results from Domain filter sub-module to standard search query and return the search result to user.

The function of Speech tagging and lemmatization sub-module and Stop word processing sub-module is similar to the function of which in the Document processing module, not repeat them.

3.3 System Workflow

First, preprocess the documents and create index file for them. The documents are sent to the Speech tagging and lemmatization sub-module to get POS and lemma, then the results are sent to Stop word processing sub-module for the removal of stop words.

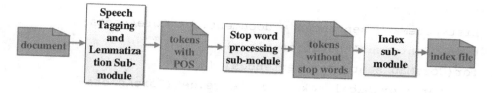

Fig. 2. Workflow of the document processing

Eventually the Indexing sub-module accomplish the indexing. The document processing workflow is shown in Fig. 2.

Second, process the user query. The user input is sent to Speech tagging and lemmatization sub-module to obtain the lexical form consistent with the processed documents and get the POS. The Stop word processing sub-module remove the stop words as in the workflow of the document processing. The results are sent to Word sense disambiguation sub-module, and the sub-module use Wordnet, related tools and specific semantic similarity algorithm to acquire the exact meaning of each word of query. Extension sub-module extends the query according to the word meaning. Domain filter sub-module filter out the pre-extended words to get the word with the highest similarity result as the extended word. Searching sub-module generate the search query and return the search results to user. The workflow of searching is shown in Fig. 3.

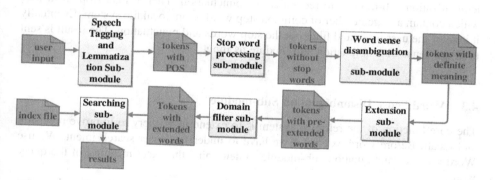

Fig. 3. Workflow of searching

4 Technical Implementation

4.1 Speech Tagging and Lemmatization Sub-module

By comparison of the existing tools, we choose the Standford CoreNLP, which has a fast speed of processing and high accuracy, to conduct lemmatization and POS annotation. The POS annotation function helps to recognize the noun words from the user query and the Extension sub-module's extension is based on this information. The core code of lemmatization is as follows.

```
List<CoreMap> sentences = document.get(CoreAnnota-
tions.SentencesAnnotation.class);
for(CoreMap sentence: sentences) {
    for (CoreLabel token: sentence.get(CoreAnnota-
tions.TokensAnnotation.class)) {
        String word = token.get(CoreAnnotations.TextAnnota-
tion.class);
        String lema = token.get(CoreAnnotations.LemmaAnnota-
tion.class);
        word2originalMap.put(word, lema);
    }
}
return word2originalMap;
```

4.2   Stop Word Processing Sub-module

Stop word processing sub-module takes advantage of the result of Speech tagging and lemmatization sub-module to recognize the punctuation. Then it load stop word files which contain a large number of common stop words from local file system. Eventually it iterator the user input and filter out the stop words and punctuation. The result is sent to Word sense disambiguation sub-module as input.

4.3   Word Sense Disambiguation Sub-module

The core function of the retrieval system is to extend user query to improve precision and recall. Before word extension we have to understand user search intent. We use Word sense disambiguation sub-module to determine the exact meaning of the query word.

This paper proposed a semantic similarity algorithm based on Wordnet, Wordnet Domains and Semcor to measure the semantic word similarity. First compute the word similarity based on Wordnet. Then compute the word similarity based on Wordnet Domains. Eventually add the two results up according to the different weights to get the final result. Formula is as follows.

$$\begin{aligned}
&Similarity(Word_A mean_i, Word_B mean_j) \\
&= \alpha * WordSim(Word_A mean_i, Word_B mean_j) + (1 - \alpha) \\
&\quad * DomainSim(Word_A mean_i, Word_B mean_j)
\end{aligned} \tag{1}$$

In formula 1–3, Similarity represent the similarity between the i-th meaning of word A and the j-th meaning of word B. WordSim is the word similarity calculated by WordNet and DomainSim is the similarity calculated by Wordnet Domains. α is a regulating factor.

Word Similarity Based on Wordnet. In Wordnet, the hyponymy take up more than 80 % of all the relationship between synsets, and it's the most important synset relationship. This paper bases on this relationship and consult some of the existing similarity algorithms and proposed a similarity calculating algorithm. The formulas are as follows.

$$WordSim(Word_A mean_i, Word_B mean_j) = \mu/(1 + Dis(Word_A mean_i, Word_B mean_j)) \tag{2}$$

$$\begin{aligned} Dis(Word_A mean_i, Word_B mean_j) = IC(Word_A mean_i) + IC(Word_B mean_j) - \\ 2 * IC(LSuperWord_A mean_i, Word_B mean_j) \end{aligned} \tag{3}$$

$$IC(Word_x mean_k) = -\log(P(Word_x mean_k)) \tag{4}$$

$$P(Word_x mean_k) = frequency(Word_x mean_k)/TotalNum \tag{5}$$

$P(Word_x mean_k)$ is the probability of the emergence of the this word meaning. We use the quotient of the frequency of this word meaning and the frequency of all the word meanings get the probability. IC represents the information content of the meaning.

LSuper the minimum common parent of the two word meanings. $Dis(Word_A mean_i, Word_B mean_j)$ is the semantic distance between the two meanings.

Word similarity based on Wordnet Domains. This part use the domain labels of Wordnet Domains to calculate the word similarity. We only use the basic domain labels to classify the word meanings. The formula is as follows.

(a) if $conDom(Word_A mean_i, Word_B mean_j) = 0$

$$DomainSim(Word_A mean_i, Word_B mean_j) = 0 \tag{6}$$

(b) if $conDom(Word_A mean_i, Word_B mean_j) \neq 0$ 且 $Domain(Word_A mean_i) \neq$ {"factotum"}

$$DomainSim(Word_A mean_i, Word_B mean_j) = 0 \tag{7}$$

(c) if $interDom(Word_A mean_i, Word_B mean_j) = $ {"factotum"}

$$DomainSim(Word_A mean_i, Word_B mean_j) = 0 \tag{8}$$

The interDom is the intersection of the labels of the two meanings, and the comDom is the union labels. f_1, f_2 is the frequency of the word meanings respectively. According to Marin Dantchev, the word meanings are ordered based on their relative frequency in tagged corpora [12]. We use the order of the meaning in the Wordnet as the frequency.

Determination of the Meaning of Query Word. First, calculate each one of the meanings of the any word A with each one of the meanings of another word B, and we regard the meanings with the highest similarity score as the real meaning of the two words respectively. And then calculate each meaning of other words with these two meanings to acquire the meanings of each word.

4.4   Extension Sub-module

According to the definite meaning we acquired by Word sense disambiguation sub-module, Extension sub-module extends the instances of the synonyms and direct hyponyms of this synset. However, some of the synset has a number of hyponyms or the hyponym synset has a lot of instances. Only one or two of them are acceptable to be extended. We have to filter out the inappropriate pre-extended words.

4.5   Domain Filter Sub-module

The Domain dictionary is chosen to be "Microsoft Press Computer User's Dictionary", which has more than 4700 entries. First use regular expressions to extract the English Interpretation of each word. Then compare this interpretation with the one given by Wordnet for the synonyms, and select the synonyms whose interpretation has the maximum number of same word as the extended synset.

4.6   Indexing Sub-module

The function of Indexing sub-module is accomplished using Lucene's API. Lucene is an open source, high performance, and extensible information retrieval software library for java. It provides the core function of the search engine, indexing and searching.

Before the performing the indexing, we have to choose or customize the Analyzer since we have to lemmatize the words. Currently there are no existing Analyzer satisfying the require, so we have to inherit and modify the Lucene Analyzer and Tokenizer interface to create our own lemmatizing analyzer.

4.7   Searching Sub-module

In the procedure of searching, we also use the function provided by lucene. The Searching sub-module generate the search query. In the generating process, the original query words and the extended words have different weights and similarity the weight of words in title is heavier than the one of the abstract words.

5   Experimental Analysis

To test the semantic retrieval system, we randomly choose 10 groups of query words, "networks security technologies", "distribute compute", "network LAN", "WAN LAN", "OS unix", "Windows Linux", "processor hardware", "memory storage", "network TCP", "route protocol". Experiment shows the difference of precision and recall between the semantic retrieval system and key word based retrieval system.

The experiment environment includes dual core 2.13 GHz Intel Core2, Windows 7 operation system, IntelliJ IDEA compiler. The data is the English metadata of IR of BUPT. The result are shown as Figs. 4 and 5.

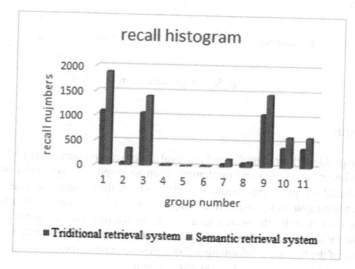

Fig. 4. Recall histogram

In Fig. 4, we can see that the recall of the semantic retrieval system has been greatly improved in comparison to the traditional key word based retrieval system. Taking "networks security technologies" for example, the recall document number of the semantic retrieval system increased by 71.8 %. And as is shown in Fig. 5, the precision also has been improved. Taking "distribute compute" for example, the hit rate of the first 20 documents increased by 28.6 %. In general, the average recall document number of semantic retrieval system is 599.5 which is 56 % more than the traditional retrieval system. And the average precision is about 62 % which is also greater than the one of the traditional retrieval system. The experiment results show that the semantic retrieval system has improvement on both recall and precision.

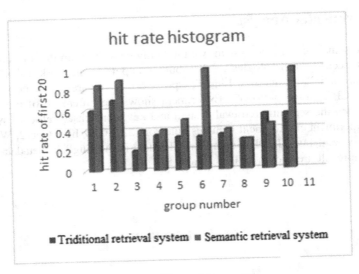

Fig. 5. Hit rate histogram

6 Epilogue

To solve the problem that the traditional retrieval system cannot accurately understand the user search intent, we design and implement a semantic retrieval system of institutional repository based on query expansion. We can see from the experimental result that the semantic retrieval system to some extent. Improve the recall and precision, and it's more suitable for IR. Currently the search result of the semantic retrieval system is acquired based on the information user provided only time. In the subsequent work, may consider adding some of the historical information about the user, and analysis the user interests to obtain results more in line with the user requirement.

Acknowledgements. This work was supported by the Major Research Plan of the National Natural Science Foundation of China [91124002] and National Culture Support Foundation Project of China [2013BAH43F01].

References

1. Bobay, J.: Institutional repositories: why go there? Indiana Libr. **27**(1), 7–9 (2014)
2. Silverstein, C., Marais, H., Henzinger, M., et al.: Analysis of a very large web search engine query log. ACM SIGIR Forum **33**(1), 6–12 (1999)
3. Yu, H., et al.: Research in search engine user behavior based on log analysis. J. Chin. Inf. Process. **21**(1), 109–114 (2007)
4. Furnas, G.W., Landauer, T.K., Gomez, L.M., et al.: The vocabulary problem in human-system communication. Commun. ACM **30**(11), 964–971 (1987)

5. Wang, F., Lin, L., Yang, S., et al. A semantic query extension-based patent retrieval approach. In: 2013 10th International Conference on Fuzzy Systems and Knowledge Discovery (FSKD), pp. 572–577. IEEE (2013)

6. Zapatrin, R.: Quantum emulation of query extension in information retrieval (2014). arXiv: 1411.3843

7. Lyons, J.: Linguistic Semantics: An Introduction. Cambridge University Press, Cambridge (1995)

8. Jiang, J.J., Conrath, D.W.: Semantic similarity based on corpus statistics and lexical taxonomy. arXiv preprint cmp-lg/9709008 (1997)

9. Balakrishnan, V., Lloyd-Yemoh, E.: Stemming and lemmatization: a comparison of retrieval performances. Lect. Notes Softw. Eng. **2**(3) (2014)

10. Pal, D., Mitra, M., Datta, K.: Improving query expansion using WordNet. J. Assoc. Inf. Sci. Technol. (2014)

11. Kolte, S.G., Bhirud, S.G.: Word sense disambiguation using wordnet domains. In: First International Conference on Emerging Trends in Engineering and Technology, 2008, ICETET 2008, pp. 1187–1191. IEEE (2008)

12. Dantchev, M.: WORDNET 2.1 Overview EECS 595/SI 661&761/LING 541 Natural Language Processing Fall (2006)

Author Index

Printed in the United States
by Bookmasters

Printed in the United States
By Bookmasters